Everything you always wanted to know about...

American Government and Politics

4th edition

STERLING
Education

STERLING
Education

4   3   2   1

ISBN-13: 978-1-9475565-4-6

Sterling Education
6 Liberty Square #11
Boston, MA 02109

info@sterling-prep.com

© 2021 Sterling Education

Published by Sterling Education

 Printed in the U.S.A.

Highest quality guarantee

Be the first to report a content error for a $10 reward
or a grammatical mistake to receive a $5 reward.

info@sterling–prep.com

*We reply to all emails – **check your spam folder***

From the founding of the American government to the present-day political and societal challenges, this clearly explained text is a perfect guide to study the democratic system and the laws that affect the lives of Americans. This book elucidates the complexity of the U.S. political system and provides readers with the information necessary to be more engaged and competent participants in the American system of government.

Created by highly qualified political scientists, teachers, scholars, and researchers, this book educates and empowers both average and highly informed readers, helping them develop and expand their understanding of American democracy. Readers will develop a better understanding of American political culture, institutions, governmental functions, and the relationships between the branches of government.

The content is clearly presented and systematically organized to provide a thorough review of essential facts, concepts, and theories of U.S. government and politics. Learn about historical figures and important events that established the American government's foundations, the meaning and significance of the United States Constitution and the Bill of Rights. Discern how each branch of government functions and how they interact with each other. Understand the influence of special interest groups on policy and politics.

We commend your desire to learn about the structure, function, and political apparatus of the United States government. The editors sincerely hope that this guide will be a valuable resource for your education.

201228mnk

Your purchase helps support global environmental causes

Sterling Education is committed to protecting our planet by supporting environmental organizations committed to conservation, research, and preservation of vital natural resources. Your purchase helps support these organizations so they can continue their critical missions.

The Ocean Conservancy advocates for a healthy ocean with sustainable solutions based on science and cleanup efforts.

The Rainforest Trust saves critical lands for conservation through land purchases and protected area designations in over 16 countries.

Pacific Whale Foundation saves whales from extinction and protects our oceans through science and advocacy.

Table of Contents

Table of Contents (*continued*)

Everything you always wanted to know about...

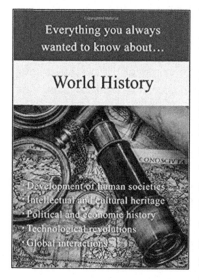

World History

ISBN-13: 9781947556881

Learn the world history starting from the early Neolithic period to the present-day events. This guide is a must-have book for anyone who wants to be knowledgeable about the history of human civilizations. As it goes through the sequence of the major events of the past, it provides readers with the analysis necessary to make them more educated and appreciative participants in the global future. Develop a better understanding of important civilizations, their economic and cultural growth and declines, the political and social challenges they went through, as well as the relationships between different historical events. Learn about historical figures and important events that set the foundations of influential civilizations, the meaning and significance of the historical shifts, as well as how each important historical event shaped its country's cultural heritage and political development.

American History

ISBN-13: 978-1947556553

From the founding of the United States of America government to the present-day challenges, this guide is perfect for anyone who wants to be knowledgeable about the history of America and its democracy. As it goes through the sequence of the events of the past, it provides readers with the analysis necessary to make them more engaged and appreciative participants in the American future. This book was designed for those who want to develop a better understanding of America's founding, economic and cultural growth, the political and social challenges it went through, as well as the relationships between different historical events. Learn about historical figures and important events that established the foundations of American government, the meaning and significance of the various social movements, as well as how each important historical event shaped the country's cultural heritage and political development.

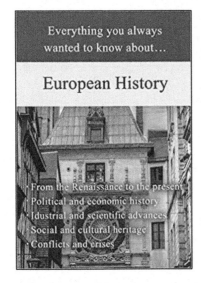

European History

ISBN-13: 978-1947556980

Perfect guide for anyone who wants to learn about European history. From the rise of humanism and Renaissance to the 21st century developments, it goes through the sequence of the events of the past, providing readers with the information necessary to make them more engaged and knowledgeable learners of European history. This book was designed to help readers develop a better understanding of what shaped European governments, their economic and cultural underpinnings, political and social challenges they went through, as well as the causal relationships between different historical events. Learn about historical figures and important events that established the foundations of the European governments, the meaning and significance of the social movements, and how each important historical event shaped regional cultural heritage and political development.

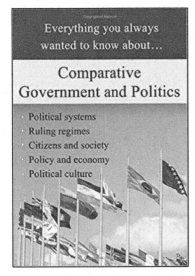

Comparative Government and Politics

ISBN-13: 978-1947556584

Why different countries have different forms of government and political institutions? Why some countries exist as democracies and others are authoritarian regimes? Why are some revolutions successful and others fail? This book was designed for those who want to develop a better understanding of political systems and regimes that affect the lives of people around the world, as well as political cultures, structures, governmental functions, and the relationships between the governments and the governed. Readers will learn about major events that shaped how governments function, the different institutions of government and political cultures that exist around the world, how branches of governments interact with each other and the governed, and how these institutions may be affected by the input from the populace. This clearly explained text is a perfect guide for anyone who wants to be knowledgeable about comparative government and politics.

Environmental Science

ISBN-13: 978-1947556645

From the foundations of Earth systems to the present-day climate challenges, this book is aimed at providing readers with the information necessary to make them more engaged and appreciative participants in the global environment. This guide is designed to help develop a better understanding of ecosystems, population dynamics, use of natural resources, as well as the political and social landscape of environmental challenges. The content is focused on an essential review of all the important facts and events shaping the natural world we live in. You will learn about Earth's biochemical cycles, land, and water use, energy resources and their consumption, the significance of the various environmental movements and global initiatives, as well as how different human actions affect the overall balance within ecosystems.

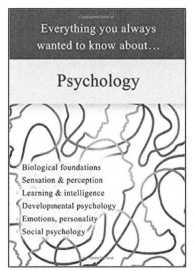

Psychology

ISBN-13: 978-1947556560

This book was designed for those who want to develop a better understanding of the human mind, emotions, feelings and behaviors, as well as the relationships between different historical events. Readers will learn about historically significant psychology researchers, the biological basis of human behavior, basic principles of consciousness and cognition, what drives human emotions and motivations, how early childhood psychological development affects human behavior, as well as develop the ability to compare and interpret theories and scientific methods, and to apply different theoretical frameworks to analyze a given situation. The book also describes all major groups of psychological disorders and covers the foundations of social psychology. From the foundations of human mind theories to the modern neuropsychology challenges, this clearly explained text is a perfect guide for anyone who wants to be knowledgeable about human psychology.

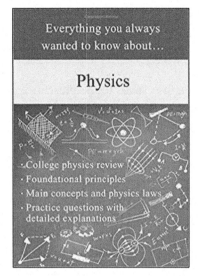

Physics

ISBN-13: 978-1947556621

From the foundations of Newtonian physics to atomic and nuclear theories, this clearly explained text is a perfect guide into standard college physics topics. As it navigates through the material, it provides readers with the information necessary to define and understand physics concepts, develop the ability to comprehend basic physical laws that govern our universe and skills to apply the theoretical knowledge to solving conceptual and quantitative problems. This book was designed for those who want to develop a better understanding of our physical universe, as well as the relationships between different laws of physics. The book describes all major topics covered in a standard college physics course and walks you through solving different types of problems. You will learn about kinematics and dynamics, statics and equilibrium, foundations of gravity, energy, work, sound and light, electricity and magnetism, basic principles of atomic physics, as well as heat and thermodynamics.

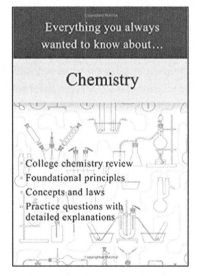

Chemistry

ISBN-13: 978-1947556874

From the foundations of the chemical reactions to the complex mechanisms of atomic particles, this general chemistry guide provides readers with the information necessary to be better equipped to understand these multifaceted chemistry topics. This book is a detailed review of all the fundamental processes and mechanisms affecting general chemistry and physical processes at the atomic level. The content was designed for those who want to develop a better understanding of the electronic structure of elements, principles of chemical bonding, phases of matter, types and mechanisms of chemical reactions, as well as essential principles of solution chemistry and acid-base equilibria. Learn about rate processes in chemical reactions, empirical and molecular formulas, bond dissociation energy for the heats of formation, Gibbs free energy, enthalpy, entropy, oxidation number, the laws of thermodynamics, and electrochemistry.

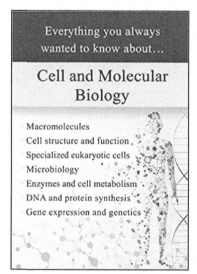

Cell and Molecular Biology

ISBN-13: 978-1947556683

Created by highly qualified science teachers, researchers, and education specialists, this book educates and empowers both the average and the well- informed readers, helping them develop and increase their understanding of biology. From the foundations of a living cell to the complex mechanisms of gene expression, this self-teaching guide provides readers with the information necessary to make them better equipped for navigating these multifaceted biology topics. This book was designed for those who want to develop a better understanding of cell structure and function, cell metabolism, DNA and genetics, as well as the technological and ethical challenges of modern science. The content is focused on an essential review of all the important processes and mechanisms affecting organisms on the cellular and molecular levels. You will learn about macromolecules, enzymes, cell cycle, photosynthesis, the significance of the various DNA mutations and heredity, as well as how different cell processes affect the overall well-being of an organism.

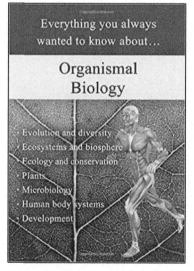

Organismal Biology

ISBN-13: 978-1947556690

Organismal biology is the study of structure, function, ecology and evolution at the organismal level. From the origin of life to the complex anatomical systems of humans, this clearly explained text was designed for those who want to develop a better understanding of ecosystems, diversity and classification, as well as anatomy and physiology. The content is focused on an essential review of all the important events and mechanisms affecting populations and communities. You will learn about evolution, comparative anatomy, plants, microorganisms, as well as human anatomical systems, along with physiological processes affecting the overall organism. Created by highly qualified science teachers, researchers, and education specialists, this book educates and empowers both the average and the well- informed readers, helping them develop and increase their understanding of biology.

Chapter 1

Constitutional Underpinnings of the U.S. Government

The Constitution of the United States of America is the "supreme law of the land." It can be and amended as the needs of the people and the country change. After the well-known Preamble or introduction, the text of the Constitution consists of seven sections called Articles. Each Article of the Constitution addresses the function and powers of the new government.

The state of modern United States politics reflects the federalism government established by the Constitution; the separation of powers, and the system of federal checks and balances.

These political developments were rooted in the Constitutional Convention's historical context and the ideological and philosophical traditions that the framers drew. These factors influenced the rationale for the framers' specific concerns and actions, such as James Madison's fear of factions or the Bill of Rights' swift adoption to protect a citizen from an overly intrusive federal government.

The United States Supreme Court interprets both legislative statutes and cases and controversies involving the Constitution. The Supreme Court rulings clarify the theoretical and practical features of federalism, the separation of powers, and the system of checks and balances. The Court addresses issues related to the Constitution.

Formulation and Adoption of the Constitution

Influences

Modern American government traces to the Enlightenment Age's philosophical traditions (1685-1815), a philosophical period in the 18th century that dominated Europe. During the Enlightenment Age, philosophers were beginning to rise against unicameral governments and absolute monarchism.

Enlightenment Age philosophers promoted the idea that people innately possess liberty, the ability to progress, the ability to reason, and a capacity for tolerance. The philosophers believed that reason, rather than tradition, could lead to a better organizational structure of government.

Thomas Hobbes (1589-1679) was a 17th-century English philosopher and political theorist whose philosophy focused on addressing conditions in which people could create and sustain peace. Hobbes argued that humans seek to gain some advantage over each other by nature rather than establish a community. He believed that this rapacious attitude could not sustain a society over time. As Hobbes stated, "*the life of man is nasty, brutish and short,*" which fundamentally represents his position on why a functioning government needs to be established and maintained.

Thomas Hobbes, English philosopher and political theorist, c. 1678

Due to this fundamental stance on the human condition, Hobbes believed that it was better to be ruled by a tyrant than live in a state of chaos and war. In *Leviathan* (1651), he wrote that the purpose of a governing body, which he calls the commonwealth, is to avoid war and allow peace to work for all people's benefit. By war, Hobbes meant conflicting forces without a universal authority.

Hobbes specified three principal causes of conflict:

- competition for resources, which inspires conflict in pursuit of material gain;

- a diffidence, which is the result of one's pursuit of safety; and

- glory, where conflict follows from the desire to protect or advance one's reputation.

Hobbes believed that the commonwealth's people are subject to the commonwealth's powers because of their desire for self-preservation and security. Hobbes stated, *"the only way to erect a common power [and secure the people] . . . is to confer all of their power and strength upon one man, or upon one assembly of men that may reduce all of their wills, by a plurality of voices, unto one will."*

John Locke (1632-1704) was a 17th-century English philosopher whose political theories greatly influenced the United States Constitution (ratified on June 21, 1788). Locke believed in natural rights. He believed that all men are born equal, free, and independent with these rights and have an inherent right to enjoy life, liberty, and property. Locke believed, concerning natural rights, that man's true freedom requires that others be naturally obligated to respect that freedom.

Locke stated, *"The great and chief end, therefore, of men's uniting into commonwealths, and putting themselves under government, is the preservation of their property."* Locke proposed that it is the need to preserve man's right over their lives, liberties, and possessions that form the basis for man's establishment of political authority. Locke believed that political authority, or political power, might only be obtained by consent or through a social contract over natural rights.

Concerning revolution, Locke believed that unbridled power over man's natural rights warrants and justified resistance by those subject to that power. He believed that a just leader is bound by the laws of the people's legislative representatives, and when a leader ceases to represent the people, he becomes a tyrant. Locke believed that the only way to protect subjects from a reversion to executive tyranny by fiat is to establish a system

---

of checks and balances. He proposed that the legislative branch always has input in the adoption of laws.

Charles de Montesquieu (1689-1755) was an 18th-century French aristocrat, author, and authority on the government who believed in the limited power of a monarch. While Montesquieu did not believe that there was a universal solution for political problems, he believed that law should be objective and evolve by society.

Montesquieu believed a monarchy, due to its inflexibility, could not adequately serve a progressing society. He ultimately concluded that government powers should be separated between an executive, a legislative, and a judicial branch to prevent the establishment of tyranny or absolutism in anyone. Montesquieu stated, "*If political liberty [or legal rights] is to be preserved for the individual, no one man or body in the state should have control of more than one of these functions.*"

Locke (left) and Montesquieu (right), Enlightenment philosophers

Jean Jacques Rousseau (1712-1778) was an 18th-century Genevan philosopher that believed humans are naturally good, free, and can rely on their instincts. Rousseau stated, "*Were there a people of gods, their government would be democratic.*" According to Rousseau, any contract whereby man alienates his freedom would be illegitimate, precisely because it is free will that constitutes man's moral nature. Like Locke, Rousseau believed that a state is made by a union freely formed by its members and that the union must consent to a set of conventions, a social contract.

Thomas Paine (1737-1809) was an 18th-century English-born American political philosopher who authored a pamphlet entitled *"Common Sense"* (1776), which greatly influenced public opinion during the American Revolution (1765-1783). Paine viewed government as a necessary evil. He felt that the government was required for the restraint of instincts and preserving larger social groups.

Paine viewed a monarchy as a form of corrupt government tied to a hereditary succession that goes against biblical principles. He viewed the monarchy as a threat to the nation's future health because it gives any king the power to leave the throne to an incompetent successor. Paine believed that a representative form of government and a rotating annual presidency that chooses each state's representatives is preferable.

Rousseau (left) & Paine (right), Enlightenment philosophers

Second Continental Congress

In 1775, as a precursor to the American Revolution and establishing an independent American government, the *Second Continental Congress* convened. This convention took place after King George III (1738-1820; 1760-1820) of Great Britain and Ireland rejected the *Declaration of Rights and Grievances* (1765), which was a petition to the King to restore harmony between Britain and the colonies after Britain passed punitive laws against the American colonies.

The Second Continental Congress (1775) consisted of delegates from all thirteen colonies. It proposed to replace state legislatures that were dissolved by royal governors. These newly formed legislatures should assume governmental duties, including regulating trade and issuance of paper money. Most importantly, the Second Continental Congress's duty was to organize a continental army and develop an institutional structure to finance the war for American independence.

By 1776, most of the Second Continental Congress members voted to instruct all thirteen colonies to establish independent governments, secede from royal authority, and approve a resolution calling for independence. Thomas Paine's pamphlet *"Common Sense"* (January 10, 1776) convinced the more conservative delegates to support American independence. In July of 1776, the Second Continental Congress signed the *Declaration of Independence,* called the American Revolution's blueprint.

Declaration of Independence

Segments of Locke's philosophy are represented in the language of the *Declaration of Independence*. Both Locke and the Declaration of Independence espouse equality, preservation of life, liberty and property, natural rights, and revolution against the monarchy. Locke and the framers of the Declaration of Independence address resistance against a tyrannical government.

Locke states, *"[w]hen any one, or more, shall take upon them to make laws whom the people have not appointed to do so, they make laws without authority. . ."*

The Declaration of Independence (1776) states, *"[w]hen in the course of human events, it becomes necessary for one people to dissolve the political bands that have connected them with another, and to assume, among the powers of the earth, the separate and equal state to which the laws of nature and nature's God entitle them [...]."*

The *Declaration of Independence* set forth a belief in self-government, a position like Locke's belief that a legitimate government derives its powers from the governed's consent. One drawback to America's Declaration of Independence was the lack of an existing central government. The Second Continental Congress attempted to convince the colonies that reliance on Continental currency and each colony's currency was harmful to the national movement, harmful to the continued financing of the war against the British, and would catalyze inflation.

In 1777, the Second Continental Congress proposed a governing document that called for a strong central government, but a majority of delegates did not favor this. By 1779, after the British began distributing the counterfeit colonial currency to thwart the colonies' war efforts, Congress ceased issuing and honoring its national currency.

Drafting the Declaration of Independence, c. 1776

Articles of Confederation

On March 1, 1781, the *Articles of Confederation* was ratified by the Second Continental Congress. The Articles of Confederation was the first governing document of the United States. The Articles of Confederation's initial purpose was to codify the Second Continental Congress's procedures and powers. The adopted Articles of Confederation changed the Second Continental Congress's name to the *Congress of Confederation*, appointed the United States of America's interim central government, and established shared responsibilities between the states and central government.

The Articles of Confederation defined the relationship between the Confederation Congress and the colonial states' sovereign governments. The Articles of Confederation established a system in which state governments had greater sovereignty and higher power than the central government.

The limited powers delegated to the central government included the power to conduct foreign policy, the power to make treaties, the power to declare war, the power to maintain an army and navy, the power to coin money, and the power to establish post offices.

The powers delegated to the states included collecting taxes, negotiating and entering into trade agreements with foreign countries, and controlling commerce. The Articles of Confederation and the Confederation Congress were vital to negotiating the *Treaty of Paris* (1783) between the United States of America and Great Britain to end the American Revolution (1765-1783).

However, the Articles of Confederation were replete with problems. Amendments to the Articles of Confederation required the colonies' unanimous consent to avoid enhancing the central government's powers. Due to the long travel time, it often took months to obtain consent from the thirteen colonies. The central government lacked any power to tax. The central government depended on the states for income. However, the central government had no way of enforcing its right to collect revenues owed by the states. The value of state currency was declining throughout this period.

The colonial states were fearing the threat of other foreign enemies. Without a strong central government and a rising war debt, there was no way of drafting an army in the event of a conflict. The central government could not regulate commerce between the states. Congress did not have law enforcement organizations or police power at their disposal. The Articles of Confederation could not adjudicate disputes between states and lacked a central executive power. The states competed in the marketplace without a centralized and regulated market and needed a unified economic system.

Shays' Rebellion

Shays' Rebellion presents an excellent example of how the Articles of Confederation were weak. By 1786, the United States was suffering from severe economic depression due to the Revolutionary War (1765-1783). States were battling over land and sea rights, taxes were extremely high, unemployment was rampant, and wages were low.

As a war tactic, the British sanctioned the colonies through curtailing trade. Daniel Shays (1747-1825), a revolutionary war veteran and farmer, led a rebellion against Massachusetts courts that were jailing debtors, confiscating property, and declaring families bankrupt. The rebellion escalated into an armed conflict between Shays' "army" of over a thousand men and the Massachusetts militia across the Commonwealth.

Daniel Shays and Job Shattuck, leaders of the Massachusetts "Regulators," c. 1787

The Commonwealth of Massachusetts sought the federal government's assistance, but without the ability to tax, the federal government could not finance an army or enforce its laws. Even though Shays' men were ultimately defeated and disbanded, his rebellion demonstrated the separate state and federal governments' weaknesses. Rebellions like Shay's commenced throughout the United States. With rebellion and economic turmoil rampant throughout the United States, political leaders determined that the next course of action was to reshape the Articles of Confederation.

Constitutional Convention

Between May 25 and September 17, 1787, delegates from the thirteen independent states (Rhode Island did not participate) met in Philadelphia, Pennsylvania, to revise the Articles of Confederation. Delegates to the Constitutional Convention included planters, bankers, businessmen, and lawyers. It was the intent of a group of delegates at the Convention, later to be called the Federalists, to replace the Articles of Confederation with a new set of governing documents.

Opponents to the Constitutional Convention, many of whom did not attend, saw the attempt to revise the Articles of Confederation as a means of usurping the independent powers of state governments. American historian Charles Beard (1874-1948) produced an interpretation of the United States Constitution from an economic standpoint.

Beard concluded that the Constitutional Convention was an attempt by the elite and wealthy leaders of government. These included the wealthy future Presidents George Washington (1732-1799; presidential term 1789-1797) and James Madison (1751-1836; 1809-1817) to turn capital forces against the agrarian stakeholders. Beard contends that much of the controversy surrounding the Articles of Confederation involved property disputes between commercial business interests and landowners.

Federalist and Anti-Federalist

During the Constitutional Convention, the delegates divided between Federalist and Anti-Federalist factions. The *Federalist* faction was the group of delegates, and eventually, the political party advocated for a stronger central government. James Madison, John Jay (1745-1829), George Washington, and Alexander Hamilton (c. 1755-1804) were among the Federalists at the Constitutional Convention.

The Federalists believed that a strong central government was essential to a state's ability to conduct foreign affairs, regulate disputes between states, collect taxes, and defend the nation. This proposal still allowed most lawmaking to be designated by the states; however, they advocated that a strong central government was essential to create an environment where the individual states could thrive.

The *Anti-Federalists* believed that a stronger federal government would tyrannize the people without restraint. Anti-Federalists included Patrick Henry (1736-1799), who refused to attend the Constitutional Convention, Samuel Adams (1722-1803), George Mason (1725-1792, he refused to sign the Constitution), and future President James Monroe (1758-1831; 1817-1825). The Anti-Federalists believed that a stronger federal government would result in a monarchy and repress individual liberties. They proposed that stronger state governments would better preserve the individual liberty of citizens.

The Anti-Federalists were fighting on behalf of the small colonial states to ensure that states maintained vigorous checks on any central government's power. They wanted mechanisms to prevent the usurpation of power from states if the central government attempted regulatory overreach. The Anti-Federalists insisted on creating a Bill of Rights to codify the rights provided to any citizen of the United States and protect them from the potential tyranny of an unchecked central government.

Virginia Plan

The key to establishing a new structure of the federalist government was building a stronger, more organized central government to work in conjunction with the established state governments.

James Madison, Edmund Randolph (1753-1813; Secretary of State 1794-1795), and other Virginia delegation members devised a plan for a new government. The *Virginia Plan* was a blueprint of a federalist government system and was the blueprint for the *United States Constitution*.

Delegates took the Virginia Plan seriously, believing that the plan would be the new government. The following decisions were taken from the Virginia Plan, agreed upon by the delegates and incorporated into the U.S. Constitution, ratified on June 21, 1788:

- Expansion of the powers of the federal government while granting state governments the power to self-govern

- Creation of a bicameral legislative branch of the federal government consisting of an upper house (Senate) and a lower house (House of Representatives) of the legislative branch. Together, these are Congress

- Creation of an executive branch to execute and enforce the laws

- Creation of a judicial branch to review the laws and arbitrate disputes between the other branches of government

- Creation of a system of governance based upon checks and balances among the three branches (i.e., legislative, executive, and judicial branch)

James Madison (left) and Edmund Randolph (right)

Delegates disagreed on apportionment's specifics for the legislative branch of government and how its members would be elected. In the *Connecticut Compromise*, the delegates finally established the bicameral structure of Congress.

Delegates agreed that the voters of each state would elect the members of the lower house of Congress. After much dispute, it was agreed that the number of representatives from each state would be apportioned based on the state's relative population (i.e., a fixed number of representatives).

Although there was much dispute, the delegates eventually agreed that two individuals from each state would be elected to Congress's upper house (Senate) by the state legislatures. In 1913, the election of Senators by state legislatures was abolished under the Seventeenth Amendment. Three-quarters of the states ratified the Amendment on April 8, 1913.

Under the *Three-Fifths Compromise*, it was agreed that slaves would be considered three-fifths of a person to measure each state's population for apportionment of the number of elected members for the House of Representatives for each state. This compromise could be argued to reduce the legislative influence (i.e., number of proportionate members to the House of Representatives) by the slave-holding states. Slaves were not permitted to participate in government by voting. Some argue that the apportionment of "three-fifths" transfers the voting rights to the slaveowner and others with vested interests in preserving this injustice.

Amendments to the Constitution

Delegates agreed that there should be a complicated amendment process for the United States Constitution. Under Article V of the Constitution, the framers provided several mechanisms for ratification of the Constitution.

According to Article V of the Constitution, the Constitution may be amended if:

- the amended language receives a two-thirds majority vote from each House of Congress, as well as ratification by three-fourths of each state's legislature, or

- the language receives two-thirds majority vote from each House of Congress as well as ratification by a convention in at least three-fourths of the states, or

- at least two-thirds request a national convention of state legislatures. Three-fourths of state legislatures vote to ratify the amendment. The language is proposed by a national convention and ratified by a specially called convention of at least three-fourths of the state's vote. This mechanism has never been used.

There are currently 27 ratified amendments to the United States Constitution.

The 13th Amendment (ratified on December 6, 1865) abolished slavery.

The 14th Amendment (ratified on July 9, 1868) provides that most federal legal rights and protections granted under the 5th Amendment Due Process Clause of the Bill of Rights (ratified on December 15, 1791) and the 14th Amendment Equal Protection clause apply equally to the states as they do to the federal government.

The 15th Amendment (ratified on February 3, 1870) granted voting rights to African American men. The 15th Amendment prohibited the states from denying men the right to vote based on "race, color or previous condition of servitude,"

The 16th Amendment (ratified on December 3, 1913) allows Congress to levy an income tax without apportioning it among the states or basing it on the United States Census results.

Bill of Rights: First Ten Amendments

The framers of the United States Constitution attempted to expedite the ratification of the *Bill of Rights* (ratified on December 15, 1791). The Bill of Rights is the first ten amendments to the Constitution. The Bill of Rights was passed by Congress and ratified by states to appease the fears of Anti-Federalists. They believed that a strong federal government would oppress individual freedoms and liberties. Without the crucial additions

---

and promises included in the Bill of Rights, some colonial states might not have ratified the U.S. Constitution.

The Bill of Rights guarantees Constitutional protection of individual freedoms and rights against abridgment by the federal (but not state) government. The Bill of Rights espoused fundamental rights not set forth in the Articles of the Constitution.

These fundamental (Constitutional) rights include:

- freedom of religion

- freedom of speech

- a free press

- free assembly

- the right to keep and bear arms

- freedom from unreasonable search and seizure

- security in personal effects

- freedom from warrants issued without probable cause

- guarantee of a speedy trial

- guarantee of a public trial with an impartial jury

- prohibition of double jeopardy

Other plans were introduced at the Constitutional Convention by both proponents and opponents of a federal government system. William Paterson (1745–1806; U.S. senator 1789–90, governor of New Jersey 1790–93, and an associate justice of the U.S. Supreme Court 1793–1806) introduced the *New Jersey Plan*. The New Jersey Plan proposed revising the Articles of Confederation so that each state would receive equal representation in a unicameral federal legislative branch of government.

The New Jersey Plan granted the United States the power to levy taxes, established a multi-person one-term executive branch of government to be elected by Congress and a judicial branch. The New Jersey Plan proposed that federal law would take precedence over state law.

Alexander Hamilton proposed a government blueprint inspired by the British parliamentary system. The *Hamilton Plan* proposed eliminating state government sovereignty, establishing a federal bicameral legislature, creating a national governor with a lifetime appointment, and creating state governors. The delegates of the Constitutional Convention rejected both the New Jersey plan and the Hamilton plan.

Thirty-nine delegates from eleven states signed the final draft of the United States Constitution. Delegates from Rhode Island (who did not participate in the Convention) and New York were not present to sign the document.

William Paterson, Supreme Court justice and pioneer of the New Jersey Plan

The United States Constitution was ratified (June 21, 1788) by nine of the thirteen colonial states, as required by Article IV of the Constitution. The Bill of Rights was not included in the draft of the Constitution signed by the 39 delegates in 1787. The Bill of Rights was drafted by Congress as Amendments to the Constitution and ratified on December 15, 1791. As formal Amendments to the Constitution, they are incorporated and given the same effect as the original seven Articles specified in the Constitution.

The Federalist Papers

To encourage the hesitant states to ratify the Constitution, James Madison, John Jay, and Alexander Hamilton wrote the *Federalist Papers*. The three authors contributed to 85 articles and essays under the pseudonym "Publius." The series was published in two volumes beginning in March and May 1788.

In *Federalist 10*, James Madison argued that factions exist in society as a derivation of passion and political interests. Madison believed that a more extensive united republic would better protect the majority's interests against a minority faction. He posited that in a representative democracy, individual liberty is protected from majority rule, where the majority's interests act as a detriment to the public interest.

Madison stated, "*[t]he smaller the society, the fewer probably will be the distinct parties and interests composing it; the fewer the distinct parties and interests, the more frequently will a majority be found of the same party.*"

James Madison stated that the smaller the number of people in the majority, the more efficiently the majority may collaborate to execute their oppression plan. "*Extend the sphere, and you take in a greater variety of parties and interests; you make it less probable that a majority of the whole will have a common motive to invade the rights of other citizens; or if such a common motive exists, it will be more difficult for all who feel it to discover their own strength and to act in unison with each other.*"

Federalist 10 argued that the United States Constitution's principles guard against the majority's tyranny in direct democracy to protect the public's interests.

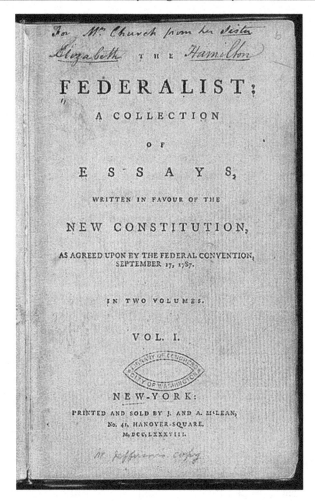

Title page, The Federalist Papers *by Alexander Hamilton, James Madison, and John Jay*

The issue of majority rule was important to the framers of the Constitution. The framers implemented the *Electoral College* so that the more populous states could not have excessive regional influence in the President's national election.

The framers established staggered election terms for the Congress and the Senate to reduce the potential factions developing to influence policy disproportionately.

The Bill of Rights was drafted to protect 1) the minority against the majority and 2) people from the federal government. It explicitly enumerates fundamental rights retained by the people in the democracy.

In *Federalist 48,* Madison argues for separate branches of government. He asserts that the three government branches should remain divided, but they should not be so divided to diminish their control (checks and balances) over each other. He warns against those with encroaching power and their attempt to control.

Madison asserts that merely defining the branches of government is insufficient to guard against encroachment by another branch. He states, *"[t]he legislative department is everywhere extending the sphere of its activity and drawing all power into its impetuous vortex."*

In *Federalist 51*, Madison wrote that the Constitution's safeguards establish three separate and independent branches of government and limitations to restrict them from usurping power. He writes, *"[t]he framers recognized that, in the long term, structural protections against abuse of power were critical to preserving liberty."*

Madison asserted that if men were angels and chaos did not exist; the government would not be necessary. He stated the *"great security against a gradual concentration of the several powers in the same department consists in giving to those who administer each department the necessary constitutional means and personal motives to resist encroachments of the others."*

Federalist 51 is the basis for a bicameral federal legislative government. Madison states, *"The legislative branch is the strongest, and therefore must be divided into different branches, be as little connected as possible and render them by different modes of election."*

In *Federalist 78*, Alexander Hamilton explained to the Anti-Federalists the importance of a federal judicial system that is not beholden to political interests and is therefore not elected. According to *Federalist 78*, the federal courts must interpret and apply the Constitution and disregard any statute or legislative action that is inconsistent with the Constitution. Hamilton states that the judicial branch has the power of judicial review to determine whether Congress or the executive branch acts are constitutional.

The judicial branch of government may be considered the weakest branch because it lacks the power of the purse, the power to declare war, and does not set policy. However, the judicial branch could be the most influential of the three government branches because the judges are appointed for life. Their court decisions and published opinions can last decades (as binding precedent) or indefinitely (not overruled by a future case on point).

Alexander Hamilton, political theorist, and author of the Federalist Papers

Hamilton defined the role of *stare decisis* (i.e., let the decision stand; precedent) for the judiciary. He stated, "*to avoid an arbitrary discretion in the courts; it is indispensable that they should be bound down by strict rules and precedents, which serve to define and point out their duty in every particular case that comes before them.*" Hamilton believed that the reliance on precedent would prevent judicial activism's imposition or application of jurists' independent principles and philosophy.

Citing *Federalist 78*, the United States Supreme Court in *Obergefell v. Hodges* (2015) same-sex marriage case stated, "*the people who ratified the Constitution authorized courts to exercise 'neither force nor will but merely judgment.*" By design, judges and justices (justices are the judges sitting on the highest court in the jurisdiction) are not subject to the will of the people or politicians but subject to the will of the U.S. Constitution.

Philosophical elements from Hobbes, Locke, Rousseau, Montesquieu, and Scottish philosopher David Hume (1711-1776) are throughout the explicit text of the Constitution. Some political commentators feel that the framers of the Constitution did not align their principles entirely with the political philosophers' egalitarian harmony but were, instead, inspired by those philosophies to establish a functioning government.

Thomas Paine wrote that "*government even in its best state is a necessary evil; in its worst state, an intolerable one.*" Hobbes emphasized the need for the state to limit its concerns to peace and common defense matters. Paine's philosophical influence is evident in the language of the Constitution.

The framers of the Constitution's primary goal was to establish a unified government for the thirteen states' common defense. The framers placed the role of Commander in Chief with the President. The power to declare war was given to Congress instead of delegating duties of defense to state governments.

Hobbes believed that man's passion is the foundation for war, which is why the framers of the United States Constitution emphasized dividing the military's power among two government branches, the legislative and the executive.

Locke's beliefs are evident throughout the Constitution. Locke believed that each person is entitled to life, liberty, and property that inspired the framework of the 5th Amendment *Due Process Clause* and the 14th Amendment *Equal Protection Clause* and *Privileges and Immunities Clause*.

Locke's belief that the consent of the governed is needed to legitimize the power of government. This belief is evident in the framers' decision to make the United States government a representative democracy where people elect government officials. Locke and Montesquieu's belief in a checks and balances system is reflected in the Constitution's language. This belief of checks and balances is evidenced by the Senate's requisite power to approve treaties and judicial appointments by the President.

Notes for active learning

Separation of Powers

Inspired by Charles de Montesquieu, the United States Constitution's framers believed that the U.S. government's power should be divided based on administrative duties. As in *Federalist 51*, the United States government is divided into three branches: the executive, the judicial, and the legislative.

The legislative branch is charged with the power to make the laws (i.e., statutes). The executive branch must execute (i.e., administer) the laws. The judicial branch must review the constitutionality of laws. The framers divided national powers among three branches to prevent an abuse of power by one person or group and safeguard freedom for all Americans.

The framers established a cautious and deliberative system of government, not an impulsive government ruled by one. Therefore, they wanted three independent branches of government, governed by its own rules, elected or appointed by independent laws set forth by the Constitution, and holding power for varying terms.

Legislative Branch

Article I of the Constitution established the legislative branch of the United States government. Article I established the Senate and House of Representatives' legislative chambers, each charged with creating the laws, regulating interstate and foreign commerce, the power to investigate the executive branch, tax and spend, raise an army, and declare war. Both Houses of Congress have the authority to subpoena and oversee laws by demanding select members of federal agencies appear before them to provide testimony.

The House of Representatives must initiate all bills related to revenue.

The Senate is uniquely charged (i.e., imposed upon) with the power to advise and consent (i.e., confirmation) to executive appointments. It is charged with the power to ratify treaties and charged to hold a trial and convict the accused (e.g., the impeachment of an executive or judicial officer) after impeachment by the House.

Under Article I of the Constitution, Congress has the power to create all laws *necessary and proper* for the carrying out of its duties.

Seals of the House of Representatives (left) and Senate (right)

Members of the House of Representatives are elected every two years. Each member of the lower house must have attained the age of twenty-five, be an inhabitant of the state in which they shall be elected, and have been a citizen of the United States for seven years before the election. Senators are elected every six years. Each member of the Senate must attain the age of 30 and be an inhabitant of the state in which they shall be elected and be citizens of the United States for nine years.

The U.S. Constitution provides a blueprint for the government, but it is in a minimalistic form. The Constitution's genius is its ability to evolve and allows the government to interpret, review, and amend the document's language. Powers expressly set forth by the Constitution's language and ratified Amendments are 1) enumerated powers of the federal government, 2) reserved fundamental individual rights, and 3) powers reserved for the states. The implied powers are those powers established by court decisions (i.e., judge-made case law). One such mechanism is the power of judicial review granted to the United States Supreme Court by its rendering of case law. Courts make case law. The legislature enacts statutes. The executive branch issues executive orders and promulgates rules and regulations related to laws.

In *McCulloch v. Maryland* (1819), James McCulloch of the First Bank of the United States sought review of the State of Maryland's decision to levy taxes on the federal bank. Even though Article I of the Constitution did not grant Congress the power to establish a bank. The Supreme Court held that the federal government could establish a bank under the Necessary and Proper Clause of Article I. Chief Justice John Marshall (1755-1835; 1801-1835), writing for the majority, stated that Article I is not dispositive of congressional authority but provides a mechanism for the expansion of its authority.

Chief Justice Marshall stated that for Congress to seek an objective within its enumerated powers, it is proper for Congress to interpret those powers if the interpretation is rationally related to the objective and not forbidden by the Constitution.

Chief Justice John Marshall of McCulloch v. Maryland, 1819

In *Gibbon v. Ogden* (1824), the Supreme Court held that Congress has the authority to regulate interstate commerce. Article I, Section 8, clause 3 provides Congress *"with the power to regulate commerce with foreign nations and among the several states and Indian tribes."* The purpose of the *Commerce Clause* was to curtail state-imposed discrimination on commerce between the colonial states that arose under the Articles of Confederation and remedy the absence of federal commerce power under the Articles of Confederation. In *Gibbon*, Justice Marshall held that the power to regulate interstate commerce relates to economics and expands interstate navigation regulation, impacting commerce.

The Commerce Clause of the Constitution is a crucial component of congressional power. The Commerce Clause and case law in *Gibbon* and other decided Supreme Court cases have expanded the federal government's powers over the state's powers by directly regulating commerce distribution between the states. This power is enumerated explicitly in the Constitution.

The Commerce Clause has been used to limit state policies that discriminate against out-of-state motorists or establish monopolies. The Commerce Clause has been invoked to enforce the protection of civil liberties and civil rights violations against protected classes of people.

In *Heart of Atlanta Motel, Inc. v. United States* (1964), the Supreme Court determined that Congress may regulate private businesses' actions that violate the 1964 Civil Rights Act. The Heart of Atlanta Motel practiced racial discrimination policies despite implementing the Civil Rights Act, which banned discrimination in public accommodation places by refusing to rent rooms to Blacks.

The motel filed suit against the United States on the grounds that Congress exceeded its authority in regulating interstate commerce. The Supreme Court held that the motel's policies violated the Constitution because they infringed on interstate commerce. The motel was in a strategic location that depended on interstate commerce. The hotel's policies impeded Blacks' ability to freely travel because 75% of the motel's guests were from out-of-state (i.e., interstate commerce).

Executive Branch

Article II of the United States Constitution established the executive branch. The executive branch consists of the elected President and Vice President who hold office for four years. Article II charges the executive branch with the duty to execute the laws passed by Congress, enforce laws, command the military as Commander in Chief, make treaties (with the advice and consent of the Senate), appoint ambassadors and executives to government agencies, appoint judges to the federal courts, and advise Congress on the state of the union.

The President has the authority to propose legislation to Congress, call a special session of Congress, veto legislation passed by Congress, remove executive appointments, oversee foreign affairs, enter treaties and agreements with foreign governments, and deploy troops once Congress has declared war.

The President has the power to enter into executive agreements without ratification by the legislature. These agreements are solely agreements between the President and another nation for foreign policy issues, the President's power as Commander in Chief, or a prior Act of Congress. These agreements are politically binding but not legally binding because the Senate does not ratify them.

Under the *Case Act*, the President must notify Congress about implementing an executive agreement within 20 days of execution. Article II powers are unique in that they fail to delineate the specifics of any power of the President. The President is the Commander in Chief of the armed forces, but the Constitution fails to define this role or authority. Therefore, the courts interpret the powers of the President not enumerated within the Constitution.

Under Article II of the Constitution, the President must be a natural-born citizen of the United States. The President must have attained thirty-five years to be eligible for the Office and must have resided in the United States for the previous 14 years. The President may not be elected to office, with a four-year term, more than twice under the 22nd Amendment, ratified on February 27, 1951.

Suppose the President is removed from office due to death, resignation, impeachment, or inability to discharge the office's duties and powers. In that case, the office shall devolve to the Vice President. Congress enacted the Presidential Succession Act of 1792 under Article II, Section I, Clause 6. The Act specifies that if the Vice President is unable to accept these duties, the President's office devolves, in succession, to the Speaker of the House, the president *pro tempore* of the Senate, and the individual cabinet members.

Under the election's clause of Article II, Section 1, Clauses 2 and 3 of the Constitution, each state must appoint electors (i.e., electoral college) equal to the number of Senators and Representatives that states may be entitled in Congress. The *Electoral College* is a proportionate number (equal to the number of the state's congressional delegation) of electors casting votes in the presidential election based on the state's popular vote. The state decides if the electors vote in a winner-take-all system or based on the percentage of votes cast for each candidate. After the populace election, these electors shall meet in their respective states and vote by ballot for the President and the Vice President. In the event of a tie in the cast number of electoral college votes, the House of Representatives chooses the President and Vice President. The presidential nominee (the nominee is the winner of the primary) with the most electoral votes is elected.

The President's powers are not absolute. In *Youngstown v. Sawyer* (1952), the Supreme Court limited the power of Democrat President Harry S. Truman (1884-1972; 1945-1953) during the Korean Conflict (June 25, 1950, to July 27, 1953). The Court held that the President's issuance of an Executive Order to seize and operate steel mills during a labor strike was unconstitutional. The Supreme Court held that, according to the

Constitution, the act of taking dominion over private property is not included in executive function but is a legislative act granted solely to Congress.

In *United States v. Curtiss-Wright Export Corporation* (1936), the Supreme Court upheld the plenary authority of Democrat President Franklin Delano Roosevelt (1882-1945; 1933 to April 12, 1945) over foreign relations. Curtiss-Wright was indicted for violating a federal embargo by sending arms to Bolivia. Curtiss-Wright argued in defense that the embargo was an unconstitutional delegation of legislative authority to the executive branch. The Supreme Court stated that while the Constitution does not explicitly specify that all power to conduct foreign policy is vested in the President, it is implicitly given. This power is suggested because the executive branch is empowered to conduct foreign affairs so that Congress cannot.

In *United States v. Belmont* (1937), President Roosevelt agreed with the Soviet Union to confiscate Soviet corporations' wealth being held on U.S. soil. Belmont, who held funds on behalf of the former Soviet corporations, sued the United States to recover those funds. The Supreme Court held that the President has the authority to enter into executive agreements with a foreign government without the Senate's advice and consent. The Court held that these executive agreements preempt state constitutions, laws, and policies under the federal government's exclusive authority over foreign policy.

Judicial Branch

Article III of the Constitution establishes the judicial branch of the United States government. The Constitution does not define the number of federal justices (i.e., judges sitting on the highest court in the jurisdiction) appointed to the bench, as determined by statute. Article III provides for the Supreme Court to be presided over by one Chief Justice.

Article III established one court, the Supreme Court, which holds:

1) original jurisdiction over the adjudication of cases involving ambassadors, public ministers, cases in which a state is a party to the lawsuit, controversies between a state and the federal government and cases between states, and

2) appellate jurisdiction to review cases from the highest state courts and the federal appellate (regional Federal Circuit) courts.

Marbury v. Madison (1803) is a Supreme Court holding that defined the Supreme Court's power of judicial review over the legislative branch's decision, which is a power not specified in the U.S. Constitution. The Supreme Court is charged with reviewing legislation and executive action's constitutionality by reviewing court decisions of lower federal courts or each state's highest court.

If the Supreme Court intends to review a lower federal or state court's decisions, it is deemed to have granted a *writ of certiorari*. Certiorari (Latin for "to be more fully informed) is a court process for invoking judicial review by a higher court. Judicial review is granted if four of the nine Supreme Court justices (i.e., rule of four) determine that the case arising from a lower court satisfies the *case and controversy requirement* (i.e., pending litigation seeking a court resolution) and involves constitutional interpretation.

Suppose, upon reviewing the facts and disposition of the case, the Supreme Court decides not to hear oral arguments (i.e., no legal issue requiring review) because the lower court applied the law correctly in resolving the dispute (i.e., lawsuit), the *writ of certiorari* is denied.

In writing about the judiciary's powers over the federal government, Thomas Jefferson (1743-1826; 1801-1809) believed that the issue's strict constitutional construction is essential for narrowly ruling on federal powers.

Congress has plenary power to establish, terminate, and delegate the duties of all other federal courts. State courts are autonomous from federal courts except that federal courts have the power to review a state court decision where the constitutionality of the state court's decision is at issue.

Constitutional interpretation of statutes, powers, and policies are concerned with the justification, standards, and methods by which courts exercise judicial review. The problem of constitutional law is that it permits majorities to rule politically in broad areas of life as the majority. The dilemma is that neither the majority nor the minority can be trusted to define the proper spheres of democratic authority and individual liberty related to the Constitution (i.e., the supreme law of the United States).

President Thomas Jefferson, and political theorist, c. 1809

Balancing the majority's desires with the rights of the minority lies in the constitutionally constructed rulings of the judiciary. *Constitutional absolutism* is a form of judicial review whereby judicial review rests on the premise that there is no necessary inconsistency between the practice of judicial review and the principles of democratic government (within the constraints of the Constitution). This principle is required because the American system is based on the principles contained in the Constitution.

In *Fletcher v. Peck* (1810), the Supreme Court reviewed the constitutionality of a state statute. Georgia enacted a law claiming possession of Native American lands and then selling land tracts to development companies. Peck sued Fletcher after a tract of land sold by Fletcher to Peck did not have a clear title of ownership. The Georgia legislature repealed the law after Peck's purchase. The Supreme Court ruled that the repeal of that state law was an unconstitutional invalidation of a binding contract.

The *Fletcher* case is the first instance in which 1) the Supreme Court ruled on the constitutionality of a state statute and 2) as a precursor court ruling to the *contract clause* that restricts states from invalidating or interfering with binding contracts between private parties.

Checks and Balances

The separation of powers doctrine in the Constitution establishes the Federalists' desires to establish independent governmental administrations. In *Federalist 51*, Madison argues that it is crucial to make each institution autonomous in a constitutional system, that is, independent of each another. However, there must be a balance contained in that autonomy. Madison states that to avoid governmental tyranny by a branch, the other branches must be diligent in assuring that they always monitor the others' actions.

Checks and balances are a system for each branch of government to regulate the actions of the others. Checks and balances provide a system whereby each branch must cooperate to accomplish a task of great importance. Article III provides that the President has the authority to veto legislation passed by both Houses of Congress. Although not enumerated in the Constitution, the judicial branch has the power (i.e., *Marbury v. Madison*) to review the constitutionality of Congressional laws.

The Constitution does not specify the judicial branch of government's appellate jurisdiction, the judicial branch's judicial review power. In *Marbury v. Madison* (1803), the Supreme Court defined the Court's power of judicial review over the legislative branch's enactment.

In *Marbury*, the Supreme Court held a congressional statute expanding the Supreme Court's original jurisdiction and requiring that the Supreme Court issue a *writ of mandamus* to federal officers is unconstitutional. The Supreme Court stated that the court must ascertain and resolve a conflict between the two branches and the meaning of any act proceeding from the legislative body.

Article II grants the President the power to veto bills passed by Congress as a part of the checks and balances power. An example of checks and balances is that the President has two veto options: a regular veto and a "pocket veto." The regular veto is negative, whereby the President returns the unsigned legislation within ten days to Congress. President Washington first used this veto on April 5, 1972. Article I, Section 7 of the Constitution states that Congress has the power to override a presidential veto by a two-thirds majority vote in both Houses of Congress.

President Madison first used a *pocket veto* in 1812. However, a pocket veto is where "the Congress by their adjournment prevent its return, in which case, it shall not be law." The executive branch and legislative branch have disagreed about the definition of "adjournment." (i.e., postpone with the intent to resume).

Other checks and balances in the system include, but are not limited to:

- Presidential treaty power requires the advice and consent of the Senate.

- Presidential appointment power requires the advice and consent of the Senate.

- Congress has the sole power to declare war and raise an army, while the President is the Commander in Chief.

- Congress has the power to investigate the actions of the executive branch.

- Congress has the power to delegate legislative powers to the executive agencies if Congress maintains oversight over those powers.

- The President nominates judicial appointees, while the Senate confirms (*advice and consent*) presidential judicial appointments and senior administration (cabinet) appointments.

- The House of Representatives has the power to impeach an executive or judicial officer. The Senate has the power to try, with the Chief Justice of the Supreme Court presiding, the impeachment proceedings in the Senate. If convicted, the Senate has the power to remove that individual.

Article II, Section 3, Clause 1 of the Constitution grants the President the power to advise Congress on the state of the union and recommend legislative measures to Congress.

In 1996, Congress passed the Line-Item Veto Act authorizing the President to veto portions of a fiscal bill, The City of New York sought judicial review of this Act. In *Clinton v. City of New York* (1998), the Supreme Court held that Democrat President William Jefferson Clinton's (1993-2001) line-item veto was an unconstitutional usurpation of legislative power by the executive branch.

The Supreme Court held that the President is authorized to approve or reject bills, in whole, as a member of the executive branch. However, the President is not authorized by the Constitution to enact, amend, or repeal legislation, as that function lies solely within the legislative branch's authority.

Supreme Court building, Washington, D.C.

In *INS v. Chadha* (1983*)*, Jagdish Chadha, born in Kenya to Indian parents, was deemed by the United States, Kenya, and the United Kingdom to be a stateless person after Kenya was declared independent of the United Kingdom. Chadha sought suspension of his deportation proceedings due to hardship. The Attorney General granted his request. The House of Representatives unilaterally overruled the Attorney's General's suspension of his deportation proceedings.

In *INS v. Chadha,* the Supreme Court held that the House of Representatives could not enact a statute that permitted it to overrule unilaterally or veto the executive branch's decision. To hold otherwise would be inconsistent with the bicameral principle of government established by the Constitution. The Supreme Court stated that the government's bicameral system was established to hinder encroachment by the legislative branch on the other government branches.

Notes for active learning

Federalism

Federalism is a system of government whereby the federal government exists in conjunction with state and local governments to execute the powers of government for the welfare of the people. The idea of federalism was central to the creation of the Constitution and the subsequent American political system.

Unlike unitary governments, the federal government is more democratic and is more effective in protecting its citizens' rights. Under the government's confederal system (e.g., the government under the Articles of Confederation), state governments held higher power than the federal government. This confederation of sovereign states believed that the states should act independently of the federal government.

Under federalism, some governmental powers are exclusive to the federal government, some powers are exclusive to the state governments, and some powers are shared. The modern system of government is an amalgamation of federal and confederal systems of government. The powers are shared or at least intertwined.

This concept is dual federalism. Dual federalism is the role state government has in the political electoral process and the Constitution's amendment process. Additionally, the power to operate courts of law, build roads, regulate traffic, and collect taxes are powers shared by both the federal and state governments.

Grants

Through a block or categorical federal grant, state governments have the sole authority to regulate and implement state programs for the impoverished, specific programs to clean the environment, oversee local primary and secondary education, and enhance programs to protect the disabled or underrepresented groups.

A block grant provides federal funds given to state and local governments with only a policy (general indication) of how (often nonbinding) the recipient state or local government should spend the money. These federal grants are distributed in blocks to state and local governments and are generally welcomed by local governments due to their flexibility in utilizing the funds.

Categorical grants are given to the state government with a specific provision recommended. Medicaid, the Food Stamp Program, and Head Start are categorical federal grants given to states. Some of these grants require that the states match the funds provided by the federal government. In the 1980s, Republican President Ronald Reagan (1911-2004; 1981-1989) set forth a plan to move much federal grants' spending power for these programs to the states by his Anti-Federalist stance.

President Ronald Reagan's policy permitted the states more governance powers and was called the "New Federalism." Reagan's program encouraged reduced government spending and incentivized efficiency. Some might construe President Reagan's policy as devolution of federal power to shift the decision-making authority to the state and local level. The argument is that the local governments can and should be more responsive than the extensive federal government to its constituents' local needs.

Mandates

The federal government sets mandates on state governments. These mandates require that states comply with specific federal rules and guidelines by limiting certain activities by the state. Often these limits on activities and mandates are tied to the awarding of federal grants. Other supreme federal oversight imposed on the states apply to such issues as civil rights or environmental protections.

The federal government may place restrictions on state and local governments' grants where those governments fail to establish anti-discrimination protections, environmental protection, or emissions regulations. Federal mandates include the Social Security Amendments, the Hazardous and Solid Waste Amendments, the Highway Safety Amendments, the Asbestos Emergency Response Act, the Drug-Free Workplace Acts, the Ocean Dumping Ban Act, and the Clean Air Act Amendment.

Enumerated and Reserved Powers

The enumerated powers described in Article I, Section 8 of the Constitution remain exclusive to the federal government. These specific powers are enumerated powers because they are explicitly stated in the Constitution. Under these powers, the federal government holds power and responsibility for its citizens without regard to their residence state. The federal government holds the exclusive authority to print money, regulate interstate commerce, declare war, and enter into international trade and foreign policy agreements.

However, the federal government does not have the power to spend without the passage and approval of an appropriations bill, impose export taxes, pass *ex-post facto* (i.e., retroactive) laws, or grant titles of nobility.

State governments have independent governing powers. Under their reserved powers, state governments have the exclusive power to issue licenses, regulate intrastate commerce if that regulation of commerce does not interfere with interstate commerce, oversee local, state, and federal elections. Under the Tenth Amendment, all other powers explicitly delegated to the states nor prohibited by the Constitution are reserved for the states.

Other reserved state powers include establishing local governments and establishing state taxing mechanisms (e.g., real estate and sales tax). States have police power and the corresponding authority to legislate to protect its constituents' health, morals, safety, and general welfare. The state government has the responsibility of regulating social, moral, and family policies.

State governments do not have the authority to regulate or enter treaties with foreign nations, declare war, print money, interfere with contracts, maintain a standing army, and impose import or export duties. States may not abridge the privileges and immunities of any state citizen by restricting the citizen's ability to obtain police protection, the ability to access state resources, or access state courts.

The federal government does have some authority over the state governments in the Federalist system. Under the Full Faith and Credit Clause of Article IV of the Constitution, states are obligated to accept the court judgments, contracts, and other civil acts granted in another state. States are prohibited from subdividing or combining without congressional consent.

The precise language of the Constitution enumerates the specific federal versus state powers. Other laws defining these powers have been created by case law (i.e., judge-made law) through the doctrine of judicial review. Because of federalism, the courts can enhance the federal government's specific powers or diminish the federal government's powers because the legislative boundaries on issues evolve. The state and federal governments' powers are designed to always conflict (i.e., intentional tension built into the American system of government). Therefore, at one time, the Supreme Court favors specific states' rights over federal rights, and at another time, the Supreme Court favors the conflicting federal rights over states' rights.

Many conflicts between state and federal governments arise where there is a state law in conflict with federal law. Conflicts between state law and federal law are resolved in favor of federal law (i.e., the Constitution's supremacy clause). Under the Supremacy Clause in Article VI, "*this Constitution, and the laws of the United States which shall be made in pursuance thereof; and all treaties made, or which shall be made, under the authority of the United States, shall be the supreme law of the land; and the judges in every state shall be bound thereby.*"

In *Martin v. Hunter's Lessee* (1816), the Supreme Court held that its judicial review power expanded its authority to review a decision from the highest court of a state where a federal law or the Constitution conflicted. Denny Martin sought a review of a Virginia law that permitted the confiscation of property owned by foreigners after the American Revolution.

Martin argued that his property rights were protected by a treaty, not subject to Virginia law. The Virginia Supreme Court held that the United States Supreme Court lacked the authority to review a Virginia law. However, the United States Supreme Court held that it had appellate jurisdiction and, therefore, the right to overrule any state law that conflicted with a federal treaty.

In *McCulloch v. Maryland (*1819), the United States Supreme Court held that federal law shall prevail (i.e., supremacy clause) for conflicts between federal law and state law, federal law shall prevail. James McCulloch of the First Bank of the United States sought a review of Maryland's decision to levy taxes on the federal bank. Even though Article I of the U.S. Constitution did not grant Congress the power to establish a bank, the Supreme Court held that a state government could not tax a federal agency.

Article I, Section 8, clause 3 provides Congress with *the power to regulate commerce with foreign nations and among the several states and Indian tribes*. The purpose of the Commerce Clause was to curtail state-imposed discrimination on commerce that arose under the Articles of Confederation and remedy the absence of any federal commerce power under the Articles of Confederation.

Gibbon v. Ogden (1824) is a federalism case. The Supreme Court held that Congress has the authority to regulate interstate commerce by preempting state regulations on interstate travel. The State of New York, along with other states, awarded exclusive licenses to navigate rivers in each state to specific steamboat lines.

In *Gibbon*, Justice Marshall held that the power to regulate interstate commerce not only holds in matters of economics but expands to the regulation of interstate navigation, which impacts commerce. The Supreme Court determined that while states and the federal government have concurrent power over the navigation of its waters, federal licenses to navigate take precedent (i.e., judicial decision) over any similar licenses issued by the states.

In *United States v. Lopez* (1995), Alfonso Lopez sought review of a federal regulation declaring schools to be gun-free zones on the grounds that the Act was an unconstitutional regulation of education, a regulation under the exclusive authority of the states. The federal government argued that the statute was enacted under Congress' power to regulate commerce because guns in an educational environment cause violence, raise insurance rates, and relegate educational institutions to unsafe environments.

In *Lopez,* the Supreme Court held that while there are individual extensions to the commerce clause, regulating the carrying of handguns where there is no evidence that carrying them would affect the economy on a massive scale is an invalid commerce clause extension.

Chief Justice Rehnquist (1924-2005; Associate Justice 1972-1986; Chief Justice 1986-2005) wrote the majority opinion in *Lopez*. Chief Justice Rehnquist stated that *"to uphold the Government's contentions here, we have to pile inference upon inference in a manner that would bid fair to convert congressional authority under the Commerce Clause to a general police power of the sort retained by the States."*

In reviewing these cases, there are advantages and disadvantages of a federalist system. Scholars have proposed that federalism mobilizes political activity among the people because it nationalizes political issues. However, the system's analysis may confuse political issues for those uninformed about the functions and issues relevant to the federal and state governments.

A federalist system diminishes the power of special interest groups due to the size of the national platform. Likewise, it makes it prohibitively expensive for local activists to receive widespread attention as they advocate for specific issues that emanate locally. Federalism provides a system where policy ideas can be challenged on a smaller, state-level before being implemented on a larger, national scale. Some founding fathers considered the states of being incubators to test ideas locally before introducing these ideas to a larger society.

The dual court system of federal and state courts may be a disadvantage of federalism because it confuses people about legal issues and laws (i.e., federal vs. state laws). This intertwined complexity makes it difficult for citizens to remain abreast of the multitude of interrelated and evolving laws.

Theories of a Democratic Government

The notion of democracy dates to Ancient Greece (700-480 B.C.) and was characterized before the Classical Age (480-323 B.C.). The term *democracy* means the rule (*kratos* or *cratos)* of the populace (*demos*). The Anglicized version is the word democracy. In the Classical Age, the prominent philosopher Plato (c. 428-348 B.C.) believed that philosophers were the natural rulers of their time, rivals to the monarchs, and revolutionaries against regimes where a man cannot live free and happy. Although they were not necessarily proponents of a democratic government, these Classical Age Greek philosophers believed in the people's power to rise against tyranny. They advocated that tyranny occurs when unitary and corrupt leaders concentrate absolute power.

Plato, philosopher of ancient Greece, c. 350 B.C.

Plato lived in a democratic regime where all males could directly participate in legislative action and had a voice in deciding important government positions. In that government, the legislature excluded women, children, slaves, and foreigners from making government decisions. Plato thought that democracy was an unjust form of government replete with disorder and desire for excessive liberty. The people's needs could never be met in this form of government because the democratic government would focus on excess, not moderation.

Democracy is a form of government that places the ultimate political authority in the people's will instead of individual authority. Democracy espouses the theory of popular sovereignty, a policy like Locke's theories in which power to govern belongs to the people governed by consent. Direct democracy is derived from ancient Athens' philosophies, wherein the citizens debated and voted directly on all laws. Democracy is an effort to bring about a compromise between the power of majorities and the power of minorities.

In a *direct democracy*, citizens debate and vote directly on all the laws of the community. The shortcoming of direct democracy is that it requires a high level of participation and is based on a high degree of confidence in citizens' judgment and integrity. Democracy often leads to majoritarianism, a system in which the government is ruled solely by the majority's decision. This rule by the majority at the behest of the others living in a democracy can lead to a system of governance known as "tyranny of the majority," In tyranny by the majority, a slim majority can mandate government and people's decisions as a whole.

Constitutional Convention of 1787

The Constitutional Convention members believed that a *representative democracy*, in which the people elect representatives to govern and make laws, is the most efficient government form. The framers of the Constitution established a representative democracy out of fear that the majority would overly influence policy, counter the influence of underrepresented factions, and reinforce federalism. There are benefits and detriments to establishing a representative government.

Representative democracy is a more efficient form of government because it allows people who are knowledgeable about the issues to decide instead of relying on uninformed individuals' decisions. One of the pitfalls of representative democracy is the inability of constituents to control the actions of their representatives effectively. Representative democracies increase the chances that elected officials succumb to factions' influence to the detriment of their constituents' interests. The oversight of representative democracy is performed by the people who hold the ultimate power to remove an elected official from office through the election process.

There are two schools of thought on whether representative democracy is efficient.

The *elite theory* stems from a belief that representative democracy is not a democracy but a system in which an elite class, not a representative body, makes decisions for the democracy. The belief is that large corporations, policymakers, and financial institutions can exert significant power over policy decisions.

What sets elites apart from the general populace are their resources, intelligence, skills, and a vested interest in government decisions. This type of governance is an oligarchy, where a select few or a plutocracy controls the government. The government is controlled by those who have access to resources (e.g., money, access, agenda) that are not within the populace's reach.

Pluralism proposes that the members of a representative democracy base decisions on a group's will to protect the individual's interests. It is the proposition that in a diverse society, too many interests exist to allow one cohesive group to decide the interests of the populace.

Pluralism is based on dialogue and a spirit of compromise, necessarily entailing concessions by individuals or groups. These compromises are justified to maintain and promote the ideals and values of a democratic society. Theorists generally believe that autonomy only exists when the governing body has members from disparate functional and cultural groups within society.

Notes for active learning

Notes for active learning

Notes for active learning

Chapter 2

Institutions of Federal Government:
The Congress, the Presidency, the Federal Courts and the Bureaucracy

The United States Congress, the presidency, federal courts, bureaucracy, and other major political institutions are organized differently, and each possesses both formal and informal powers. This arrangement of sharing power carries implications. Explore the functions these institutions perform and do not perform, and the powers they do and do not possess are essential.

These balances of power and institutional relationships may evolve gradually or change dramatically because of crises. There exist numerous types of relationships between the branches of the federal government and political parties, interest groups, the media, and state and local governments. These relationships can explain, for example, why Congress struggles to adopt a federal budget.

.

The Major Formal and Informal Institutional Arrangements of Power

The Presidency

One of the United States government's formative ideas rests on the premise that power should be subject to checks and balances. The government is divided into three branches to ensure proper checks and balances: the executive, the legislative, and the judicial branch.

The executive branch is headed by the President, whose power derives from Article II of the United States Constitution. The powers outlined by the Constitution give the President command of the Armed Forces, although Congress must approve a declaration of war. In the post-World War II era, Presidents have increasingly taken their position as Commander in Chief to mean that they can initiate foreign hostilities without a declaration of war from Congress.

The last formal declaration of war passed by Congress was World War II (June 1942), when the United States declared war on Hungary, Romania, and Bulgaria. Since then, military actions are encompassed under the *"authorization to use military force"* in the title of several joint resolutions by Congress. These newer conflicts were initiated through the office of the President (Commander and Chief).

Franklin Roosevelt signs the declaration of war against Japan in 1941 starting America's involvement in WWII

Given that Congress controls budgetary bills, these executive-initiated wars have needed to request funding from Congress. While funding authorization is not an explicit declaration of war, Presidents have increasingly interpreted Congress authorizing funds for "authorization to use military force" as tantamount to sanctioning a declaration of war.

From Article II, Section 2, the other significant power that the President holds is making treaties. The President can negotiate and sign treaties with foreign countries, subject to a two-thirds approval vote from the Senate. While Article II outlines the President's treaty-making power, it is less clear about whether the President has the power to break treaties. Republican President Abe Lincoln (1809-1865; 1861 to his assassination on April 14, 1865) and Democratic President Jimmy Carter (b. 1924; 1977-1981) both interpreted the ability to make treaties to mean they could break treaties.

Under Article II, Section 1, clause 1, the President has the power to appoint a Cabinet (i.e., advisors and heads of agencies/departments) and ambassadors to other countries. The President's power to appoint members to the judicial branch is critical. Since federal judges are appointed for life, these appointments grant the President considerable power. The impact of judicial appointments remains after the President has left office.

The President's authority concerning the judicial branch extends the ability to grant federal pardons. A presidential pardon allows people to get out of jail or have their sentences changed (e.g., changing a sentence from the death penalty to life in prison, vacate the court decision). The President usually decides whether to grant most federal pardons at the end of their term in office. Given the nature of pardoning someone convicted of a federal crime, pardons tend to be controversial and publicly scrutinized.

Article II outlines that the President is a legislative facilitator. The President can advise Congress about policy and request specific legislation to be enacted by Congress to fulfill the executive branch's objectives. In the 20th century, Presidents increasingly took more power for driving legislation. This power is so pronounced that the President's cabinet is where much legislative policy originates, instead of Congress.

Under more recent Presidents, there was a spike in the use of executive orders. These executive statements were attached to bills passed by Congress and mostly outlined the President's opinion on the bill.

The number of executive orders (EO) signed, in descending order, by Presidents is:

Democratic President Franklin D. Roosevelt (1933-1945) – 3723 EO

Democratic President Thomas Woodrow Wilson (1856-1924; 1913-1921) – 1803

Republican President Herbert Clark Hoover (1874-1964; 1929-1933) – 968

Democratic President Harry S. Truman (1945-1953) – 907

Democratic President William Jefferson Clinton (1993-2001) – 364

Republican President George Walker Bush (2001-2009) – 291

Democratic President Barrack Hussein Obama (2009-2017) – 276

The American Bar Association has criticized the use of executive signing statements as undermining the separation of the legislative and executive powers. These signing statements enable a President to tell Congress how to enact legislation, often inconsistent with Congress's will.

President Ronald Reagan and Vice President George H. W. Bush, c. 1988

The President is responsible for delivering a yearly State of the Union Address. Initially, this meant that the President wrote a letter to be read in Congress that explained the President's opinion of the country's general status. The framers of the Constitution intended the State of the Union Address to keep the executive and legislative branches in conversation.

With the advent of mass media (e.g., television and digital media), the State of the Union Address has evolved into a means for the President to speak directly to the American people. While congressional leaders are given airtime to comment on the address, the State of the Union Address's intention and thrust have changed dramatically over time.

In addition to Article II's (i.e., executive branch) importance, Article I (i.e., legislative branch) outlines the President's power concerning the legislature. The President must sign (i.e., thus authorize) bills passed by Congress for the bills to become law. If the President does not wish a congressional bill to become law, the President can veto the bill. A presidential veto either nullifies the bill, or it is sent back to Congress for modifications and resubmission.

A presidential veto can be over-ruled by Congress with a two-thirds majority vote of the members present. With a note of the President's reasons, the House that originated the legislation may attempt to override the presidential veto with a vote receiving a majority of two-thirds. If successful, the bill then moves to the other House for a two-thirds vote to override the veto and have the congressional legislation become law.

The Executive Orders, or comments included by a President on a signed bill, are controversial because they are not directly a veto. Thus, Congress has no opportunity to override either the President's comments or Executive Order.

Interpretation of Powers

The powers and role of the executive branch are outlined in the Constitution. However, some of these powers are subject to interpretation. A general trend cited by political scientists is that in the 20th century, Presidents increasingly interpreted their powers more broadly. Recent Presidents assert more authority than Presidents in the 18th and 19th centuries.

The increase in executive authority has been slow. Scholars have argued that this amounts to a natural evolution of the position to meet modern politics' demands. Conversely, other scholars argue that the executive branch's powers' contemporary interpretation has become far too broad. The framers of the Constitution intended for Congress to be the most powerful of the three balanced government branches.

Several factors explain the expansion of presidential power. Against the backdrop of partisan bickering in the House of Representatives and the Senate, the President represents a singular and decisive voice on issues. This is primarily valid when the House and Senate are held by a majority of opposite parties, creating a situation of executive and legislative deadlock that beckons for consolidated authority.

During disasters or national emergencies, the President speaks for the nation and thus is popularly viewed as holding the actual seat of power. The role of mass media plays to this perception that the President essentially is the governmental spokesperson. When the public supports the President, it is easier for presidential powers to be expanded. The President is the most visible politician, leading to an association in the public mind between the President and overall governmental authority.

A counterpoint to this trend of increasing presidential power has been the institution of term limits. Before the 22nd Amendment was ratified in 1951, Presidents could hold office for as long as they could be re-elected. Although Presidents historically had voluntarily limited themselves to two terms, Democrat Franklin Delano Roosevelt (1882-1945; 1933 to April 12, 1945) exceeded this precedent. Roosevelt won four elections and served three full terms before dying while in office early into his fourth term. After Roosevelt's unprecedented 12 years in office, the 22nd Amendment was passed, establishing term limits to inhibit the executive branch's abuse of power.

President Franklin Delano Roosevelt at his fourth inaugural address, 1945

Choosing the President

In addition to outlining the powers of the President, Article II sets the qualifications to be elected President. The President must be a natural-born citizen of the United States, over the age of 35, and lived in the United States for the preceding 14 years.

In 2008, the natural-born citizen clause was an issue of dispute. The natural-born clause is subject to interpretation. In 2008, the Republican presidential nominee John McCain was born on a U.S. Air Force base in the Panama Canal Zone, temporarily under American control. McCain was deemed eligible for the presidency.

In 2016, Republican presidential candidate Ted Cruz's eligibility was questioned because he was born in Canada. He has revoked his Canadian citizenship, but it has been debated whether this meets the natural-born qualification.

An essential part of understanding the President's election is to understand that the President is not elected directly through popular vote. The President is elected by the Electoral College, which comprises 538 electors (one elector for each member of Congress from each State and three for Washington, D.C.) and is assigned proportionally to each state using data from the 10-year census. Under the 23rd Amendment (ratified March 29, 1961), the District of Columbia is allocated three electors and treated like a state for the Electoral College. Each state decides how to appoint its apportioned electors.

Based on its population, Texas has 38 electors in the Electoral College. These 38 votes out of 538 are awarded to whichever presidential nominee won the most votes within Texas. Thus, to get elected, a President needs to win states, preferably ones with more Electoral College votes. When a candidate wins the most votes in a state, the media tends to label this state a "red state" if they voted for the Republican nominee (i.e., the nominee is the candidate selected through the primary process and enters the general election). The state is labeled "blue state" if they voted for the Democratic nominee.

The Electoral College system is a Constitutional safeguard that some assert as controversial. The system prevents densely populated cities from determining elections (i.e., more voters with a vested, collective interest) at the expense of a representative voice to the citizen in rural America. However, the system gives disproportionate power to *swing states*, which do not consistently vote for one party. For example, Texas tends to vote Republican, meaning that presidential candidates focus less of their time there as they have a reasonable expectation of whom the citizens will vote for before the election.

In Ohio, voters vacillate between the Republican or Democratic nominee. This uncertain outcome of voting preference results in most candidates focusing their time and resources on these swing states because issues can influence the voters. The candidates aligned with issues relevant to most voters are selected. This selection of a candidate then decides the election's outcome by awarding the state's Electoral College votes.

As more and more states solidify behind one major political party, the fewer swing states become more critical. The presidential election can be decided by the Electoral College votes from just a few states. This can discourage people in non-swing states from voting because they feel that their vote does not decide the election. A Democratic voter in Texas, or a Republican in California, may feel that their vote does not count. Both states tend to vote the same preference in every national election.

The Electoral College system may cause distortions in voting. In the 2000 presidential election won by George W. Bush, Bush won 30 states for 271 Electoral College votes, while his challenger Al Gore won 20 states for 266 Electoral College votes. In terms of total votes, however, Bush received 47.9%, and Gore received 48.4%. More people voted for Al Gore to be President than voted for Bush. However, Bush was declared the winner because he won more Electoral College votes. The Electoral College inherently favors a two-party system. A strong third party would have trouble gaining momentum when Electoral College votes are awarded on a winner take all basis.

If the President dies in office, new elections to replace the President are not held. Instead, there is an order of succession (adopted in 1947 and last revised in 2006). This order begins with the Vice-President, followed by the Speaker of the House, and lists a ranked order of 18 positions. The purpose of having a long succession list is to ensure that the President's office will be filled even in a catastrophe killing of senior members of the government.

The succession list came into effect just after World War II and at the beginning of the Cold War. President Gerald Ford (1913-2006; 1974-1977) has the distinction of being the only unelected President; Senator Ford was appointed Vice President by Richard Nixon after Nixon's running mate and Vice President, Spiro Agnew (1918-1996; 1969-1973), resigned. After Nixon resigned on August 9, 1974, Vice President Ford became President. This a rare example of someone who never ran for President or Vice President assuming the top office.

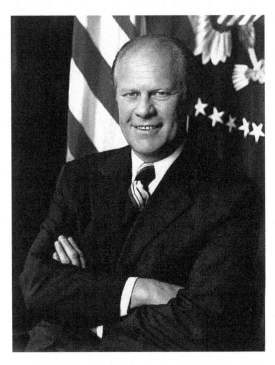

President Gerald Ford, c. 1977

The Congress

The United States Congress is bicameral, meaning it has two chambers: The House of Representatives and the Senate. As the legislative branch of government, Congress is vested with the power to make laws. While the House and the Senate are equal partners in the legislative process, meaning bills need to pass both chambers to become laws; the two bodies do have some unique powers set in the Constitution.

The Senate has the power to approve or deny appointments (e.g., judicial, cabinet) made by the President. The House of Representatives controls money-related bills. From Article I of the Constitution, all revenue-raising bills must originate in the House of Representatives.

The Sixteenth Amendment, ratified in 1913, extended the House's taxation powers to include the levy of income tax without apportioning it among the states based on population. The House of Representatives has the final say on matters related to finance and the federal budget. This power includes setting the tax rates, duties, tariffs, and control over funding for expenditure programs (e.g., military. social security). With financial authority vested in the legislative branch, the President cannot directly raise or lower taxes, as such legislation must originate in the House of Representatives.

Congress has exclusive authority over national defense matters, including the power to declare war and determine the military's internal function rules. Scholars have highlighted that the executive branch has increasingly wielded these powers, leading to a decline in congressional authority over military matters.

Before World War II, the President needed to ask Congress to declare war, which required a vote by the people's representatives. At the time, this was considered an essential check on the power of the President. However, since then, Presidents have initiated wars without direct approval from Congress. The Korean War (June 25, 1950, to July 22, 1953), the Vietnam War (November 1, 1955, to April 30, 1975), Desert Storm (August 2, 1990, to February 28, 1991), Iraq War (March 20, 2003, to December 18, 2011) were all initiated by the President without a formal declaration of war from Congress.

Congress is vested with some latent powers which are less noticeable. Congress has the power to issue patents and copyrights, establish post offices, and institute courts subordinate to the Supreme Court. Article IV gives Congress control over granting new states entrance into the United States. While this was a necessary congressional power as the country grew from 13 to 50 states, this power is less practiced today. However, it is still vital if, for example, Puerto Rico wished to become the 51st state – it would have to petition Congress for a decision.

Outside of Congress's legislative powers, it plays an essential role as a check on executive authority. These checks involve the ability to approve and reject presidential appointments (e.g., Supreme Court justices) and the ability to control the military and as a general investigative check on the President. Congress can wield this power by setting committees to investigate whether the President has overstepped executive authority's bounds. If Congress deems so, they have the authority to instigate impeachment proceedings.

The House of Representatives can initiate impeachment against the President, Vice-President, or any United States civil officer. If the House votes in favor of impeachment, the proceedings move to the Senate, where a trial takes place. The Senate then votes, based on the trial proceedings, whether the impeached official is indeed guilty.

Impeachment does not mean the removal of office, but merely being charged with an offense that the House deems worthy of removing someone from office. Three Presidents were impeached. Democrat Andrew Johnson (1808-1875; 1865-1869; 1868), Democrat Bill Clinton (1993-2001; 1998), and Republican Donald Trump (2017–2021; December 18, 2019, to February 5, 2020) were each impeached by the House of

Representatives, but each found not guilty after the trial by the Senate. Republican Richard Nixon (1913-1994; 1969 to August 9, 1974) resigned before his impeachment trial.

U.S. Senate in session during the impeachment trial of President Bill Clinton, 1999

In addition to passing legislation, the other primary role of Congress is to represent the American people. District Representatives are responsible for addressing issues and concerns from constituents and helping them navigate the bureaucracy.

Democratic President Barack Hussein Obama (b. 1961; 2009–2017) publicly argued that it is the President's role to represent the entire American public; this has traditionally been Congress's role. Against the backdrop of increasing partisan deadlock in the House and Senate, Barak Obama's attempt to position the President as the singular representative of all Americans could be interpreted as an example of either a continued decrease in the power of Congress or as an attempt to overcome the continuous (by design) partisan deadlock in Congress. The framers envisioned a cumbersome legislative process to ensure deliberation and debate before laws are enacted; prevent overreach by a single branch of government.

Bicameral Structure

The framers of the Constitution envisioned two chambers of Congress as ensuring that legislation would be passed through a combination of popular participation (via the House of Representatives) and after consideration by those generally more experienced and wiser (via the Senate). When the Constitution was drafted (May 25, 1787) and adopted

(September 17, 1787), there was a real fear that allowing typical Americans (which excluded women, Native Americans, African Americans, and men without property) to vote could lead to irresponsible decisions threatening the status quo.

To combat this fear of popular democracy, the Senate devised a second legislative body, which was intended to be upper-class elites. The term was set for six years because the Senators were assumed to be experienced and enlightened compared to the House's directly elected representatives. Before the Seventeenth Amendment in 1913, Senators were chosen by state legislatures rather than being popularly elected as they are now.

The House of Representatives is designed to represent each person as a constituent equally. The Senate provides the states equal representation regardless of their population. Each state has two Senators, while more populous states have more seats in the House of Representatives.

This balancing between representation by population and by the state was called the *Connecticut Compromise.* To serve as a House of Representatives member, one must be at least 25 years, while a Senator must be at least 30. While the House has elections every four years for all Representatives (elected for two-year terms), Senators serve six-year terms, and one-third of the Senate is up for election every two years. The longer-term and lack of total turnover in the Senate insulate Senators from public opinion.

As part of a rigid two-party system, the House and Senate are controlled by one of the two parties. The party with the most seats is called the majority party, and the party with fewer seats is called the minority party. While Representatives do not officially have to vote the same way as the rest of their party, it is the party Whip's job to rally support and ensure the party votes the same way. One of the primary ways the Whip rallies support is through dealing with caucuses.

Caucuses are non-official groups of Representatives who share a common goal or concern. Some prominent caucuses include the Congressional Black Caucus, the Congressional Internet Caucus, and the Out of Iraq Caucus. The Whip negotiates with caucuses by trading favors to get the caucus members to vote the way the Whip wants. For instance, if the majority party leadership wants to pass a bill on education, the Whip may promise that the majority party will support a bill related to the internet in exchange for the Internet Caucus voting in favor of the education bill.

The leader of the House of Representatives is the Speaker of the House. The Speaker is elected by the majority party to preside over and control the house's legislative agenda. The Whip helps the Speaker ensure that the Speaker's legislative agenda has enough support to prevail by votes. By contrast, the President of the Senate is the Vice President of the United States.

However, in practice, the Vice President is not incredibly involved with the Senate, which is *de facto* led by the most senior member of the Senate's majority party. Senators are less subject to whipped votes, as they are supposed to act as independent voices of wisdom, but in practice, most Senators follow the party line.

Founding members of the Congressional Black Caucus, c. 1971

Initially, the House and Senate engaged in a vigorous debate on the proposed legislation, but this is rarely the case in practice. The most common way for Senators to show disapproval with a piece of legislation is through a filibuster. The filibuster is a formal process whereby a member(s) of the Senate delay the passage of a piece of legislation by taking the floor and talking for as long as possible. This delay does not allow a vote to take place for the legislation in question.

A vote in the Senate can change the rules for filibusters. Filibusters can be stopped with a 60% supermajority vote. Even if a party does not have a majority in the Senate, they can filibuster legislation if they can maintain 40% or more of the seats. Senators can attach riders to legislation, which are additional clauses to the bill. Often this is done to ensure support for a piece of legislation, but sometimes these riders have little relationship with the bill under consideration. This is pork-barreling and involves a Senator attaching a clause that supports their home state but is unrelated to the original bill.

Outside of voting on bills and responding to constituents, Congress members' most crucial role is their time spent serving on Committees. Committees are small groups that study bills in-depth; they are entrusted with informing Congress whether they should vote for a bill. However, this allows Congress to work on more bills at once, an in-depth study is divided among members, but it can lead to Representatives voting on bills they have not read or even do not understand.

There are four types of congressional committees. *Standing committees* are most common and focus on reviewing specific legislation types and deciding what funding levels for public programs are most appropriate.

Select committees address a specific issue and dissolve after their work is over.

Joint committees are like select committees but have members from both chambers.

Logo for the U.S. Senate Select Committee on Intelligence

Committees are extremely powerful as they determine what bills are sent to the floor for voting. Most bills are killed in committees before Congress's general members have a chance to vote on them. This ensures that only significant and essential bills are subject to debate, as committees weed out bills that they find problematic or think will not prevail a general vote.

Congress can, however, overrule the decision of a committee to kill a bill and not send it to the floor for a general vote if they feel the committee has misbehaved. This termination involves passing a discharge petition.

The majority party chooses a chairperson as the leader of each committee. The minority party chooses their committee leader, who is called the ranking member. Given that committees do essential work, leadership and membership in a committee grants a member of Congress significant power, making committee positions highly sought after.

Committee members do not have to do all their committee work by themselves, as they are assisted by staffers whom they hire directly. These staffers engage in committee work nuts and bolts, including researching legislation, assisting committee members with general duties, and even writing the legislation's text.

While the idea behind a bicameral Congress was to ensure that the Senate would act as a check on the House of Representatives, in practice, this system has produced a deadlock, as bills require double approval. When different parties control the Senate and the House, passing legislation is complicated, as rigid partisan views tend to interfere with legislative judgment.

If the same party controls both houses of Congress, but the President is from the other party, then the President is more likely to veto bills, causing more deadlock. Scholars have argued that the persistent deadlock in Congress in the modern era explains why the executive branch's increasing power at the legislative branch's expense has not upset the American people.

The Legislative Process

Passing bills through committees and then voting and amending them in both Houses of Congress can make the legislative process entirely drawn out. This is by design, as the Framers of the Constitution did not want Congress to hastily pass ill-conceived legislation that might limit the American people's freedom.

There are two types of bills, *public bills* (which affect everyone) and *private bills* (aimed toward a person). The process by which a bill becomes a law begins with its introduction by a House of Representatives member. The bill is then referred to the appropriate committee for further study and analysis. The committee can then refer it to a subcommittee for hearings or more detailed study, kill the bill or approve it.

Upon approval, the bill is sent back to the House of Representatives for debate and voting by the legislature's full body. The Rules Committee and voting procedures limit the house's debate through a roll call where each member registers their vote. If the House of Representatives approves the bill, it moves to the Senate, where each Senator can speak about or propose amendments to the bill.

If the Senate and House agree to pass a piece of legislation but differ slightly in how it should be worded, the bill is referred to a conference committee. The conference committee has members from both chambers of Congress, who work together to reach an agreement on the bill's final wording. The bill is then sent to the President, who can sign it to make it law or veto it to quash it. The veto can be overridden by a two-thirds vote in both the Senate and House. A veto override is extremely difficult, so a presidential veto almost always quashes a bill.

The Judiciary

The Supreme Court acts as the ultimate check on the power of the legislative and executive branches. The judiciary's primary role is to uphold the Constitution and ensure that no legislation is passed, which is inconsistent with the Constitution and Bill of Rights. When an individual or group feels that a piece of legislation violates the Constitution, they can challenge this legislation in court, rather than trying to have to convince the politicians that passed it that the law violated the Constitution. For this reason, lawyers and judges play an essential part in the American political system.

In addition to Congress's laws, it is the Supreme Court's role to interpret the Constitution and make judgments regarding case law (which are previous court decisions). One of the most critical functions of the Supreme Court is its ability to overturn precedents. *Stare decisis* (let the decision stand) is the principle that court decisions should be respected. *Stare decisis* is most evident in the Supreme Court's reluctance to overturn its rulings from prior Supreme Court cases.

However, the overturning of prior judicial decisions does happen when interpretations of the law change or faulty decisions. Wrong decisions arise from changes in public policy or societal needs/values change but still consistent with the limits of permitted government intervention (e.g., prohibitions on same-sex marriage) contained in the Constitution. May the government regulate the activity, or is the right reserved for the citizens (i.e., natural law). For instance, in *Roe v. Wade* (1973), the Supreme Court ruled that the choice to have an abortion is a fundamental right covered by the Ninth and Fourteenth Amendments, overturning past court decisions and invalidating state laws prohibiting abortion.

The precedent overturned by the Supreme Court is often from a lower court (i.e., highest state court or Federal Circuit Court). Lower court judges rely on case law (i.e., prior issued decisions) to rule in cases. However, if situations change and individuals feel that past rulings have become unjust, they may appeal to have the precedent reviewed by the Supreme Court; this requires a current "case and controversy" before the court.

The Supreme Court reviews legislation, precedents, and constitutionality based on court challenges (*case and controversy*) filed by *parties to a lawsuit* (i.e., litigant that initiates the action is the plaintiff). The Supreme Court retains the power to initiate judicial reviews of legislation passed by Congress when the issue is challenged in court. Without a lawsuit, there is no review of statutes or interpretations of the Constitution. This power of review is not specified in the Constitution but is based on precedent from *Marbury v. Madison* (1803).

Supreme Court building, One First Street, NW, Washington, D.C.

The federal judiciary uses a hierarchical structure of authority. At the top of this hierarchy is the Supreme Court; below it is the Courts of Appeals (i.e., Circuit Courts), and below those are the 94 federal district courts. As the highest court, the Supreme Court is the highest court of appeal, and thus it has the final say in all rulings.

The Supreme Court is composed of nine justices, led by the Chief Justice and eight associate justices. Supreme Court justices are appointed for life but can choose to retire. The President appoints the justices which are approved (consent and advice) by the Senate.

Congress has the power to change the number of justices on the Supreme Court, but the current number of nine justices has remained unchanged since 1869.

Seal of the United States Court of Appeals for the First Circuit, Boston MA

While the Supreme Court receives many appeals to review cases, they do not review all requests. The justices decide which cases should be reviewed based on a minority vote and generally only review cases they deem significant. If four of the justices agree a case should be heard (rule of four), the court issues a *writ of certiorari*, which orders a lower court to send a case to the Supreme Court for review.

When the Supreme Court reviews a case, briefs (i.e., proposal of legal arguments) are submitted by both sides of the case summarizing their position for the justices. People or organizations not directly involved in the case may submit briefs outlining their position on the issue by submitting *amicus curiae* (friend of the court) briefs. After reading the briefs in detail, the justices may hear oral arguments from the parties involved. The litigants (or their attorney) usually have half an hour to present their case directly to the justices. The justices use the oral arguments to ask both sides of the case to clarify the issue and statements made in the written briefs.

Rather than an ordinary court trial where lawyers present their arguments mostly uninterrupted by the judge, Supreme Court justices interject with questions and comment frequently during oral arguments. After reading the briefs and hearing the oral arguments, the justices then hold a judicial conference to discuss and debate the case. These conferences are secret to ensure the integrity of their rulings.

Upon the judicial conference's conclusion, the justices can decide that the lower court ruling was adequate; they do not wish to register a formal decision or opinion on the case. This is a *per curiam* (i.e., by the court) rejection, and upon reviewing the case in detail, the Supreme Court does not feel the case is worth hearing (no issue requiring review), as the lower courts did an adequate job with it. If the justices agree the case merits a ruling, they issue a decision and a written opinion (i.e., establish a precedent for future cases). The decision determines which side of the case prevails. The issued opinion (often more than 100 pages long with detailed legal reasoning) provides a legal analysis of why and how the court decided.

There are four main types of decisions the Supreme Court makes.

A *majority opinion* is when at least five justices agree with the decision and support the opinion's reasoning.

A *plurality opinion* occurs when a majority of the justices agree on the decision but not the reasoning. For example, seven judges may decide a case in favor of one side but disagree on why it should be decided this way; a plurality opinion can be issued. If four of these justices support one set of legal reasoning and three support another, the opinion of the four is presented as a plurality opinion since the majority does not support it.

A *concurring opinion* is issued by justices who agree with the decision, but not the opinion. The three justices' opinions would be concurrent, while that of the other four remains a plurality opinion.

A *dissenting opinion* is issued by the justices who disagree with what the majority ruled. If four justices issue a plurality opinion in favor of the decision and three issues a concurring opinion in favor of the decision, then the other two justices issue dissenting opinions against the decision.

A *memorandum opinion* decides a case without setting a precedent. This involves cases where the individual circumstances (facts for the dispute) were exceptional. The justices feel that their ruling is narrow and pertains to these unique facts, not on becoming case law (i.e., precedent, binding on lower courts).

The Supreme Court has exercised its power to issue some landmark rulings (e.g., desegregation, abortion, same-sex marriage, 2nd Amendment rights to possess firearms), which have fundamentally altered America's political landscape.

In *Marbury v. Madison* (1803), the Supreme Court ruled that it had the power to overturn unconstitutional laws. This established judicial review as the purview of the Court.

In *Dred Scott v. Sanford* (1857), the Supreme Court decided to permit the forceful return of a slave to his owner, which increased tensions on the issue and contributed to the Civil War's onset.

In *Plessy v. Ferguson* (1896), the Court upheld the legality of racial segregation, which was consequently overturned in *Brown v. Board of Education* (1954).

In *Gideon v. Wainwright* (1963), the Supreme Court ruled that a person who cannot afford a lawyer when charged with a crime punishable by a loss of freedom (i.e., jail time is a possible sentence) must be provided a lawyer (at no cost; public defender) by the state.

Miranda v. Arizona (1966) established the requirement that the police must read "Miranda rights" (right to remain silent) to anyone arrested.

Roe v. Wade (1973) legalized abortion.

Bush v. Gore (2000) provided a ruling about recounts of presidential ballots.

Obergefell v. Hodges (2015) legalized same-sex marriage.

Some Supreme Court decisions are controversial and sometimes contradictory. The decision on an issue may change over time and demonstrate that the Court's primary role is to interpret the Constitution overlaid with society's interests.

It is important to note that the Constitution must be interpreted and that these interpretations can change over time. Therefore, a Supreme Court is needed as the final arbitrator of these interpretations. The Supreme Court can change its opinions and overrule past decisions. The fact that the President appoints the justices is vital. Presidents generally seek to appoint justices who agree with them politically.

While the framers intended the Supreme Court to be legal experts free of partisan influence, the situation's reality has evolved in practice over time. The judicial branch's ability to act as a check on the executive and legislative branches is questionable when the Supreme Court can be "stacked" with those inclined to agree with the President. This "stacking" has not always worked out as anticipated.

Members of the Warren Court, who made the unanimous decision for
Brown v. Board of Education, 1954

Republican President Dwight Eisenhower (1890-1969; 1953-1961) appointed former Republican California Governor Earl Warren (1891-1974; 1953-1969) as Chief Justice in 1953. Eisenhower expected Warren to be politically conservative in his rulings. However, Chief Justice Warren was less inclined to follow a conservative ideology, much to President Eisenhower's dismay.

Since justices are inclined to make rulings based on their political views, the President and the Senate's vetting committee take special care to select Supreme Court justices who rule consistent with the President's positions. Vetting of the nominee is accomplished by trying to understand the judicial philosophy of a potential justice.

Judicial philosophy can differ in how the Constitution is interpreted. Some judges are *loose constructionists* "legislate from the bench." They believe that the spirit of the Constitution is evolving. The Constitution means what they propose is in the best interest of society when creating judge-made law. This effect is like a legislative statute because, in contrast, *strict constructionists* posit that the judiciary must only consider what is explicitly written in the Constitution; the four walls of the document, and not subject to the judge's opinion as to what it should say.

Some judges believe in *judicial activism*, which means that they have the power to overturn laws (disregard *stare decisis*) and change precedence that they deem unfavorable. Some activists interpret the Constitution as a living document that can be amended to meet citizens' changing circumstances and temperament. An advocate of judicial activism would propose that the court decide society's values without input from society members. Judges are educated and can decide what the law should be without the constraints of adhering to the Constitution.

In contrast, *judicial restraint* advocates that the Supreme Court should only interpret existing laws under the framers' intent when the states ratified the document. An advocate of judicial restraint would hear such an appeal. However, if they deemed the existing law inadequate, it should be up to Congress (hearing from their constituents on the issue) before changing the law (i.e., draft a new statute in a democratic process). The change should not be imposed on society by the Supreme Court's unelected members, without voter input in the process. They argue that the original document must not be contravened, and original intent eclipses the changing present-day concerns. The law should be stable (not depend on the judge's views of how society should be), predictable (easy to understand and comply), and respect the Constitution (the supreme law of the land) from which democracy in America was founded.

In combination with the justices' personal political views, the different judicial philosophies factor into how the Supreme Court rules on cases. This has ramifications well beyond mere legal interpretation. In this sense, the judiciary may (for activist courts) a political institution that imposes its values on people. Nine justices decide for millions of Americans without considering the people's will – no elections to remove them if they digress from societal values.

The Constitution does not outline any specific requirements or qualifications to become a federal court judge; thus, a person need not be a lawyer to be appointed to the Supreme Court. In practice, federal court appointees are almost always lawyers, usually with previous experience as a judge. Some political scientists argue that a degree of legal training and experience is necessary for federal judges to interpret complex legal arguments. In contrast, others point out that lawyers are good at following legal precedent but lack the philosophical training and understanding to create binding legal principles.

While the Supreme Court is the last resort of appeals. The Court's function is a final check to ensure that the legislative and executive branches do not pass laws that violate the Constitution. The executive and legislative branches do have a way to check the judiciary's power.

For instance, if the Supreme Court rules that a law be unconstitutional, Congress and the President can move to amend the Constitution. If the Supreme Court rules that a law be unconstitutional but should be replaced with better legislation, the legislative branch can simply not put forward any such new legislation. Congress can refuse to provide funding (appropriations), thus undermining the impact (or execution) of a Supreme Court decision.

The Bureaucracy

Bureaucracy, which comes from the French word *bureau,* meaning "desk," and the ancient Greek *cracy,* which means "rule of," gives the meaning "the rule of desks." The word applies to government workers as executing legislature statutes, though not participating in the political process. While the name suggests a somewhat negative connotation, there are arguments for and against bureaucracy.

The German sociologist Max Weber (1864-1920) presented one of the most detailed accounts of why bureaucracy is essential in modern, functional government. Weber points out that without a slew of professional government employees, dealing with the government would be a nightmare of inefficiency based on personal favor (e.g., to plead with a congressional representative to embrace the constituent's concern).

Max Weber, German sociologist, c. 1920

The bureaucracy plays a vital role in professionalizing government to ensure that dealing with it is based on consistent rules and not politicians' whims. Before the professionalization of the bureaucracy, a spoils system was in place. The President would fire all existing government workers and replace them with his friends and supporters, resulting in an incompetent government unable to execute the President's and Congress's orders properly.

Simultaneously, the expansion and professionalization of the bureaucracy have created vast amounts of "red tape." Bureaucratization was designed to increase efficiency. The critics of bureaucracy argue that dealing with bureaucratic rules and procedures is dehumanizing because government workers merely follow the rules without sympathy for an individual's plight. They point to a decline in personal responsibility in bureaucratic systems, as the bureaucracy's hierarchy enables government workers to shift responsibility away from themselves. Regardless of one's opinions on bureaucracy's effectiveness, the sophisticated modern government requires a professional, non-partisan workforce as the intermediary between citizens and government.

The first responsibility of a bureaucrat is to implement government policy. When Congress and the President decide they want something done, it is the bureaucracy that puts these laws and directives into practice. Putting government directives into practice can range from policy analysis, which takes government directives and creates rules for how this law will be applied to a specific situation, to public administration that delivers these policies to the public.

If Congress passes legislation stating that they wish to see better health care for military veterans, policy-makers in public service take this directive and write policies and rules for how the Veteran Affairs (VA) will improve health care in specific ways. Public administrators, ranging from those who run VA hospitals to the nurses and doctors who treat patients, implement the policy. The bureaucracy is responsible for promoting government policy, national security and policing, and various economic functions via the Federal Reserve Bank.

The bureaucracy is responsible for regulation, in addition to policymaking and implementation. Regulation ensures that existing rules are followed. Regulatory bureaucracies include the Environmental Protection Agency (EPA), which addresses regulations on pollution and environmental issues, and the Securities and Exchange Commission (SEC), which regulates publicly traded companies' stock market.

The federal bureaucracy employs approximately 2.6 million people and is mostly directed by the executive branch. The President appoints cabinet secretaries, who oversee the bureaucracy branches, so the bureaucracy is primarily an instrument of presidential power. Ninety-seven percent of government employees are members of the federal civil service. Ten percent work in Washington, D.C. Congress and the judiciary have bureaucracies, but these are smaller and less powerful than the executive branch.

Congress' most powerful bureaucratic branches are the Library of Congress and the Congressional Research Service. These are minuscule compared to federal bureaucracies such as the Federal Bureau of Investigation (FBI) or the Department of Homeland Security (DHS). Congress does, however, act as a check on the power of the bureaucracy. It has oversight power enabling Congress to monitor the federal bureaucracy is acting correctly in executing its duties.

For much of American history, the bureaucracy was relatively small. In part, this was simply because the population was much smaller, and society was less complex. Part of the government bureaucracy's growth resulted from the change in the federal government's scope and function. Democratic President Franklin D. Roosevelt's New Deal (1933–1939) and Democratic President Lyndon Johnson's Great Society (1964–1965) policies sought to increase the bureaucracy's size to expand its capacity.

Democratic President Franklin D. Roosevelt (1933 to April 12, 1945) created an unprecedented number of new agencies (including the defunct CCC, CWA, FSA, NIRA, and several others). Also, Democratic President Lyndon Baines Johnson (1963-1969) implemented almost 200 pieces of legislation. These agencies and programs expanded the federal government's size beyond reasonable predictions for the people's anticipated needs.

President Lyndon B. Johnson at the University of Michigan commencement in 1964, where he made his first public reference to his Great Society policies

There has been a shift since the 1980s toward accepting "big government" in the form of an enormous bureaucracy. Critics assert that this amounts to a prohibitive taxpayer-supported cost for a bloated and intrusive federal government. In the wake of the September 11th, 2001 terrorist attacks, under Republican President George W. Bush, there was a second major expansion of the bureaucracy as new departments related to national security were created, most notably the Department of Homeland Security (DHS). Some critics are concerned about expanding the federal government that requires federal borrowing (increasing national debt), which has ballooned in the last few decades.

The Cabinet

The most critical positions in the bureaucracy are the cabinet. These are leaders (officially called secretaries, but sometimes informally called "czars") of essential government departments (e.g., Housing, Health, Defense, Treasury). The President appoints the Cabinet, and the Senate approves (consent and advice) each cabinet member.

The Cabinet is important not just because they are the heads of the principal executive departments and oversee the bureaucracy but because they are included in the order of succession should the President and Vice President be unable to continue in office.

The main branches of the bureaucracy and their functions are below.

The Secretary of State heads the United States Department of State, focusing on foreign affairs.

The Department of the Treasury oversees financial and monetary policy.

The Department of Defense oversees the military.

The Attorney General is the country's top lawyer and oversees the Justice Department (e.g., FBI, DEA), which handles criminal matters and policy.

The Department of the Interior concerns itself with geographical issues, land management, and national parks.

The Secretary of Agriculture. The Secretary of Commerce. The Department of Labor enforces workplace regulations and manages laws related to labor unions.

Next in succession are the Departments of Health, Housing and Urban Development (HUD), Transportation, Energy, Education, Veterans Affairs, and Homeland Security. These departments of the bureaucracy form the bulk of government employees and provide the services to citizens.

In addition to the heads of each bureaucratic department, the Cabinet includes the White House Chief of Staff, who is the President's primary assistant, the Director of the Office of Management and Budget, the Administrator of the Environmental Protection Agency, the U.S. Trade Representative, the Ambassador to the United Nations, the Chairman of the Council of Economic Advisors, and finally the Administrator of the Small Business Association. The President has people whose purpose is to give advice and oversee functions to ensure that the government operates effectively to provide for its citizens.

Appointees and the Civil Service

The President appoints cabinet secretaries, but the bulk of the bureaucracy is part of what is referred to as the civil service. At the President's discretion, approximately 2,000 positions, called presidential appointments, are filled as part of the bureaucracy. When the President rewards loyal allies or fundraisers with a bureaucratic appointment, it is called patronage. Before the professionalization of the bureaucracy, the President's influence in appointing the bureaucracy was more significant.

The spoils system, in which the President may award jobs to supporters, was generally seen as corrupt. The spoils system was officially abolished after the assassination by a supporter of Republican President James Garfield (1831-1881; 1881 to September 19, 1881). The assassin was angry that Republican President James A. Garfield did not appoint him to the desired bureaucratic position (per the phrase "to the victor belong the spoils" c. 1831).

The assassination of President James Garfield, 1881

After Garfield's assassination, America moved toward a professional bureaucracy consisting of specialized experts rather than presidential appointees. By 1900, most of the civil service was no longer subject to the spoils system. This shift in staffing significantly increased efficiency and reduced executive authority and the potential for corruption.

At the state and city level, however, spoils systems lasted well into the 20th century. Civil servants were to be selected based on competence and knowledge instead of political loyalty, beginning with the 1883 Pendleton Act or the Civil Service Reform Act. The Pendleton Act was signed by Republican President Chester A. Arthur (1829-1886; 1881-1885). The Act was expanded under President Carter in the 1978 Civil Service Reform Act to ensure that the civil service was free (theoretically) of political interference.

To become a civil servant (e.g., postal worker, police officer, air traffic controller) requires passing an entrance exam to ensure that job appointments are based on merit. The goal of this requirement is to hire civil servants who are the most qualified to increase efficiency. Civil servants have strong protections against political interference, which gives them remarkably high job security. This prevents the President from firing civil servants. It is challenging to fire incompetent civil servants because courts have ruled that civil servants have a property interest in their job.

Unlike the limited number of elected politicians, the civil service may better represent America's demographic diversity. Given that bureaucrats have the power to write policy, which determines how laws and directives passed by Congress and the President are administered, many scholars question the bureaucracy's role concerning the system of checks and balances.

Dissatisfied citizens can vote out (i.e., not reelect) ineffective Presidents and members of Congress. However, some data shows that incumbents are re-elected in more than 95 percent of the studies. Some commentators conclude that incumbent elected officials have dramatic advantages (e.g., media exposure, name recognition).

Civil servants are not fired based on public opinion. This job protection for professional bureaucrats (i.e., civil service employees) raises issues of democratic accountability. Additionally, some departments, such as the Central Intelligence Agency (CIA), have extraordinarily little transparency. For national security reasons, the public cannot know what civil servants in the CIA are doing.

Seal of the Central Intelligent Agency (CIA)

These realities of unfettered job security, independent actions disconnected from the voters' will, and other meaningful issues raise concerns that the bureaucracy has expanded its power to be detrimental to democracy. For example, when high-ranking officials of the CIA refuse to answer questions (e.g., due to the issue of national security) in congressional committee hearings, it can seem that such secret agencies are more powerful than Congress. This refusal to disclose details of the bureaucratic operations is a problem because Congress is vested with the power of oversight for the bureaucracy. In extreme cases, Congress has the power to stop funding (i.e., deny appropriations) to an uncooperative department of the bureaucracy.

However, denying appropriations would likely instigate a conflict with the President, who could retaliate by vetoing Congress' laws. The President's initial check is the ability to appoint the heads of each department, but the President has the power to reorganize the bureaucracy and create new departments. The judiciary acts as less of a direct check. The judiciary is mainly concerned with ensuring that bureaucrats have not engaged in illegal activity or overacting their delegated powers.

In response to the fear of an undemocratic overgrowth of the bureaucracy's power, there have been several attempts to reform the bureaucracy's authority to execute its function. Republican President Gerald Ford signed the Sunshine Act of 1976. The Act forced many bureaucracy departments to open themselves up to public inspection by forcing them to hold public meetings and proceedings to shine a light on their activities. This Act made the bureaucracy more transparent and increased public confidence in the bureaucracy by revealing their inner workings.

Congress can place sunset provisions onto government programs, which require the program to meet specific standards for it to be renewed. The goal of such provisions is to maintain congressional oversight and reel in the power of the bureaucracy. Congress and Presidents have tried to tie financial incentives to exemplary job performance, providing bonuses when bureaucrats increase efficiency.

Further measures try to protect whistleblowers, which are civil servants who report the misdeeds of their superiors. The results of such whistleblower protections have been mixed, as often the government does not like what the whistleblower has to say. Reporting illegal activity, corruption, or inefficiency as a whistleblower is still a risky and dangerous activity. A few examples of recent high-profile whistleblowers include Edward Snowden (2013) regarding the National Security Agency (NSA) and Chelsea Manning (2010) regarding issues in the U.S. Army that were published by WikiLeaks. Some civil service whistleblowers are hailed as heroes, while others are demonized as traitors.

Another approach to reforming the bureaucracy began in the 1980s when Republican President Ronald Reagan adopted neoliberal economics's ideology. Neoliberal economics argues that government is inherently inefficient because there is no profit motive or competition to drive it. Attempting to increase governmental efficiency through privatization, Republican and Democratic Presidents since Reagan sought to privatize several bureaucracy functions (e.g., prisons, airport operations, water and wastewater service). The proposition is that private corporations competing in the marketplace can do a better job of delivering public services than the monopoly power of governmental control.

President Ronald Reagan, 1989

Government services do not lend themselves to privatization because they tend to be unprofitable by nature – these services are "public goods." Privatized bureaucratic functions tend to create monopolies in which one company is awarded the contract and receives all government contracts without competition. The initial process of awarding the bids for services must be open and competitive. The danger is that corruption and spoils can occur if governments award these contracts to companies operated by their political supporters. Privatization can be viewed as a reintroduction of the spoilage system.

Other privatization problems relate to the military, especially with the use of "no-bid" contracts in the Iraq War of 2003. Politically connected organizations were able to receive contracts from the federal government without having to bid for the contract (e.g., Halliburton for logistics, Blackwater for private security). Additionally, the requirements to be considered a qualified bidder (i.e., has the expertise, experience, and ability to perform as specified by the contract) limit the number of companies awarded the contract to provide services to the government.

Notes for active learning

Notes for active learning

Relationships Among Institutions and Varying Balances of Power

The four institutions of the federal government have different powers but are continually interacting with one another. The idea behind dividing the government into different branches is the principle of the separation of powers. The idea of separating governmental powers into different branches was developed by the French political theorist Montesquieu. His work greatly influenced the constitutional framers.

By separating the government into executive, legislative, and judicial branches, the idea was that each branch checks the power of the other two. The goal of separating the powers is to ensure that no one branch accrues too much power. Montesquieu was anxious about unchecked executive power becoming despotic or tyrannical, and thus the legislative and judicial branches needed to have the power to keep the executive restrained.

Montesquieu, French political theorist. 1750

By balancing these three powers equally, the goal was to ensure that no one branch could abuse its power and get away with it. In the United States, this system of separating powers is called checks and balances. The downside of such a system is that it tends to make it challenging to get things done, as there are several ways another branch can block progress, leading to a deadlock.

As the executive power, the President is elected independently of Congress, which is part of the separation of powers. It is much easier for the President to advance the agenda if the majority party in both Houses of Congress is the same as the President. This is a significant difference from the Westminster system used in Canada and the United Kingdom; in these governments, executive power is simply the legislature's largest party leader and is not elected independently.

In the American system, the executive and legislative branches' separation diminishes and enhances the executive's power. Compared to the Canadian or British systems, the President has less power than a prime minister. The executive does not directly control the legislature in the United States as in Canada or the UK. In the United States, Congress can vote contrary to the President's wishes, and a different party than the President can control Congress. The President's power is checked and makes the position less potent than that of a Prime Minister.

Conversely, the President of the United States' separation from the legislature makes the President more powerful in that they are not beholden to their political party's wishes. If the Republican Party in Congress, for example, were to turn against President Trump, Trump would remain President and continue to exercise presidential authority even without general support from his party.

If the Prime Minister loses the party's confidence in a parliamentary system, the party can remove the Prime Minister without an election. This happened in Australia four times between 2010 and 2018. The governing party decided they did not like the current Prime Minister and replaced him with another member of their party, all without an election. This is impossible in the United States and is an example of how the President can be more potent than a Prime Minister.

In America, each branch has a set of powers to exercise to check the other branches' power and maintain a balance between the three. The executive branch's initial check on the legislative branch is the bill's presidential veto, preventing the law from passing.

The President has the power to direct the course of a war. Even though Congress has the power to declare war, once the war is declared, it is up to the President to decide how that war will be fought. The President has the power to make decrees and declarations that override the usual procedure, for example, declaring a state of emergency in the event of a natural disaster or a terrorist attack.

The President may influence the other branches' agenda through the State of the Union address. The State of the Union address outlines the President's government's agenda directly to the American people. The President's ability to appoint judges and bureaucratic leaders is an essential check on the judiciary and the bureaucracy, as they continue to serve at the President's discretion.

The President can check the judiciary's power by granting pardons to anyone convicted of a federal crime by the court system. A similar pardon is available by the governor for persons convicted of a state crime. This check is used if the President or governor feels the court system has acted unfairly or has convicted an innocent person.

Congress has an internal check and balance as it is divided into two houses. On a broader system of checks and balances, it is peculiar that the legislative branch should have an extra check and balance built into it. As discussed earlier, part of this legislative structure stemmed from a distrust of popular democracy in Congress (i.e., House of Representatives and Senate). However, part of this bicameral legislative design involved copying the United Kingdom's (UK) established system. Without separation of powers, the two-chamber legislature in the United Kingdom served as an example of checks and balances, albeit not as sophisticated as established in the United States.

Since the United Kingdom had no separation of executive power, the two Houses of Parliament in the legislative branch provide something of a check. Agreeing with this general rationale of checks and balances, a two-house, or bicameral legislature, was adopted in the United States. Such a bicameral legislature system in America has drawn criticism for creating a partisan deadlock and being unnecessary in the broader context of checks and balances. Many countries use unicameral systems, where the legislature is only one directly elected house, and there is no equivalent of a Senate.

The legislative branch in the United States balances the President and judiciary's power by writing laws and controlling the budget. Congress is supposed to have the exclusive power to declare war, although this power has been ceded significantly to the executive branch in the post-World War II era.

Congress can check the President's power, the Supreme Court, or the bureaucracy by initiating investigative committees with the legal authority to compel truthful testimony from all witnesses. These investigative committees have played an essential role in ensuring the President's power is moderated.

Congress initiated investigations into the Watergate scandal from the June 17, 1972, failed break-in attempt of the Democratic National Committee (DNC) at the Watergate Office Complex. This investigation revealed that President Richard Nixon tried to bug the offices of political opponents. Once exposed, Nixon attempted to cover up this break-in committed to stealing information from the opposition. The investigative committee's findings led to President Nixon's resignation before what appeared to be his inevitable removal (impeachment in the House and trial in the Senate) from office. His successor, President Gerald Ford, pardoned Richard Nixon.

President Richard Nixon, c. 1972

The Senate has the power to check the President by being able to reject any presidential appointment, such as a Supreme Court judge or bureaucratic official. In 2005, President George W. Bush's nominee for the Supreme Court, Harriet Miers, was criticized by the Senate. It was expected that the Senate would have voted not to approve her. To avoid the embarrassment of being rebuffed by the Senate, President George Bush withdrew Harriet Miers as his nominee.

The Senate has the power to ratify or reject treaties with other countries. This power to ratify or reject treaties is a check on both the President and bureaucracy's power. The House of Representatives can impeach, and the Senate can remove executive and judicial branch members. This power is exercised rarely but is critical to balancing and checking power. Congress has the power to change the number of Supreme Court justices and can overturn presidential vetoes with a supermajority vote.

The judicial branch's separation from Congress and the President ensures that they do not act contrary to the Constitution. While the framers of the Constitution sought to create a judiciary branch that would be completely free of political influence, this separation of powers has diminished over time. Given that the President appoints members to the Supreme Court not on their legal merits but based on the President's belief that the justice makes rulings he or she agrees with, the Supreme Court's power is often conditional on the power of the President.

In other countries, such as Canada, the Supreme Court members are appointed based on judicial merit. It may create a contentious public debate if the Prime Minister appoints a justice by his or her political views. In countries with a parliamentary system, the judiciary is more independent of the political system and more independent of the executive and legislative branches. Though the American system is based on separate powers, this is often not the reality.

The primary checks that the judiciary, primarily the Supreme Court, can balance the executive and legislative branches' power are numerous. Primarily, the Supreme Court can invalidate a law by determining it to be unconstitutional. This is a necessary power and checks on Congress, as it enables the judiciary to protect the rights of the minority against majority votes in Congress.

Congress should not pass a law that violates an individual's rights specified in the Bill of Rights, even if the majority votes to violate these rights. The judiciary is a vital check on the possible formation of a "tyranny of the majority." The tyranny of the majority happens when the majority vote to thwart away rights from the minority.

The Supreme Court interprets laws; they determine if a law passed by Congress satisfied the Constitution's limitations. This is an essential power because often, Congress passes vague laws (i.e., vague statutes are unconstitutional). Vague laws allow the potential for injustice because people do not know when and how the law applies to their behavior.

The judiciary is responsible for policing its members, which means that if a judge or lawyer misbehaves, the court system should be the first one to seek to punish them. Strict standards are applied to lawyers and judges to maintain the integrity of the justice system. If Congress must intervene to remove a judge, this is a significant failure of the justice system because it is supposed to regulate itself.

The cabinet members are the heads of the departments of the bureaucracy. The Cabinet is appointed by and functions as senior advisors of the President. The Cabinet has a check on the President's power as cabinet members advise the President on their department's issues. The President is not an expert in all matters. The President often defers to the appointed cabinet secretaries' experience and expertise, giving cabinet members vast power.

In parliamentary systems, cabinet leaders, called ministers, are chosen by the Prime Minister from those elected to the legislature. The advantage of the American system is that the President can appoint experts in their respective fields to lead government departments without the limitation that they are elected. The disadvantage is that the people can not democratically remove these cabinet secretaries if they do a poor job.

Abraham Lincoln with his cabinet, c. 1865

Relative Powers

While the idea is that each branch should be equal in power to act as a sufficient check against the others, most political scientists agree this is not the case. The power of the executive branch has been expanded in the modern era. The expansion of this power has been at the expense of the legislative branch.

Most experts agree that the judicial branch is by far the weakest. The primary check on power exercised by the Supreme Court is to nullify laws by its ability to rule laws unconstitutional. This power was not granted in the Constitution but resulted from the *Marbury v Madison* (1803) decision.

Even the Constitution sets the judiciary branch as having significantly less power than the other two. While the Supreme Court does have this power now, significant rulings that render laws unconstitutional are relatively rare, demonstrating that Congress is significantly more powerful than the judiciary. The Supreme Court often defers to the legislative branch to enact laws and is reticent to deem laws unconstitutional unless fundamental rights are violated. Further deference is granted to the bureaucracy in the *Chevron* doctrine, case law from 1984. The *Chevron* doctrine stands for the proposition that administrative agencies have considerable latitude in determine rules and regulations applicable to the enactment and enforcement of legislation. However, the Chevron doctrine has recently come under additional court challenges, and the Court has yielded less deference to the bureaucracy.

By contrast, the Supreme Court of Canada struck down as unconstitutional at least one major law per year passed by Prime Minister Stephen Harper's government from 2006 to 2015. Whether this was because the Canadian Supreme Court was more powerful than the American Supreme Court, or simply because the Canadian government under Harper tried to pass more overreaching laws than the U.S. Congress does, is open to debate.

President Barack Obama with Canadian Prime Minister Stephen Harper, c. 2011

The balance of power between the branches has seen significant shifts throughout its history. As outlined above, the Supreme Court started very weak but carved out the power of judicial review to strengthen its power.

Immediately after the Civil War (April 12, 1861, to April 9, 1865), Congress passed some Acts to make the President subordinate to Congress. This included passage of the Tenure of Office Act (in effect from 1867-1887), which was legislation to diminish the power of Democratic President Andrew Johnson's presidential veto after the assassination of Republican President Abraham Lincoln. With the onset of World War II (September 1, 1939, to September 2, 1945), power shifted back to Democratic President Franklin Delano Roosevelt as he requested broad authority to conduct a major war.

After World War II, presidential powers continued to expand to support Roosevelt's New Deal and Johnson Great Society. Since then, several Presidents have invoked national security as a reason for greater presidential secrecy and power. Examples include President Nixon's impediment of the Watergate Investigation, President Bush's emphasis on Homeland Security, and President Obama's increased utilization of FISA Court warrants, which many scholars criticize as usurpation flagrant disregard for the protection of the 4th Amendment against unlawful search and seizures.

The Foreign Intelligence Surveillance Act was introduced by Democratic Senator Ted Kennedy on May 18, 1977, and signed into law by Democratic President Jimmy Carter on October 25, 1978. President Obama dramatically increased the use of FISA warrants. The FISA warrants were included in whistleblower complaints that alleged improper use of the powers because the warrants targeted American citizens and were not limited to foreign powers or suspected agents of a foreign power suspected of espionage or terrorism.

Alleged abuses include FISA warrants issued against American citizens George Papadopoulos and Carter Paige. These allegations extend to the highest branches of the CIA and FBI. The issue of impropriety has not been resolved despite several investigations by the Senate Judiciary Committee, House Intelligence Committee, Inspector General of the United States, and special counsel John Durham appointed in May 2019 by the justice department.

Notes for active learning

Notes for active learning

Linkages Between Institutions and Political Groups

While the three branches of government and the bureaucracy have checks and balances to ensure that no branch can abuse its power, the American government's institutions are influenced and checked by other political actors. The government does not operate in isolation, and there are some linkages between institutional, governmental authority, and other aspects of society.

Public Opinion and Voters

As a democracy, the United States' government's primary responsibility is to carry out the American people's wishes. American citizens hold the ultimate check on the President's power through their ability to elect the executive. If the voters feel that the President is not competent, they can exercise their power to elect someone else in the next election. While the President's Constitutional role does not explicitly represent the American people, if they appear to ignore public opinion, their re-election chances are significantly diminished.

When the President has public opinion on his or her side, it becomes easier to advance the executive's agenda, especially if Congress attempts to prevent the President's actions. However, in the President's second term in office, public opinion becomes less influential when they cannot be re-elected as the President is not concerned with being re-elected. Conversely, towards the end of their second term, Presidents may consider how they will be remembered in history and continue to seek widespread approval for their acts hoping that they will be remembered favorably in the history books.

Since public opinion is so important, polling organizations play an essential role by conveying what people think about an issue. Polling firms contact a small number of people and ask what their opinion is on an issue or approve or disapprove of the President's or Congress's performance. People often complain that polls are inaccurate. With statistical sampling, voter preference polls provide a somewhat accurate assessment of the general popular opinion with an acceptable margin of error.

These polls are crucial because they discover people's opinion on any given issue, which helps the President and Congress decide where to give their support. The government is interested in public opinion polls to successfully change its public messaging to encourage people to agree with government actions. In this sense, public opinion is a two-way street. The people's opinions can push the government, while the government continually tries to shape and manipulate public opinion.

Logo for the Gallup Corporation, a leading polling firm in the U.S.

Congress, and especially the House of Representatives, is constitutionally expected to represent public opinion directly. Members of the House of Representatives are concerned with being re-elected, as they have no term limits which last two years. Representatives usually pay close attention to public opinion in their home districts. This leads to clashes between a house member and their party if the member's district is opposed to the party favored policy.

In this situation, the Whip tries to convince this member to vote with the party rather than the district. Situations like this pose a dilemma for a member of the house. Voting against the wishes of those in the home district could mean not being re-elected. Voting against one's political party's wishes could mean that the party chooses someone else to run in that district's next election, making re-election difficult.

While Senators are subject to re-election, their longer six-year terms insulate them somewhat from public opinion. Senators were unelected to ensure that only sage and experienced people could become Senators; their job requires them to consider issues outside public opinion demands. Being elected, however, makes Senators subject to the same need to appeal to voters in their home state as do the members of the House of Representatives. This undermines the framers' intent to make the Senate a bastion of worldly wisdom capable of acting as a buffer against public opinion.

Public opinion and voting play no role in the bureaucracy or federal judiciary, although lower court justices at the state and local level are often elected. Judges are to consider the law and Constitution, regardless of popular opinion. The bureaucracy, mostly getting jobs through experience and expertise, is not subject to public approval, even if people have opinions on their job.

Interest Groups

Taking part in a public interest group requires dedication to a cause apart from personal gain. If a cause is successful, it is theoretically beneficial to everyone, even those who did not lobby the government. Political scientists call this the "free rider" effect, and it demonstrates how people uninterested in political activity can benefit from the hard work of others.

To advance their cause, lobby groups engage in a variety of tactics. Primarily, they want access to a government representative to directly tell a member of Congress or the President about their cause. Given how many lobby groups there are relative to politicians, gaining access can be exceedingly difficult. One of the primary ways that lobby groups gain access to politicians is through large campaign donations. A well-funded interest group will donate a large sum of money to a politician trying to get elected.

If that politician wins, they feel a debt of gratitude for the large donation and offer more donors access. This is a controversial aspect of lobbying, as it dramatically favors corporations and labor unions, who can buy access to politicians. Another effective method is to recruit a high-profile celebrity to the cause. Celebrities command much public attention, and if a politician should refuse to meet with a celebrity promoting a popular cause, this can hurt the politician's reputation. As such, many interest groups actively seek out celebrities to endorse their campaign to win political access.

If interest groups cannot win direct access, they attempt to influence politicians via public opinion campaigns. This is usually accomplished by running high profile media campaigns about an issue to get the public talking and asking questions. If an interest group raises public awareness of an issue to a high enough level, it can become impossible for politicians to ignore it. Such campaigns rely on celebrities and require large sums of money for advertising, favoring wealthier people, labor unions, and corporate interest groups.

If both methods fail, then lobby groups can turn to the judicial system and attempt to instigate change through litigation. For example, the National Association for the Advancement of Colored People (NAACP) used lawsuits in the 1940s and 1950s to overturn racial segregation laws.

President John F. Kennedy meets with representatives from the NAACP:
Dr. E. Franklin Jackson (left) and Bishop Stephen G. Spottswood (right), c. 1961

Suppose all three methods fail to bring change or the attention of politicians. In that case, interest groups can engage in protests and civil disobedience to force politicians, the media, the legal system, and public opinion to pay attention to their cause. Having been ignored by all the forms of government, Martin Luther King Jr. (1929 to April 4, 1968) led the civil rights movement in non-violent protests and civil disobedience to finally bring the cause of racial equality to the attention of the government. While such disruption techniques tend to be the last resort of frustrated interest groups, if the government refuses to pay attention to important issues, protests and civil disobedience can be a highly effective means of political action.

Civil Rights leader Martin Luther King Jr.

Other successful civil disobedience and protest campaigns included the eight- hour workday (reduced from the previously allowed 12-hour workday). The women's suffrage movement culminated in women winning the right to vote. More recently, the gay rights movement has affected legislative change concerning gay and lesbian rights and led to more knowledge and acceptance of these issues. Such protest-based lobbying tends to be favored by those who lack the money to buy access to politicians.

Interest groups serve to hold members of the bureaucracy accountable. They report violations of the policy to the media and lawmakers and challenge them in court. They sometimes demand the removal of offending government workers who are obstinate. In America, many members of the bureaucracy are elected by voters, including district attorneys, police chiefs, county clerks. Interest groups can influence these elections.

An excellent example is from the civil rights era in Alabama. When Congress passed the Voting Rights Act, Selma's black population turned out at the next election and defeated the police's racist chief. Members of interest groups may also be members of the bureaucracy. Interest groups interact with the courts as well. They are usually the first to bring court cases against civil servants. The cases against civil servants allege violations of their constitutional rights. The case could have the government named as a defendant if Congress enacted legislation violative of the Constitution.

A recent case of how interest groups use the court system is the lawsuit filed in November 2015, by the Libertarian Party and the Green Party of America as joint plaintiffs, against the Federal Debate Commission. They complain that the Commission refuses to allow presidential candidates other than Republicans and Democrats to participate in the election debates, which the plaintiffs see as a violation of the Sherman Anti-Trust Act.

Political Parties

Political parties play an essential role in the legislative branch, as the majority party leader in the House and the Senate control the legislative agenda. When different parties control the executive, the House of Representatives, and the Senate, obstruction and deadlock can occur.

The checks and balances system, which is meant to prevent abuse, can prevent legislation altogether due to partisanship. Engaging in partisan-based obstruction and blocking leads to political parties developing poor reputations with generally low public support for Congress. For example, a Gallop poll for November 13, 2013, showed an approval rating for Congress of 9%, a disapproval rating of 86%, and no opinion rating of 5%. The range of ratings dating back to 1974 ranged from approval of 84% (November 2001) to a low of 9% (November 2013) with many variations at other time intervals. The checks and balances system designed by the framers of the Constitution applies to situations without political parties. Thus, they could not have foreseen how introducing parties into these checks and balances could lead to government shutdowns and unnecessary legislative and executive obstacles.

As with Congress, the President is a member of a political party. For a short time at the beginning of the Republic, the President and Vice-President were of different parties. The winner of a presidential election would become President, and the second-place candidate – the President's political opponent – would become Vice-President. This was changed in the early nineteenth century. Now, the President and Vice-President are elected in separate votes.

The presidential candidates have running mates from the same party, and there has not been a case of a President elected without their running mate. Once in office, a President may be facing members of another party in the upper bureaucracy, and federal courts and opponents may hold the majority in either or both houses of Congress. This demands that a President be a strong negotiator. The President's partisan power is with the executive branch. An incoming President appoints members of the executive branch (e.g., secretaries of defense, justice, education), and these are usually appointed on a partisan basis

Presidents have appointed executive members from a different party if they share some shared vision with the President. For example, an exception to this partisan nature was Republican President Trump's (2016) appointment of life-long Democrat General Michael Flynn as National Security Advisor. The critical thing to note is that the President has the power to appoint executives of his party and do so immediately on being sworn in. Many times, these same people were part of the "transition team" of the president-elect.

In contrast to the President's freedom to appoint members to the executive branch, federal judges (judicial branch) can only be appointed if a vacancy occurs (and must be confirmed by the Senate). The President can not select members of the legislative branch to serve in Congress. Many states permit the governor to appoint interim legislative members (e.g., Senators) when a vacancy occurs before the next scheduled election. An example of this power abuse occurred with Democrat Rod Blagojevich (2011; 14-year conviction) as Governor of Illinois attempting to trade favors for filling the vacant Senate seat available when Senator Obama was elected President.

The process of appointing bureaucrats who are members of one's party is called the "spoils system." In exchange for support during elections, party members expect to be rewarded with government appointments, while vocational merit is a secondary consideration. This is how bureaucracy appointments are made and have been since the beginning of the multi-party democracy in the early nineteenth century. Partisanship in the bureaucracy affects how policies are implemented – in extreme cases, even to the extent of blatant violations of the law.

Although government workers are expected to uphold the law with impartiality, in theory, they are opinionated human beings as much as any politician is. They can be held accountable for egregious breaches of the public trust. There are many ways that an unsympathetic bureaucracy can retard the implementation of a policy. When a problem arises, it is frustrating for people dependent on their function (citizens, legislature, president, cabinet members). For example, the bureaucracy can interpret a policy's wording in extreme ways to obstruct or take excessive amounts of time to do what is required. Adding qualifications that are not expressly prohibited by the law is a frequent strategy.

The most publicized recent example of this is the finding, in 2014, that the I.R.S. made partisan decisions in applying a political funding law. I.R.S. employees were accused of deliberately failing to apply a tax exemption to a disproportionate number of political activist groups that supported conservative causes and candidates. The I.R.S. employees, like other professional bureaucrats, are overwhelmingly Democrats. Under Democratic Attorney General Eric Holder, the Department of Justice closed the case in 2015 with no convictions. Many people have raised the issue that the Department of Justice is partisan.

The federal court system includes the Supreme Court, 94 federal courts, 13 courts of appeal, and three special courts (U.S. Court of Appeals for Veteran Claims, U.S. Court of Appeals for the Armed Forces, and U.S. Tax Courts). Nine judges sit on the Supreme Court and rule as a committee. Under Article III (i.e., District Courts, Circuit Courts, and Supreme Court), federal judges and justices are appointed by the President and confirmed (*advice and consent*) by the Senate.

Internal Revenue Service Building on Constitution Avenue in Washington, D.C.

Appointments are usually partisan. This matters because, while it might seem like a judge cannot choose the outcome of a trial based on personal opinion, the reality is that compelling legal arguments can be made to support any point of view in a complex disagreement. Supreme Court hears only legal disputes most challenging to resolve since its purpose is to rule on such significant and complex cases. Thus, partisanship matters. Presidents tend to appoint federal judges aligned with the President's political beliefs.

When the President and the majority in the Senate are from different parties, it can be difficult for the President to make appointments since an unsympathetic Senate can block them. Presidents get around this problem by negotiation. Presidents can agree to things the majority party wants to get some support for judicial appointments. When a Senate is unsympathetic, the President does not need the support of the entire opposing party; all that the President needs to do is sway the minimum number of Senators needed to win the confirmation vote. Alternatively, a President can choose a moderate candidate (seems to be rare in recent times) who is likelier not to be rejected by the other party.

As with appointments, the outcomes of Supreme Court decisions often hinge on swaying at least one justice, which is of an opposing point of view. In 2020, there were five sitting Republican appointees and four sitting Democratic appointees among the

Supreme Court's justices. However, many "liberal" rulings were made because at least one of the conservative justices was convinced to rule with the more liberal ones (e.g., upholding the tax for the Health Care Act). The reverse of a liberal justice voting with the conservatives is not frequent.

Many decisions of the Supreme Court are decided with a 5-4 vote by the justices. Therefore, the swing vote (sometimes favoring liberal causes and sometimes conservative) is critical. This role was held by Justice Kennedy (appointed by Republican President Reagan; 1988-2018) until his retirement. Since then, the swing vote has been cast by Chief Justice Roberts (appointed by Republican President George W. Bush in 2005).

The Media

The news media and social media are two of the most vital tools the public has as an indirect check on the government's power abuse. Members of the public can expose incidents of corruption and violations of the law by politicians and bureaucrats, either to the news agencies or personally, on social media.

However, these tools are not infallible. Political parties demonstrated their willingness and ability to co-opt the news media, beginning shortly after the development of "muckraking journalism" in the 1890s. Today, news articles shape public opinion and are not used only to report facts in nonpartisan ways. Thus, social media has a different use as a public check on the opinionated and agenda-setting news media. The news media can be a tool for exposing incidents of corruption and violations of the law by civil servants and politicians if the facts support the news organization's narrative slant.

However, to the extent that the exposed targets of wrongdoing are members of the same party that the media staff is sympathetic to, the media can use strategies and spin to defend the accused or to squelch coverage of the story. Social media keeps the traditional news media honest because any member of the public can publish something that is not being covered in the news or expose irresponsible journalism. A weakness of social media is that it is unfiltered. There is no vetting or corroboration of the story. Inaccurate information can be posted with no professional editing.

The bureaucracy has a formal role in regulating the media. The Federal Communications Commission (FCC) acts as a kind of "media police," and its primary job is to ensure that broadcasters obey public decency standards. If a radio or TV station continually violates these standards, the FCC can revoke its license, and the station is shut down. Usually, the FCC imposes monetary fines based on the severity and frequency of individual incidents.

The FCC imposed significant fines on radio talk show host Howard Stern for profanity on the air. CBS was fined for violating public decency over the 2004 Super Bowl halftime show in which singer Janet Jackson had her infamous "wardrobe malfunction." Many have argued that the FCC's public decency rules amount to censorship and that the American people are mature enough to decide what to watch and what not to watch. While the FCC is controversial, it generally does not censor political matters and promotes fairness during political campaigns.

Logo of the Federal Communications Commission

Congress and the President have a two-directional power relationship. The government created goals that the FCC enforces and laws that it must follow in its operations. The FCC sets out the rules for how political campaigns during an election can use the broadcast media. The FCC enforces the *equal time rule*, ensuring that every broadcaster must give equal time to all candidates who request it.

If a local news station allows a candidate to run a one-minute advertisement in prime time, the opposing candidates can demand to receive a one-minute advertisement in the same time slot. The goal of this rule is to prevent a media outlet from favoring one candidate over another. Commentators question the neutrality of several prominent "news" outlets. The audiences of these stations show a polarized, definite bias (i.e., conservative or liberal) in the information they seek to obtain from watching or listening to the station.

However, it is vital to note that although America is a multi-party democracy with registered alternative parties who run candidates, the equal time rule mentioned above mainly only applies to the Republican and Democratic parties. Parties in America are categorized by law into "Major," "Minor," and "New" parties, with different requirements for media time.

The *right to rebuttal* is the second significant FCC rule for political campaigns. The broadcast outlet must offer a candidate a chance to respond if another candidate criticizes them on air. This rule prevents the media from allowing one candidate to attack the others without the recipient being able to respond publicly to those attacks.

The Fairness Doctrine was the third FCC political rule. It has not been enforced since the mid-1980s and was removed as a rule in 2011 under President Obama's administration. This rule required broadcasters to balance out viewpoints in the media and present multiple sides of a controversial issue. Many political scientists believe that the decline in enforcement and the eventual overturning of this rule has contributed to partisan polarization, as news outlets no longer must present opposing viewpoints to the public.

It is important to distinguish that the FCC can only regulate public broadcasts over the air (i.e., radio waves from the TV station's transmitter), which means cable television and the internet are exempt. The FCC has sought to expand its reach to regulate all media. The FCC found some supporters in Congress, and some opposed to this expanding jurisdiction to regulate content delivery.

State and Local Governments

The United States government is a federal system, meaning that there are layers of governmental authority. The federal government is the top layer of government (supremacy clause in the Constitution), with state governments and local governments below it regarding overall authority and power. Article VI of the Constitution sets out the *supremacy clause*, which declares that the federal government has power over the state governments and that state governments cannot pass laws that contravene the Constitution or laws passed by Congress at the federal level. State governments can pass nonconflicting laws, which makes state governments relatively powerful units of government.

The federal government has some exclusive powers which state governments do not. Its enumerated powers involve the ability to declare war, manage the currency system, and regulate commerce. For example, Alaska could not declare war on Canada, nor could it make its currency. The federal government has implied powers, meaning it oversees national concern issues, such as building interstate highways, managing air traffic control, or regulating the public airwaves.

The inherent powers of the federal government mean that it has the responsibility to protect its citizens. If Canada decided to attack Alaska, it would be the federal government's responsibility to intervene and defend Alaska. The federal government cannot merely leave a state to fend for itself in the event of an external attack. The Constitution outlines powers that the federal government is not allowed to exercise, called prohibited powers. Congress cannot tax the exports of an individual state or dictate (i.e., commandeer) how a state chooses electors in the Electoral College. Appropriations are a mechanism used by Congress to encourage states to cooperate with federal policy; states receive money if they comply or are denied funds if they deviate from the policy.

Each state government uses a three-branch structure; legislative, executive, and judicial branches. The balance of power and the number of checks is often different in each state. The Governor may hold the most power in some states, while the legislative branch is the most powerful in others.

The amount of relative state power has been an issue throughout American history, beginning with the Federalist Papers' arguments (which led to Jefferson's anti-federalist political party). During the Civil War, where states' rights to set their laws relating to slavery were challenged. In the modern era after World War II, most scholars agree that the federal government has become more powerful than individual states.

Painting of Thomas Jefferson (leader of the anti-federalists) and Alexander Hamilton (author of The Federalist Papers) with George Washington in the Capitol building

At times, the 10th Amendment is used by states to push back on intrusive federal powers. At other times, the powers reserved to the states under the 10th Amendment are dormant, and the federal government seeks to encroach upon the rights reserved to the states under the 10th Amendment.

More recently, however, state governments have been driving the national agenda on social issues. Individual states, such as Vermont (civil union) and Massachusetts (same-sex marriage) in 2004 under Republican Governor Mitt Romney, forced the issue to the national stage. Under Republican President George Bush and Democratic President Obama, the federal government seemed unresponsive to the issue.

For another example of the states leading on societal issues, consider the recreational use of marijuana. Some states, notably Colorado, decriminalized the recreational use of marijuana in November 2012. Almost 40 states have either permitted medical use of marijuana, decriminalized the recreational use of marijuana, or legalized recreational marijuana despite it being illegal at the federal level.

Some political scientists view states passing legislation that forces the federal government to act on ignored or controversial issues as a resurgence of state power under the 10th Amendment.

The Constitution does not mention any specific powers for local governments. Courts have interpreted this to mean that local governments have no independent authority and are purely under the state's power. Individual states can then create or abolish municipal governments as they see appropriate.

After the financial crisis of 2008, many cities faced severe budget issues. Several state governments intervened by either providing additional funds or taking control of the city services. Such acts were controversial because they directly undermined the local government's authority, but the states were well within their constitutional rights to intervene.

In 1995, the state government of Illinois was dissatisfied with the poor condition of schools in Chicago. To fix this issue, the state government wholly re-arranged Chicago's government structure, taking away almost all authority over the school system from the local board of education and giving this power to the mayor.

For creating a local or municipal government, the state creates a charter outlining the local or municipal governmental powers. These charters usually grant some degree of autonomy to local decisions, but the localities must pay for programs without financial help from the state. Most states have different types of charters that grant different levels of power, depending on the population's size. Most states differentiate between a town, a village, a township, a county, and a city, granting each a different charter with a different set of powers and responsibilities.

For example, a large city charter may allow a city to have its police force, while a village charter may leave policing to the state or county government. Most local governments consist of an elected mayor and an elected city council. Some smaller towns use town hall meetings to make decisions. The local governments' structure is entirely up to the state, and thus the state can decide what structure these governments should have.

One notable exception to state control of the local government is autonomous Native American reservations. These are pockets of land managed by Native Americans under the U.S. Bureau of Indian Affairs' authority rather than the state government. The structure of government on reservations usually takes the form of an elected council. These territories are outside the state governments' control; therefore, reservations can pass laws that differ from their location.

For example, while gambling is illegal in New York State, Native American reservations within New York can pass laws to make casinos legal. While the reservation council is supposed to have sovereignty over the land, making it the highest authority (over the state or federal government), the situation's reality has been more complex, resulting in conflicts.

Seal of the U.S. Bureau of Indian Affairs

Notes for active learning

Notes for active learning

Chapter 3

Civil Rights
and Civil Liberties

The development of individuals' rights and liberties has had a meaningful impact on American citizens and United States politics. Intrinsically tied to this topic are the United States Supreme Court's workings and its most significant decisions.

The judicial interpretations of civil rights and liberties, such as freedom of speech, assembly and expression, the rights of the accused during a trial, and minority groups and women's rights, offer critical insight into the United States politics' evolution.

The Fourteenth Amendment and the *selective incorporation* doctrine have extended several protections of rights and liberties against the state government. Several Supreme Court decisions have been tools, either inhibiting or promoting social change.

Civil Liberties and Civil Rights by Judicial Interpretation

The theory behind civil rights or civil liberties is that people have fundamental rights that cannot be violated, especially by the government. Through the codification of these rights in the Constitution through the Bill of Rights, people have the right to seek redress through the Supreme Court if Congress should pass a federal law or if state legislatures (through reverse incorporation of rights under the 14th Amendment) pass laws that violate the rights and liberties of an individual.

Founding Father Benjamin Franklin (1706-1790) is credited with saying, *"democracy is two wolves and a lamb voting on what to have for lunch. Liberty is a well-armed lamb contesting the vote."* With a set of constitutional rights, the minority is protected from this kind of abuse by the majority. The Bill of Rights outlined what was considered fundamental and universal rights. However, these rights have not been applied equally to all segments of the population. Since the unequal application of rights usually affects only minorities, Congress has traditionally been slow to act, leaving them to the courts and popular movements on such issues.

The applicability of rights first arose to prominence over slavery, which divided American society from the Republic's establishment. While slavery was legal and practiced throughout the thirteen colonies, the American Revolution (1765-1783) sparked the idea of equality and freedom, which led to five northern states abolishing slavery by 1789 (PA in 1780, MA in 1783, NH in 1783, CT in 1784 and RI in 1784), just a few years after the formation of the United States. Despite the Constitution setting out all rights, it was silent on slavery, which would lead to problems.

The Constitution indirectly addressed slavery by stating in Article I, Section 9, that Congress may not change laws related to the migration or importation of people until 1808. At the end of 1807, Congress promptly passed a law effective January 1, 1808, which banned importing slaves and ending the slave trade. Owning slaves was still legal in America; however, importing people to make them slaves was banned.

Slavery was banned in most northern states but legal in the southern states, pursuing a divergent economic development path into the mid-1800s. Due to the lack of need for slave labor in the industrializing northern states, slavery was unnecessary. The southern states were reliant on labor-intensive cash crops, which would remain profitable

121

even if looked after by paid laborers; however, the revenues would be drastically reduced. Many opponents of slavery (active abolitionists) emerged in the northern states. These economic differences, underscored by being "free" states or slave states, led to significant cultural and political differences between the North and the South.

Slave auction in America, c. 1810

Slavery became a significant issue when considering which new states would be admitted to the Union. In 1820, Missouri applied to be admitted into the United States as a slave state. This caused a political crisis because admitting Missouri as a slave state would mean that slave states held a majority in the Senate. Northern states were strongly opposed to admitting Missouri due to opposition to slavery, but the federal government was adamant that its territory continues to expand to the west.

From this controversy, the Missouri Compromise was created. Missouri would be admitted as a slave state, but Massachusetts would be divided into two states to create a new free state (Maine). The balance of power between slave states and "free" states continued to be controversial and eventually led to the Civil War outbreak.

In addition to the role of slavery on a state level within the Union, the more liberal political climate in the North led to the first Civil Rights Movement, led by white abolitionists, who publicly advocated ending slavery. Abolitionists engaged in a variety of tactics to undermine slavery.

Before outlawing the transatlantic slave trade, abolitionists would buy people captured and sent to America to be slaves. The white northerners would then free them and pay the cost to ship them back to Africa. In the 1820s, former American slaves formed Liberia's independent state in Western Africa and joined with the American abolitionists to send freed slaves to live in this new country. This was a costly solution, and the northern abolitionists soon ran out of money to support the mission. It was a controversial solution because, by this time, many American slaves were second or third generation with little to no ties to Liberia or Africa.

The abolitionist movement's tone shifted under the leadership of Massachusetts-born William Lloyd Garrison (1805-1879). Garrison published a newspaper, *The Liberator* (1831-1865), that called for immediate emancipation rather than resettle former slaves in Liberia. At this time, the abolitionist movement was joined by many free African Americans, such as Republican Frederick Douglass (1818-1895), Robert Purvis (1810-1898), and James Fortin (1766-1842). These African American leaders wrote important philosophical works condemning the injustice of slavery and were responsible for leading organizations in the abolitionist movement.

William Lloyd Garrison, leader of the abolitionist movement, c. 1878

Many unsupportive whites saw the collaboration of black and white Americans working together to abolish slavery at the time as scandalous. The major northern universities—Yale, Harvard, and Princeton—opposed the abolitionists on these grounds. The university-sponsored opposition led to the establishment of more liberal colleges that admitted black students (e.g., Bowdoin College in Maine). New religious denominations (e.g., Free Methodists) were established. Abolitionists started their newspapers, including Frederick Douglass' *North Star* (1847-1851), to promote the fervent cause of abolition.

In the 1850s, the abolitionist movement split over the constitutionality of slavery. One side, led by William Lloyd Garrison, saw the Constitution as pro-slavery and called for a new Constitution that explicitly outlawed slavery. The other side, led by Lysander Spooner (1808-1887) and supported by Frederick Douglass, argued that the Constitution already outlawed slavery in practice and simply needed to be applied appropriately.

Around this time, the abolitionist movement split along class lines. Many wealthy northern industrialists joined and began to support abolitionism because they saw slavery as an unfair economic advantage for the South. The northern working-class opposed this argument and insisted that human equality be an essential principle.

In addition to internal efforts at societal reform, abolitionists played a prominent role in developing the Underground Railroad. The Underground Railroad was a network of safe houses set up by Abolitionists to allow escaped slaves to travel to the North and, eventually, Canada. The Underground Railroad was led by prominent activists such as Harriet Tubman (died March 10, 1913); the network transported approximately 30,000 people to freedom; most of the freed slaves settled in Canada because of their illegal status in the United States under the Fugitive Slave Law of 1850 signed by Whig Party President Millard Fillmore (1800-1874; 1850-1853).

In some cases, abolitionists took more direct action to free captured escaped slaves. In 1858, abolitionists were able to free an escaped slave who was captured by a U.S. Marshal in Ohio, allowing him to escape to Canada. This was the Oberlin-Wellington Rescue, and the abolitionists who took part were put on federal trial. This trial allowed the accused a national stage of arguing the case for emancipation.

Another prominent abolitionist was Connecticut-born John Brown (1800-1859), who advocated for armed insurrection to overthrow slavery. Brown attempted to spark a national slave revolt by seizing arms at a U.S. military arsenal in Harpers Ferry, Virginia, between October 16-18, 1859. Brown gathered twenty men and attempted to seize control of the arsenal. After the insurrection, only a few local slaves joined the revolt. Brown was defeated by a detachment of U.S. Marines led by Colonel Robert E. Lee (1807-1870). Seven people (including three blacks) were killed and ten more injured. Brown was the first person convicted of treason in U.S. history. After being found guilty on all counts, he was hanged.

The Harpers Ferry raid was considered too risky by most abolitionists, including Douglass and Tubman. Garrison called it "misguided, wild, and insane." The trial, conviction, and punishment by death turned John Brown into a hero in the North. His supporters included prominent philosophers such as Henry David Thoreau (1817-1862) and Ralph Waldo Emerson (1803-1882). After the state of Virginia executed Brown, abolitionism became more vocal and active in the North, where Brown was a martyr.

In the South, Brown was portrayed as a petty criminal trying to take away people's property. This difference in opinion revealed and exacerbated the dominant cultural and political differences between the North and the South that would culminate in the Civil War. Abolitionists strongly supported the Union and the Republican Party during the onset of the Civil War, which eventually led to Lincoln's Emancipation Proclamation that ended slavery.

U.S. Colonel Robert E. Lee, c. 1865

With the Union victory in the Civil War and the end of slavery, abolitionists such as Garrison considered the movement a success. These prominent abolitionists sought to disband the organizations they founded. The Reconstruction Amendments (13th, 14th, 15th) were passed, which outlawed discrimination against former slaves and black Americans, but some states passed legislation that skirted these significant Amendments' intent.

Southern states passed the Black Codes immediately after the Civil War, which dramatically restricted African Americans' freedom by preventing them from serving on a jury, voting, owning guns, and even gathering in public in a group for any purpose, including education or religious service.

Although slavery was no longer legal, blacks were still not free in the South. To remedy these injustices, Congress passed the Civil Rights Act of 1866, which was intended to overrule the Black Codes. The successor to the assassinated Republican President Abraham Lincoln was Democratic President Andrew Johnson (1808-1875; April 15, 1865, to 1869). Johnson used his presidential veto on the Civil Rights Act of 1866. However, in a rare action, Congress used its ability to override a presidential veto (the first successful congressional override of a presidential veto in 1845). The congressional override by a two-thirds vote in each house ensured that the Civil Rights Act of 1866 became law.

After the defeat of the Black Codes, the southern states-initiated Jim Crow laws. The Jim Crow laws mandated racial segregation in all public facilities, alleging that blacks and whites were equal but should remain separate. Public schools, public spaces, public transportation, public restrooms, restaurants, drinking fountains, and even the U.S. military were all segregated; blacks and whites had to use separate facilities.

By 1883, the Supreme Court ruled that Jim Crow laws were the Civil Rights Cases. The Civil Rights Cases consisted of five Supreme Court rulings in 1883 that challenged the 13th and 14th Amendments' validity. The court ruled that Congress can prohibit government discrimination based on race but lacked authority to enforce civil rights in areas not related to the federal government.

In *Plessy v. Ferguson* (1896), the Supreme Court again held the legality of segregation by declaring that the separate but equal reasoning was valid. The challenge was initiated after a man who was seven-eighths white and one-eighth black had been denied a seat in the "whites only" section of a train.

Since the 15th Amendment (ratified 1870) outlawed discriminating against people based on race for voting, southern states used other means to prevent blacks from voting. Many southern states adopted clauses that said one's grandfather must have been able to vote in order for one to vote legally. The southern states adopted property requirements and poll taxes, which were only applied when African Americans would try to register to vote. Some states even instituted biased literary tests that disenfranchised black Americans.

The Jim Crow laws and racial segregation remained in effect until a new Civil Rights Movement challenged them in the 1950s. In the landmark *Brown v. Board of Education* (1954), the Supreme Court held that racially segregated schools were unconstitutional. This holding was a significant advance against segregation, spurring renewed activism. The Supreme Court ruled that racial segregation in schools must be dismantled with "all deliberate speed." Federal court judges were charged with devising and overseeing desegregation in public schools.

During the 1950s, the Civil Rights Movement, emboldened by the *Brown v. Board of Education* ruling, began to challenge segregation in all aspects of society. In 1955, Rosa Parks made civil rights for black Americans a globally recognized issue after refusing to give up her seat on a bus for a white passenger. After Parks was arrested, the Montgomery Bus Boycott began, pushing for desegregation of public transport, which was achieved the next year. Dr. Martin Luther King Jr. led the bus boycott, and the Civil Rights Movement gained momentum.

Medals that commemorate the leaders of the desegregation of public schools that led directly to the Supreme Court case of Brown v. the Board of Education

In 1957, Arkansas Democratic Governor Orval Faubus (1910-1994; 1955-1967) announced he would deploy the National Guard to prevent desegregation in Little Rock schools. This provoked a crisis with fears of another Civil War. The issue was resolved when Republican President Dwight Eisenhower sent federal troops to escort black students into a newly integrated high school. Desegregation in public schools continued to be a controversial issue, especially with schoolchildren as pawns in the political posturing.

Led by Dr. Martin Luther King Jr., the Civil Rights Movement engaged in sit-ins, boycotts, and marches to draw attention to the southern Jim Crow laws' injustices. The Civil Rights Movement campaign spread and was supported by people of all races, leading to the Freedom Riders. The Freedom Riders were a mix of black and white students who booked bus trips across the United States, purposely choosing mixed-race seating to force desegregation of intercity bus trips. These civil rights activists were met with violent resistance from local authorities. Eventually, the national and global media began to cover local police violence against the civil rights demonstrators. American public opinion began to favor Dr. King and the Civil Rights Movement overwhelmingly.

By 1963, President Kennedy (1917-1963; 1961 to November 22, 1963) asked Congress to pass a law banning racial segregation in public places. Dr. King believed the law was inadequate and wanted a ban on all forms of racial segregation. King organized a march of over 250,000 people in Washington, D.C., culminating in his famous "I Have a Dream" speech. Meanwhile, President Kennedy was assassinated. His successor, President Lyndon Baines Johnson (1908-1973; 1963-1969), advocated for the bill in Congress, which was filibustered by Democratic Senators from the southern states, despite the 100 years since the end of the Civil War.

The Civil Rights Act of 1964 eventually passed. This Act outlawed segregation on interstate transportation, allowed the federal government to withhold funding from institutions or groups engaged in racial discrimination, and explicitly enshrined protection against discrimination by race, color, religion, sex, or national origin into law.

In the South, the Civil Rights Movement led by King saw this law as progress, though they believed it to be mostly inadequate in addressing the day's central race-related issues. Meanwhile, blacks in northern states faced economic issues, and a new movement led by Malcolm X (1925 to February 21, 1965) emerged. Malcolm X called for more direct forms of protest and action against racial and economic discrimination.

Initially, Malcolm X advocated for Black Nationalism and argued that blacks needed to make their own country in America because living equally with whites was impossible. Eventually, he came to see these views as racist and supported King's Civil

Rights Movement. However, Malcolm X favored more aggressive protest tactics and argued to link the blacks' plight in America to human rights issues worldwide.

Voting rights continued to be an issue after the passage of the Civil Rights Act of 1964. A march from Selma to Montgomery, Alabama, in March 1965, protested discrimination against the right of blacks to vote. A mob of vigilantes and state troopers attacked the marchers. Local organizer Amelia Boynton (1911–2015) was beaten unconscious.

A second march was planned for two days later, to be led by Martin Luther King Jr. despite several threats on his life. King led the march to the bridge, where the demonstrators were attacked two days later. After a standoff, the police and vigilantes stepped aside. King decided to lead the marchers back into Selma to wait for possible federal protection. That night, activist James Reeb (1927 to March 11, 1965), a white minister from Boston who come to support King, was beaten to death by vigilantes.

Reeb's murder catalyzed public opinion in favor of the civil rights marchers. President Johnson asked Congress to immediately put forward a voter protection act and offered federal troops to protect the marchers. After leading the push for equal rights in housing, the movement spurred Congress to pass the Civil Rights Act of 1968 in the wake of King's assassination and a renewed push from protestors. The Civil Rights Act passed despite another filibuster attempt from southern Senators. The Civil Rights Act of 1964 primarily addressed discrimination issues in the right to vote and employment. The Civil Rights Act of 1968 addressed discrimination issues in housing (e.g., renting, buying, selling).

Women's Rights and the Suffragette Movement

As with the issue of slavery, the status of women was left to individual states. Shortly after independence, women's status was unclear, and women with property could vote in states such as New Jersey. As states adopted their legal frameworks, however, women's political rights were quickly outlawed, and the women who could vote in individual states lost that right by 1807. The abolitionist movement gained momentum in the 1830s and 1840s. Participants started to question the second-class status of women as well as slaves.

In 1848, prominent abolitionist Elizabeth Cady Stanton (1815-1902) organized the Seneca Falls Convention. This was the first gathering of women's rights activists and the suffragette movement's birth in the United States. Suffragettes were women who advocated for universal suffrage (i.e., everyone should be able to vote), whether man or woman. This convention set the stage for the women's rights agenda, advocating for changes in social and legal codes to grant women more of a voice. The issue of voting rights for women was controversial even within the women's rights movement.

Elizabeth Cady Stanton, Susan B. Anthony (1820-1906) and Lucy Stone (1818-1893) began to organize women after the Civil War to promote voting rights. In 1867, they addressed state governments in New York and Kansas. They started to form more explicit links with African American groups who were facing similar issues of disenfranchisement.

Around this time, the passing of the 14th Amendment divided the women's movement. Most suffragettes were abolitionists. The 14th Amendment specified representation for male citizens, which suffragettes felt was discriminatory language.

Suffragettes Stanton (l) and Anthony (r)

The 15th Amendment was problematic for the abolitionist movement. It outlawed discrimination based on *race, color, or previous condition of servitude for voting* but made no mention of sex as a possible basis of discrimination.

The women's movement felt that the Reconstruction Amendments (13th, 14th, 15th) were a lost chance to remedy the injustice of their inferior position in American society, as they felt that women's issues could have been linked to the injustices suffered by slaves. After initially opposing the 14th Amendment, the suffragettes changed their strategy and decided that it could be the legal basis for women's right to vote.

In 1871, Victoria Woodhull (1838-1927) spoke at the House of Representatives and argued that the 14th Amendment should grant women the right to vote, but the house disagreed. In 1872, Susan B. Anthony registered to vote in Rochester, N.Y., citing the 14th Amendment, which led to her arrest and, ultimately, jail time. During this time, the United States was expanding west. Many new western states were granting women the right to vote, creating inconsistent human rights (much like slavery) across the United States. Victories for the right to vote in the West emboldened the East's suffragette movement to continue lobbying Congress to legislate national voting rights for women.

Feminist and suffragette Victoria Woodhull, c. 1926

Throughout the 1880s, many states revoked women's voting rights, while other states, including Rhode Island in the East, granted women the right to vote. This frustrating reversal of rights continued into the early 1900s. American suffragettes joined with suffragettes in ten other countries to form an international movement. By 1910, the suffragette movement grew and held mass demonstrations, with over 3,000 women marching in New York City demonstrations.

In the 1910s, the movement continued to pick up steam as more western states adopted universal suffrage. In 1912, former Republican President Theodore Roosevelt (1858-1919; 1901-1909) included women's voting rights as part of its election platform.

After intensive lobbying by women's groups, in 1916, Woodrow Wilson promised that women's suffrage would be part of the Democratic Party's platform in the next election. In the same year, Republican Jeannette Rankin (1880-1973) of Montana was elected to the House of Representatives, becoming the first female member of Congress when many states did not allow women to vote.

Spurred by a wave of protests and more western states granting women's suffrage, in 1918, the 19th Amendment was passed in the House of Commons after Rankin opened the debate. The 19th Amendment was initially proposed in 1872 by a Senator who become friends with Susan B. Anthony. The Amendment was similar to the 15th Amendment, except it outlawed voting discrimination based on sex.

After the 19th Amendment passed in the house in 1918, it failed to pass in the Senate by just two votes. The Senate's failure caused Democratic President Wilson to finally get involved and directly support the cause of suffrage, which eventually led to the Amendment being ratified in 1920, granting full suffrage to women across the country.

From the victory of 1920, the women's rights movement was quiet until the 1950s and early 1960s. Women participating in the Civil Rights Movement began to see parallels between the lack of proper rights and African Americans. In 1961, women were not allowed to serve on juries in many states, including Florida.

In *Hoyt v. Florida* (1961), a woman was convicted by an all-male jury of killing her abusive husband. She filed an appeal to the Supreme Court. After the *writ of certiorari*, her lawyers argued that she was insane. The male jury refused to consider this; therefore, the women should be allowed to serve on juries to balance potential bias. However, the Supreme Court upheld the ability to discriminate against women by preventing them from serving on juries. This ruling angered women across the country and spurred a new push for women's rights. The *Hoyt* ruling was not overturned until 1975.

The 1960s saw two significant legal advances. The first was the Presidential Commission on the Status of Women (PCSW) initiated by President Kennedy in 1961 and revealed its findings in 1963. The PCSW garnered a tremendous amount of public attention as it criticized the unequal status of American women in what was supposedly free society. This work culminated in the 1963 Equal Pay Act, which prohibited employers from purposefully paying women less than men for doing the same job. The next significant advancement was the inclusion of a ban on sex discrimination in the Civil Rights Act of 1964.

Eleanor Roosevelt (left) and Esther Peterson (right)
of the Presidential Commission on the Status of Women, c. 1961

The ban on sex discrimination was added to the Civil Rights Act of 1964 by Democratic Senator Howard Smith of Virginia. Smith thought that by adding women's rights to the Act, he would make the Act fail passage by Congress. He erroneously believed that even if civil rights were widely supported, rights for women were not.

Senator Howard Smith of Virginia was embarrassed when the Act passed, and then publicly argued that he was a strong supporter of women's rights and was not merely trying to make the Act fail to pass Congress. Many commentators and historians are skeptical of his later claims and believe his real motivation was to kill the bill. By having women's issues included in the Civil Rights Act, the women's rights movement was emboldened and became more active now that it had a legal basis to challenge discrimination.

In 1973, the women's movement begun to focus on issues related to reproductive freedom. The landmark *Roe v. Wade* (1973) case was a massive victory for women's rights. The Supreme Court ruled that women have a constitutional right to privacy. Thus, the decision to terminate a fetus was a right that the woman held, and the state could not infringe on this right. State laws criminalizing aborting fetuses were struck down as a violation of a women's right to privacy and the ability to make her own choices.

In *Reed v. Reed* (1971), the Supreme Court ruling interpreted the 14th Amendment as covering sex discrimination. Throughout the 1970s and into the 1980s, the Supreme Court. The Court was led by Republican Chief Justice Warren E. Burger (1907-1995; 1969-1986), and Republican Chief Justice William Rehnquist (1924-2005; 1972-2005). The Bergin and Rehnquist court began to interpret the 14th Amendment as protecting women's rights. The Court increasingly ruled in favor of women's rights, using the *Reed* ruling as legal precedent (*stare decisis*).

Continuing Rights Issues

The civil rights and women's movements were two early and significant movements for fundamental rights. Other disenfranchised groups who were denied rights or equal treatment have been active in fighting for their causes more recently. Hispanic Americans began pushing to end discrimination in the late 1960s and early 1970s.

The Mexican American Legal Defense and Education Fund (MALDEF) has played a prominent role. MALDEF has pushed to end discrimination against migrant workers and has fought to ensure that redistricting does not lead to deliberate attempts to disenfranchise Hispanic voters. In May 2006, MALDEF organized a massive one-day march to oppose new immigration restrictions and oppose proposals to build a physical wall to regulate immigration along the Mexican border.

Native Americans fought to end discrimination and have their rights recognized. While indigenous peoples have had the right to vote since 1924, they began to organize as a collective force against discrimination in the 1960s. In 1968, the American Indian Movement (AIM) was formed to promote civil rights for Native Americans, ensure treaty rights were recognized, and advocate for indigenous people's economic well-being.

AIM was one of the FBI's highly secret COINTELPRO program's main targets, which used covert and often illegal tactics to infiltrate and discredit activist groups from the 1950s to the 1970s. The FBI's COINTELPRO infiltrated and attempted to spread malicious disinformation and internal dissension in the Civil Rights Movement, targeting Martin Luther King Jr. and Malcolm X.

While COINTELPRO was initially designed to spy on suspected communists in the 1950s, it quickly morphed into a mechanism through which the FBI attempted to disrupt the growing social activists of the 1960s. These targeted groups were trying to end discrimination and assert their fundamental rights. The committee was named after Democratic Senator

Frank Church from Idaho (1924-1984; 1957-1981). The Senate's Church Committee led an investigation into the COINTELPRO program's impropriety and subsequent closure.

Amid FBI infiltration and internal division, AIM's most famous action was the occupation of the town of Wounded Knee, South Dakota, in 1973. Through protests, AIM was trying to draw national attention to the mistreatment of Native Americans from local authorities. The FBI sent in U.S. Marshals, who escalated the situation into a violent siege. One AIM activist was killed, an FBI agent was shot and left paralyzed, and a dozen activists were wounded during the seventy-one-day siege. Eventually, the FBI arrested 1,200 members of AIM, but all charges were dismissed at trial due to the overreaching and heavy-handed actions of the federal government.

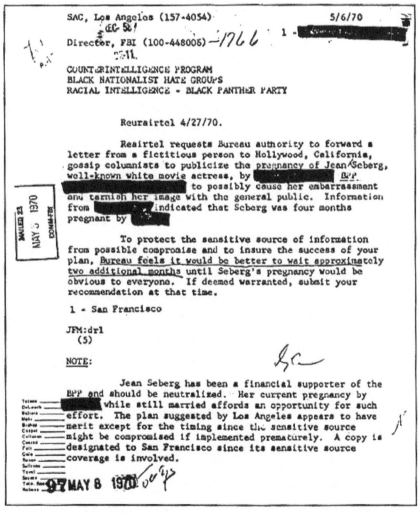

A COINTELPRO document outlining the FBI's plans
to 'neutralize' activist Jean Seberg for her support of the Black Panther Party, 1970

The treatment of Native Americans has since improved, with many Native American groups winning land sovereignty. Native Americans form self-government within the broader American context. More recently, Native American groups have been turning to the formal political process and organizing people to elect Native Americans to the House of Representatives to give their issues official representation.

One aspect of the sovereign land situation is that the Constitution does not apply to legally recognized sovereign tribes. These sovereign rights of autonomous authority became an issue in 2015 with the Supreme Court legalizing same-sex marriage. While virtually all tribal laws defer this issue to federal or state legislation, the Navajo nation explicitly forbids same-sex marriage. The Supreme Court ruling cannot override this prohibition for the sovereign nation status of Native American reservations. Lesbian and gay activists within the Navajo community are fighting to have their autonomous government recognize their rights.

In 2015, lesbian activist Cleo Pablo launched a challenge of the Navajo ban on same-sex marriage, arguing that it violates the Navajo constitution, which guarantees equal rights for all. This case presents an interesting and ongoing collision between an individual's rights, as what is beneficial for one group is problematic for another. Thus, while sovereignty rights ended discrimination against Native Americans, individuals within the group can still feel that their rights are not adequately recognized. They became targets of discrimination within their group for being a sub-set minority within a more substantial minority.

One aspect of the sovereign land situation is that the Constitution does not apply to legally recognized sovereign tribes. These sovereign rights of autonomous authority became an issue in 2015 with the Supreme Court legalizing same-sex marriage. While virtually all tribal laws defer this issue to federal or state legislation, the Navajo nation explicitly forbids same-sex marriage. The Supreme Court ruling cannot override this prohibition with respect for the sovereign nation status of Native American reservations. Lesbian and gay activists within the Navajo community are fighting to recognize their autonomous local governments' rights.

The issue of colliding rights claims is becoming increasingly prominent about the First Amendment's separation of church and state. Many Christian groups have begun to challenge this separation backed by changing legal interpretations. Minority religious groups such as the Church of Satan have taken the opportunity to cite these public displays of religion by Christians to allow them to demonstrate in favor of Satanism openly.

The issue for the Church of Satan is ironic because they do not believe in Satan. Their religion's public displays are often enough to make Christian groups ponder whether they want to open the public realm up to religion. After a Christian group's installation of a monument depicting the Ten Commandments outside a courthouse in Oklahoma was ruled constitutional, the Church of Satan installed a monument beside it depicting a goat-headed Satan. Under the Equal Protection Clause of the 14th Amendment, the Church of Satan argued that if Christian symbols can be displayed on government property, Satanic imagery must be legally protected.

People with disabilities faced extensive discrimination in the past as well. Often led by veterans wounded in the war, the disabled Americans' movement culminated in 1990 with the Americans with Disabilities Act (ADA). The Act was signed by Republican President George W. H. Bush (1924-2018; 1989-1993) and banned discrimination based on physical limitations or mental disability.

The ADA legislation required that public facilities (e.g., courts, restaurants, offices) be accessible to people in wheelchairs. Other required services are provided to deaf and hard of hearing people. Employers must be flexible in accommodating people with disabilities (reasonable accommodation). This Act has been subject to litigation and Supreme Court rulings, which held that the Americans with Disabilities Act protects pregnant women and people living with AIDS from discrimination.

President George H. W. Bush signs the Americans with Disabilities Act of 1990

In 2004, the *Tennessee v. Lane* case was an important ruling on the ADA, as it set a precedent enabling the federal government to enforce it. The plaintiffs argued that a Tennessee courthouse violated the ADA after a man in a wheelchair had to crawl up the stairs to meet a court appointment to avoid being jailed. He asserted that this amounted to discrimination. Tennessee argued that the federally enacted ADA did not have jurisdiction in a state courthouse, but the Supreme Court ruled that the ADA did apply.

One of the enduring controversies today is affirmative action (i.e., policy favoring people belonging to specific groups). In general, affirmative action is based on restorative justice principles and helps people from groups suffering from historical discrimination. Critics of affirmative action argue that it is a form of discrimination itself as the policy disadvantages others.

Bakke v. Regents of the University of California (1978) was the first Supreme Court that ruled on affirmative action. Bakke argued that U.C. Davis discriminated against him because they had two separate admission criteria, one for black students and one for white students. Several minority applicants with lower test scores were admitted while he was twice denied admission. Additionally, some seats reserved (quota) for minority students went unfilled.

The court ruled that this amounted to discrimination and ordered U.C. Davis to not use racial quotas (target numbers of a specific group) in its admissions. Affirmative action programs were still legal, but only if they did not have strict quotas, and there was evidence of past historical discrimination. Republican President Regan's Supreme Court appointee Republican William Rehnquist became Chief Justice (1986). The Court increasingly ruled against the constitutionality of affirmative action programs that disadvantaged members of excluded groups (i.e., whites) when these affected persons did not participate in discrimination.

The Democrat-controlled Congress passed the 1991 Civil Rights Act, which affirmed affirmative action's legality if quotas were not used. Throughout the 1990s, the Supreme Court continued to rule against affirmative action, including significant rulings in Texas and California, when alleged reverse discrimination was raised as an issue.

Supreme Court Chief Justice William Rehnquist, c. 2000

In *Grutter v. Bollinger* (2003), the Supreme Court upheld the legality of the University of Michigan Law School's affirmative action plan because it was in the public interest to ensure that diversity was represented in the legal profession. The ruling meant that considerations such as race, or economic class (rarely invoked), could be a factor in college admission. However, every applicant for admission needs to be considered based on merit. The Court again held that any quota system which might bar someone from being admitted to college based on race would be unconstitutional. *Grutter* was important because it reframed affirmative action to ensure that student populations would represent the diversity within American society instead of extending rights to people from protected classes (i.e., experienced discrimination in the past).

While previously affirmative action was argued to overcome past injustices of discrimination that targeted specific groups, the Court was now interpreting affirmative action to promote diversity. The plaintiffs successfully used this approach of "reframing the argument" in cigarette litigations (among other aggrieved parties in court cases).

A ruling based on the precedent set in *Grutter* (2003) was at issue in *Parents Involved in Community Schools v. Seattle School District No. 1* (2007). In this case, schools were alleged to use racial classifications to assign children to school districts to ensure that individuals were not "racially isolated." The Supreme Court upheld that diversity was in the public interest but ultimately ruled that these programs should be stopped because they were not being implemented according to their objective.

Gay Rights

One of the most recent groups to win legal protection against discrimination has been the LGBTQ+ community. The bulk of the progress on gay rights has come through activism and Supreme Court decisions, with the congressional branch often lagging with legislation. Laws against same-sex activity date back to well before the founding of America. Originally punishable by death, by the late 1700s, the most common punishment for engaging in same-sex activity was life in prison. The issue remained mostly taboo until the 1940s and 1950s, when the scientific study of human sexuality (i.e., *The Kinsey Report*) provided a counter-narrative to the Christian-dominated sexual mores.

Some Supreme Court rulings have advanced the cause of ending discrimination against gays and lesbians. The first of these rulings came when the gay liberation movement was in its infancy. In 1957, the Ninth Circuit ruled that a gay-themed magazine could not be banned as this was a violation of the 1st Amendment. In *One, Inc, v. Olesen* (1958), the Supreme Court overturned the Ninth Circuit decision by merely citing its ruling in *Roth v. United States*. The holding in *Roth* (1957) resulted in a new test for the courts. It ruled what speech (e.g., magazine content) could be prosecuted under obscenity laws and what speech was protected under the 1st Amendment. The ruling in *One, Inc.* was a landmark decision as it was the first Supreme Court ruling to address the issue of fundamental rights by gays and lesbians.

Amid the sexual revolution of the late 1960s and the general upheaval in civil rights and women's movements, the Gay Liberation Movement was formed in the late 1960s. A significant turning point in the movement came in June 1969 when police in New York City raided the popular gay and transgender bar Stonewall Inn. While police regularly conducted raids on gay bars, jailing those they caught inside for crimes. The raid on Stonewall was different because the patrons inside the bar actively resisted the police and fought against arrest.

Stonewall was a significant event because it demonstrated to gays and lesbians that they did not have to accept persecution and police brutality but could assert their rights. Various activist groups were formed in the 1970s with the intent of liberalizing laws against same-sex activity. Many of these groups explicitly linked gay rights to human rights. They positioned themselves as part of the broader movement to push governments to not discriminate against groups of people for any reason.

In the early 1970s, there was a trend toward gay migration, in which gays and lesbians would move to cities that were deemed less hostile. In particular, San Francisco attracted many gays and lesbians in the 1970s. This activism was supported by the openly gay city councilor Harvey Milk (1930 to November 27, 1978). Milk played a prominent role in the Gay Rights Movement, being perhaps the first openly gay prominent politician in American history.

However, like several other civil rights leaders of the time, he was assassinated in 1978. Milk's assassin was convicted of voluntary manslaughter (the light sentence) for killing both Milk and San Francisco Mayor George Moscone (1929 to November 27, 1978). In response, riots erupted in the streets as people were outraged by a political assassin's light sentence. Later that year, the first gay rights march in Washington, D.C., was attended by an estimated 100,000 people.

San Francisco politician and gay rights activist Harvey Milk, c. 1978

The next wave of the Gay Liberation Movement began in the early 1980s when the AIDS (autoimmune deficiency syndrome) epidemic swept through the gay community. This era was focused on sexual education and ending the stigma against gay men and people with AIDS. After the invention of HIV (human immunodeficiency virus) drugs, which dramatically increased the life expectancy of people with AIDS in the late 1990s, the movement shifted again to promoting same-sex marriage.

In 1972, a teacher in Tacoma, Washington, was fired for being gay. The Supreme Court refused (denied *writ of certiorari*) to hear his appeal. The lower court held that being gay was inherently immoral, and thus having immoral people as teachers would corrupt the young, vulnerable, and impressionable students. In 2014, the Tacoma, Washington school board issued an apology to the teacher after 42 years. This case was important because it was among one of the first times the nightly television news reported an issue related to gay rights. Thus, an estimated 60 million Americans learned about this discrimination that had been previously taboo to speak about publicly.

In *National Gay Task Force v. Board of Education* (1984), the Supreme Court ruled on the issue of gay teachers. The Supreme Court was divided (establish no case law on the issue). A divided Supreme Court decision meant that the lower court's holding that permitted the firing of gay teachers stood. The case was argued in terms of the rights contained in the 1st and 14th Amendments.

National Gay Task Force was the first case where the non-discrimination clauses of the 14th Amendment were applied to discrimination against sexual orientation, thus setting a different approach to framing the issue. In *Gay Student Services v. Texas A&M University* (5th Cir., 1984), the Supreme Court denied a request to hear an appeal (denied *writ of certiorari*) by a gay student association at Texas A&M banned by the university.

Bowers v. Hardwick (1986) was a significant defeat for gay rights. In *Bowers*, the Supreme Court ruled that gays and lesbians do not have the right to privacy afforded by the 14th Amendment. Thus, Georgia laws banning homosexual acts in private among consenting adults were upheld as constitutional.

In *Boy Scouts of America v. Dale* (2000), the Supreme Court ruled that the Boy Scouts have a right to exclude gay Scout leaders against a challenge under the 1st Amendment. This ruling was later overturned in *Lawrence v. Texas* (2003), where the Court held that laws against same-sex acts be unconstitutional under the 14th Amendment's due process clause. It was not until *Lawrence* that the Supreme Court treated sexual orientation as discrimination. Before 2003, same-sex sexual activity was illegal in 14 states. *Lawrence* held the fundamental right of gays and lesbians against state and federal governmental discrimination.

The Supreme Court has acted swiftly since *Lawrence*. In *Windsor v. United States* (2013), the Supreme Court ruled that Democratic President Clinton's Defense of Marriage Act (DOMA) was partly unconstitutional. The Court held that the federal government's prohibition of marriage between same-sex couples violated the 14th Amendment *due process clause*.

In *Goodridge v. Department of Public Health* (2003), the Supreme Judicial Court of Massachusetts led with the first state to rule in support of same-sex marriage. In *Obergefell v. Hodges* (2015), the Supreme Court struck down all state bans on same-sex marriage. Therefore, same-sex marriage became legal nationwide. The due process and equal protection clauses of the 14th Amendment formed the basis for this ruling. In the *Obergefell* holding, the Court cited *Loving v. Virginia* (1967), which removed bans on interracial marriage as precedent.

Notes for active learning

Notes for active learning

Notes for active learning

Knowledge of Substantive Rights and Liberties

The legal basis of American citizens' fundamental rights against federal government intrusion is derived from the Bill of Rights and the later Amendments that addressed these rights. The Bill of Rights became the First Ten Amendments to the Constitution and was proposed to ease the Anti-Federalists' fears who believed that the new American federal government (as opposed to state government) would have too much power. This extensive power would be prone to abuse by the federal government.

The authors of *The Federalist Papers*, including Alexander Hamilton and James Madison, were initially leery of including a set of rights in the Constitution because they were concerned that it would be assumed that any rights not explicitly mentioned would be assumed not to exist. As a result of this concern, a bill of rights was not included in the Constitution.

Prominent Anti-Federalists such as Patrick Henry and Samuel Adams argued that the new Constitution did not protect individual rights against the federal government. Thus, they inverted Hamilton's fears by pointing out that if rights are not explicitly expressed in the Constitution, it is assumed that no such fundamental rights exist.

Ratifying the original Constitution without a Bill of Rights was controversial, especially in Massachusetts, where the state convention on ratification turned ugly. Massachusetts Anti-Federalist Elbridge Thomas Gerry (1744-1814; ninth governor of Massachusetts 1810-1812; fifth Vice President 1813-1814) was not allowed to speak to the assembly. A fistfight broke out between Gerry and the Massachusetts Federalist delegate Francis Dana (1743-1811).

The melee was stopped after Samuel Adams (1722-1803; Fourth Governor of Massachusetts 1794-1797) and John Hancock (1737-1793; First and Third Governor of Massachusetts 1787-1793) intervened. A compromise was agreed that Massachusetts would ratify the Constitution if specific Amendments were proposed, outlining citizens' fundamental rights. These demands became the genesis of the 5th and 10th Amendments.

After the Anti-Federalists' success in Massachusetts by adding conditions to ratification, similar conditions were put in place by Virginia and New York. After his initial opposition, James Madison agreed with the necessity of a Bill of Rights. Madison drafted the Bill of Rights for consideration by Congress.

Elbridge Gerry, American politician, and Anti-Federalist, c. 1814

Federalists in the House of Representatives were initially strongly opposed. They felt that amending the Constitution so soon after its ratification might shake the public's faith in the new government's stability. Eventually, the House passed seventeen of Madison's proposed twenty amendments to the Senate.

The Senate reworded many of these amendments and reduced them to just twelve proposed amendments. A joint committee between the House and Senate eventually got the language of the amendments agreed upon and, in 1789, passed the proposed twelve amendments onto the states for ratification. Articles III to XII (ten amendments in total) were ratified in 1792, and these became the first ten Amendments, which comprise the Bill of Rights.

After the Bill of Rights was ratified, it mostly lay legally dormant for 150 years. The Supreme Court made no critical rulings based on these fundamental rights contained in the Bill of Rights, and they were rarely invoked in the context of legal arguments. For example, the Supreme Court did not make a ruling on the First Amendment issue of free speech until 1931.

Part of the reason for this delay in widespread addressing of these fundamental protections outlined in the Bill of Rights is that these rights were thought of only between citizens and the federal (but not state) government. Therefore, state governments passed laws that essentially contravened the Bill of Rights without concern from purported protections contained in the Bill of Rights. It was not until the 14th Amendment declared that many of these fundamental rights (i.e., using *reverse incorporation*) limit state governments.

First Amendment

The 1st Amendment states: "*Congress shall make no law respecting an establishment of religion or prohibiting the free exercise thereof; or abridging the freedom of speech, or of the press, or the right of the people peaceably to assemble, and to petition the Government for a redress of grievances.*"

This 1st Amendment is perhaps the most complex, as it includes some different and even unrelated fundamental political and human rights. The basis for the 1st Amendment stems from similar statements in nine of the state government constitutions. The 1st Amendment was strongly supported by Anti-Federalists, who argued that civil liberties needed to be explicitly protected in the Constitution.

The first part of the 1st Amendment relates to freedom of religion and is based on Thomas Jefferson's argument that there needed to be a "*wall of separation between church and state.*" Jefferson argued that religion was a matter between "man and his god," Thus, the government should have no role in legislating religious matters.

Jefferson saw this right as protecting the beliefs of minority religions from persecution and protecting the right to hold any personal religious opinion. For Jefferson, religion happened in the church, politics happened in government, and any overlap between the two would infringe on the freedom of both. In an early Supreme Court ruling on this issue (*Reynolds v. United States*, 1878), the court held that freedom of religion, under the 1st Amendment, applies to belief and opinion, but not to actions supporting these religious beliefs. A person is not protected (i.e., exempt from laws) by claiming legal protection of freedom of religion as a justification. Freedom of religion equates to freedom of belief, not to freedom of action.

Generally, the Cold War period is considered to span from the 1947 Truman Doctrine until the dissolution of the Soviet Union on December 25, 1991. During the Cold War, Jefferson's wall of separation between the government and religion, which was guaranteed by the 1st Amendment, began to unravel. The religious language was added to money. The pledge of allegiance and court rulings interpreted the 1st Amendment differently and allowed taxpayer money for religious primary and secondary schools.

During the Cold War, the constitutional framers' secularism yielded new interpretations that allowed what might have seemed like egregious breaches of Constitutional authority in Jefferson's day. Displaying religious symbols is permitted in courthouses in some states. This is increasingly being interpreted as compatible with the 1st Amendment.

Free speech is the second aspect of the 1st Amendment to prevent the prosecution of people who are openly critical of the government. The Supreme Court was silent on this issue until the 20th Century. Under the second President, John Adams, the Alien and Sedition Acts were four laws passed in 1798, banning advocating to overthrow the U.S. government.

Jefferson and Madison argued that laws banning public discourse were a flagrant violation of the 1st Amendment, but the court did not rule on it. Adams' anti-free speech laws were publicly very unpopular. Massachusetts Federalist John Adams narrowly defeated Virginian Democratic-Republican Thomas Jefferson in 1796. In 1800, Jefferson defeated incumbent John Adams to become the third President. President Jefferson eliminated Adam's laws prohibiting public discourse about the government.

During World War I (1914-1918) and after the Communist Revolution in Russia (October 1917; 1917-1924), Congress passed the Espionage Act of 1917. The Act placed restrictions on what American citizens could say about the U.S. military. Specifically, any attempts to promote insubordination were punishable with twenty years in prison.

In 1918, American socialist Eugene Debs (1855-1926) gave a speech criticizing prosecution under the Espionage Act as violating Americans' freedom of speech, leading to his arrest under the Act. He challenged the case, but again, the Supreme Court upheld his conviction, claiming that his words presented a clear and present danger to America.

In *Schenck v. United States* (1919), Schenck, a socialist party member, challenged his conviction for handing out pamphlets advocating for Americans to resist the draft. He argued that the conviction was a violation of his 1st Amendment rights to freedom of speech. The Supreme Court ruled against Schenck, and his conviction was upheld.

The Supreme Court has not always upheld the fundamental rights contained in the Bill of Rights. As the political context of mass hysteria about Communism led to rulings which later legal scholars have asserted were erroneous.

Eugene Debs, political activist, c. 1926

Throughout the 1920s, the Supreme Court issued some rulings that continued ruling against freedom of speech. In *Herndon v. United States* (1937), in a narrow 5-4 ruling, the Supreme Court struck down Georgia's insurrection statute as unconstitutional, as it violated the 1st Amendment. Herndon (1913-1997) was a Black Communist leader charged with insurrection under a Reconstruction Era law in Georgia to outlaw rebellions by former slaves. He was arrested after his hotel room was searched, and Communist Party literature was found. In Herndon's favor, the Supreme Court ruling marked the first significant court victory to uphold the right to free speech as protected speech under the 1st Amendment.

In 1940, Congress passed the Smith Act, which jailed Communist leaders. In *Dennis v. United States* (1951), the Supreme Court upheld this law after Dennis, general secretary of the American Communist Party, was accused of having spoken, so grave to be a threat to national security. The plurality opinion (i.e., controlling opinion when no unified controlling majority opinion exists) stated, "Certainly an attempt to overthrow the government by force, even though doomed from the outset because of inadequate numbers or power of the revolutionist, is a sufficient evil for Congress to prevent."

In 1957 the Supreme Court ruled that the Smith Act could not be applied to those who simply believed in Communism. The Act could only be used to prosecute a person who explicitly acted to overthrow the government. This ruling was a significant victory for freedom of speech and the 1st Amendment. By the late 1960s and early 1970s, the Supreme Court shifted and began to accept that freedom of speech included the right to openly criticize the government in significant rulings, upholding the 1st Amendment rights of those protestors opposed to the Vietnam War (1955-1975).

The third aspect of the 1st Amendment is the right to freedom of the press. Through reverse incorporation by the 14th Amendment, the federal government and state government cannot control what is published. The language of the First Amendment refers to printing presses and, thus, newspapers. It has been interpreted by the Court to include any form of public media (e.g., radio, television, video games).

In 1931, the first significant test of freedom of the press came when Minnesota passed a law that enabled the state to shut any newspaper it deemed to be publishing malicious or scandalous writing. The Supreme Court ruled that this law was an unconstitutional violation of the 1st Amendment. The Court quoted James Madison's argument that a courageous and vigilant press was necessary to preserve democracy.

James Madison, fourth President of the United States, c. 1817

In 1971, the Supreme Court again upheld freedom of the press when President Nixon tried to prevent the *New York Times* from publishing leaked governmental documents. The documents, called the Pentagon Papers, proposed that the United States secretly began bombing campaigns and deploying ground forces to Laos and Cambodia without congressional consent. President Nixon argued for prior constraints (injunction or prohibition before the act) that these documents' publication threatens national security by disclosing troop movements. However, the Court ruled that these documents did not threaten national security because they described past events rather than plans for future military actions.

The fourth and fifth clauses of the 1st Amendment guarantee citizens' right to petition the government and assemble peacefully. The right to petition means that citizens have the right to contact government officials and politicians, engage in lobbying, and file political grievances with the courts. In 1830, the petition clause was first challenged when Congress banned petitions from abolitionists. Congress retracted the law a few years later before the Court could rule (i.e., review requires a case and controversy).

In the early 1920s, those signing petitions in favor of repealing the anti-freedom of speech Espionage Act were jailed. The Supreme Court did not rule on this violation of the 1st Amendment. Freedom of assembly means that groups can get together for political purposes, including petitioning the government, such as in a public protest.

Non-violent protests were broken up by police intervention (e.g., during the Vietnam War), are cited as a violation of the right to freedom of assembly. In the assemblies protesting the Iraq War (2003–2011), police established "free speech zones" for protesters. These established zones implied that freedom of speech and assembly were permitted but limited in location.

For public protests, the Court has used the following definitions:

Traditional Public Forum – places traditionally considered available for public assembly and debate (e.g., streets, sidewalks, public parks). The state and federal government's authority to restrict public speech (except speech that incites imminent violence) in traditional public forums is limited.

Designated Public Forum – a public property that is not traditionally open for 1st Amendment activity may be made available (e.g., meeting rooms in a public building, public libraries) by the government for that purpose. Suppose the government adopts rules and policies, allowing 1st Amendment activity on public property. In that case, the public has a right to exercise their right to free speech and peaceful assembly in that designated space.

Nonpublic Forum – other public property that is not a traditional or designated forum (e.g., jails, public schools, courthouses) is considered a non-public forum. Courts have ruled that the "*First Amendment does not guarantee access to property simply because it is owned or controlled by the government.*" Therefore, citizens do not have a right to assemble and protest in nonpublic forums.

Second Amendment

The 2nd Amendment states, "*A well regulated Militia being necessary to the security of a free State, the right of the people to keep and bear arms shall not be infringed.*"

The 2nd Amendment is the most controversial Amendment and open to the broadest range of interpretation. The context of adopting this Amendment comes out of the early Revolutionary period in American history. American rebels fought British authority. They relied on personal firearms to start an insurrection against British rule. There was a strong thrust of the intent behind the 2nd Amendment, which invoked the pre-independence period. It implied that citizens have the right to violently overthrow the government should they deem it to be tyrannical. The 2nd Amendment was used to get support from the Anti-Federalists. It preserved state militias and provided reassurances against the central authority of the federal government.

In the first decades after the 2nd Amendment was ratified, the focus was on militias. Many Americans were intensely opposed to the idea of having a standing federal military and instead argued that the 2nd Amendment outlawed such a professional military in favor of citizen militias. This interpretation focused on the right to form a militia rather than gun ownership. Such early militias were considered a civic duty and often involved weapons other than guns (e.g., clubs, farm tools, pitchforks).

In 1792, the 2nd Amendment was invoked by farmers in Pennsylvania who argued that the government had become tyrannical. Thus, they had a right to use their firearms to overthrow it violently. Neighboring states invoked the 2nd Amendment to fight against the Farmers' Insurrection by attempting to raise a militia to fight against the insurrectionists. The government found few people willing to join the militia and resorted to drafting people into the militia (i.e., conscription), which was an unpopular decision.

Eventually, President George Washington personally led a militia of 7,000 men, who put down the rebellion through negotiation. The lack of a standing army was criticized for allowing the insurrection to last longer than it should have and was blamed for the unpreparedness when British Canadians succeeded in burning down the White House during the War of 1812. Washington's army was not an official army of the United States. On September 29, 1789 (the last day of the first formal first session of Congress), an Act was passed to establish the "United States Military." Eventually, a standing army was adopted, and the 2nd Amendment interpretation shifted to emphasize the "bear arms" portion of the amendment rather than the "militia" portion. Multiple legal scholars developed conflicting interpretations, which continue the controversy.

Some argue that gun ownership is dependent on being a member of a well-regulated militia, which implies that gun ownership is not an individual right but a collective one. This argument states that the 2nd Amendment means that individual states have a right to arm their militias. Another proposed interpretation of this collective rights interpretation argues that part of a well-regulated militia has the right to own guns personally. If a person is not part of a militia, there is no individual right to gun ownership.

A third interpretation argues that the 2nd Amendment outlines the right for individual Americans to own guns. This interpretation rejects the idea that the lack of militias' existence today invalidates the fundamental right to gun ownership and argues that the prefatory clause about a militia is merely a philosophical statement and not a dependent clause upon which gun ownership must rest.

In District of Columbia v. Heller (2008), the Supreme Court (in a 5–4 majority split along partisan lines) that the Second Amendment guarantees an individual the right to possess firearms independent of service in a state militia and to use firearms for traditionally lawful purposes, including self-defense within the home. The Supreme Court overturned the District of Columbia Firearm Regulation Control Act (1979) that made it illegal to carry an unregistered firearm and prohibited handguns registration. The Chief of Police had the discretion to issue a one-year license for handguns.

Dick Heller was a special police officer in the District of Columbia authorized to carry a handgun while on duty. He applied to the Chief of Police for a one-year permit to keep a handgun at home but was denied. Heller sued the District of Columbia and sought an injunction asserting an abridgment of his 2nd Amendment rights. He prevailed on appeal to the Supreme Court, and the District of Columbia's Firearm Regulation Control Act of

1979 was deemed unconstitutional. The Supreme Court held that this right, explicit in the operative clause, exists independently of a well-regulated militia.

The burning of Washington during the War of 1812

Third Amendment

The 3rd Amendment states: "*No Soldier shall, in time of peace be quartered in any house, without the consent of the Owner, nor in time of war, but in a manner to be prescribed by law.*" The 3rd Amendment states that the government cannot force an individual to house soldiers in their home.

While in today's context, this may seem unusual to include in the Bill of Rights, this was a symbolically important right when the 3rd Amendment was adopted. In 1765, the British Parliament passed an Act that required American colonists to pay the costs of quartering British soldiers in the thirteen colonies. After the Boston Tea Party on December 16, 1773, the British Parliament passed another Act requiring American colonists to house British soldiers in their private homes if necessary. If there were not enough space in the local military barracks, colonists would have to house soldiers at local inns and taverns. This Act was listed as one of the Intolerable Acts cited by the American revolutionaries because they were demanding independence from Britain. The Supreme Court has never heard a case involving the 3rd Amendment, and it is rarely a source of litigation (case and controversy) in federal district court.

Throwing tea overboard during the Boston Tea Party, December 16, 1773

Fourth Amendment

The 4th Amendment states: "*The right of the people to be secure in their persons, houses, papers, and effects, against unreasonable searches and seizures, shall not be violated, and no Warrants shall issue, but upon probable cause, supported by Oath or affirmation, and particularly describing the place to be searched, and the persons or things to be seized.*"

The 4th Amendment protects against unreasonable searches of persons and seizures of property. The government (e.g., police) cannot merely search people at random and cannot take their things without prior court authorization (i.e., search warrant). For police to search, they need to be issued a prior warrant by a neutral third party (e.g., judge), and the request for the warrant needs to be attested by the governmental agent (police officer) to the judge that they have probable cause (more than a mere suspicion). The request for a search warrant requires evidence of behavior that emanated from illegal activity and that the search will likely yield evidence (proof) of that illegal activity.

In *Weeks v United States* (1914), the Supreme Court held that evidence obtained from a 4th Amendment violation is generally inadmissible in criminal trials. This decision provides a meaningful way that the rights granted by the 4th Amendment are preserved. The Exclusionary Rule (*fruit of a poisonous tree* doctrine) bars the introduction in a court proceeding of illegally obtained evidence. The fruit of a poisonous tree doctrine extends to any evidence (not justly likely to be found) obtained from an illegal search. For example, if the police execute an unauthorized warrant for drugs and discover counterfeit equipment, it is generally not permitted as evidence of counterfeiting activity due to an illegal search.

In *Katz v. United States* (1967), the court ruled that the 4th Amendment applies to "people and not places." A wiretap on a public payphone without a warrant was held to be an unconstitutional search. This ruling established the provisions for a general right to an expectation of privacy. Despite using a public payphone, the person making the phone call had a reasonable expectation that only the listener would hear the conversation. There was no expectation that the FBI or others would be privy to the conversation.

In *Chandler v. Miller* (1997), the Supreme Court held that probable cause must be based on individual suspicion of wrongdoing. This ruling struck down a Georgia law requiring all state employees to undergo drug testing. The Court held this law amounted to an unreasonable search because it targeted a large group of people with no past evidence or future suspicion of drug use.

It is unclear if the 4th Amendment applies to online activities and web browsing. Some civil liberties groups claim that government spying programs are a violation of the 4th Amendment. The government programs collect information without a warrant. Such a case has yet to be heard by the Supreme Court.

There are exceptions to the preservation of rights under the 4th Amendment. If a person consents to the search, 4th Amendment protections are waived. In *Schneckloth v. Bustamonte* (1973), the Supreme Court ruled that the police do not need to inform a person that they have the right to refuse a warrantless search.

In *United States v. Matlock* (1974), the Court ruled that a third-party occupant could give consent for police to search a house co-occupied by another. If the police want to search a location, a roommate can consent to search any area that the roommate can access (i.e., not a locked bedroom of another roommate). The police can then search without a warrant or explicit consent from the target of the search.

Police, without a warrant, can perform a "search" of objects in plain view. For example, if someone steals a car and parks it in a driveway and the police can see (from a

---

public vantage point) it while driving down the street, this observation is probable cause for arresting without a warrant. The stolen automobile (in plain view) can be introduced into evidence against the defendant at the criminal trial.

Motor vehicles are an exception. Automobiles move on public roads and are not considered a private residence. Police can search a car with probable cause (not requiring a warrant) and seize items in plain view but cannot search the driver or passenger without a warrant or consent. An exception is that the police can search a person using probable cause to check (pat-down) for weapons. If a weapon is suspected as the officer feels outside the garment (pat-down), the officer may reach for the object and remove it.

Fifth Amendment

The 5th Amendment states: "*No person shall be held to answer for a capital, or otherwise infamous crime, unless on a presentment or indictment of a Grand Jury, except in cases arising in the land or naval forces, or in the Militia, when in actual service in time of War or public danger; nor shall any person be subject for the same offence to be twice put in jeopardy of life or limb; nor shall be compelled in any criminal case to be a witness against himself, nor be deprived of life, liberty, or property, without due process of law; nor shall private property be taken for public use, without just compensation.*"

The 5th Amendment harbors many rights. It protects against self-incrimination (the compelling of self-incriminating evidence), prevents double jeopardy, guarantees due process in court (notice and right to be heard; to mount a defense to the accusations), and compensation if private property is seized by the government using eminent domain.

The *double jeopardy* clause ensures that people cannot be punished for the same crime more than once. Therefore, the government (with virtually unlimited resources) cannot appeal an acquittal (i.e., not guilty verdict for the crime charged, not the same as a verdict of innocent). The prosecution has the burden to advance its most compelling case in the first criminal trial. The clause does not prevent appeals or new trials if there is significant new evidence that could not be discovered before trial (e.g., located inside a locked safe that was no subject to inspection). In a civil action (non-criminal case), either side may appeal the verdict.

The *right against self-incrimination* is used more often than double jeopardy. The state cannot force someone to give testimony about a crime of which they are accused. Called the *right to remain silent*, if asked a question about guilt in a crime, the person can "plead the Fifth" and not answer the question by invoking the right against self-incrimination. Initially, this right protected against confessions obtained under torture.

The Miranda warning states, *"You have the right to remain silent and refuse to answer questions. Anything you say may be used against you in a court of law. You have the right to consult an attorney before speaking to the police and to have an attorney present during questioning now or in the future."*

Today, the *right to remain silent* is interpreted more broadly. The right to not incriminate oneself and remain silent can be invoked if the government impels testimony. During the McCarthy era (the 1940s to 1954), the House Committee on Un-American Activities subpoenaed famous Hollywood actors to question Communist affiliations. Many of the accused invoked the Fifth Amendment (right to remain silent) when asked if they were communists to avoid prosecution.

House Committee on Un-American Activities, 1938

In *United States v. Sullivan* (1927), the Supreme Court ruled that the 5th Amendment could not be invoked to avoid paying income taxes. In 1976, the Supreme Court ruled that it did not violate the 5th Amendment for income tax records to be used at the trial. The case related to a man convicted of conspiracy to fix sports matches and illegal gambling. He declared on his income taxes that he was a professional gambler. He argued that this was self-incrimination, but the Supreme Court disagreed.

A contemporary issue relates to computer passwords, as giving up one's password could produce self-incriminating evidence. The Supreme Court has yet to rule on this issue, but district courts have given conflicting interpretations. In 2007, the Federal District Court in Vermont ruled that one cannot be forced to reveal a password or to unencrypt data on a USB drive.

However, the Massachusetts Supreme Judicial Court (2015) ruling required a defendant to provide the password to an unencrypted drive. So far, the trend has been that encrypting one's data protects it from authorities, but unencrypted data that is password protected can result in the court ordering someone to give up a password.

The 5th Amendment has been used to justify eminent domain. Eminent domain allows the government to seize private property when it is in the public interest, so long as the government provides fair compensation. This eminent domain clause was often invoked during the development of the railway system during the westward expansion.

The public-use clause has proven to be controversial. In *Kelo v. City of New London* (2005), the Supreme Court ruled 5-4 that a city which seized private land to transfer it to a private developer is public use because it would provide housing and jobs. The dissenting opinion was written by President Reagan's' 1981 nominee, Republican Sandra Day O'Connor (b. 1930; 1981-2006), who was extremely critical of the Court's rationale. She asserted that this ruling provided a license for the rich to take property from the poor. She asserted that public use was not justified as the property seizure was transferred from one private agent (homeowners) to another private agent (a biopharmaceutical company).

Sandra Day O'Connor, first woman Supreme Court Justice, c. 2005

Sixth Amendment

The 6th Amendment states: "*In all criminal prosecutions, the accused shall enjoy the right to a speedy and public trial, by an impartial jury of the State and district wherein the crime shall have been committed, which district shall have been previously ascertained by law, and to be informed of the nature and cause of the accusation; to be confronted with the witnesses against him; to have compulsory process for obtaining witnesses in his favor, and to have the Assistance of Counsel for his defense.*" This Amendment outlines the rights to a fair trial and provides a legal framework for defendants in a criminal trial.

In *Barker v. Wingo* (1972), the Supreme Court set out a four-factor test that would determine if a federal criminal prosecution complied with the *right to a speedy trial* under the Sixth Amendment. The Court did not set specific time limits but suggested that the proceeding (e.g., indictment, the commencement of a trial) should occur within a defined period. The holding states that there should not be any delays in court proceedings of more than one year. Any such delay must be reasonable and not designed to advantage either party in the trial, resulting in the presence or absence of prejudice. In 1973, the Court ruled that any case which violates the accused right to a speedy trial be dismissed. The accused cannot be tried later (double jeopardy) under the original indictment.

The *impartial jury* clause guarantees the right to a jury trial for any crime that, upon conviction, would result in a prison sentence of more than six months. It requires juries to reach a unanimous verdict (i.e., all jurors agree on the guilty verdict). Unanimity does not apply to state-level criminal jury trials, as only a majority is needed for such verdicts. Impartial jurors mean that lawyers from each side can question the potential jury (*voir dire*; to speak the truth) to evaluate that jurors are not biased before the trial begins.

In *Gideon v. Wainwright* (1963), the Supreme Court decided a 6th Amendment issue. For criminal proceedings (i.e., loss of liberty for guilty verdicts), the Court ruled that defendants who could not afford legal representation would be provided a lawyer at no cost (*pro bono*) by the court. The right to court-appointed legal representation in criminal proceedings applies at the state (14th Amendment reverse incorporation) and federal levels (6th Amendment). Gideon was a Florida man that was too poor to afford a lawyer. He represented himself because the state court would not provide a lawyer for the charges of petty burglary. Gideon was found guilty in state court, and he appealed to the Supreme Court from his prison cell. Upon hearing oral arguments on the matter, the Supreme Court ruled that any defendant at risk of incarceration (i.e., loss of freedom) as a penalty for their crime must be provided *pro bono* legal counsel. Thus, 2,000 people in Florida were freed, and Gideon had a retrial. He was acquitted of all charges after his court-appointed lawyer successfully proved that the defendant did not commit the robbery.

Seventh Amendment

The 7th Amendment states: "*In suits at common law, where the value in controversy shall exceed twenty dollars, the right of trial by jury shall be preserved, and no fact tried by a jury, shall be otherwise reexamined in any court of the United States, than according to the rules of the common law.*"

The 7th Amendment guarantees a jury trial in federal civil suits over twenty dollars and ensures that judges cannot overturn juries' decisions. The twenty-dollar amount has not been indexed for inflation since the Bill of Right's ratification in 1791. Effectively, all civil suits today may be tried by juries. This Bill of Rights Amendment (i.e., protection against the *federal* government) has not been held applicable to the states under *reverse incorporation* by the 14th Amendment. This right does not apply to state-level trials (federal courts only). A bench trial has the judge act as the arbiter of law (elements of the crime) and the finder of fact (is the evidence believable). In jury trials, fact-finding – did the defendant do what he/she is accused of – is performed by the jury.

Eighth Amendment

The 8th Amendment states: "*Excessive bail shall not be required, nor excessive fines imposed, nor cruel and unusual punishments inflicted.*" This Amendment is inspired by the 1689 English Bill of Rights, which Madison studied in detail. The question of what excessive bail or excessive fine entail is open to judicial interpretation.

Stack v. Boyle (1951) was an early ruling on *excessive bail* under the 8th Amendment. Under the Smith Act (Alien Registration Act of 1940), Communist Party members were arrested and bail set at $50,000 each. The Supreme Court ruled that this amounted to excessive bail. In previous arrests under the Smith Act, bail had been set much lower. This established the precedent of "excessive" bail relative to similar cases.

In *United States v. Bajakajian* (1988), the Supreme Court decided the first issue of an *excessive fine*. Hosep Krikor Bajakajian attempted to leave the United States for Cyprus to pay a substantial debt he owed. Bajakajian was carrying $357,144 and failed to report it to customs, requiring declaring all-cash exceeding $10,000. The government seized the entire

$357,144. The Supreme Court ruled that this fine was grossly disproportionate to the crime of failing to report an international currency transaction. There was no evidence to suggest that this money was intended for use in criminal activity. The *Bajakajian* ruling held civil forfeiture (e.g., cash, jewels, automobiles) as a violation of the 8th Amendment, even though it was not technically imposed as a fine.

Citing the excessive fines clause of the 8th Amendment, the Court held that asset forfeiture is unconstitutional when it is "grossly disproportional to the gravity of the defendant's offense." Several challenges are alleging excessive civil forfeiture challenges percolating at the lower courts. It is expected that one of these cases will be granted a *writ of certiorari* to address this contentious, contemporary issue. Plaintiffs (aggrieved citizens) are suing in state courts (state laws at issue) to demand the return of valuable assets (e.g., automobiles, boats, cash) seized, in non-criminal allegations, and therefore without the justified, proper authority by the police.

In *Furman v. Georgia* (1972), the Supreme Court addressed the issue of *cruel and unusual punishment*. The Court ruled that the 8th Amendment explicitly outlawed torture, severe punishments inflicted arbitrarily, any severe punishment that is "clearly and totally rejected throughout society," and any unnecessary punishment.

In 2003, it was discovered that the U.S. government was torturing prisoners in Guantanamo Bay and the Abu Ghraib prison in Iraq. Activists asserted that it was a direct violation of the 8th Amendment. The alleged victims were not U.S. citizens, and the activities did not occur on American soil. However, the behavior was recognized as abridging human rights and violating prisoners of war's proper treatment. As a result, eleven American soldiers were charged with dereliction of duty, maltreatment of prisoners, aggravated assault, and battery. These soldiers were court-martialed, convicted, dishonorably discharged, sentenced to military prison (up to ten years).

The Brigadier (one-star) General, as commanding officer of the Abu Ghraib prison in Iraq, was reprimanded and demoted to the rank of colonel. Several others (including high ranking military personnel) who were accused of perpetrating or authorizing the measures were not prosecuted. President Bush and Defense Secretary Donald Rumsfeld (b. 1932; Defense Secretary under Gerald Ford 1975-1977 and George Bush 2001-2006) apologized in 2004 for the Abu Ghraib abuses.

Guard tower at Abu Ghraib Prison. C. 2003

Some legal scholars sympathetic to the Bush administration's war on terrorism argued that the court ruled that cruel and unusual punishment depended on society's interpretation. Since the American public was divided on the issue, alleged terrorist prisoners' torture did not consist of cruel and unusual punishment. They asserted that the military's means of interrogation helped the government locate additional terrorists and ultimately protect innocent Americans from future attacks by this terrorist network.

Several philosophers and ethicists saw this argument as weak. If the public (even out of fear of future terrorist attacks) were to become morally depraved, then there would be no limits on the government's ability to inflict cruel and unusual torture.

In *Wilkerson v. Utah* (1878), the Supreme Court held that punishment by drawing and quartering, burning alive, or disemboweling was cruel and unusual punishment.

In *Tropp v. Dulles* (1958), the Supreme Court ruled that stripping a natural-born citizen of their citizenship is a cruel and unusual punishment worse than torture, as it deprives an individual of all legal rights.

In *Robinson v. California* (1962), the Supreme Court ruled that drug addicts could not be jailed for being an addict in and of itself. Being addicted to (contrasted with possession, distribution, or use of) illegal substances was not expressly prohibited.

In *Thompson v. Oklahoma* (1988), the Court ruled that executing people under 16 amounted to cruel and unusual punishment. This holding was updated in 2005 and increased the age of execution to 18 years or older.

In *Solem v. Helm* (1988), the Supreme Court ruled for the first time that the length of a prison sentence could be construed as cruel and unusual under the 8th Amendment if the sentence were disproportionate to the crime. This case involved a man who was convicted of writing a check from a fake account for one hundred dollars and, under South Dakota state law, received a life sentence. The Court held that this sentence was cruel and unusual punishment because it was grossly disproportionate to the gravity of the crime.

In *Harmelin v. Michigan* (1991), the Supreme Court largely overturned the *Solem* (proportional sentence) precedent, as the Court upheld a life without parole sentence for the crime of possessing about 1.5 pounds (650 grams) of cocaine. The Court held that although the punishment was cruel, it was not unusual, relying on the fact that the 8th Amendment places a cruel and unusual dependency.

In 2002, the *Harmelin* ruling was upheld on a challenge to the constitutionality of California's "Three Strikes" laws. The Court held that a sentence of fifty years to life for the *third strike* crime of shoplifting $150 worth of videotapes was not a violation of the cruel and unusual punishment clause of the 8th Amendment.

In *Atkins v. Virginia* (2002), the Court ruled that executing someone with mental disabilities was cruel and unusual punishment.

In *Miller v. Alabama* (2010), the Supreme Court ruled that for persons under the age of 18, any punishment of life in prison without parole was cruel and unusual, except for murder convictions. This holding is consistent with the precedent established in 1977 and 2008 that held that the death penalty sentence for cases other than murder amounted to cruel and unusual punishment.

In *Furman v. Georgia* (1972), the issue of whether the death penalty itself is cruel and unusual punishment was before the Supreme Court. In a 5-4 decision (with each justice in the majority writing a separate opinion), the Court ruled that capital punishment (sentenced to death), as it was currently applied, consisted of cruel and unusual punishment. As a result, a moratorium on executions took effect, and the death penalty became *de facto* illegal in the United States.

In *Gregg v. Georgia* (1976), the Supreme Court reversed and reaffirmed the death penalty's legality, ending the moratorium on executions in the United States. The ruling did add stipulations to death penalty eligible cases and requirements on how executions (i.e., achieving the sentence) are to be conducted. Worldwide, the death penalty remains controversial, as the world, except for a few dictatorial regimes (e.g., China, Saudi Arabia, North Korea), have outlawed the death penalty. Several states have banned punishment by death as cruel and unusual punishment under the 8th Amendment.

Ninth Amendment

The 9th Amendment states: "*The enumeration in the Constitution, of certain rights, shall not be construed to deny or disparage others retained by the people.*" This Amendment clarified that the Bill of Rights does not constitute a definitive and exhaustive list of people's fundamental rights. The 9th Amendment was adopted to appease the Federalists, who were concerned that an explicit listing of representative fundamental rights would be considered exhaustive. Thus, any right not listed in the Bill of Rights might be assumed not to exist. The 9th Amendment was adopted to ensure that the federal government could not arbitrarily infringe on fundamental rights in such a way that it did not violate any of the explicitly listed rights but was nonetheless recognized as an infringement of individual liberty.

The Supreme Court has relied on the 9th Amendment to rule that Americans have a right to privacy. Even though the right to privacy is not explicitly in the Bill of Rights, the Court has held that the 9th Amendment covers fundamental rights. These unenumerated rights, such as the right to vote, travel, and keep personal matters private) are judicially recognized but not explicitly stated in the Constitution or the Bill of Rights.

In *Griswold v. Connecticut* (1965), the Supreme Court held that the *right to privacy* was protected under the 9th Amendment. In *Griswold,* Connecticut had passed a law banning all contraception. The Supreme Court held that this law was an undue intrusion into citizens' intimate lives and violated the right to privacy. The majority decision invoked the 5th Amendment's right against self-incrimination to justify the ruling. A consenting opinion was written by Associate Justice Arthur Goldberg (1908-1990; 1962-1965), which asserted that the right to privacy was a constitutional right embedded in the 9th

Amendment. Goldberg's consenting opinion invoking the 9th Amendment to protect privacy is an essential precedent for social liberties.

Supreme Court Justice Arthur Goldberg, c. 1965

In *Roe v. Wade* (1973), in a 7-2 decision, the Supreme Court relied on the 9th Amendment and *due process clause* of the 14th Amendments. The Court held that the right to privacy included the woman's right to an abortion. Plaintiff Roe (Norma McCorvey) argued that women have a right to privacy under the 9th Amendment. Thus, she asserted that the states against abortion were unconstitutional. Enactment of such prohibitive laws would make a woman's reproductive choices a matter of public opinion or concern.

Norma McCorvey (1947-2017) did not receive an abortion because abortion was prohibited, and her third child was born during the litigation phase. There were three years of lower court trials supported by pro-abortion attorneys seeking a pregnant woman named plaintiff (needed standing; *case and controversy* requirement for judicial review). As her attorneys' advocated on her behalf, McCorvey never attended a single trial. After her Court victory in legalizing abortion, she was a vocal critic of abortion. She became a Roman Catholic activist in the anti-abortion movement. McCorvey frequently toured college campuses and other venues and advocated against the right to have an abortion. She stated that her involvement in *Roe* was "the biggest mistake of my life."

Abortion is a polarizing political, moral, and religious issue. Since the decision in 1971 through 2015, Harris (polling organization) records surveys of people's opinions regarding abortion. Harris poll results show support for the right to an abortion ranging from about 27% to 48%. During the same period, Harris poll results show opposition to the right to an abortion ranging from about 50% to 65%. Several other polling surveys have been conducted over the years, showing adamant support for and opposition to abortion. This remains a profoundly ingrained personal issue that may never achieve a consensus.

In *Lawrence v. Texas* (2003), the Supreme Court considered the right to privacy under the 9th Amendment. The Court held that a fundamental right to privacy included same-sex sodomy. The Court ruled that people have a right to privacy, and a person's sex lives should not be a public concern; the statute prohibiting same-sex sodomy was deemed unconstitutional.

In the internet age, the 9th Amendment is often invoked as protection against electronic spying by the federal and state governments. If citizens have a fundamental right to privacy, then the government should not be able to spy on what people assume are reasonably private activities. While internet activists such as the Electronic Frontiers Foundation often make this 9th Amendment argument, the issue of online spying has yet to be heard by the Supreme Court.

Tenth Amendment

The 10th Amendment states: "*The powers not delegated to the United States by the Constitution, nor prohibited by it to the States, are reserved to the States respectively, or to the people.*" The 10th Amendment reaffirms the separation of powers between the federal government and state governments. The states, subject to the federal system, want to ensure that they can enact laws on matters not covered in the other nine Amendments. Madison generally saw the 10th Amendment as unnecessary but included it to ease Anti-Federalists' fears and some hesitant state governments to ratify the Bill of Rights. Anti-Federalists and some colonial states thought the Bill of Rights would dramatically undercut their autonomy and authority.

In *United States v. Sprague* (1931), the Supreme Court ruled that the 10th Amendment was a truism that added nothing new to the Constitution. However, it merely reaffirmed what was written elsewhere within the Constitution. Occasionally, state governments have attempted to invoke the 10th Amendment to argue that federal legislation should not apply to state governments. The 2010s saw a renewed vitality by the states attempting to reclaim sovereign state rights and rebuff, what some state allege, is an overly intrusive power of the federal government. Some of these challenges were successful in recent years. However, the Supreme Court has consistently tempered a broad interpretation of the 10th Amendment. Rulings in the 1940s upheld the legality of federal minimum wage and labor standards legislation.

An occasion where the Supreme Court has struck down legislation for violating the 10th Amendment was when legislation compelled state governments to administer federal programs (i.e., commandeering).

For example, in *Printz v. United States* (1997), the Supreme Court ruled that a gun control law requiring state officials to perform background checks violated the 10th Amendment because state officials were burdened with implementing and executing a federal program.

Later Amendments

In addition to the Bill of Rights and the Reconstruction Amendments (13th, 14th, 15th) banning slavery and racial discrimination, some later Amendments were ratified, which protected civil rights.

The 19th Amendment (1920) granted women the right to vote.

The 23rd Amendment (1961) gave voting rights to residents of Washington, D.C. The court ruled that since residents of the capital district are citizens and have all the accompanying duties, such as military service and paying taxes, they could not be denied the right to vote. By 1960, Washington, D.C. had a larger population than thirteen states; this was relevant legislation that granted Electoral College votes to Washington, D.C.

The 24th Amendment (1964) was another famous civil rights era Amendment that made poll taxes illegal. Before the 24th Amendment, many southern states required a person to pay a sum of money to vote. These states used a poll tax to prevent poor white people from voting and indirectly discriminate against blacks since they were disproportionately impoverished in the post-slavery era. President Lyndon B. Johnson called the 24th Amendment a "triumph of liberty over restriction" and a "verification of people's rights."

The 24th Amendment significantly increased suffrage (i.e., the right to vote in political elections) in the South, allowing impoverished white males and blacks equal access to the right to vote regardless of their ability to pay a state-imposed poll tax. Although the 24th Amendment was meant to remove undue obstacles to voting, Alabama retained a literacy test to exclude people from voting. Congress eventually banned literacy tests in the Voting Rights Act of 1965 and the updated Act of 1970.

36th President Lyndon Baines Johnson, c. 1965

The 26th Amendment (1971) lowered the national voting age from twenty-one to eighteen. The impetus for the 26th Amendment was the upsurge in student activism in the late 1960s and early 1970s with protests against the Vietnam War. University students argued that they become the most politically engaged segment of the population, yet they could not exercise their voting rights. Congress drafted the 26th Amendment, and it was ratified after votes by the 38 state legislatures. The 26th Amendment was the fastest ratification of any Amendment. It was proposed by Congress on March 23, 1971, and ratified by the requisite three-fourth states' affirmed votes on July 1, 1971

While the Constitution and Bill of Rights provide a robust framework of rights and liberties held and exercised by all American citizens, the government and Supreme Court do not always apply these rights. It is up to the people to continually test their rights to ensure that the Constitution continues to be the supreme law.

Governments and courts' political flavor may change with time, but Constitutional rights are a bulwark against governmental abuse. The long history of activism and litigation to ensure that the government and courts upheld these rights is evidence that Americans cannot take these fundamental rights for granted; they must be continually exercised and fought for.

Notes for active learning

Notes for active learning

The Impact of the Fourteenth Amendment

The 13th, 14th, and 15th Amendments are the Reconstruction Amendments and were adopted in the wake of the Civil War (1861-1865). The Reconstruction Amendments transformed the United States from a country that was, as Abraham Lincoln put it, "half slave, half free" into a united country where freedom would be constitutionally guaranteed. The civil rights Amendments guarantee the freedom of former slaves and their descendants.

Celebrating the passage of the Fifteenth Amendment to the United States Constitution

The 14th Amendment (see appendix for the text of the amendment), ratified on July 9, 1868, is especially crucial to guarantee fundamental rights. It empowers the federal government to protect the rights of citizens against state governmental intrusions. The 14th Amendment has been the basis of successful state court challenges seeking to bring Americans new rights. Section 1 of the 14th Amendment guarantees citizenship rights for natural-born and naturalized persons and ensures that individual states cannot pass laws that violate these citizenship rights without due process.

Section 1 of the 14th Amendment was vital because it overturned *Dred Scott v. Sandford* (1857), in which the Supreme Court ruled that Americans descended from slaves could not be citizens. The *due process clause* of the 14th Amendment grants the federal government the authority to ensure that states do not pass legislation violating rights granted by the Bill of Rights by reverse incorporation. The *equal protection clause* ensures that state governments treat everyone equally under the law. This clause was vital as the basis of *Brown v. Board of Education* (1954), where the Supreme Court held that racially segregated public schools (i.e., *separate but equal*) be unconstitutional.

The other four sections of the 14th Amendment have been less critical for court rulings. However, they set out the proportion of Representatives for each state in the legislature, bar people who participated in insurrections against the U.S. government from holding office, and outlaw questioning the validity of the public debt related to putting down rebellions. The 14th Amendment gave Congress the ability to enforce the provisions of the 14th Amendment.

While the 14th Amendment was passed to ensure that the rights of former slaves were protected after emancipation, the Amendment retains its importance as the basis for other disenfranchised groups (i.e., deprived of rights and privileges) acquiring fundamental rights, which were denied to them. The 14th Amendment was significant in the wake of the Civil War, as it gave the federal government the power to enforce the Bill of Rights against the states, which it was unable to do before the 14th Amendment.

In *Barron v. Baltimore* (1833), the Supreme Court ruled that the Bill of Rights restricts the federal powers but does not apply to state governments. As such, slave states used this ruling as the basis of their claim that the Bill of Rights did not outlaw slavery because the Bill of Rights had no jurisdiction over state (only the federal) governments. Given the national unity problems caused by the *Barron* ruling, the 14th Amendment was an important step both for individuals' rights and for ensuring that the United States remained a single country and did not break again as in the Civil War.

The three primary protections outlined in the 14th Amendment became the basis for Supreme Court decisions. Due process, which ensures the opportunity for trials to be heard fairly and without discrimination, was the basis of *Roe v. Wade* (1973), which legalized abortion. The court ruled that the 14th Amendment's *due process clause* establishes a right to personal privacy. A state government cannot violate a woman's privacy by telling her whether she can terminate a pregnancy.

In *Obergefell v. Hodges* (2015), the Court ruled that the liberty of individuals guaranteed by the due process clause and the equality of individuals guaranteed by the equal protection clause were both significantly burdened by state-level restrictions on same-sex marriage. The court ruled that states cannot pass laws banning same-sex marriage, thus violating the 14th Amendment.

The equal protection clause, which guarantees that all citizens must be treated the same, has been the basis of famous rulings like *Brown v. Board of Education* (1954), which struck down racial segregation in schools.

In *Loving v. Virginia* (1967), the Supreme Court unanimously (9-0) struck down laws against antimiscegenation (i.e., interracial marriage) statutes under the *equal protection* and *due processes* clause of the 14th Amendment to invalidate the Virginia statute prohibition on interracial marriage. Republican Chief Justice Warren, citing the holding in *Korematsu v. United States* (1941), invoked the highest judicial standard (strict scrutiny). He wrote that "*and if they [statutes] are ever to be upheld, they [statutes] must be shown to be necessary to the accomplishment of some permissible state objective.*"

In *Eisenstadt v. Baird* (1972), the ruling invoked the equal protection clause to ensure that contraception was available to people who were not married.

In *Bush v. Gore* (2000), the Supreme Court ruled, used the equal protection clause of the 14th Amendment as the basis of ruling related to presidential ballot recounts in Florida in the 2000 presidential election. The court ruled that a statewide recount of Florida votes would violate the equal protection clause because of how different counties tallied votes. The ruling was that recounts stop, and the initial result of Bush winning the state's vote was upheld.

The *privileges and immunities* clause is the third crucial clause of the 14th Amendment. The privileges and immunities clause guarantees that all American citizens have the same rights, regardless of which state they reside.

In *United States v. Wheeler* (1920), the Supreme Court used the *privileges and immunities* clause to rule that it was up to state governments to prosecute kidnappers. More importantly, this case set the standard for citizens' legal right to travel freely within the

United States. This right to travel between states was later upheld in *Saenz v. Roe* (1999). Although this right is not explicitly mentioned in the Constitution, people have a fundamental right to move between states (i.e., the right to travel or establish domicile).

Republican Congressman John A. Bingham (OH), a principal framer of the Equal Protection Clause of the Fourteenth Amendment, c. 1868

In the 1940s (i.e., at the time of World War II), a Supreme Court ruling used the privileges and immunities clause of the 14th Amendment to set a precedent that was used by the California Supreme Court to strike down California State laws against landownership by non-citizens, aimed at Japanese immigrants.

The 14th Amendment remains the most actively litigated aspect of the Constitution. Given that the 14th Amendment grants a fundamental right against state-sponsored discrimination. The 14th Amendment is likely to continue to be the basis of future court challenges if state-sponsored discrimination exists.

Notes for active learning

Notes for active learning

Chapter 4

Political Beliefs and Behaviors

Individual citizens hold various beliefs about their government, its leaders, and the U.S. political system. Taken together, these beliefs form the foundation of U.S. political culture. The formation, evolution, and transmission processes of these beliefs are essential.

Equally important is why U.S. citizens hold certain beliefs about politics and how families, schools, and the media act to perpetuate or change these beliefs. Political culture affects and informs political participation profoundly.

Individuals often engage in multiple forms of political participation (e.g., voting, protests, and mass movements) for various reasons. This participation may affect the political system.

What leads citizens to differ from one another in their political beliefs, behaviors, and their views about the political process and the political consequences of these differences is the subject of constant analysis. Demographic features of the American population can inform understanding of these differences

Beliefs of Citizens About Their Government and Its Leaders

The United States is a large and diverse country where people hold a broad spectrum of political views and beliefs. The Bill of Rights guarantees freedom of conscience, which means that every American is free to hold whatever political beliefs they choose. The consequence is that there is no official belief system that people must hold.

An American citizen cannot be jailed merely because of their political views. The fact that citizens are free to believe whatever they wish enables a wide range of views or "plurality." The German American political theorist Hannah Arendt (1906-1975) argued that plurality is a part of the human condition. Each person born into the world is unique, meaning each person has their own set of views and beliefs about the world.

The First Federal Congress, 1789, where the Bill of Rights was created

While many factors can affect different people's beliefs about politics, people tend to associate general groups of ideas broadly. These general groupings are called ideologies and include liberalism, conservatism, socialism, and libertarianism. Someone who identifies as a libertarian may do so because they generally agree with the idea of less government involvement in the economy and one's social life.

However, a libertarian may have vastly different views from another libertarian about specific details. In many cases, someone identifying with a significant ideology may do so because they agree with one or two significant aspects of the ideology while disagreeing with other major aspects. Even within ideologies, there is a plurality of views. Thus, viewing political beliefs solely in terms of ideologies can be complicated, as people rarely agree with every aspect, making lumping people together into groups problematic.

Due to the two-party system in the United States, there tends to be an oversimplification of the range of views people believe. In the mass media, it is presumed that one is either liberal or conservative, each corresponding with a political party. Due to human plurality, it can be challenging to lump people together into broad ideological groupings; narrowing those groups into just two ideologies is a gross simplification. One may be a liberal on one issue but conservative on another.

At the same time, there are broader political ideologies besides liberalism and conservatism. While every person has a different set of opinions, studying broad ideologies is mainly essential for their relation to what type of government they prefer.

Political theorists as far back as Plato (c. 428-348 B.C.) and Aristotle (385-323 B.C.) in the Greek classical age (480-323 B.C.) have sought to classify the different types of government to determine which type might be best. For Aristotle, there were only three government types, and each could be either good or bad for six possible political structures.

According to Aristotle, the government was either ruled by one person, a few people, or many people. When one person ruled it, it was either a monarchy (if it was good) or a tyranny (if it was bad). When the government comprised a few people, it was either an aristocracy (if it was good) or an oligarchy (if it was bad). The government of the many was a polity (if it was good) and democracy (if it was bad).

Aristotle defined a pure democracy as bad because he believed the "*rule of the people*" meant that the more impoverished masses would use and control state resources. However, the rich would need to be taxed heavily for the system to work. Thus, through taxation, the wealthy are exploited by the poor.

Aristotle believed that a polity (or politeia), in which citizens are bound by a governing constitution that served the interests of both the rich and poor, to be most favorable. Except for how "democracy" is defined in today's vernacular, these governmental classifications are still useful today, as they inform much of the discourse around positive and negative governance in the modern world.

Aristotle, classical Greek philosopher, c. 325 BC

A monarchical system is a mode of governance where a monarch rules on behalf of his people. In contrast, a tyrannical mode of governance occurs when the "governance of one" turns into governance in the interests of only the monarch and his inner circle.

An aristocratic (i.e., *rule of the best*) mode of governance is one in which a select segment of society is chosen to govern the population. This group is assumed to be representative of the wisest members of the given polity. If this select group begins governing its interests and explicitly against its constituency interests, the aristocratic form of governance has become an oligarchy.

The United States Senate was designed to represent the ideals of the aristocratic mode of governance. Since the rich are the few, accusing the government of being an oligarchy is generally meant today to imply that the wealthy have too much influence. For a "government of the many," Aristotle believed that democracy represented a bad form of governance because it tended towards the tyranny of the majority.

Aristotle argued that having a mixed regime (polity), which combined a king, an aristocracy, and a democracy, was the best form of government due to each constituent's ability to balance against the other. This corresponds to the American political system's arrangement, with a single President, a Senate theoretically composed of the wisest few, and the House of Representatives as a democratic institution representing the many.

Aristotle would likely approve of the American system of government. However, he did think that a monarchy is the best and, at the same time, the most dangerous form of government because it could quickly turn into a tyranny, which he considered to be the worst form of government.

Generally, those who believe in a type of government believe in a corresponding set of ideological beliefs. These beliefs, however, may not support their type of government. For example, a liberal might support monarchism, and one in favor of democracy might be a communist. Different ideologies can mix and correspond to different forms of government. Consequently, there are seemingly countless combinations of significant ideologies and corresponding types of government.

For the sake of brevity, the next section discusses five significant ideologies and the most common type of government that each ideology endorses. Again, it is essential to remember that each person may have a different perspective and interpretation of the ideology. Thus, even two people who claim to support the same ideology could have vastly different beliefs regarding the specific ideology's constraints and details.

The Five Major Political Ideologies

Before looking into the dominant political ideologies, it is crucial to understand that all politics exist on a right-left spectrum. Right-wing policies tend to be more conservative, and left-wing policies tend to be more liberal. However, this spectrum should be a circle where the further a proponent goes on the spectrum of either side, the closer they get to authoritarianism.

Though Soviet Communism (all property is owned publicly) and Fascism (dictatorial power) are extreme representations of the left and right on the political spectrum, respectively, they should "touch" due to their authoritarian nature. Most political ideologies are not as extreme as the above example. However, it is essential to understand the specific characteristics of ideology and its position on a circular spectrum.

It is essential to realize that ideologies existing on the left-right spectrum may be better indicators than the typical American descriptors of being conservative or liberal.

These interpretations are inherently subject to framing the narrative and therefore are not truly representative of an individual's or party's beliefs.

The Democratic Party is considered liberal in the modern American political lexicon; however, some of its policies may be slightly right of center on the political spectrum. Looking back to Republican Dwight Eisenhower's presidency, many of his policies were to the left on the political spectrum. Consider the actual policies and not party affiliation of politicians when evaluating ideology.

Democratic President Kennedy was a co-called blue-dog democrat identified as fiscally responsible and centrist (commentators call them a rare breed today). Kennedy had several policies that many today would consider to be firmly on the right side of the political spectrum. For example, his 1961 presidential inaugural speech included the words, *"And so, my fellow Americans: ask not what your country can do for you – ask what you can do for your country."*

President Dwight D. Eisenhower, c. 1960

The most basic type of government is a monarchy. Monarchists believe that one person should oversee all decisions and enact legislation. This was the predominant form of government during the Middle Ages (476-1453). In a monarchy, people (i.e., subjects) believe that kings and queens have a divine right to rule. Divine right means that the monarch derives his or her authority directly from God, and thus the monarch would rule society subject to no external (e.g., citizen) control.

It was then extrapolated that due to their divine mandate, questioning the monarch was not only an act against the government but against God himself. Since it was accepted that the monarch was essentially chosen to rule by God, monarchies tended to be hereditary, meaning that the son (or sometimes the daughter) of the monarch would take over after the current monarch died.

While few Americans today would consider themselves monarchists, it is a critical historical ideology in American political society. The American Revolution was a categorical rejection of monarchism as an ideology. The idea that society should be founded on a secular principle of government that is not grounded in God's authority, but the authority derived from the governed's consent is republicanism (i.e., natural rights, popular sovereignty, social contract).

Republicanism, as an organizational principle for the government, is almost universally accepted in the United States. Due to the republican revolutions in the United States and France, which overthrew monarchies and led to the increase in secular ideas, absolutist monarchism as an ideology has mostly died out. However, some notable exceptions exist in the Gulf States (seven Arab states that border the Persian Gulf: Bahrain, Kuwait, Iraq, Oman, Qatar, Saudi Arabia, and the United Arab Emirates), Swaziland, Brunei, and the Vatican.

A variant of the absolute control of a divine monarch is embodied in a constitutional monarchy. The most famous constitutional monarchy is in the United Kingdom, where the monarch's role has become mostly ceremonial. The executive function is performed by the Prime Minister (appointed by the Monarch) and ministers.

Another example of constitutional monarchy is the sovereign-city state (country) of Monaco. Monaco is a principality, like Andorra and Lichtenstein, governed as a form of constitutional monarchy, with Prince Albert II (b. 1958; House of Grimaldi) as head of state (2005 to present). The House of Grimaldi has ruled Monaco, with brief interruptions, since its forbearer, Rainier I of Monaco (1267-1314), left the Kingdom of Naples in Italy and conquered the region, known as present-day Monaco in 1297.

General George Washington in the American Revolution, c. 1783

According to monarchy supporters, the monarchy's main advantage is that it gives the monarch (e.g., king, queen) the ability to act quickly without having to overcome the hurdles of pluralistic modes of governance. Monarchists claim that this makes the government more responsive to the people than a democracy, which has slow deliberations before enacting legislation.

However, the absolute power of one person can be the most flawed aspect of the monarchy. If the king is unpopular and engages in destructive policies, there is no mechanism to stop him or her, and the monarch can quickly turn into a tyrant.

The principle of having a government ruled by one person or one grouping without any provision for the opposition is not exclusive to monarchism. Advocates of various forms of absolutism agree that the government should be decisively united. Absolutism has many forms, including dictatorship by one person or political parties, such as the dictatorial regime of Adolf Hitler's (1889 to April 30, 1945) Nazi Party (1921-1945) in Germany in the 1930s and Joseph Stalin's (1878-1953) Communist Party in Soviet Russia (1912-1991). Both the Nazi and Communist parties were the only ideologies allowed in government. The dictators had absolute rule without permitted debate, dissent, or opposition.

Absolutism can be divided into authoritarianism and totalitarianism. Authoritarian governments are concerned primarily with ensuring everyone follows their rules at whatever cost. In contrast, a totalitarian government wants to control how people think, not just how they act. One can disagree with an authoritarian government and not be persecuted, so long as one does not act against the government. A totalitarian government insists that citizens believe in it and agree with it. Both the Soviet Union in Russia (1922-1991) and the Nazi Party of Germany were totalitarian, as they wanted to control people's beliefs. Examples of authoritarian governments that were overthrown recently are the dictatorships in Tunisia (2011) and Egypt (2011), among others stemming from the Arab Spring, protests against oppression between c. 2010-2014.

While few people would openly identify their political views as totalitarian or even authoritarian because of their association with complete destructive regimes of the past, these are fundamental ideologies in the context of American political culture. Many people believe that the government should rule unopposed or that holding political views should be outlawed. It is crucial to understand how authoritarian and totalitarian thinking may exist in American political culture even if people do not identify with these terms.

For example, after the 9/11 terrorist attacks, President George W. Bush declared in 2001 that *"you are either with us, or you are with the terrorists,"* implying (to some) that Americans agreed with everything the President was doing. Otherwise, they were enemies of the American government. While this is not to say that President Bush transformed the country into a totalitarian mode of governance, he was implicitly referencing that only through adhering to a set of principles (that he and the government defined) could citizens show support for the American policies to fight terrorism.

Presidential portrait of George W. Bush, c. 2006

Another example of such totalitarian rhetoric was Senator Joseph McCarthy (1908-1957) in the 1940s and 1950s, who headed the House Un-American Activities Committee, which sought to target the thousands of "communists" living in the United States. During the McCarthy era (1950-54), the United States was not governed by authoritarianism principles, but McCarthy's rhetoric was authoritarian.

If absolutism is one extreme of government, the other extreme is anarchism. Anarchists believe that government is inherently oppressive, and people can only be free when there is a minimal form of government or no government at all. While this may sound ridiculous or merely unrealistic, anarchism advocates for self-government instead of traditional government.

Within the United States, there are two main branches of anarchism. One branch of anarchism endorses capitalist economics, and another endorses socialist economics.

Anarchist capitalism, usually referred to as libertarianism, is the more popular variant in the United States. Libertarians such as former Congressman Ron Paul (1935–

2020) and Senator Rand Paul (b. 1963) believe that the government is oppressive by nature. Libertarians tend to advocate for a policing government reduced to the smallest size possible; for example, the government should only provide citizens' national security from foreign or domestic threats. Many libertarians call for what they term a "night watchmen state," meaning the government's role is only to intervene in criminal cases.

Libertarians support liberal social policies because of their distrust of government and favor same-sex marriage, drug legalization, and pro-choice on abortions. Many libertarians see government regulation on these issues, as promoted by conservatives, as taking away individuals' free choice.

On economic matters, libertarians tend to take a very pro-capitalist and right-wing point of view, believing that corporations should have extensive freedom. For these economic issues, libertarians tend to align with what Americans label a conservative economic perspective. They oppose environmental regulations, labor unions (employees are free to quit and seek better working conditions), minimum wage (market sets the value of services), and workplace safety laws. Generally, libertarians do not believe the government should regulate the economy or the participants within.

Anarchist socialists (sometimes called libertarian socialists) agree with libertarians on social issues but believe that corporations form an oppressive government. Anarchist socialists believe that workplaces should be run through democratic committees. The large-scale federal government should be replaced by small-scale democratic councils that form governments at the local level. Unlike Soviet communism, which was economically left-wing but politically right-wing and totalitarian, socialist anarchists oppose government control of the economy while supporting socialist and sometimes communist principles of collective ownership.

Libertarians such as Ron Paul have recently become more popular, while socialist anarchists like Lithuania Emma Goldman (1869-1940) were instrumental in their time in influencing American political culture. Their activities in the late 19th and early 20th centuries led to the shortening of the standard workday from twelve to eight hours.

Liberalism is a prominent political ideology in contemporary American political culture. However, as with conservatism, liberalism has evolved. Originally liberalism was a less extreme version of Libertarianism. Liberals generally believed that governments were a restriction on freedom, but a necessary one.

Liberalism originally meant limited government, which was curbed by the American system of checks and balances. In the light of Democratic President Franklin D. Roosevelt's New Deal, American liberalism shifted and regarded an expanding government as a source of progress whose role was to redistribute wealth.

President Franklin Delano Roosevelt, c. 1938

Today, liberals generally want less government regulation on social issues, such as drugs, marriage, abortion, but want substantially more government regulation for the economy. Liberals want the expanding government to use its power to promote their self-defined social good. Capitalism is not an economic model endorsed by most liberals.

One of the main contrasts between today's liberalism and conservatism is that liberals believe that a drastic change of American values leads to progress. In contrast, conservatives are skeptical about change (especially imposed by the federal government) and feel that the gradually evolved traditions are generally superior.

The American version of liberalism tends to promote a progressive income tax system. A progressive income tax system means that higher wage earners (some would argue more productive people) pay a higher percentage of their revenue to the government. American liberalism promotes welfare programs to help the poor (historically supported by charitable and religious organizations), programs to help reduce unemployment, increased spending on public education, affirmative action programs to bolster minorities and immigrants, and a general expansion of explicit and implicit civil rights. Liberalism differs from anarchism in that liberals believe the expanded government (supported by taxpayers) can be a force for good and is not inherently oppressive.

Liberalism differs from socialism in that liberals generally support a modified capitalist economy. However, liberals believe that there should be extensive checks on free enterprise with intertwined oversight and intrusive government regulation. This notion of liberalism only relates to the modern context of liberalism in American politics, as the term liberal has a different meaning in the sphere of economics. Liberal economics is a theory that argues that economic decisions should be made by individuals, not by governmental or other institutions.

Conservatism has evolved and is more complicated in America. The original conservatives in Europe were mostly monarchists, whose goal was to conserve the monarchy and against growth in republicanism after the successful American Revolution (1765-1783) and French Revolution (May 5, 1789, to November 9, 1799).

After General Napoleon Bonaparte (1769-1821) swept across Europe (1789-1792), most absolutist monarchies yielded some power to legislatures due to the widespread demand for constitutional monarchies. Along with the growing demand for constitutional monarchies, there was growth in industrialization and urbanization.

Conservatives were deeply skeptical of this trend as the new industrialists began to amass power outside of the traditional means of acquiring assets from family holdings. Therefore, these conservatives generally supported legislative checks on the monarchy. The monarchists were unwilling to support the requested changes during this period of revolution.

In the United States, the meaning of conservatism was different and has since evolved with time. Some of the first conservatives (e.g., southern Democrats) were those who wanted to conserve the institution of slavery in the South. These large landowners were the equivalent of European aristocrats and believed the radical change of ending slavery would disrupt the entire economic and social fabric of the American South. These were the first real conservatives for the preservation of the status quo) in American history.

With the New Deal's rise in the early 1930s, conservatism in the United States shifted in position. The new conservatives favored the traditional concept of American liberalism, which promoted limited government in an economic sense. Beginning in the Cold War (1947-1991) and reaching full steam in the 1980s, American conservatism remade itself into an ideology promoting government regulation on social and moral issues.

Conservative Christians urged for government deregulation of the economy as a means of conserving classical American economic liberalism. Today, the American version of conservatism supports increasing the influence of Christianity in government, traditional social and family structure, lower taxes, regulated legal immigration, and a strong military for national defense.

Since the new millennium, there have been two major movements in American conservatism: President George W. Bush's neoconservatism and the restrained government of the Tea Party's fiscal conservatism. The Tea Party was grass-roots activism founded in 2009 in response to the perceived increasing governmental regulations under Democratic President Barak Obama. President Bush's neo-conservatism was centered on foreign policy and was widely supported in the wake of the 9/11 attacks when terrorists hijacked commercial planes and destroyed the occupied World Trade Center, killing almost three thousand people. The American people were looking for a government response; George W. Bush and his advisors provided this through their interventionist foreign policy.

Traces of this interventionist foreign policy legacy were seen in President Barack Obama's foreign policy. This was mainly at the behest of the former Secretary of State Hillary Clinton. She proposed intervention in many conflicts around the world. However, President Obama did not always act on her recommendations. Obama's interventionist policies were focused primarily on domestic issues. President Obama campaigned on the promise to fundamentally change America.

In 2009, the Tea Party arose as a spontaneous movement in response to several government programs, including the massive economic stimulus package of 2009, healthcare reform legislation, and the government bailout of the large publicly traded banks in the banks in the aftermath of the 2007–08 financial crisis. The new Tea Party formed in 2009 advocated for fiscal restraint, limited government, reduced federal budget, and the reduction of the recently ballooning federal debt. The national debt is the amount imputed to be owed by each citizen in America. The national debt results from excessive spending when expenses are higher than tax revenue.

For example, the national debt was $3.23 trillion in 1990, $5.67 trillion in 2000, $13.56 trillion in 2010, and almost $23 trillion in 2020. The national debt amounts to an almost $20 trillion increase over just the last 30 years. Commentators point to a rapid increase in the national debt (38% over two years) under the Obama administration. The national debt matters to Americans because future generations of taxpayers will be burdened with the financial obligation to retire this ballooning debt.

As of September 17, 2019, the obligation to retire the debt is $68,400 per citizen (including children, retired and unemployed persons) or a stunning $183,000 per taxpayer, which is 6.8 times the federal revenue per taxpayer. As the national debt increases, the phrase *"kick the can down the road"* is invoked to describe the future, unsustainable financial burden placed on each taxpayer to satisfy the country's financial obligation. It becomes more alarming when these figures are compared to the Gross Domestic Product (i.e., market value from all goods and services). The national debt is 106% of GDP. This unsustainable amount of debt sobering and invokes the expression that *"each taxpayer is underwater concerning the national debt."* Even if the national debt, based on overspending by the government, remained flat, the interest payments would increase taxpayers' obligations. The expected interest-only (interest payment is recurring; the principal remains the same) is estimated at $593 billion ($593,000,000,000) for 2019.

One of the main quirks in the American interpretation of political ideology is the confusion between what a specific term means in a theoretical sense (abstract, academic definition) and the term means in practice (i.e., the reality of its application). In the academic, theoretical world, the definition of liberalism is closer to that of non-interventionism in all spheres of life. However, this is divorced from the everyday colloquial use of the word liberalism. According to the theoretical ideology of liberalism, there should be a limited government that protects citizens' general welfare. However, the people under the jurisdiction of a liberal government should generally be allowed to make their way, both personally (without restraint on civil liberties) and economically (under the free markets of capitalism).

This confusion dates to the New Deal era when a large portion of the socialist programs enacted by Democratic President Franklin D. Roosevelt was not labeled "socialist" to distinguish between New Deal activism and the Soviet Union. Since this time, when the government has proposed socialist ideas (e.g., a mandatory minimum wage, taxation for the creation of the interstate governmental regulation, Obamacare), these programs have tended to be called "liberal" as opposed to "socialist." More pronounced as of 2020, the *socialist agenda* entered the mainstream dialogue (no longer cloaked as *democratic* ideals only). In the realm of conservatism, the American definition is focused on limited government, fiscal responsibility, self-reliance (fewer social programs supported by higher taxes), and free-market economics (fewer governmental regulations).

One example of a peculiar confusion between the liberal and conservative party ideologies (Democrats vs. Republicans) in the mainstream American political media is gun control. Conservative Americans are more inclined to support the right to own a gun, and liberals are more inclined to want the government to prohibit gun ownership; these positions are seemingly contrary to the expected position for these two ideologies.

Since liberals usually want less government control on non-economic issues and a general expansion of civil liberties, liberals should be pro-gun-ownership (personal freedoms). Some commentators propose that since conservatives want the government to regulate social issues and argue that security and law and order should be more important than individual liberties, conservatives would be expected to regulate guns in the name of security and public order. However, this analysis is a specious argument because conservatives do not (in any appreciable number) advocate or condone illegal uses of guns. This applies if the gun is in the rightful (permitted) possession of the assailant or used by a criminal who was barred from the legal possession (no permit) of gun ownership. Neither liberals nor conservatives legitimately advocate for guns to be used for illegal purposes.

In general, most of the political ideologies in America are like the rest of the world. One area where American political culture is unique is gun ownership because of gun ownership's explicit language as a fundamental right in the Bill of Rights' Second Amendment. Some commentators propound if one amendment is more critical than another. A hypocritical approach is that the most significant amendments (deserving expanded protections) favor a person. In contrast, the least important (trampling or deny those rights) are contained in those amendments that a person opposes. From this shallow perspective, well-reasoned arguments are futile and worthy of abandonment.

The next central ideology is socialism, though often under a different name. Socialism has played an important role in American politics and is increasingly taking center stage for recent political debates. There are varieties of socialism, but the general idea is that the government should regulate capitalism.

In theory, socialist governments generally see their primary goal as promoting economic equality and fairness by limiting corporations' power. Social democrats and democratic socialists promote universal healthcare programs, which provide governmental-sponsored healthcare to all, relying on taxpayers to fund this proposition.

Social democrats promote strong legislation protecting workers while increasing wages are passed to the consumer. They believe in taxpayer-funded social welfare programs to help those unable or unwilling to work. Socialism is not based on *equal opportunity but equal results* because equality is the goal of socialism.

In contrast, capitalism requires capital at risk and does not guarantee rewards because customers select among competing firms. The firms that satisfy customers with price, quality, and service survive and are profitable. Profitable companies remain in business when revenue is higher than the costs of production.

Socialism is different from communism. Socialists generally do not promote government ownership of the means of production but believe the government should focus on promoting equality and helping the poor. Socialism advocates a redistributive tax policy of shifting resources *from the haves to the have nots*. Communism involves the state assuming ownership of the economy's central planning rather than free markets.

Furthermore, socialists recognize that there are "public goods," such as transportation infrastructure, power distribution infrastructure, and there is a need for the government to provide these goods and services, which are often not profitable because the cost of production is higher than the revenue generated.

Vermont Senator Bernie Sanders (b. 1941, Vermont Representative 1991-2007, Senate 2007-) and other socialists see America's social assistance programs enacted under Democratic President Roosevelt's New Deal (e.g., social security, minimum wage laws) as proof of America's unacknowledged socialist tendencies. Socialists differ from liberals in that socialists generally see corporations and capitalism as inherently and irredeemably problematic and need oppressive regulations to protect people. Much of the socialist agenda in the United States was cloaked under other names until the late 2010s.

Ideologies can have a tremendous impact in determining people's political beliefs. Many people do not spend much time thinking about their political beliefs. Their beliefs on one issue may lead them to identify as part of a specific ideology, even if they have not thought about the other beliefs within that ideology. Individuals may defer to the overall ideology, groupthink, rather than thinking for themselves.

For example, suppose a person feels strongly that the government should not regulate social issues because they believe marijuana should be legal. In that case, they may identify as libertarian. If this person has no explicit beliefs about what they think about the economy, they may defer to conventional libertarian thinking when asked about economic questions. When such a situation occurs, ideology is a general description of what people believe and determine how people behave.

Many political theorists have sought to critique ideology, as they see ideology as more like brainwashing than as a simple description of what people believe. These critics of ideology are not opposed to people having their own set of political beliefs. Their goal is to get people to arrive at beliefs through thinking rather than merely buying into a system without questioning it.

These critics point to how easily the Nazi ideology swept across Germany, allowing Hitler to come to power with popular support, as an argument that not thinking for oneself and merely subscribing to a popular ideology can be extremely dangerous.

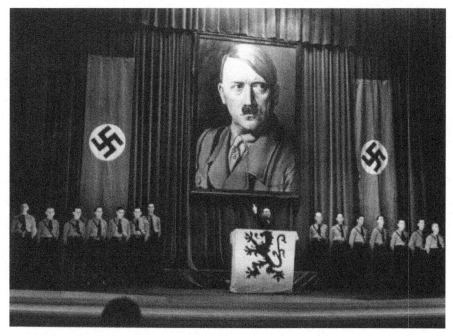

Portrait of Hitler at an SS meeting during the German occupation of WWII

Some political scientists argue that, based on political beliefs, people should not be categorized into five significant ideologies. Instead, examine the opinions of people on certain essential aspects of politics. Ideology in this negative context can make people believe in political causes that harm their self-interest.

Many political scientists seek to uncover how ideology causes people to vote for a political party that would seemingly harm them. While the Southern states are, on average, more impoverished than other states, they tend to support Republicans. The economic policies of Republicans tend to favor free markets and self-reliance, which are valued by people in the south.

According to economic theory, people are supposed to act in a self-interested fashion, so the poorest states should have the least support for the Republicans, not the most. Political theorists know that ideology can play a role in shaping people's political actions in such a way as to make their choices seem strange. It is best to be critical of everything that one hears about politics and form opinions based on one's thinking rather than relying on what others say.

Political Beliefs and Concepts

Since no two people have identical political views, even if they both identify as part of the same broad ideological grouping, it can be more informative to analyze how people feel about politics and government concepts. More can be learned about the average American by asking what they think should be the government's role in regulating the economy, regulating social issues, and taking in immigrants, than merely asking if they are liberal or conservative.

While a person may identify as part of one ideology, their beliefs may orient them entirely differently. Instead of asking if someone is a conservative, ask instead what they believe the government's role should be in maintaining law and order, what they think the place of religion should be in society and government, and how much they value freedom relative to equality. By asking more specific questions, political scientists can better determine what people believe, rather than asking them to answer in terms of liberal or conservative, resulting in misleading answers.

In American political culture, certain positions on significant issues have changed with time and have either become dominant or divisive. Concepts such as freedom, equality, and democracy are often taken for granted as the pillars of American political culture, in that everyone believes in these three concepts. If someone is asked what they think freedom is, they talk about the right to own guns.

At the same time, another person answers that freedom means voting and participating in government; it is easier to deduce a lot more than merely relying on ideological labels. This is the inherent problem with the descriptive terms listed above: they fit into a category with their support being "trivially true."

The real knowledge of the individual's political beliefs stems from asking them what this concept means to them. Freedom can have many interpretations. The gun owner may say that they are free because the government cannot take away their guns, while they believe that governments should take away the freedom for people to marry whom they choose or to terminate a pregnancy by aborting the fetus.

Freedom can mean the ability to participate in government, criticize authority, and hold any political opinion, all of which are unconnected to whether guns, abortions, or gay marriage are legal. Another person may interpret freedom in economic terms, like the ability to start one's own business or to quit a job when one chooses, which can happen regardless of whether there is much social or political freedom.

Similarly, equality can have multiple aspects. The term "equality" shares the position of being "trivially true." This is a term that has been popular since the onset of American democracy. At one stage, equality among the states meant that one slave was counted as 3/5 of a person in determining proportional representation. Equality is transient just as freedom is, and to understand one's position relative to this concept. It is similarly vital to ask base-level questions to ascertain what one believes.

Most Americans believe in political equality, in that every person should have one vote; stilted economic equality is controversial. Many people do not believe that the government should engage in extensive welfare programs to help the poor, believing they demotivate the labor force. Instead, they believe that everyone must compete in the free market. Someone making this claim is probably a conservative. A socialist would complain that the government spends too much money helping corporations while ignoring the poor, thus exacerbating inequality.

Economic inequality has skyrocketed since the mid-1980s and is increasingly becoming an issue with protest movements, such as "Occupy Wall Street." According to some studies, the top 0.1% of people in the United States control as much wealth as the bottom 90%. However, many economists disagree with this number. From 1929 to 1980, Americans progressively became more equal in wealth. Issues of social equality are controversial, especially concerning race. African Americans are disproportionately incarcerated for committing crimes, suffer higher unemployment, and are more financially burdened to meet their living and housing needs.

While these issues are strongly linked to economic inequality, many people argue that structural discrimination persists. By asking people about their opinions on concepts of equality or freedom about political, social, and economic issues, a clearer picture of their opinions emerges.

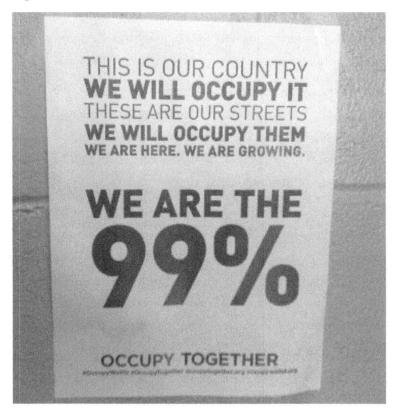

Occupy Wall Street poster, c. 2011

The same concern is valid for democracy, which is a vague term and has many possible implementations. Two people may both claim to be firm believers in democracy. One person might see voting in elections every couple of years as exercising their rights in a democracy. The other person sees voting as hardly democratic; real democracy means people must be more involved in directing government policy through direct participation.

Someone else may argue that democracy is a great ideal that should be applied to the economy as well, as socialist anarchists argue that workplaces should be democratic and that the workers should elect the bosses, rather than appointed by the founders and capitalist owners.

Again, political beliefs are complex, and various ideologies and political concepts can mix in several ways. Thus, talk about universal political values that define America is inherently misleading because what defines America is a plurality of different opinions whose expression is guaranteed by the 1st Amendment.

Democracy is the final "trivially true" term. Most Americans believe in democracy; however, many people do not understand what specifics this entails. Some express a minimalist view, where the simple ability to participate in free and fair elections is enough to declare the polity a democracy. Others are maximalists, who believe that democratic principles should be expanded to include all aspects of political participation, with far more inherent mechanisms for the public to voice their opinion and change the political landscape.

Notes for active learning

Notes for active learning

Notes for active learning

Processes by Which Citizens Learn About Politics

The first exposure to political beliefs and viewpoints usually comes through one's family. From a young age, children may hear their parents talking about politics, which is often the start of a child's political education. Some parents may seek to actively teach their children about politics and the political system, and some may try to ensure that their children have the same political views. A person's family's political identification is an influential factor informing a person's political beliefs. For example, if one's parents are both liberals and strongly support Democrats, chances are their child will be a liberal and support Democrats as well.

Even though children and teenagers cannot vote, political scientists are interested in studying these groups' political opinions. Information on these opinions helps political scientists understand the political socialization process and measure how much of a role family plays in shaping one's political views.

In 2005, a major study was conducted where researchers found that 71% of Americans aged 13-17 said they held the same political views as their parents. 7% said they were more right-wing than their parents, and 21% said they were more left-wing than their parents. It is popularly assumed that young people would be more liberal than their parents. In general, teenagers have the same views as their parents, which indicates that the family is the predominant means of political socialization for young people.

This continuation of the political views and alliances of parents and children is seen in politicians. The Kennedy family, through multiple generations, were liberal Blue Dog Democrats. The Blue Dog Democrat coalition is fiscally conservative and centrist that occupy 25 of the 232 Democratic seats in the 2020 congressional delegation. President George H. W. Bush (1924-2018; 1989-1993) and his son President George W. Bush, were conservative Republicans. President Bill Clinton and his wife Hillary Clinton share similar liberal political views.

Young voters, broadly classified as those twenty-four years of age and younger, tend to be much less attached to a political party than older voters. This detachment is partly because young citizens are still deciding about their political views and therefore are less inclined to identify with one party. While family inculcation can lead a young voter to identify with one party rather than the other, young people are more likely to switch parties than older voters.

As young people leave high school and attend college or enter the workforce, they usually move out of their parents' homes, diminishing the influence of their parents' political views. Also, young people find themselves in a new social situation, which leads to various influences that can affect their political beliefs. For older citizens, especially when they retire, there is a tendency toward partisan stabilization. When a voter retires, they tend to vote for the same party without regard for the election's specific circumstances.

Education is a critical aspect of the political process for new citizens. Thomas Jefferson is famous for stating that an educated citizenry was a requirement for America to survive as a free democracy. Through the education system, young citizens learn about the government's workings and their political process role.

For most Americans, this political education comes in public elementary, secondary, and high school. After graduating from high school, people may forget these lessons later in life. Often, young people who just completed a high school politics course are some of the most knowledgeable citizens on the government's technicalities. However, suppose these young citizens do not continue to engage with the political process and continue learning about the government's contemporary aspects. In that case, they become less informed about the evolving political landscape.

College students tend to absorb more information about government function, even if political science is not their primary field. Citizens with higher education levels are less inclined to be swayed by politicians' continual emotional pitches, such as fear-based politics. They are more likely to analyze the rallying statements of politicians critically.

As Thomas Jefferson pointed out, educated citizens are essential to a well-functioning democracy because they use their votes to make an informed choice for the country's future direction. Those with less education are more likely to vote irresponsibly by being swayed by attack ads, voting for a party without considering the campaign issues, or merely voting for superficial reasons such as which politician they would most like to have over for dinner. Jefferson feared that if the population were politically uneducated, the government could become tyrannical and take advantage of the population instead of governing for the population's benefit.

After a person is out of school, their primary means of learning about politics comes through the news media. Citizens who pay attention to the news tend to be better informed than those who do not. Reading the news in a newspaper or online or watching it on TV is critical to ensuring citizens stay informed. The media has an enormous responsibility to educate the public about political issues in an unbiased, sensible manner. However, the news reporting may not be objective because the truth is filtered through peoples' bias; the news media should strive to present multiple sides to an issue that ensures balanced and wholistic news coverage for the viewers to draw their conclusions.

Those who own the media can use their control of news to shape what citizens know and think. Media can shape what people know about politics by neglecting to report individual stories or presenting commentators and opinions from only one side of an issue. While the media rarely lies outright, as this would cause the public to lose all trust, they engage in subtle manipulations.

However, with the rise of the Internet and an individual's ability to select which news media one consumes, there has been a shift in the direction of individuals seeking out media sources that support the views an individual already holds. This is called *confirmation bias*, in which an individual seeks out facts that support their previously held conception of an issue or set of issues.

One example of confirmation bias comes from a study conducted in 2005 comparing people's beliefs regarding whether the U.S. found weapons of mass destruction in Iraq after the 2003 invasion. After the invasion, it was determined that Iraq had conducted biological weapons production research that likely ended in 1996. However, the U.S. did not find weapons of mass destruction (WMD), so researchers analyzed the percentage of people who falsely believed WMDs were found.

The study found that people who got their news from specific sources were more likely to believe that WMD were not found. This study demonstrates that the news can play a critical role in informing Americans about what is happening politically or play a critical role in misinforming Americans. As in all aspects of politics, people need to be aware of the news media's biases and critically think about what is presented.

With the emergence of the 24-hour cable TV news networks (e.g., CNN, Fox News, MSNBC), some political scientists have argued that these news networks can lead to people becoming less informed due to how one-sided they have all become. These news outlets are more like ideological apparatuses meant to convince viewers of their point of view rather than inform viewers of what is happening and provide commentary from multiple angles and multiple opinions. It can be imperative to analyze the bias of a news source to determine the validity of its reporting and the opinions it is presenting.

Fox News has a conservative bias, and CNN and MSNBC have a liberal bias. Thus, a Fox News commentary that defends a conservative politician and MSNBC commentary that defends a liberal politician should be taken cautiously; it is presumed that each of these networks simply defends its side.

Alternatively, suppose Fox News is criticizing a conservative or MSNBC is criticizing a liberal. There ought to be more attention given to that commentary because the networks are not merely following their standard partisan lines.

Thus, it is essential to understand news sources' bias, especially since most news networks are not forthcoming about their bias. Politics can never be neutral, so media claims as neutral or objective must be met with skepticism, as people reporting the news are almost always biased. By acknowledging the inherent bias, a viewer determines if the commentary is simply an expression of bias or contributes something unique and exciting.

Studies have recently shown that younger Americans learn about political issues from social media and comedy programs, such as *The Daily Show* and *The Colbert Report*. Through social media, friends can help others learn about political issues by sharing links to news stories and articles. People now use sites like Facebook and Twitter, so their social media reach has become extremely large.

With overall trust declining in the American news media, the popularity of comedy programs that make fun of the news has increased. Although these shows are not news in the proper sense, they can also be inherently biased and educate their audience about critical political issues. Comedian Stephen Colbert won a Peabody Award in 2012 for making Americans aware of the issues surrounding the Supreme Court's *Citizens United v. FEC* (2010) ruling and the establishment of Super PACs, which allowed unlimited, anonymous spending by labor unions and corporations during an election campaign. The holding in *Citizens United* is often falsely reported to permit unlimited spending for only corporations and ignores holding granting labor unions' the same rights.

Stephen Colbert at the 71st Peabody Awards, c. 2012

Taken together, how Americans learn about the political system is "political socialization." This process is most intense when citizens are younger and learn about politics for the first time but is a continual process that occurs throughout life. Especially when experiencing a significant change, such as moving to a new city, changing jobs, or finding a new circle of friends, a person can be introduced to a new set of political beliefs previously unconsidered (i.e., reference group changes).

The process of adapting to new beliefs of acquaintances can be positive or negative but is still an example of political socialization. The more people can encounter different and new viewpoints, the more likely they are to change their opinions.

People who do not encounter contrasting views tend to keep the same opinions they have always had. Sometimes people actively seek out new means of political socialization because they are interested in challenging their own opinions and learning others' opinions. However, in general, people actively avoid hearing opinions they may disagree with because they do not want to think about the underpinnings of their political beliefs and reconsider their ingrained or nebulous political views.

Notes for active learning

Nature, Sources and Consequences of Public Opinion

Public opinion is complex and continually evolving. The first question to consider is whether public opinion exists. While it is quite apparent that individuals have opinions, it is more contentious to consider whether people can have a collective opinion.

An opinion is formed through the processes outlined in the previous section, namely through education, consuming the news media in various guises, and discussing politics with others. An individual can easily do this, but it makes less sense to think of a group forming an opinion unless every member of that group is the same. Some political scientists prefer to talk about public moods or public interests because they see opinions as reserved for the individual.

Issues of trying to measure public opinion or the public mood relate to issues regarding knowledge and change. A complex political issue that requires a lot of thought and study may be outside of the realm of public knowledge. If the public is asked their opinion on something they know little about, their answers are not an expression of public opinion but public ignorance. If "public opinion" is reframed as "the public mood," it can gauge the public's general attitudes.

Take the example of the Electoral College and its procedures of electing the President. Trying to determine the public's opinion on the Electoral College would likely yield unreliable answers since most people do not know much about how it works or its purpose. Instead, consider the public's sentiment toward the Electoral College. It would be possible to discern whether there was a general desire to change, despite the lack of knowledge, how the Electoral College works, or keep it the same. The opinion does not require a person to understand the issue, but only a vague sense if something is "broken" with the Electoral College.

The concept of public opinion is problematic because it is continuously in flux as an aggregation of individual opinions. Even on matters as simple as whether same-sex marriage should be legal, public opinion has changed. A politician ten years ago who said that public opinion opposed same-sex marriage might be just as correct as a politician who said that public opinion supported same-sex marriage.

Politicians on different sides of an issue who appeal to public opinion can claim that the public is their side, an assertion that often has no basis. However, due to the prevalence of confirmation bias, their supporters likely reinforce such beliefs.

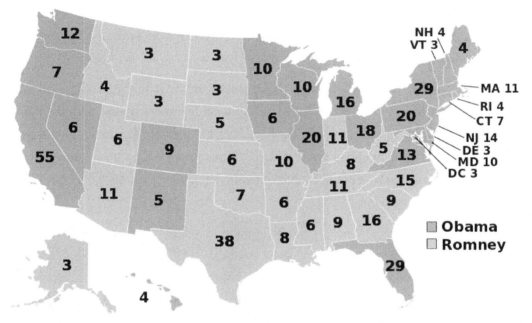

Electoral College map of the 2012 United States presidential election

Public opinion and public mood are challenging to measure. The usual method is through opinion polling. A certain number of people are called, usually at least 1,000, and asked their opinion. If the sample of people called represents the wider public, the principles of statistics dictate that the respondents' answers reflect the public's sentiment.

People criticize polling by saying that they were not asked for their opinion. Therefore the poll is not accurate. This is not an accurate statement as not every person needs to be asked to get a reasonably accurate picture of the population's broader views. There are issues regarding how public opinion is measured through polling.

The wording of questions in a poll can have a dramatic effect on the results. If the questions are worded in a biased way towards one answer or another, responses may not truly reflect the polled beliefs. A poll to discover public opinion on the issue of whether to accept refugees from a war-torn country needs to frame questions in a neutral way to get an accurate result.

If the question is biased, then it can change the results. If the question was framed in such a way as to imply the refugees were violent or possible terrorists, this might lead people to oppose accepting refugees. If the question is worded to emphasize the refugees' suffering, it may influence people to give answers that are more inclined to support allowing refugees into the country. Thus, for cited opinion polls, look at what questions were asked to decide if the questions were biased toward one response.

Another issue with measuring public opinion through polling relates to creating a representative sample. For political purposes, evaluate if likely voters were sampled if the intended purpose is to evaluate political support for an issue. For general polling, those contacted (how they are contacted – daytime, evening, mobile phones or landlines) should represent the spectrum of the American public. If not, then the poll may not provide information about the views of the wider public.

The most famous example of a political poll using an unrepresentative sample was the magazine Literary Digest poll for the 1936 presidential election. The poll sampled 2.4 million people, a large sample that should have given extremely accurate results. The poll predicted that Republican nominee Alfred Landon would easily win the election with 50% of the vote and win 32 of 48 states in the Electoral College.

In the election, Democratic candidate Franklin Roosevelt won a landslide victory with over 60% of the popular vote, winning all but two states in the Electoral College. This poll got the results spectacularly wrong because the sample was not representative of the broader American public. The poll only asked subscribers of the *Literary Digest* magazine whom they planned to vote for. The problem was that *Literary Digest* subscribers were overwhelmingly wealthier than the average American, especially during this period in the Great Depression. This demographic disparity caused the opinion poll to overwhelmingly favor the Republicans while Americans, in general, favored the Democrats.

A second problem related to representative sampling relates to evolving technology. Traditionally, polls have been conducted by randomly selecting numbers from the phone book. By using random selection, the problems of the *Literary Digest* poll would be avoided.

Today, however, fewer people have landlines as most younger people shifted to cellular phones. While many polling firms are adapting by calling cell phones and using online questionnaires, some polling firms still use the outdated (and less representative) random phone book method. Since people with landline telephones tend to be disproportionately older, their polling sample is not representative as it is made up of people mostly over the age of fifty.

There are considerations of how random these polling samples are. While they may contact people at random, many people may refuse to answer the questions. The polls are biased toward people who want to give their opinion on political matters, usually those who have already formed strong opinions. Those who do not feel strongly about political issues are often not adequately represented in polling.

There are multiple consequences of public opinion and the public mood. Public opinion is most notable during elections, where pollsters closely monitor public opinion to predict who will win an election. Politicians campaign on issues that they think the public supports, and thus public opinion can shape the election platform of parties and candidates. Once in office, public opinion is polled on specific issues to inform politicians.

While politicians do not always do what public opinion suggests, they do closely monitor it. If a politician is going against public opinion, they may try to keep this policy out of the media and make it less visible. Suppose a politician believes he or she has public opinion on their side. In that case, the politician may talk to the media as much as possible to ensure the public has a favorable opinion.

Public opinion is essential for the general attitude of what people think about the President and Congress. This is called "approval rating," and if it drops too low, the President takes measures—perhaps even reverses course—to appeal to the public to win reelection or leave a positive legacy.

In addition to merely using polling to evaluate the population's percentage for or against a specific action on an issue, other characteristics can be measured. Saliency measures how important an issue is and is measured with targeted groups.

Saliency polling may be used if a candidate is trying to win votes from a population segment. If the target audience is young people, then polls may evaluate this group's most critical issues. Suppose the polling finds that young people care most about education and do not care about social security. In that case, the campaign can target young voters on education issues and avoid messaging them about social security.

Intensity polling is like saliency but measures how strongly people feel about an issue rather than how important they feel. Again, this is usually conducted on targeted groups. An intensity poll about gun ownership might reveal that NRA members feel strongly about this issue. Others in the population might feel it is an important issue but not have strong opinions on it.

Friends of the National Rifle Association (NRA) logo

Stability polling measures how susceptible a group is to change its opinions. Stability polling is especially vital for political parties. They want to identify districts held by the opposition in which the electorate might change their minds and vote for them.

Suppose a stability poll finds that most voters in a district have already made up their minds and are not open to changing their vote. In that case, political parties generally dedicate less time to campaign in that district. They know that places where opinion is less steadfast provide better opportunities to convince people to change their minds.

Notes for active learning

Voting and Other Civic Participation in Political Life

There are many ways to participate in politics, and voting is the most common way to participate in the formal governance process. While the federal government has jurisdiction over federal elections, individual registration laws vary by state.

The Constitution has three significant Amendments (15th, 19th, and 26th) that address voting rights upon which states cannot infringe. The 15th Amendment guarantees citizens the right to vote regardless of their "*race, color, or previous condition of servitude.*" The 15th Amendment was passed (1870) in the wake of the Civil War to address voter registration discrimination against former slaves.

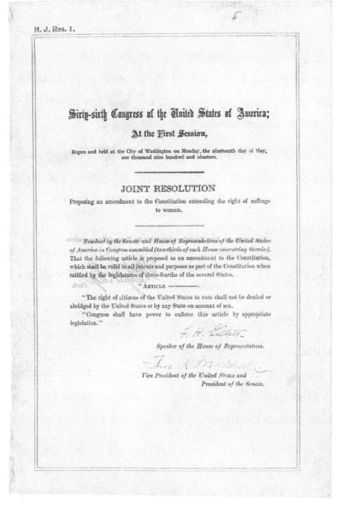

Nineteenth Amendment, voting rights for women, passed in 1920

The 19th Amendment was passed by both Houses of Congress in 1919 and ratified by the 36th state in 1920. This enfranchised 26 million women voters in time for the 1920 presidential election. In 1920, Republican President William G. Harding (1865-1923; 1921-1923) was elected. Upon Harding's death in office, he was succeeded by Republican Vice President Calvin Coolidge (1872-1933; 1923-1929).

The 26th Amendment (1971) lowered the minimum voting age from 21 to 18. To vote, citizens must first register (except in North Dakota, where registration is not required). Unlike much of the rest of the world, people of voting age are not automatically registered, and thus registration is an extra step in voting in the United States. Until the National Voter Registration Act of 1993, citizens had to go to a government office to register. After this act, citizens in most states could register to vote when they renewed their driver's license or interacted with certain other government services.

In 2015, Oregon became the first state to automatic voter registration upon receiving or renewing a driver's license. Registration laws vary between states, and several states even allow citizens to register to vote on Election Day. In contrast, some other states only have a limited window during the campaign when one can register. Several states allow voters to register online to make voter registration more convenient.

Some argue that the extra step of registering to vote is why voter turnout tends to be lower in the United States than in other developed countries. Approximately 25% of the voting-age population of the United States are not registered to vote.

In some states, those convicted of a felony are not allowed to vote for the rest of their lives, while in other states, they can vote when they are no longer on parole. In some states, one can choose to declare a party affiliation when voting, allowing them to vote in the primary for that party. Thus, if one registers as a Democrat, one can vote in the primary elections that decide which Democrat will be the nominee to run for President.

In other states, anyone can vote in primaries, and in others, those who register as independents can vote in either party's primary. However, those who register with a party cannot vote in the other party's primaries. The rules are different in each state, and thus voters must be aware of how their state operates to ascertain their eligibility.

In addition to voting in municipal elections, state elections, and national elections for President and Senate members and the House of Representatives, citizens can vote in primary elections. Primaries are how voters choose who will represent a given political party in the general election, where they will be pitted against rivals from other parties.

In states that are solidly in support of one party, the primaries are the main path to general election victory, as support for the other party is below the level needed. Given that the United States has a two-party system, voting in primaries is just as important as voting in the national elections because it is an opportunity to choose the party's nominee.

Primaries run on a state-by-state basis and are staggered so that not all states vote at once. Each state is assigned a certain number of delegates pledged to support whomever their state voted for. Some superdelegates are unpledged, meaning they can vote for whichever candidate they want, regardless of whom people voted for in the primaries. After all the primaries have been conducted, the pledged delegates and superdelegates get together and vote to determine their party's presidential nominee.

The superdelegates' existence is controversial because they tend to be party insiders and establishment figures who can sway the result against the primary voters' wishes. The problem is that the number of superdelegates can vary from election to election, meaning that the party can essentially stack the deck in favor of an individual candidate, even if voters in the primary would prefer another candidate. For this reason, some political scientists have criticized the system of superdelegates as undemocratic.

Once the primaries are decided, and national elections are held, citizens can vote for whom they want to be President, who their local representative in the House of Representatives will be, and, in rotating years, for their U.S. Senator. The presidential election is by far the most visible, as it is national, and the President holds tremendous authority. The voter turnout in the presidential election is much higher than voter turnout in the midterm congressional elections, even when held on the same day. Many people feel that the President has real power, so it does not matter whom they elect to Congress.

The assumption that the President has the most political power is erroneous. Congress is responsible for legislation and has great power in passing laws and limiting the President's authority. The constituent's Representative in the House is a local person whose job is to respond directly to those in their district of about 700,000 people (this is more of a theory than reality). The President cannot respond to every complaint or suggestion an American sends him or her, but this is the local Representative's responsibility.

Voter turnout is an essential aspect of an election. Political scientists measure voter turnout as a way of determining how legitimate a government is. If many people vote, then it is assumed that the government is legitimate in that it represents the people well. If very few people vote, then the government has legitimacy problems, as few people selected it.

A significant trend in both the United States and in mature democracies worldwide is a significant decrease in voter turnout levels from what they were in the 1960s. In the 1960s, American presidential election turnout averaged in the 60-70% range; today, it has fallen to the 50-60% range with just 49% turnout in the 1996 election.

U.S. voting booths, Nashua, New Hampshire, 2013

The determining factors that lead individuals to participate or refrain from participating in the democratic process is a significant branch of political science. Demographics provide some clues, as wealthier Americans are more likely to vote than more impoverished Americans, and older Americans are more likely to vote than younger Americans. Whites are more likely to vote than blacks and Hispanics, though this difference disappears when wealth is factored out. More educated people are more likely to vote, but more education corresponds to more wealth, making economic differences the primary demographic factor in voting patterns.

Beyond demographics, there are many reasons why people choose to refrain from exercising their right to vote. In the popular media, people who do not vote are often portrayed as apathetic, meaning they are too lazy to vote on Election Day. Studies have found little evidence to support this claim. Some people who do not vote are merely uninterested in politics and feel that they are not informed enough to vote to make a responsible choice.

Another major factor in not voting is that some people feel that neither of the two parties can represent their views, and thus they choose not to vote rather than voting for someone with whom they disagree. In some cases, voting or not voting becomes a habit, and people who have always voted continue to vote, while those who have never voted continue not to vote. When voting is a habit, elections are simply things in which one either participates without thought or does not participate without thought.

Some political scientists, however, return to the issue of legitimacy when looking at voter turnout. Rather than figuring out why people are voting less frequently and blaming this problem on individuals, they argue that governments have become less responsive to the public and, overall, less democratically legitimate.

These scholars argue that if the government did a better job of engaging the American public and delivering its promises, Americans would trust the system more and be more inclined to vote. This position is supported by polling how much Americans feel they can trust the government to do the right thing.

Until the mid-1970s, Americans overwhelmingly believed that they could trust the government to look out for the people's general well-being, regardless of which party was in power. In the 1980s, opinion shifted. The majority answered that they did not trust the government to act in their best interest, regardless of which party was in power.

This lack of trust is especially prevalent concerning Congress. Public trust in Congress has been in steady decline since 2000, and in 2014 reached an all-time low, with only 14% of Americans feeling that Congress was doing a good job. This shift, which perhaps explains a decline in voter turnout, can be traced to some causes. The Watergate scandal, which led to President Nixon's resignation for the cover-up of his operatives spying on opponents and breaking into Democratic headquarters to steal information, shook the public's faith in the government. If the President could not be trusted to obey laws, the whole political system falls into disrepute. There were similar allegations against the Obama administration (i.e., Obamagate) for the 2016 election, albeit now the invasion was electronic instead of physical intrusion.

At the same time, the Vietnam War (November 1, 1955, to April 30, 1975) led to massive public protests. At Kent State University in 1970, the Ohio National Guard opened fire on a crowd of unarmed student protesters, killing four. This incident contributed to Americans viewing the government with growing distrust.

A further shift came in the 1980s as Republican President Reagan reoriented economic policy toward deregulation and budget cutbacks. Whereas the government had previously been an expanding entity that built or enabled things, the government now shifted its focus to increasing efficiency and lowering taxes. All these factors, which decreased people's trust in government, help explain why voter turnout has plummeted.

Watergate Complex, Washington, D.C., c. 1978

In addition to general concerns about the system's legitimacy as measured by voter participation rates, the voter turnout rate is increasingly becoming a factor that may decide elections. Given that a significant number of Americans do not currently participate in the electoral process, tapping into these groups who do not vote can lead to electoral success. Rather than merely trying to get people to switch parties, which can be difficult, candidates increasingly realize that if they can inspire people who are disillusioned with the political system to vote for them, they can win.

An example of this was the 2008 presidential election won by Democrat Barack Hussein Obama. First-term Senator Obama campaigned on an inspirational message that focused on targeting people who usually did not vote. Voter turnout in that election increased by nine million votes, and Obama beat Republican Senator John McCain by just over nine million popular votes. By convincing those who typically did not vote to show up and vote for Obama, the Democrats won the presidential election.

Rallying non-voters to vote is quickly emerging as an essential campaign strategy in an era when significant numbers of people do not vote. Canadian Prime Minister Justin Trudeau accomplished a similar task in 2015. He increased his party's vote by six million, and voter turnout increased by six million, allowing him to win the election.

Canadian Prime Minister Justin Trudeau, c. 2017

There have been many proposals to increase voter turnout. These proposals differ depending on what a group or person believes explains the cause of low voter turnout. Groups like FairVote blame the electoral system for low turnout, arguing that the winner-take-all system in congressional elections is biased against third parties. They argue that the Electoral College distorts the will of the people in the presidential vote. FairVote proposes that the President be elected directly by the people in a popular vote and that Congress should use proportional representation to decide who gets a seat.

Proportional representation is the electoral system used in most other countries. If 30% of Americans vote for Party A, Party A gets 30% of the Senate's or House of Representatives seats. In the current system, Party A could get no seats with 30%, or it could get 45% of the seats. FairVote argues that because the electoral system distorts how people voted, voters become disillusioned and decide not to participate. They point to studies showing that countries using proportional representation have a significantly higher voter turnout than countries that do not.

In 2015, the Brookings Institute published a plan to increase voter turnout by focusing on the younger generation and getting them involved. They suggest that political parties need to take the first step by recruiting younger candidates. The minimum age to run for the House of Representatives is 25. The minimum age to run for the Senate is 30. However, the average age is 57 in the House and 62 in the Senate.

By recruiting younger people to run for office, Brookings argues that the government represents Americans better. Young people will be more likely to vote when they do not think of the government as being run almost exclusively by older people. They recommend making political awareness a factor in college admissions and developing more mobile phone technologies to make political participation easier.

Another popular proposal is to develop a system to allow people to vote online. While many Americans are worried that this could lead to corruption or security problems, making people able to vote online would significantly enhance access to voting and, in all likelihood, increase voter turnout. While people often claim that online voting could be "hacked," the banking and financial system's entire infrastructure is online and is not easily "hacked." However, banks and their customers' commercial interests require a continual investment in technology to secure their systems.

Getting elected as a politician is the most direct way to participate in government. However, there are many financial barriers, even to be considered a viable candidate. Democracy is premised on the idea of equality of opportunity in that anyone can run for office and win if he or she can convince the public of their views. Many political scientists have criticized the fact that running for office has become extremely expensive as replacing democracy with a plutocratic oligarchy.

A plutocratic oligarchy is a system whereby access to the necessary capital to convince others of their viability as a candidate is a necessary condition to run for most offices. Since the 2000 presidential election, candidates from the two major parties have raised one billion dollars to remain viable. Before 1971, there were no regulations on campaign finance.

However, in 1971 Congress passed the Federal Election Campaign Act to regulate spending and make campaign donations more transparent. This Act required candidates to disclose who donated to their campaigns and how much they donated. The Act was amended in 1974 to create the Federal Elections Commission (FEC). The FEC established limits on how much money a candidate could donate to their campaign, put limits on how much Political Action Committees (PACs) could donate, placed donation limits on individuals, and set overall spending limits.

In 1976, the Supreme Court struck down parts of this act; campaign spending limits were ruled unconstitutional and removed limits on how much a candidate could donate to their campaign. In the 1990s, the issue of "soft money" became a problem. While donors were limited in how much they could give to a political party as part of an election campaign, they could give unlimited amounts of "soft money," which were donations to a party to fund its operations that were not related to election campaigns.

Even though this soft money was not supposed to be used for campaigning, parties used it indirectly to help candidates win elections by running general ads or spending it on registering potential voters. By 2002, the two main parties raised and spent over $400 million of soft money.

In response, Congress passed the Bipartisan Campaign Reform Act of 2002, which more expressly outlawed soft money for political campaigns. The Act opened the ability to use "527 organizations," which are not directly part of a political party but can spend unlimited money running ads to promote their cause during an election. Much of the soft money that was now prohibited channeled into these 527 organizations. The 527 organizations spend it indirectly campaigning for their preferred candidates.

Election finance laws became even more controversial with the Supreme Court's *Citizens United* ruling, which allowed the formation of Super PACs. These PACs allowed unlimited, virtually anonymous contributions by anyone, including labor unions and corporations, which could be spent during a campaign in any way, so long as they did not directly coordinate with a political party.

The same people who ran the campaigns of the political parties served as chairs of Super PACs. Thus, Super PACs are seen by critics as fundamentally undermining previous restrictions on campaign finance. For these reasons, it can be difficult for someone who is not wealthy and connected to run for office.

Since donating money is another way of participating in an election, campaign finance and spending are important issues. Suppose ordinary people pitching in with a few small donations end up not mattering because a Super PAC can spend unlimited corporate or union money. In that case, the democratic intent of elections is undermined.

As of the 2016 federal election, corporate donations directly to parties are banned but are funneled through Super PACs. Individuals may donate $2,700 per year per candidate. An individual may donate an additional $5,000 to a PAC, a total of $10,000 to a local or state political party, and $100,200 per year to a national political party. These numbers reflect the maximums as of 2016 and are periodically adjusted.

There is no longer a limit on the total amount of donations one can make to candidates. If someone had enough money, they could donate in one year $2,700 to every candidate in each of the 435 districts that make up the House of Representatives and an additional $2,700 to every candidate in each of the 100 Senatorial candidates. This amount applies to each of the primaries and general elections; $5,400 per candidate. Previously, there were limits on the total aggregate amount of money one person could spend, but the Supreme Court struck down these limits in *McCutcheon v. FEC* (2014).

Seal of the Supreme Court of the United States

Other Forms of Political Participation

While voting is the only official means of participating in government, there are plenty of other ways to participate in politics in a non-official capacity. Beginning with the aspects which take the least amount of effort and involve a minimum amount of participation, citizens can participate politically by sending letters or emails to their local Representative.

While a Representative may not read every letter he or she receives, someone on their staff will. This staffer then summarizes for the Representative an idea of what issues concern their constituents. Thus, by writing letters and sending emails, a constituent can request their Representative consider an issue. If persuasive, it may be passed to the Representative who reads it and replies. Similarly, one can sign petitions sent to politicians to demonstrate that the public cares about an issue enough to sign their name.

If one has more time and feels very strongly about an issue to the point that writing a letter does not seem to be enough, one can join an interest group and attempt to lobby the government. Many interest groups that defend the public interest rely on volunteers and run periodical lobbying campaigns. These groups look for supporters to help with their activities. Another way to participate politically is to talk about political issues with people.

Since some people may be reticent to discuss controversial political topics, a common source to find an in-depth discussion on political issues is on the Internet, where debaters can remain anonymous. There are websites where people can find vigorous discussions of political issues among people who want to talk about politics. Participating in these discussions can help people develop informed opinions, and it allows advocates to try to convince others of these political opinions. Democracy, in its purest sense, involves discussing and debating politics with others.

During an election campaign, the best way to participate in politics is to work on the campaign team. Candidates rely on a support team for various roles. They need people to call potential supporters, ask for donations, drive people to the polling station on election day, go door to door with the candidate, hand out flyers and campaign material, and convince other people to support them. Candidates need scrutineers to go to a polling station and make sure the voting happens without problems. Both parties may send a scrutineer to ensure that the election workers do not do anything that supports one party over the other.

The most involved someone can be in politics is becoming an activist and joining a group dedicated to a cause. Activist groups often engage in a diversity of tactics to promote their cause, including writing material to convince others to support their cause, holding information sessions, organizing people to support their cause, and participating in protests and demonstrations. A protest is the most democratic form of participation as it opens politics up to everyone, allowing anyone to participate.

Protest movements have been significant in leading to significant advances in American history, from winning the eight-hour workday to allowing women to vote, through the civil rights movement. When the government refuses to act, political participation through protest can provide an effective means of participating directly in political change.

Recently, protests such as Occupy Wall Street have made economic inequality part of the national conversation. Increasingly, these protest movements are being organized online, making them easy to find and join.

Civil Rights movement protest, c. 1965

There are reasons why activists hold a public protest. The first is to make an issue visible to the broader public. When thousands of people show up to protest and cause a disruption, the media shows up and covers the event. The cause of the protest will be discussed, and the public learns about issues that they may not have been exposed to.

Before the major protests in Seattle in 1999, few people had heard of the World Trade Organization (WTO). After the protests became national news for weeks, anyone who watched the news knew about the treaty and how it was problematic for workers' rights and the environment.

Seattle Ministerial Conference of the WTO, 1999

The second reason to protest is to demonstrate and create power. When the government sees thousands and thousands of people marching in the street, all united for a cause, it demonstrates that people are serious about an issue and that the government must do something about it.

In 2006, when the Democratic House of Representatives, under Speaker Nancy Pelosi, passed a bill calling for undocumented migrant workers' deportation, protests were organized by pro-immigrant and Hispanic groups and their allies. Half a million people marched in Los Angeles, and 300,000 people marched in Chicago. The House of Representatives noticed these demonstrations and realized that they would be in much trouble with voters if they went forward with this bill.

As a result of the protests, the deportation bill was removed from the legislative process's committee phase. The third reason for protests is to demonstrate solidarity. Sometimes something happens, which is perceived as an injustice, and people want to show that they care and support the victims of injustice.

In 2014, solidarity-based protests occurred in Ferguson, Missouri, as people took to the streets to show their support for a young man. He was shot and killed by police under suspicious circumstances. A person may join a protest on a specific issue out of solidarity. When gay and lesbian groups organized protests bans on same-sex marriage, many people who were not gay joined the protests in a show of solidarity because they believed everyone should be treated equally under the law.

Related to solidarity is that joining a protest can form political networks, leading to other forms of action. Politics is an inherently collective activity; one cannot merely engage in politics alone; it must be done against others. Protests can help people establish connections for future forms of non-protest activity.

After the WTO protests in Seattle, many people connected, leading to environmental lobbying groups and even an online news website geared towards political activists. Those non-protest political activities would not have happened if political networks were not established by individuals joining up with each other at a protest.

Protests are exciting and energizing. Marching in the street and joining up with thousands of people is exhilarating. The feeling of participating directly in political action can inspire people to do other political activities. Many of the activists who marched with Dr. Martin Luther King Jr. became prominent politicians and community leaders during the civil rights movement and beyond. Some people who are part of significant protest movements report that being involved in those protests changed their lives and made them better people.

Civil Rights leader, Dr. Martin Luther King Jr.

Even if a massive protest does not achieve its immediate goals, the inspiration that many individuals take from becoming politically engaged in such a direct way ends up having lasting effects. While the current media discourse tends to portray mass protests as ineffective, this view ignores the above factors and tends to see protests as only marching around holding signs.

Protests can take various forms, including direct action and civil disobedience. General strikes were once the primary form of protest, in which everyone would not show up for work for a day, thus shutting down the whole economy. Considering that mass public protests in Egypt and Tunisia in 2014 were able to overthrow dictatorships, protests remain a useful tool of democratic participation.

Notes for active learning

Factors That Influence Differences in Political Beliefs and Behaviors

There are various ways to participate in government and an almost limitless range of opinions people have on any political topic. What are some of the factors that lead people to hold one set of opinions over another? The family plays a significant role, as children tend to adopt the political views of their parents. The strong influence of the family demonstrates how people tend to absorb the views of those around them. *Demographics* describe statistical data related to a population. It is the term for when political scientists study these environmental factors, which influence what people believe.

Some demographic divisions are essential factors explaining differences in political views. While demographic factors do a poor job of explaining participation, they provide information on what people are more likely to believe. When political scientists analyze demographics, they do not view these relationships as causal but as correlational.

Blacks are more liberal than whites. However, political scientists should not assume that skin color is determinative of political views. Instead, the relationship establishes a correlation (statistical relationship), not causation (direct cause and effect).

Religion is one of the significant demographic factors which can lead to differences in values and belief. Sometimes the content of religious beliefs can form a causal relation with political views. However, the connection between religion and political views is merely correlational and is explained better by other factors. Over the years, political scientists studying the correlation between religion and political views have found some general correlational trends.

Roman Catholics tend to tilt to the left on economic issues, while Protestants tend to tilt to the right on economic issues. Both groups are correlated to right-wing social views. Jews tend to lean more to the left on social and economic issues than either Catholics or Protestants. It should be emphasized that these are general trends. It has been observed (i.e., correlation) that more than half of people in these groups tend to gravitate toward similar beliefs on specific issues.

Some studies of opinion polling on social and economic issues have identified a strong connection between one's political views and the intensity of religious beliefs. These studies argue this connection's main factor is not their denomination, but how devout one is.

There are noticeable differences in the voting patterns between the sexes. Since the 1960s, women have increasingly moved to support the Democrats, while men's voting patterns have stayed the same. Today, women disproportionately vote for Democrats compared to men.

Studies have shown statistically significant differences in critical social issues between men and women. Women are more likely to favor some gun control regulations and less military spending, and they tend to support legislation against workplace harassment. Interestingly, other issues seem to be more relevant to women (e.g., abortion), show no statistically significant difference in opinion between men and women.

Another primary source of demographic differences relates to race. Regarding affirmative action and treatment by police, racial differences can be significant in people's political views. On other issues, such as the length of prison sentences and whether one would vote for a black President, there were no significant differences in opinion.

Age is another significant demographic factor, as young people and older people tend to diverge on many issues. Part of this is explained because younger and older people have different concerns. However, much of it relates that older people became politically socialized in an earlier era with different political values, making their views seem more conservative.

In addition to analyzing the traits of groups of people, the second significant aspect of demographics is the study of where people live. There is a robust correlation between being more right-wing and living in a rural area, whereas living in a large city is correlated with being more on the left of the political spectrum because the large cities offer more social programs for its residents. Therefore, where government-sponsored social programs are vital, residents may move to a liberal large city with an extensive safety net.

The region in which one lives is a significant demographic factor for predicting what most people might believe. The South tends to be more conservative, whereas the west coast tends to be more liberal.

Regional factors can change over time. At the turn of the 19th century, rural areas were more likely to support left-wing economic causes, as rural farmers formed the base of support for the Progressive Party of Democratic presidential nominee William Jennings Bryan (1860-1925; 1896, 1900, 1908).

With time this has changed, and today farmers tend to be more conservative. The same is true for what parts of the country tend to believe. While the American South is staunchly conservative and overwhelmingly Republican, it used to be the base of support for Democrats. Therefore, although factors like where someone lives can be reliable indicators of political views, their beliefs, and allegiance to political parties may shift.

Campaign poster for William J. Bryan, American politician, c. 1900

A reason why a similar group shifts from one belief to another over time is related to demographic changes. If the demographic makeup of those who live in a region changes, then the dominant beliefs may change. At the same time, if someone is a member of a demographic group that tends to believe in a specific set of political values, those values may differ from the region's values in which they live. If a person lives in Texas, there is a significant chance they support the Republicans. However, with the changing demographics within sections of Texas, this supposition is becoming less valid. For blacks and Hispanic voters, they are more likely to support Democrats. However, blacks and Hispanics living in Texas are less likely to support Democrats than blacks or Hispanics living in California.

After personal traits and geography, the other major demographic factor is wealth. How wealthy someone is, usually measured by their tax bracket or the socioeconomic class of their profession, tends to be one of the most reliable indicators of political views. Very wealthy Americans tend to be more conservative, while working-class Americans tend to be more left-wing on economic issues.

Wealth and class tend to be causal factors in political beliefs. Republicans tend to favor tax cuts and programs that limit the government's size and responsibility, thus leading prosperous people to support Republicans. Working-class and impoverished people are likely to support redistributive progressive tax policies and programs that offer taxpayer-funded programs.

A significant exception includes people who strongly identify as "very religious." Even if they are relatively impoverished, the religious factor tends to be more critical in shaping their beliefs and self-reliance values. Thus, people who identify as "very religious" but are working-class are more conservative than the working class who are slightly religious or not religious.

All these factors influence each other and play a role in a person's political socialization and ideological views. While these factors can combine, and it might be tempting to conclude an individual's political beliefs prematurely, everyone is different and can be unpredictable. Most people's beliefs may not be shared in the same economic, social, geographical, or religious group.

When political scientists – and political parties looking for areas they can target to win votes – look at a district, they use all these demographic factors to predict what people are likely to believe and how they are likely to vote. A dense urban district on the west coast with more women and a majority of African Americans will likely vote for the

Democrats. This demographic contains factors that are indicators of being more on the left side of the political spectrum.

Political parties use these demographic guesses to build their campaign strategy, and policymakers use demographic information to target specific government programs in certain areas. Thus, even though demographic data cannot predict exactly what everyone might think. Demographic data can give political parties and policymakers an idea of where specific programs and campaigns are more likely to succeed.

Political scientists are generally interested in finding correlations between political views and demographics to determine how possible future population changes may affect the political climate.

Notes for active learning

Notes for active learning

Notes for active learning

Chapter 5

Political Parties,
Interest Groups, Mass Media

Political parties, elections, political action committees (PACs), labor unions, special interest groups, and mass media allow citizens to organize and communicate their interests and concerns. Historical evolutions of the U.S. party system, the functions and structures of political parties, and their effects on the political process can have been significant. Party reforms and campaign strategies, and financing in the electronic age provide essential perspectives.

Elections, election laws, and election systems on the national and state levels provide a framework for understanding parties' nature and individual voting behavior. PACs' development, their role in elections, and the ideological and demographic differences between major parties and third parties are critical factors.

Political roles played by varieties of the lobby and interest groups and what they do, how they do it, and how this affects both the political process and public policy can be critical to understanding the state of modern U.S. politics.

Equally important are the significant influences the media has in influencing public opinion, voter perceptions, campaign strategies, electoral outcomes, agenda development, and the public images and stances of officials and candidates. The relationship between candidates, elected officials, and the media is symbiotic and frequently conflicting.

The goals and incentives of the media industry can influence the nature of news coverage itself. The increasing consolidation of major media outlets and the growing role of the Internet both carry consequences.

Political Parties and Elections

The role of political parties is not mentioned in the Constitution. Political parties resulted from the natural evolution of the American political system. In a representative democracy, political parties were thought of as a necessary evil. The framers of the Constitution, especially the *Federalist Papers* authors, were extremely skeptical of political parties.

The Federalists believed that partisan attachment to a party would cause unhealthy strife and division. The current climate of extreme partisan division certainly demonstrates that the founders were correct. What the constitutional framers did not realize was that representative democracy could not effectively function without parties.

Functions

In a modern context, the most important question is not whether there should be political parties, but how many there should be. Like other nations, America has a multi-party system with several registered parties that run candidates. However, America is unique in the continuing dominance of two specific parties over a long period.

In other countries, there are more (sometimes many more) than two major parties. There are at least three major parties in Canada and the United Kingdom and several secondary parties with seats in the legislatures. In Brazil, there are often more than seven major parties elected.

In the American system, it is tough for a third party to win elections because of numerous laws, control of public opinion by the schools and news media, and how entrenched the two-party system is in the present governmental framework. Having only two parties implies that there are only two different sets of political beliefs, with voters choosing one. There are many political views and ideologies, and having more parties would allow more choice for voters and, therefore, better representation.

Approximately one-third of U.S. voters identify as independent, meaning they feel only a tenuous connection to either of the two main parties. The more precise term is unenrolled or unaffiliated because, in some states, "Independent" is a designation that a voter can select during the registration process. Some voters with strong beliefs register as unaffiliated/unenrolled or independent if they live in a state where most other voters align with the opposite major party. Since voter registration is public information, they might feel inhibited from being in the minority in their political views. In general, unaffiliated registered voters are highly sought-after during elections hoping they may be persuaded to vote for a party (swing voters).

Regardless of opinion on political parties, the parties perform necessary functions within the political system's congressional and presidential branches. One of their primary functions is recruiting candidates to run for office. Because parties want to win elections, they put much effort into recruiting "distinguished," high-profile people, which usually helps ensure that qualified candidates get elected.

Parties play an essential role during elections to convince citizens to exercise their vote and rallying supporters. When parties provide resources to help ensure their supporters go to the polling booth on Election Day, this is "getting out the vote" or GOTV. Voter turnouts in the United States are relatively low compared to most other developed, democratic nations. The ability of parties to mobilize their volunteers to ensure that their supporters vote for them is crucial—it can be enough to decide an election.

Organization

The United States uses a system called "single-member plurality." Any candidate may run for a House or Senate seat, and the winner is simply the one who scores the largest share of the votes, even if it is less than 50% (in those elections where there are more than two candidates). Each district is decided independently. Canada and Britain are the only other countries to use this system.

Much of the democratic world uses proportional representation; each party's number is matched to the party's level of support. Ballot access laws affect when a party can field candidates. They differ from state to state, but they originate with designations in federal law.

Political parties are categorized into three types: "major," "minor," and "new." New parties field candidates in an election for the first time or have sponsored candidates in elections but have not obtained more than 5% of the vote. Campaign law mandates that media corporations give a minimum amount of free advertising time to political parties and provide funding subsidies for presidential campaigns higher for the major parties than for minor or new parties. Since the elected members of Congress passed this law, it was voted into law only by members of the two major parties, which receive undue advantages.

Left: logo of the Republican Party of the United States of America.
Abbreviation GOP stands for "Grand Old Party."
Right: the official logo of the United States Democratic Party

The Green Party and the Libertarian Party are political parties still considered new. They are eligible for significantly less free media time and federal funding allowances for their presidential campaigns than the two major parties. This is true despite having fielded numerous candidates for President, Congress, and other partisan elections.

Minor parties are those that have obtained more than 5% in a previous election. Major parties are those who obtained over 15% of the vote in the previous election. Only the Democratic and Republican Parties currently qualify as major parties and are eligible for the benefits which major parties receive under this self-serving law.

The official logos of the Libertarian Party of the United States (left),
and the Green Party of the United States (right).

American political campaigns depend heavily on funding, media exposure (including advertising and debates), and mobilization of people and resources. Funding and media exposure are strongly regulated by law. The process by which federal candidates (i.e., President, Representative, and Senator) are elected is a complicated system detailed precisely in the Constitution. In practice, these have led to moral dilemmas.

Americans have been resistant to modifying the system outlined in the Constitution or supporting new parties. America had a long period of new parties in earlier years. Voters in other nations routinely facilitate newly formed parties to win legislative seats.

Development

When a group of people discusses political issues, sides naturally form over issues, leading to alliances. This is how the party system evolved in the United States. Parties are necessary for voters to choose the country's direction instead of merely voting for the person representing them.

By having political parties that set forth different visions for how the country should be governed, called a platform, voters can choose which vision they like better and thus have a say in how the country is governed. Without political parties, elections would be mere popularity contests, and voters would not choose the country's direction.

Although the Democratic and Republican Parties now seem so entrenched to the point where seemingly no new party could ever achieve significant gains, the American party system has evolved. Parties first arose over federalism, or how powerful the central government should be compared to state governments. Eventually, the split on this issue led to Federalist and anti-Federalist factions, which evolved into loose alliances seen as precursors to political parties.

Thomas Jefferson named his anti-Federalist party the Democratic-Republicans. While this name may seem strange in today's political climate, today's prevailing parties' names are not descriptive of their beliefs. Today's Democrats believe in republicanism; they wish to retain the existing system based on popular authority and do not wish to create a monarchy.

The Republican Party believes in democracy; they do not wish to replace elections with dictatorship. Jefferson's Democratic-Republican Party was an apt description of his party's ideology and not a contradiction. Jefferson's Democratic-Republican Party eventually won comprehensive support. Until Whig Party nominee Andrew Jackson won the presidency in 1824, all Presidents identified with the Democratic-Republicans, and there was no real opposition party.

Thomas Jefferson, founder of the Democratic-Republicans, c. 1804

The first real political party, in the modern sense, arose in the wake of President Andrew Jackson's loss of the 1824 presidential election to the 6th President John Quincy Adams (son of the second President John Adams). Wealthy, slaveowner planter Andrew Jackson won the popular vote for President but lost the Electoral College election.

Jackson's supporters created the Democratic Party to oppose the government of President John Quincy Adams. After Jackson (1767-1845; 1829-1837) won the subsequent presidential election, those opposed to Jackson's presidency rallied to form the Whig Party in opposition. In 1830, Jackson signed the Indian Removal Act, which forcibly relocated about sixty thousand Native Americans to Indian Reservations (Trail of Tears).

When slavery became a significant issue in 1850, both the Democratic and Whig parties split into pro-slavery and anti-slavery factions. Around the same time, the Republican Party coalesced from a combination of the anti-slavery wing of the Democrats in the South and the northern anti-slavery Whig faction.

The Democratic Party consisted mainly of pro-slavery Southerners and settlers of the western frontier. The few remaining Northern Democrats then formed their party, but this system was thoroughly disrupted with the Civil War outbreak.

After the Civil War, the current two-party system emerged, with the Republicans garnering support from the North and blacks in the South, while the white South supported the Democrats. Even after abolishing slavery, the parties were still primarily defined by whether they supported or opposed slavery before the Civil War.

Andrew Jackson, presidential candidate of 1824

In the late 1800s, a new party emerged, called the People's Party, known as the Populists. The Populist party was supported by poor cotton farmers in the South and wheat farmers suffering from drought in the West and advocated replacing the gold standard with silver. The party was critical of the urban banking system and sought sweeping agricultural reform and a better life for farmers.

In 1892, the Populist ticket of James B. Weaver and James G. Field won 8.5% of the popular vote and won five states in the Electoral College. The Populists added some members in Congress. In 1896, the prominent party member William Jennings Bryan won the Democratic nomination for President, essentially merging the Democrats and the People's Party. Bryan lost the election to Republican William McKinley (1843-1901; 1897 until his assassination on September 14, 1901)

In the early 1900s, a new faction of Progressives emerged. Progressives sought to regulate industrialists and bring more power to the average American. Members of both of the parties expressed support for Progressivism. In 1912, the Progressives officially became a political party after a split in the Republican Party between President Theodore Roosevelt (1858-1919; 1901-1909) and President William Howard Taft (1857-1930; 1909-1913).

Teddy Roosevelt led the Progressive Party (popularly called the Bull Moose Party) to a strong showing in the 1912 Presidential election. However, Teddy Roosevelt split the Republican vote, which allowed Democrat Thomas Woodrow Wilson (1856-1924; 1913-1921) to win the presidency.

Progressives contested the 1914 legislative elections and won five seats. Significantly, the party ran some women candidates in this election. By 1918, however, the party faded from a lack of electoral success. Most of those who initially split from the Republican Party did not rejoin it after the Progressive Party's deterioration; the remaining Republicans became more conservative after the split of 1912.

Theodore Roosevelt (left) and William Howard Taft (right),
26th and 27th Presidents of the United States, respectively

With the stock market crash of 1929 and the onset of the Great Depression, the Democrats shifted their political orientation with the New Deal to become more liberal. Based on the New Deal's popularity, the Democrats were able to combine their newfound support from the northern working class with traditional support in the South. The New Deal-era Democrats (1932-1969) appealed to African Americans, marking the first shift of black voters away from the Republican Party. When the New Deal Democrats under Lyndon Baines Johnson began supporting the civil rights movement in the 1960s, white southerners switched from their traditional allegiance to the Democratic Party to support the Republicans. This party system largely remains intact today, but historically, changes and party ideology shifts are possible.

Since the 1960s, there have been some significant challenges by third-party candidates. In 1992, Texas billionaire Henry Ross Perot (1930-2019) ran an effective presidential campaign as an Independent. He received a massive 18.9% of the popular vote. This was the most significant challenge to the two-party system since Teddy Roosevelt's Progressives (1901-1909). Perot did not win any states in the Electoral College, and after unsuccessfully trying to create the new Reform Party, he withdrew from the political stage.

In 2000, political activist Ralph Nader (b. 1934; consumer protection, environmentalism, government reform) ran an effective third-party presidential campaign as the Green Party leader. He won 2.7% of the vote in an election that ended as a virtual tie between the Democrats and Republicans. Many Democrats blamed the support of Ralph Nader as costing them the election. The Green Party faded from prominence.

Ross Perot, American businessman, c. 2015

Effects on the Political Process

It is at the level of policy formation where political parties are the most influential. First, an issue needing action is identified. The course of action to take can be significantly influenced by the ideology of the party in power. If unemployment becomes an issue, a pro-labor party seeks solutions that differ from the pro-business party's solution.

While both may agree that the issue demands attention, the political party's ideology drives which policy solutions are enacted. Parties have Congressional Whips whose function is to encourage individual Representatives to follow the party line. This partisan political pressure makes going against the party fraught with danger, even if the party policy is contrary to constituents' interests.

When political parties bog down the policy formation and decision process, an issue may become highly visible in the media. One political party may oppose the other party's solution to appear oppositional, even if they mostly agree in principle. Small differences in procedures and implementations can escalate into contentious issues and undermine the broad agreement. This is *partisanship* and creates unnecessary and undue obstacles by promoting a disagreement over trivial details.

Critics of partisanship maintain that these arguments over small details obscure that Congress is not considering big-picture alternatives. For example, during the occupation of Iraq, partisan arguments focused on minor details like the types of equipment supplied to the military, rather than questioning significant strategy issues and whether the occupation effectively achieved the overall policy agenda.

By engaging in complex arguments over small details, political parties generate the perception of significant differences in their ideologies. Voters believe they have an important choice to make. Some politicians try to become intentional obstacles in the policy process to curry favor (e.g., campaign donations) from special interest groups advancing an agenda.

The politician who blocks this agenda is positioned to exert disproportionate influence, even while agreeing with the policy's theory. This public perception of opposition (or even support) can be compared to their voting record to determine what a politician does (i.e., voting on issues) instead of what they say. Additionally, politicians' campaign donations are a matter of public record and can be matched to the endorser (i.e., lobbyist) of specific issues.

Electoral Laws and Systems

The Federal Election Commission (FEC) writes and publishes rules on parties and candidates' conduct and rights in all United States elections. Its publication, *Federal Election Campaign Laws*, contains the complete list of electoral and campaign funding laws and is available on their website.

Campaign funding comes in different forms and is regulated by law. Direct contributions to individual candidates' campaigns are allowed from individuals, corporations and labor unions, and even foreign contributors. However, these permitted amounts are held to specific limits. For example, an individual can donate up to $5,400 to any federal campaign. However, there are ways in which these laws can be circumvented.

Presidential Elections

Before discussing the processes by which a candidate is nominated to run for President, it is essential to understand the criteria for running for office. Article II, Section 1 of the Constitution states, *"No person except a natural born citizen, or a citizen of the United States, at the time of the adoption of this Constitution, shall be eligible to the Office of the President; neither shall any person be eligible to that Office who shall not have attained to the age of thirty-five years, and been fourteen years a resident within the United States."* This creates specific criteria required to be a candidate for President. There are additional state criteria for presidential eligibility. However, these are too numerous to be covered.

The United States has a two-party system on the federal electoral level. This section discusses how a person can be nominated by a political party to run for President at one of the two major parties' conventions. The process begins with registration as a candidate in the state and ends with the eventual nomination at the party's convention. These national conventions are usually held the summer before the November general election.

There are two major forms of primaries in the presidential nomination process: caucuses and typical primaries. Primaries are the most common way a candidate is selected to run as the party representative for President. Different parties decide the specific rules of the primary process. There is some leeway given to the states for the process of selecting a nominee.

The Democratic Party's rules insist that some degree of *proportional representation* must be used. To receive a proportional number of delegates, a candidate must receive at least 15% of the vote statewide. This minimum threshold is in place to prevent a candidate from receiving a disproportionate number of delegates in select districts through pandering to the interests of distinct communities living in a constituency. This method is like the Electoral College system of awarding votes in the general election. The minimum statewide support mechanism allows the candidates who have the broadest support to achieve the maximum number of delegates. This prevents a fractured (or brokered) convention where multiple candidates have a similar number of delegates.

1916 Democratic Party National Convention

For Republicans, how delegates are allocated is, in keeping with the Republicans' general respect for states' rights, decided on a state-by-state basis. This has been a point of contention, as some in the public claim that electoral committees in heavily Republican states use this ability to disenfranchise individual voters.

Caucuses are the second major means by which the parties select their candidate for President. Caucuses are held in Iowa, Texas, and Nevada. This type of electoral process is less organized than the more formal primary voting process. Small but vocal portions of the electorate can have an outsized influence in the nominating process.

The Iowa Caucus is an example where many of those who actively participate in caucusing are Evangelical Christians, who are unrepresentative of the nation at large. As a result, candidates that are not very prominent on the national stage (e.g., Rick Santorum in 2012) have won the Iowa Caucus even though he lacked national support.

Once an individual has won a state primary or caucus, that candidate is awarded a corresponding number of delegates at the respective party's national convention. *Pledged delegates* are those delegates awarded through an electoral process.

Presidential candidate Rick Santorum campaigning for Iowa Caucus, January 2012

Less critical, though crucial in gaining the nomination, is a smaller number of *super-delegates*, who can cast their vote in favor of which candidate they favor. These delegates are Representatives of the respective party's "establishment." They often vote as a unified block in favor of the candidate who either represents the status quo or is thought to have the best chance of victory in the general election.

Once all state primaries and caucuses have been held, a party convention is held the summer before the general election. There is usually a decisive winner regarding pledged delegates and super-delegates' support, making the convention itself merely a formality. Before the spread of mass communication technologies, conventions were an occasion for the parties and their candidate to hammer out a reliable electoral "platform" of positions on which the candidate would run. In the present day, this function continues as a formality and is not necessary.

Because one primary candidate usually has an outright majority of support, there is usually only the need for one ballot to name a nominee. Should this not be the case, there is a *brokered convention* whereby all political maneuvering is practiced by shifting delegates to one candidate. This is infrequent because even if there is a relatively equal split in electoral support, the superdelegates have enough power to sway the balance in favor of a candidate.

Once the party has chosen its nominee, the candidate gives a nomination acceptance speech to the assembled convention, stirring up enthusiasm for their proposed path to victory. The convention is often when the presidential nominee announces their choice of vice-presidential nominee, creating the presidential ticket.

Once a party has chosen the candidate they wish to put forth for President, the respective nominee begins campaigning for the general election. The winner of the presidential general election is decided through the Electoral College. The Electoral College is responsible for electing the President. It is commonly believed that the person elected to the Office of the President is chosen through direct democracy.

The person who wins the majority of the popular vote is not automatically declared the winner. This result has occurred several times throughout American history. In the United States, the Electoral College votes and decides such matters. The Electoral College is the number of "votes" each state can allocate for a presidential nominee. The number of Electoral College votes that each state is allocated is directly proportional to the relative number of people residing in the state.

The number of Electoral College votes ranges from California's 55 electoral votes to Alaska, Delaware, Montana, North Dakota, South Dakota, Vermont, and Wyoming's three electoral votes. The six states with the most electors are California (55), Texas (38), Florida (29), New York (29), Illinois (29), and Pennsylvania (20). These numbers are subject to change based on the 10-year census.

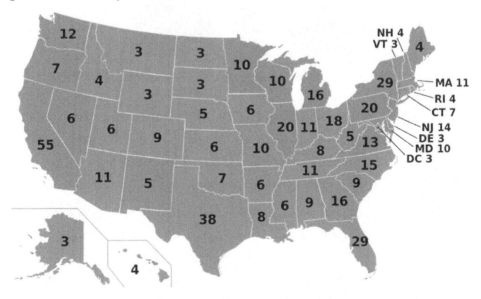

The United States Electoral College map, 2020

How one wins the Electoral College votes in each state vary, but the general rule is that the winner takes all. A candidate who receives a 50%+1 vote in the state is awarded 100% of the Electoral College votes. Exceptions of this method are for Nebraska and Maine.

Some consider this a biased system for choosing a President because votes above 50%+1 in a state are not awarded. The majority candidate has been awarded the electoral votes in that state. All voters who contributed to the losing candidate are not counted in selecting a President, with their vote essentially wasted.

Due to the Electoral College process, the elected President is often not representative of the electorate. An example of this was the 2000 General Election, where Al Gore beat George Bush in the popular vote (i.e., received more popular votes). However, George Bush won the Electoral College and was elected the 43rd President of the United States.

Al Gore, American politician and environmentalist, c. 2000.

The Electoral College process of electing the President is controversial in the modern era, as some feel that their voices are not heard and that the candidate who wins does not represent much of the country. This electoral process creates "Red States" and "Blue States," which tend to select candidates from one party in presidential elections.

Presidential candidates tend to ignore the desires of these states in favor of a strategy intended to win "purple states," known as "swing states" (which tend to be more politically centrist or mixed). This leads to candidates shifting their platforms to the political "center" to garner voters who are not loyal to one party. Partisans on either the right-wing or the left-wing of American politics argue that this process waters down the potential for change and often leads to a candidate's hands being tied when advocating policies for change.

Thus, there is a movement to abolish the Electoral College, but it has been unsuccessful so far. In Nebraska and Maine states, it has been neutralized, bypassing state laws that require that their Electoral College votes be given in proportion to each candidate's level of votes in the state rather than the winner taking all of them. However, this has a minor effect so far because these two states have a tiny share of the Electoral College.

Congressional Branch

In the United States, Congress is designed to be far more powerful than the executive or judicial branches, intended to represent the American people. However, Congress' power is more diffused. Many people incorrectly believe Congress is the weakest branch since there are 435 Representatives.

The United States Senate is the higher house of Congress with 100 members (U.S. Senators), two Senators per state regardless of the population's size. The longer-serving Senator for a state is the "senior Senator." The more recently elected Senator is the "junior Senator," irrespective of their age and political experience. The House of Representatives is the lower house but is the most populous branch of the federal government's elected portion, with 435 members as U.S. Representatives.

Senators serve staggered six-year terms in three different groups (referred to as Class I, II, and III). Every two years, approximately one-third of the seats are up for election. Additionally, they are staggered so that only one Senate seat per state is up for reelection during an election year. Members of Congress elected to the House of Representatives serve two-year terms, with all House of Representatives seats up for election on every even-numbered year.

Eligibility to become a Senator is based on three criteria detailed in Article 1, Section 3 of the U.S. Constitution. First, the individual must be at least 30 years old. Second, the individual must have been a U.S. citizen for at least the past nine years before their election bid. Third, the individual must live in the state where they are running for office.

To be eligible for election to the House of Representatives, an individual must be a resident of the state they wish to represent, a United States citizen, and at least twenty-five years of age. Each state is partitioned into congressional districts consisting of about 700,000 residents. Each constituency elects an individual member of the House of Representatives as their Representative in Congress.

The House of Representatives has a fixed number of electoral districts. However, these 435 seats of the lower house are apportioned according to each state's population, per the Constitution. Thus, every decade, according to the most recent population census, the 435 seats are redistributed as each state's share of the American population changes. This means that those district boundaries are redrawn on the electorate map. This redrawing of districts for the House of Representatives (the lower House) raises questions and criticisms because it is prone to partisan manipulation. Questions arise as to who gets to redraw the map and what criteria they use.

In 1812, the concept of "gerrymandering" was first tried by its namesake, Democratic-Republican Massachusetts Governor Elbridge Gerry. Governor Gerry chose to cynically redraw district boundaries to ensure that his candidates would have a better chance of winning. In modern times, accusations have been made that gerrymandering minimizes or "compresses" the number of electoral districts in which Blacks, Hispanics, and other minorities can vote, thus lowering the number of Representatives they can elect.

Political cartoon of the newly drawn Massachusetts State Senate district of South Essex created by the legislature to favor of the Democratic-Republican Party candidates Governor Elbridge Gerry over the Federalists (1812)

Senate and House elections occur on even-numbered years on the first Tuesday after the first Monday in November (Election Day). In election years, all house seats and one-third of Senate seats are up for contestation. In the months before Election Day, primary elections are held for each political party in different states to determine the nominees who will run in the general election for each party. Primaries give the American people more influence in the nominee selection process than party leaders to select nominees.

Not all primaries are structured the same and vary from state to state. There are six variations: closed primaries, semi-closed primaries, open primaries, semi-open primaries, partisan blanket primaries, and nonpartisan blanket parties.

Closed primaries are elections in which only people who are registered members of a political party can vote in their party's primary election. Independents, non-partisans, or unaffiliated voters, those who are not members of a political party, cannot vote.

Semi-closed primaries are like closed primaries in that registered party members can only vote for candidates in their political party. However, independents, non-partisans, or unaffiliated voters can vote and choose one of the party primaries to vote in either at the polling station or by registering with a party on Election Day.

Open primaries are elections in which registered voters can vote in any party primary of their choosing regardless of personal party affiliation.

Pick-a-party primary is a colloquial term sometimes used because voters can choose which party to vote for on Election Day. "Party raiding" can occur during open primaries, when members of one party vote in the other party's primaries to elect a perceived weaker candidate and thus increase their party's chances of victory in the general election. In open primaries, no party-specific ballots are printed, and voters can select the party they want to vote for in their voting booth on a single ballot.

Semi-open primaries are contests in which registered voters do not need to declare the party primary they will be participating in before arriving at their polling station. Instead, after being identified by election officials, voters are to request a party-specific ballot. This party-specific ballot is what differentiates semi-open from open primaries.

A *blanket primary* is a system in which voters can mix the parties they vote for according to each office. A person might vote for a Democratic Senate candidate and vote for a Republican Representative candidate on the same ballot.

A *non-partisan blanket primary* (also called "top-two primary") is a primary in which voters are not restricted to candidates from one party. All candidates run one ballot, and the top two vote-getters compete in the general election regardless of their party affiliation. These top two candidates can be from the same or different political parties.

Louisiana's primary (a state with a long history of holding nonpartisan blanket primaries) is another variation of a non-partisan primary. However, this election is held on Federal Election Day. In this primary, all candidates run one ballot. If one candidate receives most of the vote (50% + 1 vote), that candidate is declared a winner (in Louisiana). If there is no majority winner, the top two vote-getters (regardless of their party) have a runoff election in December to determine the winner.

The *partisan blanket primary* is where all candidates run on one ballot. Then, the top vote-getter from each represented party runs in the general election. Currently, Alaska is the only state that uses this type of primary election. Participation of each party is voluntary because the Supreme Court ruled (2000) that states cannot require political parties to participate in blanket primaries.

Party nominations for U.S. Senators and U.S. Representatives in some states are decided during their spring or summer political conventions instead of a ballot voting system. These conventions often rely on voice votes, indicating continued confidence in the incumbent candidate or a lack of consensus. In the latter case, a "floor fight" can ensue where delegates vote on representing their party in the general election.

Notes for active learning

Notes for active learning

Interest Groups, Including Political Action Committees (PACs)

Perhaps the most powerful nonofficial element of American politics is interest groups. Interest groups are groups of people committed to a single issue, identity, or cause. Interest groups generally attempt to persuade the government to act on their issue through *lobbying*. There can be multiple interest groups dedicated to an issue by taking different positions, or there can be interest groups dedicated to promoting broad causes rather than any specific issue. Any group trying to convince the government or politician to do something a certain way (or refrain from doing something) is an interest group.

The Range of Interests Represented

Interest groups can be organizations, informal groups of people, labor unions, or corporate-based lobby groups dedicated to pushing the government to act on an issue. Interest groups can be dedicated to virtually any issue and are therefore remarkably diverse. Some interest groups are mighty (e.g., labor union or corporate-backed), while others rely on volunteers and sheer numbers to push for action. Concerning the policymaking process, any interest group's primary aim is to push the government to make a policy related to their area of interest.

While an interest group can be dedicated to virtually any issue, it can be divided into some significant types. The first of these is *economic interest groups*, who seek to lobby the government and provide an economic advantage to group members. These groups tend to seek private advantage for their members rather than for the overall public good and are quite controversial. Corporations in the same industry form the most prominent form of economic interest groups.

For instance, oil companies may pool their resources to create a lobby group dedicated to convincing the government to provide tax breaks or relaxed environmental standards only to companies operating in the oil industry. Business interest groups tend to be well-funded and can devote considerable resources to lobbying the government, making them potent entities. Consequently, it is much easier to convince the government to act a certain way if one can pay for hundreds of experienced professional lobbyists than individuals can by writing letters, however persuasive, to their Representative.

The second category of an interest group is *professional associations*. These associations lobby the government on issues related to a specific profession. The American Medical Association (AMA) is the most influential trade union in the United States. The AMA advocates for doctors, and the powerful labor union, the National Education Association, promotes schoolteachers' interests. Professional associations are usually not engaged in full-time lobbying like corporate interest groups. However, they become active when they feel the government is doing something contrary to their profession's interests.

American Medical Association headquarters in Chicago, Illinois

Citizens groups or *advocacy groups* are those dedicated to advancing a cause or an issue that is not related to their material advantage. While economic lobby groups seek to achieve private gain, citizen groups are concerned with advancing the public good and tend to be less controversial. Given that democratic government, by definition, acts to advance the public good rather than enhance private gain by select groups, citizen groups are interest groups capable of achieving extensive popular support.

These groups, however, can have vastly different opinions on what the public good is, and conflicting citizens' groups often form around a single issue, with each group believing they are acting for the common good. These public interest groups can address any political issue. They can dedicate themselves to one issue or advocate a broad agenda.

The Activities of Interest Groups

Lobbying and attempting to convince the government to favor a position happens at all policy cycle steps. Lobbying by interest groups is aimed entirely at the President and Congress; lobbying the bureaucracy or the Supreme Court is considered "corruption," as these institutions should rely on their expertise and independent judgment.

The Effects of Interest Groups on the Political Process

The extravagance of American election spending has caused concern for many citizens. There is a strong movement to "get money out of politics." The right of corporations and labor unions to make campaign contributions was challenged in the Supreme Court case *Citizens United v. Federal Election Commission*. The court ruled that corporations and labor unions have the same right as individuals to donate to campaigns.

Associate Justice Anthony Kennedy, author of the Supreme Court's decision in Citizens United v. Federal Election Commission, c. 2018

Critics call the *Citizens United* ruling a new avenue for labor unions and corporations to spend unlimited amounts of money and corrupt democracy. They point out that only people are people. If corporations and unions can spend unlimited money influencing politicians, this ruling has damaged citizens' ability to have a voice in government. When elections can be influenced by such dramatic spending, this provides a considerable media voice to those with much money and can sway many voters.

Super PACs have been criticized as corrupting individual members of Congress. Members of Congress may be more likely to advocate a policy position that they disagree with the hope that this will catch a Super PAC's attention that spends heavily in support of their election campaign. For now, the side in favor of limiting campaign contributions has suffered a setback, with labor unions and corporations continuing to contribute to campaigns and PACs.

The Unique Characteristics and Roles of PACs in the Political Process

PACs are interest groups that target specific Congress members with substantial financial support in exchange for taking their preferred policy position. For example, an anti-abortion PAC might reward Representatives who speak out against abortion with support and funding during their reelection campaigns. PACs can lobby politicians to support their causes. However, they identify politicians who already support their policy issues and then provide funding to help them get reelected and push for their agenda.

Since PACs tend to be more reactive with their financial support by rewarding those politicians whose policy stances and voting records agree with their agenda, PACs tend to support incumbents overwhelmingly. This can make challenging an incumbent supported by one or more PACs exceedingly challenging, as the incumbent has a spending advantage during the campaign. Political Action Committees are now the largest source of fundraising for candidates. Campaign funding from PACs has increased dramatically since the 1980s and continued to do so. In 1992, PACs donated $250 million to presidential campaigns.

A new category of PACs exists, formally referred to as an "independent-expenditure only committee" and nicknamed a "Super PAC." These exist solely to raise funds to support a party, as distinct from the regular PACs, which raise money for a cause. Unlike the regular PACs, which donate directly to candidates and thus have to adhere to the legal limits, Super PACs spend as much as they want on advertising for their affiliated parties, doing so as organizations that are legally separate from the party. This could include running attack ads against the candidate they oppose or running "information" commercials designed to sway voters toward their side and thus get them to vote for their preferred candidate.

Since Super PACs are legally considered separate from political parties, they must not coordinate with the candidate or party during the election. Despite this rule, donations to Super PACs can mostly be anonymous means that political parties could funnel money into Super PACs to circumvent election financing laws.

Although many states have now passed laws requiring Super PAC donors' disclosure, these disclosures may not occur until after an election, opening avenues for impropriety or corruption of the electoral process. In this way, Super PACs circumvent election finance laws while having an impact on the elections.

Notes for active learning

The Mass Media

Given that Americans rely on the media to report what happens in government, the media is a compelling political actor. Democracy requires an informed populace, and thus a free and open media is both to inform the public of what goes on in government and hold the government accountable. The media is a tool that people can use to check government power, whether by criticizing the government or ensuring it remains transparent.

Throughout history, the media landscape has changed dramatically, with the onset of radio, television, and now the Internet. Once, small or medium-sized newspapers proliferated, while today, the media is concentrated with a few major corporations.

In previous decades, daily newspapers had such influence and authority that it was popularly believed that newspapers were the arbiters of truth. There used to be a common expression that if something was printed in the *New York Times*, it must be true. The corollary was that if it was not in the *Times*, then it could not be true. Today, many observers argue that daily newspapers have lost their credibility as arbiters of truth. However, they once played an essential role in uncovering government scandals and informing the public.

The Functions and Structures of the News Media

There are many types of media, and the prominence of each has evolved. When the country was founded, print media (e.g., newspapers, newsletters) was the primary means by which people received their news. While print media survived the advent of radio and television news, it has dramatically changed in the Internet era. People are less inclined to subscribe to a newspaper when they can read print media online from different newspapers worldwide.

Many newspapers lament the Internet as leading to the death of the daily newspaper. The Internet has led to a revitalization of printed media. As people with different viewpoints publish newspapers and newsletters, the ease with which someone can create a website leads to diversity in print media's voices.

The invention of the radio in the 1920s caused broadcast media to become a popular source of news. With the proliferation of television in the 1950s and 1960s, broadcast media became the dominant way most Americans got their political news. Newspapers criticized television and radio news broadcasts as lacking in reporting, but television news has continued to retain its popularity even into the Internet era. With the development of 24-hour news channels, beginning with Cable News Network (CNN) in 1980, it became possible to watch nothing but news on TV.

Logo for the 24-hour news channel, Cable News Network (CNN)

The need to fill 24 hours of airtime with content has led many stations to fill airtime with partisan opinions. This leads to a shift from news reporting to political commentary and analysis. This emphasis on political commentary and analysis is a significant reason for the media's criticism as shallow and lacking serious content.

While news reporting on the radio was initially frequent, the primary form of news radio is political talk shows that rely on listener input. These talk shows are less about news and more about pushing opinions on listeners. They have been criticized for creating echo chambers rather than facilitating forums for legitimate debate and discussion.

As previously mentioned, the Internet has become a prominent media actor. Traditional forms of media (such as newspapers and TV stations) have built a web presence to stay competitive. There is much debate about whether the Internet exposes people to a broader range of news and opinion or not.

However, the Internet allows the average American to easily access media from across the country and the political spectrum. Media from around the world is now easily accessible. In the era of newspapers and television dominance, most people's media consumption was limited to whatever was locally available.

The Impacts of the News Media on Politics

Some media theorists argue that this new availability of many media sources encourages Americans to become more informed, leading to a robust and healthier democracy. Suppose public opinion is no longer exclusively mediated through a few local news outlets. In that case, Americans should see the bigger picture and do a better job of holding the government accountable.

The other side of this argument about the Internet is that it enables people to "live in a bubble," with other attitudes filtered out. Since it is easier to connect with and find like-minded people online, the filter bubble theorists argue that the Internet allows people to access only those media opinions with which they already agree.

In addition to the Internet as a novel form of media, it is becoming more than just media. People can go online to debate and argue their viewpoints as a political space, just like meeting in a town hall or public square. Online avenues of popular participation in politics could work to revitalize democracy. Governments are increasingly using the Internet to deliver services to the public. The Internet can make the bureaucracy more efficient by making it easier for people to do things like filing their taxes and renewing driver's licenses through a government website.

The News Media Industry and its Consequences

Political parties are becoming increasingly aware of the Internet's power to reach people directly without relying on the media. Political campaigns increasingly use websites, email lists, and social media to speak directly to recipients and rally voters. Historically, voters decided their votes entirely through media information; now, political parties can speak directly to voters without the media spin.

This is especially important in an era where just six corporations own 90% of all media outlets in the United States. These media corporations wield a large amount of power, which they can use to sway voters. In the future, political campaigns will likely increasingly use the Internet to get around this corporate bias and speak directly to the voters.

While the Constitution guarantees freedom of the press, the practice is more complicated. In addition to the fact that a handful of corporations controls most of the media, the traditional ability to use the press to speak out freely is now severely constrained by the amount of money one has, making "freedom of speech" quite expensive to purchase.

Even then, the government still regulates the media to make sure they do not act irresponsibly. The bulk of regulation has been directed toward broadcast media (radio and television) since they have traditionally been broadcast over public airwaves. Since the public owns radio and television frequency space, sending a broadcast into public space requires a license from the Federal Communications Commission (FCC).

U.S. Federal Communications Commission (FCC) Inspector General badge

Another vital part of the political coverage is presidential debates, aired by the major news networks. The first televised presidential debate was in 1960. The FEC organizes these presidential debates, which decides the debate's rules and who participates in it. Public opinion polling has demonstrated that these debates have a substantial impact on voting decisions.

Although there are continuously numerous official presidential candidates in America, the only ones invited to participate are the Republican and Democratic Parties' candidates. An unusual exception was made for the independent candidate Ross Perot in 1992, but no other exceptions were made since the first televised debates in 1960.

In September 2015, The Libertarian and Green Parties filed a federal lawsuit against the Commission on Presidential Debates for violating the Sherman Anti-Trust Act by excluding other candidates from the debates. The plaintiffs argue that the two major parties are colluding to create a monopoly in the electoral market.

Notes for active learning

Notes for active learning

Chapter 6

Public Policy

Public policy is the result of interactions and dynamics among actors, interests, institutions, and processes. The formation of policy agenda, enacting public policies by Congress and the President, interpretation, and implementation by the bureaucracy and the courts are all distinct stages in the policy process.

Policy and issues in the domestic and foreign policy areas, affected by federalism, interest groups, parties, and elections on policy processes and policymaking in the national context, can significantly influence.

Policymaking in a Federal System

The *policy* is the set of procedures and rules to be followed to achieve specific outcomes. When the government decides on an issue, the policy is created to enact that decision and guide administrators. The policy is different from the legislation because legislation creates laws that compel or prohibit certain behaviors; the policy provides guidelines towards achieving specific goals. Policymaking, in its most basic form, is choosing how to enact a decision. For example, if the government decides it wants to reduce poverty, it makes policies to reduce poverty.

The policymaking process is complicated. Even though the policy is meant to achieve a specific outcome, the policymaking process results in unintended consequences of decisions (e.g., the Iraq War leading to ISIS). It is especially challenging to ensure that policymaking leads to the desired outcome in an extensive, complex federal system, such as the United States government. With several actors and branches of government involved, the policymaking process requires many government employees to work on these issues. The policymaking process's complexity is one of the primary reasons a vast bureaucracy becomes necessary in modern societies.

A policy can be made by all branches of government, including the bureaucracy. State and local governments can make policy, but they cannot make a policy that directly contravenes federal policy without instigating lawsuits and involvement from the judicial branch. In the modern era of American government (post World War II), the overall policy agenda is driven mainly by the President. The President's executive office, created in 1939 by President Roosevelt, is essential in the policymaking process.

When the President wants to achieve a specific outcome, they consult with the White House Chief of Staff, who bring together principal advisory office leaders. The President rarely makes decisions alone but usually consults with heads of the bureaucratic offices and cabinet members. Once the President decides, much of the policymaking specifics are transferred to experts from the bureaucracy. Suppose the President wants to enact a policy to make the internet more accessible in schools. In that case, they consult with the Office of Science and Technology Policy and the Secretary of Education. Bureaucrats would then implement the policy in those offices.

Logo of the Executive Office of the President of the United States

The role of cabinet members in the policy process has evolved. Cabinet members originally had autonomous influence. The President typically appointed advisors who were experts in their fields and, as such, could initiate policy themselves. Most political scientists observe that the Cabinet's independence has declined since the Kennedy administration, with his trusted advisors. The latter were often allowed to exercise the roles of their offices with executive-like authority. Increasingly, policy originating from the executive branch has been exclusively initiated by the President.

Cabinet members have shifted to advisors and administrators' roles who carry out the President's orders, rather than people who come to the President with their ideas and policy agendas. In the modern era, the White House staff tends to control the policymaking agenda. Under Franklin Roosevelt, policymaking authority was more distributed to the cabinet members and departments of the bureaucracy. The decline in cabinet members' influence correlates to the general increase in executive power in the modern era.

The control that the White House now exerts over the policy agenda was Democratic President Obama's intervention in the Attorney General's work concerning prisoners in Guantanamo Bay. As part of Obama's decision to try to close the Guantanamo Bay prison holding terrorism suspects, the Attorney General decided that some of these suspects should be tried in a criminal court in New York City. The Attorney General initiated this policy himself, but President Obama intervened and decided these trials would not happen after public outrage. Guantanamo Bay's policymaking shifted away from the Attorney General's office and has since come from inside the White House.

Guantanamo Bay, Cuba map

Policymaking in the legislative branch usually stems from committees and sub-committees who specialize in specific areas. The judicial branch can make policy through its interpretation of the law. By a court ruling that creates a new interpretation, policy changes may implement it. The bureaucracy is tasked with fine-tuning policy details and has some room to maneuver in policy crafting.

While the bureaucracy cannot make decisions or act independently of the executive branch, if the policy that comes from the President is vague, the bureaucracy must transform it into specific, actionable steps for administrators to take. The President might decide to increase energy efficiency and that this should be done by promoting energy-efficient housing. The bureaucracy would then develop specific policy incentives (e.g., tax rebates for buying green homes) that would lead to the desired outcome.

The Policy Cycle

The policymaking process generally goes through steps which political scientists use to analyze how policy is made. *Agenda-setting* is the first step, which involves the government identifying that a problem exists and needs to be acted upon. Problems can come to the attention of the government through a variety of means.

Interest groups can lobby the government, activists can engage in protests, and the media can bring issues to the government's attention. Next, the policy formation process step involves considering various options and methods to deal with the established problem. This may involve the President consulting with advisors or hearings and discussions within a legislative committee. The goal of this step is, generally, to discuss and formulate options that may solve the problem.

Decision-making is the next step, where the previously considered options are discussed, and a choice is made to best address the issue. This decision could enact some policy to address the problem, pass the issue to the legislature to create a law to address it, ignore the problem, or dismiss it as not a problem.

Policy implementation is the next step, after a decision for action is made, where the participants formulate how to translate their intended policy into action. Implementation is usually done at the bureaucratic level, as government agencies create guidelines, detailed procedures, and funding allocation to implement the decision.

Policy evaluation is the final step, which assesses how effective the policy implementation step was at turning the decision into action to solve the problem. Those inside and outside the government evaluate the policy and determine if it successfully solved the problem. If the policy failed to solve the problem, the policy cycle could start over at any step.

Types of Policy

Policies may be divided into different types depending on how they are implemented and what goals they seek to accomplish. The type of policy a government may seek to implement depends on the problem being addressed and the government's general ideological orientation. Whether the government seeks to implement a redistributive policy to solve an issue tends to be driven more by ideological beliefs than whether this is the most suitable way to address a problem. The primary policy types are distributive, redistributive, regulatory, and constituent.

Distributive policies seek to distribute government goods to the population. Examples include funding schools, building highways, and promoting public safety.

Redistributive policies seek to reallocate government goods from one sector of the population to another. For example, if the government is seeking to increase economic equality, it may make wealthier people pay more taxes to allow more impoverished people to pay fewer taxes. This would be a redistributive policy.

Regulative policies attempt to compel the behavior of individuals or organizations by putting in place limitations. These policies work best to control excessive behaviors. Examples include speed limits, limits on pollution for industry, and limitations on the types of stock trading that are possible.

The *constituent policy* creates an authoritative body to address a problem. For example, after the 9/11 terrorist attacks, President Bush created the Department of Homeland Security to solve the problem of keeping Americans safe from terrorist attacks.

President Bush signs the Homeland Security Appropriations Act of 2004

Due to the checks and balances system between the three branches of the federal government, the United States' policy process is protracted. Policy proposals must filter through various branches of government and are subject to interest group lobbying throughout. When Congress is studying an issue, they hear compelling arguments from interest groups against or in favor of an issue. Congress may hear from others that believe an entirely different approach should be taken toward the issue.

The government tends not to act quickly on an emerging issue of public concern. The policy change process is referred to as *incrementalism*, meaning change comes slowly. The process of legalizing same-sex marriage is an example of policy incrementalism on the federal level. The issue first received public awareness in the 1970s when LGBTQ activists attempted to marry and were denied. Continued activism eventually led to court challenges and rulings throughout the 1990s. This activism and court decision led Congress to pass (with Democratic President Clinton's support) the 1996 Defense of Marriage Act (DOMA), explicitly banning same-sex marriage on a Federal level.

In the early 2000s, courts began to rule that same-sex marriage should be legal, spurred state legislatures to consider making policy on the issue, with some states moving to legalize it. Most changes came at the state level, but meanwhile, the federal government was continually being lobbied by both sides of the issue. Eventually, some states adopted same-sex civil union clauses as an incremental compromise. By 2011, under Democratic President Obama, the government no longer actively enforced DOMA but refused to repeal it.

Democratic President Bill Clinton signs the Defense of Marriage Act (DOMA) in 1996

The executive branch led policy while Congress was profoundly split on the issue. Since Congress alone has lawmaking powers, the executive could not overturn the law, decide not to enforce it. As more state courts and legislatures passed rulings on same-sex marriage legality, a case was brought to the Supreme Court in 2015.

In *Obergefell v. Hodges* (2015), the Supreme Court ruled that all bans on same-sex marriage be unconstitutional and effectively legalized it across the country. Many same-sex marriage advocates complained about the slow pace of policy change coming from the President and Congress. The fact that this change emanated from the judicial branch demonstrates the slow and incremental nature of policy change in the American federal system.

Notes for active learning

Notes for active learning

The Formation of Policy Agendas

Policy agenda formation is the process by which specific issues are raised to demanding government action. This is the first and generally the most critical step in the policy cycle. Advocates are successful if the government pays attention to an issue, even if no policy changes are initiated. The formation of policy agendas is significant, being the primary mechanism through which citizens, corporations, and interest groups can try to get the government to act on issues they care about.

There are various ways an issue can be raised to a matter of national concern, placing it on the government agenda for action. In many cases, issues get placed on the policy agenda because they arise as part of a new trend or changing circumstances. As the internet became more prevalent in daily life through the late 1990s and into the 2000s, it became an issue that the government felt it must make policy on to keep up with changing technological trends. This trend-based policymaking is often reactive; governments see overall societal changes and generally act after the fact. They can consider these changes as a good thing and try to encourage the trend or determine them as unfavorable and enact policy to reverse the change.

Significant events can be reliable drivers of forming new policy agendas. The media gives major events coverage, pushing issues to the forefront of citizens' and politicians' minds, leading to policy change. When something exceptional happens, it becomes front and center in both the public and government officials' minds. Given the prominence of significant events in the media, such events are reliable drivers of policy change. After the 9/11 terrorist attacks, the government quickly brought about policy changes to prevent future attacks and increase national security.

In certain circumstances, government policy is dramatically sped for more immediate results. The advocates of incrementalism have criticized the speedy policy. They see fast government action in the wake of a significant event leading to poorly thought out policies that can have unintended negative consequences. An example was President Bush's Patriot Act, which was quickly passed in the wake of 9/11, but was criticized as curtailing civil liberties. Incrementalists argued that such dramatic changes should have been carefully considered, like other issues, and the urgency to act led the government to create and pass bad legislation.

President Bush signs the Patriot Act, October 26, 2001

Interest groups, social movements, and advocacy from individual citizens can provide a strong impetus to put an issue on the national agenda for policy action. Interest groups lobby the government, often spending large amounts of money hiring professional lobbyists who spend their time directing the government's attention to the issue. Lobby groups can donate large sums of money to political candidates' campaigns, which may buy them direct access to Congress members to advocate for issues they want to push to the national policy agenda. Often this is practiced through promising well-paid jobs to members of the bureaucracy or politicians when they leave office, the "revolving door" between government and the private sector industry they are tasked with regulating.

Social movements rely on the large numbers of people participating rather than large sums of money to get the government to pay attention to their issue. When the numbers of people involved in these movements (e.g., the Civil Rights movement in the 1960s) become large enough, eventually, the government is forced to address the issues they raise. This may take time, but social movements tend to have a snowball effect. They start small and with little attention, but once a social movement reaches a critical mass of supporters and participants, media coverage increases, forcing the government to address the issue. In some cases, individual citizens can push an issue onto the policy agenda. This is rare, but occasionally a citizen meeting or exchanging letters with a politician can convince the politician of the need to act on an issue. This can be done by meeting with one's local Representative or writing letters to politicians.

Leaders of the Civil Rights March on Washington, 1963

Politicians themselves sometimes drive the policy agenda. Someone who is passionately interested in a specific issue may run for Congress and win, allowing them to use their influence as a politician to advocate for a specific issue. Sometimes politicians become convinced of the worthiness of a cause after they are in office and decide to dedicate their time to push for that issue.

Vice President Al Gore became an advocate for addressing climate change after he first became a politician. Once he realized the severity of the issue, he began to attempt to put the issue on the national agenda.

Once issues are raised to a national agenda, policymakers need to decide which issues to act upon. Deciding which issues to move forward on involves a variety of considerations. To choose, they must consider any constitutional issues involved and if this issue might be better dealt with through the court system. Returning to the example of same-sex marriage, Democratic President Obama decided not to use executive power to push same-sex marriage onto the national policy agenda.

The second consideration for policymakers is whether the issue under consideration is a new problem. The policy process is slow, and Congress does not want to pass redundant legislation. Politicians must carefully consider whether an issue might be addressed under existing legislation or added to another issue's policy agenda.

The final and perhaps most important consideration is what would happen if the government does not act on this issue. Congress and the executive want to be actively doing things in response to the demands of the people. If the government ignores an issue that has been brought to their attention by many people, there could be major political consequences. Consequences include not being re-elected if an opposing party promises action on the issue. Such issues that one party may deem unimportant but the other party sees as extremely important are *wedge issues*. The party that believes the issue is essential uses it aggressively to rally voters to their side.

Wedge issues are priorities that one group of people care passionately about, but most of the population is not interested in. Supporting action on wedge issues can win many votes and is unlikely to cost votes because those who are against action on the issue think it irrelevant.

The other significant consequences for inaction on a publicly raised issue are potential long-term consequences. If scientists tell the government that they need to reduce greenhouse gas emissions; the government needs to decide if the long-term consequences of inaction are worth it or not.

Often, the government will not act on an issue because they believe it will be forgotten in a few months. Politics is inherently risky because the outcomes of policy action can never be known in advance. Governments must continually weigh the risks of not acting against the risks of acting. Sometimes issues do fade (they are not that important and were over-hyped). However, the government misjudges the importance of some issues and acts in a way that becomes widely resented.

There are many ways that issues can become included in the policy agenda; which methods are most potent and effective at driving the policy agenda? Political scientists have developed three competing theories to explain who has real power to make policy agenda.

Pluralists believe that issues become part of the policy agenda by different groups and individuals pushing the government to act. They believe that the government is continuously bombarded by demands to act on various issues from people and disparate groups with a range of views. According to *pluralism theory*, this bottom-up bombardment with demands drives the policy agenda in a democracy and gives the people the real power.

In contrast to the bottom-up idea of pluralist theory, the *elitist theory* argues that policy is top-down. Issues that make it onto the national policy agenda are those that are personally important to the President. The elitist theory acknowledges that labor unions and corporations with lots of money can influence their actions.

Powerful labor unions and corporations drive policymaking by the interests of the well-endowed rather than the average American. The elitist theory claims that people's issues, the media, interest groups, and social movements should be generally ignored. That power over the policy agenda comes from the top. There is a growing body of political scholarship supporting this position, the most well-known of which is a study published by Princeton University in 2014, which showed that over the last 30 years, public opinion had zero correlation with the policies implemented by the government.

Institutional theory is the third theory of policymaking. It proposes that the bureaucracy sets the policy agenda based on issues that are important to those institutions. For example, the Department of Homeland Security pushes terrorism as a significant issue because it is in their interest to keep this issue relevant to maintain their institutional and bureaucratic power.

Institutional theorists argue that policy agenda-setting power is neither exerted top-down by the President and large corporations and labor unions nor bottom-up by the people but is almost exclusively the bureaucracy's role. The latter seeks to strengthen institutional power at the expense of both big money and the wider population.

Seal for the Counter Terrorist Unit, Department of Homeland Security

Economic Policy

Policy agendas can be divided into foreign and defense policy, economic policy and social welfare, and domestic policy. The concerns of the political economy drive economic policy. *Political economy* is the interaction between government and markets. When governments enact policies to shape the economic situation, they engage in a political economy. One of the significant issues in the political economy is the balance between government regulation and capitalist markets.

There are different theories within the political economy dedicated to arguing the exact amount of government regulation of markets. Some theorists argue that the government should heavily regulate all the economies. Some argue that regulation is only needed in specific industrial sectors, and others argue that government regulation should be minimal.

As with all contentious issues in politics, there is not a single correct theory. As such, elections play an essential role in allowing voters to indicate what direction economic policy should take by supporting the party whose economic policy they agree with.

However, there have been broad, global economic trends that dictate American economic policy direction. Before the stock market crash of 1929 and the Great Depression, it was believed that governments should generally refrain from regulating domestic markets and should instead regulate external markets. However, these policies worsened the economy during the Great Depression, and it became necessary for the government to intervene in the domestic economy to correct market failures. This policy has now become commonplace.

From the 1980s, there was another shift in policy toward deregulation and the opening of transnational corporations' borders. The role of the United States has been significant in setting global economic trends. Democratic President Roosevelt's New Deal to end the Great Depression and Republican President Reagan's embrace of deregulation and government non-intervention. American economic policy influences the domestic economy and can dramatically influence the economic policy of other countries.

President Roosevelt signs the Tennessee Authority Act, part of the New Deal, 1933

The primary economic policy tool is the *annual budget*. Setting the budget is used for various purposes, depending on the government's economic theory embraced by the current administration. By changing tax rates, the government can promote economic equality or give tax incentives for policy agendas (e.g., sustainable energy tax credits).

The overall amount of spending in the budget is also a policy tool. Unlike when a business or individual manages their finances, the government spending more money than it brings in can be economically beneficial. If this happens, the government is said to be running a deficit.

Deficit spending can help stimulate the private economy as the government pumps more money into the economy, making up for the slack produced by a decline in private economic activity. Conversely, when the government brings in more money (primarily through taxation) than it spends, this is a budget surplus. While some political economists argue that running budget surpluses and deficits can be an essential tool to stimulate sluggish economies and slow down bubble economies, other theories argue that this form of fiscal policy is ineffective.

The second primary form of government economic policy is *monetary policy*. Unlike fiscal policy, monetary policy is controlled entirely by the bureaucracy of the Federal Reserve Bank form. The Federal Reserve Bank determines the interest rate. Therefore, the Federal Reserve Bank stimulates the economy by making it less costly to borrow money by lowering the interest rate. Conversely, it slows a heated (i.e., inflation prone) economy by raising the interest rate and borrowing (loans) is more expensive.

Monetary policy and fiscal policy work best in combination. However, since different branches of government control them, cooperation and collaboration do not always occur. The Federal Reserve Bank may see the economy as sluggish and want to lower interest rates. At the same time, Congress may view that the economy is doing well and seek to run a budget stimulus, thus slowing the economy. The same objective with the implementation of two different policies. When these two forms of economic policy work in opposition, they may cancel each other, causing the economic policy (e.g., slow the economy and minimize inflation) to fail.

The Federal Reserve headquarters in Washington, D.C.

Some crucial issues directly affect the economic policymaking process. The ideological approach to these issues determines what economic policies will be implemented. Four major economic factors come into play when configuring the direction of economic policy. The first is *inflation*, the overall average increase in the country's price of goods and services. The bureaucracy monitors inflation by choosing a "basket of goods," which are everyday items that people buy, and tracking the changes in price over time.

If the economy is growing, prices go up; this is inflation. Inflation can become a problem if it gets too high, called hyperinflation, making money less valuable. What could be bought this week for $5 might cost $9 next month during hyperinflation. Since wages usually do not grow at the same rate as prices during hyperinflation, it is unfavorable for the economy, and people become impoverished. Generally, economic policymakers target small amounts of limited and controlled inflation.

Deflation is the inverse of inflation. Deflation has worse consequences than hyperinflation. Even a little bit of deflation is concerning since the economy is shrinking, and everything is getting cheaper. Initially, this might sound good; what costs $5 today might cost $3 next week, making money more valuable. However, if prices keep going down, it reduces the incentive for people to spend money, knowing that the price will be lower the longer they wait. This causes a deflationary spiral, as it slows the economy even more since consumer purchases plummet.

Controlling inflation became one of the primary objectives of economic policy from the 1970s to the 1990s. In the wake of the 2008 financial crisis, deflation and disinflation have become more significant threats. Inflation and deflation can be manipulated through fiscal policy and monetary policy. Increasing the interest rate encourages saving, which can be deflationary, and lowering it encourages spending, leading to inflation.

Unemployment is the second primary consideration for economic policy. Depending on which economic theory one follows, there are different approaches to dealing with unemployment. Some theories see unemployment as a positive, as it helps keep wages low and thus increases profitability. Other theories see unemployment as a problem because it leads to less consumer spending in the economy and more poverty, which means more government spending on social assistance.

Balance of trade is an economic policy concerned with the value of imports compared to exports. If imports vastly outnumber exports, it can affect the American dollar's value relative to other countries. In contrast, more exports mean that the economy is doing well; its production is more than what is needed domestically. While the trade balance is generally essential, it is less of an issue for the United States, which has the world's largest economy. The U.S. dollar is considered the world's reserve currency. Governments and corporations worldwide perceive the U.S. dollar as safe and tend to exchange their local currency for U.S. dollars if the local currency's value fluctuates. The status as reserve currency keeps the U.S. dollar's relative value reasonably steady.

The *environment* is the fourth economic issue. Many industries are inherently harmful to the environment because of pollution or the emission of greenhouse (CO_2) gasses. A conservative economic policy should balance economic growth with environmental concern, though this has not always been the case.

When making economic policy, environmental considerations have not been as prominent due to corporations' and labor unions' extensive lobbying influence. The Kyoto Protocol (1992), an international agreement to regulate economies to reduce greenhouse gasses, was not signed by the United States. There are several reasons, but the standard response is that environmental concerns have a lower priority than economic issues.

Often the environment and the economy are opposites, though many industries are environmentally friendly or do not produce carbon dioxide emissions. These industries tend to be less prominent in lobbying the government than "dirty industries," such as oil and coal, which make more substantial profits and therefore have the "deep pockets" to influence the political process.

Foreign Policy

Foreign and military policy is the second primary policy type. Policymaking power in military and foreign policy is almost exclusively the prerogative of the executive branch. As the Commander in Chief of the military, Presidents since World War II have carved out the power to determine military policy exclusively; Presidents now send the military into other countries without approval from Congress, despite congressional authorization being required in the Constitution.

Senior cabinet members are vital for setting foreign and military policy, making the Secretary of State and Secretary of Defense powerful positions for setting the policy agenda. In negotiations with other countries, the President has the power to meet with other world leaders and come up with policies and resolutions that are not subject to congressional oversight. Trade policies can be negotiated by the President but must be approved by the Senate.

The most important drivers of the foreign policy agenda are the National Security Council and the Central Intelligence Agency (CIA). The National Security Council consists of the President, Vice President, Secretary of State, Secretary of Defense, and any other leaders the President wishes to hear from, such as the Joint Chiefs of Staff. The Joint Chiefs of Staff has senior members of the several branches of the military.

When developing a foreign policy agenda, the President consults the National Security Council and use intelligence gathered by the CIA to make decisions. Foreign policy can cover virtually anything related to the United States' interaction with other countries. Examples range from negotiating climate change treaties to condemning the actions of other countries. The American approach to foreign policy has changed dramatically in the modern era.

President Barack Obama and Vice President Joe Biden meet with members of the
National Security Council in 2014

Before the early to mid-20th century, American foreign policy was premised on the idea of isolationism. This was based mainly on the Monroe Doctrine: President Monroe declared that the United States would only be involved in Western Hemisphere interventions. American leaders saw the United States as removed from the old conflicts in Europe and its colonial possessions. American leaders generally did not wish to entangle itself in the foreign wars of the European powers. During this period, the priority was developing a policy on internal issues while leaving Europe and the rest of the world alone.

This policy changed with World War II and the Japanese attack on Pearl Harbor on December 7, 1941. Before this attack, the United States did not see itself as a world power or a major player in world politics. This attack forced the United States to realize its emerging position as a superpower and ended the isolationism policy.

After World War II, the U.S. adopted a policy of aggressive interventionism around the world. The U.S. sanctioned covert actions, endorsed governments fighting Communism, and supported military invasions during the Cold War. The communist regime of the Soviet Union collapsed in 1991. Then the U.S. was the world's only superpower. Many analysts inside the government's foreign policy circle saw the United States' role as an obligation for policing the world.

The USS Arizona burning after the Japanese attack on Pearl Harbor, December 7, 1941

There are two main theoretical approaches to foreign policy within the modern interventionist era: realism and idealism. *Idealism* witnessed World War I's horror and argued that a global body was needed to ensure international cooperation. This international cooperation would serve to prevent a future world war. The League of Nations (1920-1946) and later the United Nations (founded 1945) supported idealists as mechanisms to promote international cooperation. Idealists generally wanted American foreign policy to support democracy, human rights, and the peaceful resolution of conflicts.

Realism argued that international cooperation is impossible and that every nation-state advances its selfish interests. This does not mean that states cannot cooperate. Instead, it means that cooperation should only be undertaken for pragmatic, self-interest reasons. During the Cold War, realists in American foreign policy supported anti-communist dictatorships that tortured and murdered their people. They argued that it was better to have allies against the Soviets than to focus only on human rights and democracy.

During the Cold War, idealism was generally promoted by liberals and realism by conservatives. There was a reversal in this alignment, beginning with the Presidency of George W. Bush. The Bush Doctrine (published September 20, 2002), called *neoconservatism*, was a conservative idealism. President Bush argued that it was now the United States' responsibility to promote democracy and human rights worldwide, even with military intervention at the end of the Cold War. This policy was evident in the invasion of Iraq in 2003. At the same time, realism became the preferred stance of liberals, who argued that invading Iraq, criticizing Iran, and supporting Israel was against American interests in the global war on terror. Changing course, liberal realists now argued that America should be willing to support dictators like Saddam Hussein, who were potential allies against al-Qaeda.

Saddam Hussein, Iraqi dictator and terrorist shortly after his capture, 2003

After the invasion and occupation of Iraq, some advocated for the U.S. to return to its pre-World War II policy of isolationism. These proponents argue not only that foreign intervention tends to lead to entangled issues in the future, but that America should focus on helping Americans before the rest of the world.

The military policy comes from the President but more heavily involves the Secretary of Defense and the Joint Chiefs of Staff. Military policy is most apparent when there is a decision to attack another country, such as in the 2003 invasion of Iraq, but has other less obvious aspects. The military actions of other countries are closely monitored by the Department of Defense and the military. The President is briefed continuously on these evolving situations. The President must decide if such matters are worthy of American involvement and to what degree.

The Joint Chiefs of Staff photographed in the Joint Chiefs of Staff Gold Room, more commonly known as The Tank, in the Pentagon on December 14, 2001.

From left to right are: U.S. Air Force Chief of Staff Gen. John P. Jumper, U.S. Marine Corps Commandant Gen. James L. Jones Jr., Vice Chairman of the Joint Chiefs of Staff Gen. Peter Pace, U.S. Marine Corps, Chairman of the Joint Chiefs of Staff Gen. Richard B. Myers, U.S. Air Force, U.S. Army Chief of Staff Gen. Eric K. Shinseki, U.S. Navy Chief of Naval Operations Adm. Vern E. Clark.

While wars and invasions are the most extreme outcomes, the President can issue warnings to countries, such as when President Obama warned Russian President Vladimir Putin to move troops from the Ukraine border. The policy decision resulted in calls for corrective action against the aggressor. The U.S. threats were hollow as Ukraine's continued request for help from the Obama administration remained unanswered. Some analysts argued that, when America enters the world stage with stated policy, such threats must be backed by action. Ukraine had a vast region of its southern territory (Crimea) seized under hostile Russian actions as President Obama made hollow threats and other countries stood idle.

The President can utilize the CIA to engage in intelligence monitoring or to implement covert actions. The President may order a small-scale use of the military, such as a drone strike, or send in a small team of elite military forces, such as when President Obama authorized Seal Team 6 to kill the reputed al-Qaeda terrorist Osama Bin Laden (1957-2011).

Domestic Policy

There are five broad categories of domestic policies that have driven the American policy agenda in the modern era: welfare, crime and law enforcement, the environment, social security, and education. While not all issues fit under these categories, these issues have achieved considerable attention in the post-WWII era.

Welfare policies are a redistributive tax policy designed to help people in need of financial and social assistance. Helping these people in need is paid for by taxpayers. Welfare and public assistant programs first became prominent drivers of the policy agenda in the 1960s when Democratic President Lyndon B. Johnson declared war on poverty. President Johnson saw income inequality as inherently harmful to America's national fabric and sought to instigate additional policy programs to help the poor.

Some programs were driven by welfare policy (i.e., income transfer to assist the poor). These include the food stamps program (which gives low-income Americans vouchers to exchange for food), the creation of public housing (which subsidizes housing costs for low-income people to reduce homelessness), and Medicaid programs (which assists low-income people with medical bills).

President Lyndon B. Johnson signs the Economic Opportunity Act of 1964

Unfortunately, the empirical data does not support the effectiveness of these welfare programs. Using data collected by the U.S. Census Bureau, America's poverty rate was approximately 15% in 1965 and 15% in 2015. During these 50 years of numerous Democratic initiated redistributive policies, the rate has ranged from about 12% to the more common value of 15% of Americans suffering from poverty. The years 2010 to 2015 witnessed a relatively steady value of 15% of Americans classified as living in poverty. Economists and commentators question the ineffectiveness of such policies to reduce the number of Americans suffering from poverty.

In the wake of the 2008 financial crisis, under Democratic President Obama, the government engaged in welfare programs for corporations. In 2008, the U.S. government bailed out publicly traded banks and automotive companies as "corporate welfare." Critics of such bailouts complained that the government was helping corporations, while the average Americans received no direct government support under the campaign promises of the democratic administration. This seemingly misguided policy gained much attention with the bailout of the banks and the auto industry. Many profitable publicly traded companies, such as General Electric, have a negative effective tax rate after accounting for deductions and subsidies when they adhere to specific governmental policy objectives.

As a policy driver, congressional mandates provide tax benefits to companies and individuals when they satisfy requirements incentivizing specific behavior. For example, tax deductions are offered to a corporation for shifting to manufacture an automobile or electric appliance that reduces energy consumption. Personal tax deductions for a homeowner are incentives for implementing energy conservation measures such as installing solar panels or purchasing insulation to reduce energy consumption. Some tax incentives target people that do not own homes. For example, there are tax incentives to encourage public transportation or the purchase of energy-efficient automobiles. These are a few examples for companies and people contained in the voluminous U.S. tax code. The earned income tax credit provides monies for low-income wage earners. In effect, a low-income wage earner may receive a refund larger than the amount they paid in taxes. Welfare payments and associated benefits are not taxed.

Some economic and policy think tanks report an after-tax benefit for a single-headed household with two children receives, on average, $28,500 per year in available public assistance programs. There are approximately ten states where these social welfare benefits total more than $35,000 per year. At a 28% effective tax rate, a typical wage earner would need to earn about $49,000 from employment to have a take-home pay and provide for them and their family the same $35,000. A granular understanding of these issues opens the debate. It encourages civic discourse about the approximately thirteen welfare government policies designed to help the vulnerable and economically challenged population needing assistance.

Crime is another primary driver of the policy agenda. In the 1970s, violent crime began to increase, and politicians were quick to place crackdowns on criminals at the top of the policy agenda. Cracking down on crime is generally an accessible policy since few people, other than criminals, favor more crime, and thus, this issue tends to get acted on more quickly than others. Since the 1990s, crime rates across the country have been in decline. Politicians still push crime and law and order issues to the top of the policy agenda, though earlier efforts in the 1970s have reduced crime. More recently, issues around gun control and the war on drugs have dominated the policy agenda. This renewed focus demonstrates how crime and law issues tend to get elevated to the policy agenda quickly.

The *environment* became an important policy issue in the 1960s. An oil spill in 1969 led to the first legislation to protect the environment, and legislation passed the next year, under Republican President Richard Nixon, was intended to reduce the amount of air pollution. Issues related to clean water, pesticide use, and toxic waste dominated the 1970s and were led by the Environmental Protection Agency (EPA), created in the early 1970s by Republican President Richard Nixon. For the past several decades, the issue of climate change has been significant. However, recent administrations have become much slower to act on environmental issues than in the 1970s and 1980s.

The official logo of the Environmental Protection Agency

Since its creation in 1935 by Democratic President Roosevelt as part of the New Deal, the social security pension has continued to be an essential issue. By having every American working pay a small portion of their salary into one federally administered fund, the government attempts to ensure that retired senior citizens do not live in poverty. Preventing the elderly from dying in poverty was the program's original intent and impetus to advance the policy agenda.

Today, the issue is significant because the largest cohort of the population is the 76.4 million baby boomers born between 1946 and 1964. The baby boomers are entering their retirement years after decades in the workforce. Many people are worried that, despite their regular contributions to social security, there is not enough money in the social security system since soon the number of retired people be the most substantial proportion in American history.

An *entitlement* is a right granted by the government to citizens and certain non-citizens. Programs such as Social Security and Medicare provides benefits to any person meeting a set qualification. These programs are divided between contributory and non-contributory programs. For example, unemployment, Medicare, and Social Security are contributory programs. Medicaid (free or low-cost health coverage), SNAP (Supplemental Nutrition Assistance Program, formerly known as food stamps), Supplemental Security Income (SSI), and Section 8 Housing Vouchers are non-contributory programs.

Education has always been a significant driver of the policy agenda. This is a complicated issue because it affects all Americans but tends to be controlled by state governments. The federal government provided no funding for education until 1965, when the Higher Education Act and the Elementary and Secondary Education Act were passed. The federal government became much more involved in education policy in 1979 under Democratic President Jimmy Carter. In 1979, Carter's administration created the federal Department of Education as a prominent bureaucratic entity with a cabinet secretary. In 2001, under President George W. Bush, the federal government became involved in regulating public schools' quality, with the No Child Left Behind Act. This Act promoted standardized testing and punished schools whose students had low scores.

The issue of student college debt, which is the largest source of personal debt in the U.S., is receiving increased attention. The financial obligations arising from student loans cannot be discharged even upon the death of the debtor. This issue is becoming more urgent and could drive future policy agendas.

President George W. Bush signs the No Child Left Behind Act, January 8, 2002

Notes for active learning

Notes for active learning

The Role of Institutions in the Enactment of Policy

Each of the institutions of the American government has a role to play in enacting and implementing policy. The bulk of the power in enacting public policy rests in the executive branch and the bureaucracy. The bureaucracy is considered an extension of the executive branch for the implementation of policy agendas.

As the most public figure of the government, the President focuses on public opinion. The President pushes the public policy agenda in such a way so that he or she can maintain widespread approval by pointing to programs, policies, and projects which affect positive change. The President is often motivated by a desire to get re-elected during the first term in office. In the second term, the President is driven by the need to "leave a legacy." Presidents want to be remembered in history for having completed significant accomplishments. For example, everyone remembers Franklin Roosevelt for his expansive federal government programs of the New Deal.

The President's staff in the White House is usually highly active in monitoring public opinion. They help the President find issues that lead to re-election or a legacy. President Obama's Affordable Healthcare Act, signed into law on March 23, 2010, is an example. President Obama decided that health care was too expensive for the average person and found that many citizens supported making health care more affordable. Obama saw this as a chance to win votes to help him get re-elected and leave a lasting, positive legacy.

After consulting with interest groups who lobbied for reform, Obama put health care reform on his policy agenda. The issue was then discussed in Congress, and a bill was created to advance the policy agenda. Congress approved the bill, and Obama signed it into law on March 23, 2010. Then policymaking authority passed to the bureaucracy, which follows the President and the enacted legislation to develop procedures to get the desired results. The bureaucracy's policy procedures are then acted upon by front-line administrators who interact with the public to provide the intended services.

Congress' role in the implementation of the policy comes mainly through its legislative powers. Congress tends to take policy direction from the President, but it still has the power and freedom (subject to a presidential veto) to draft legislation. Congress can influence the policy agenda, as the House of Representatives is supposed to present issues relevant to the public for consideration. This happens if an issue becomes so paramount that it threatens the re-election chances of a Representative. The reality is that individual Representatives have very little power to advance a policy agenda.

Barack Obama signing the Patient Protection and Affordable Care Act, March 23, 2010

The President and the political parties' leadership have most of the power to set the policy agenda and decide what issues are acted on. Through committees and sub-committees, Congress decides which legislation to focus on, based on discussion and deliberation. When members of these committees have connections to like-minded people in interest groups and the bureaucracy, an issue network is formed, which can help advance policy. Congress is in control of money bills and can influence the enactment of policy by providing money. If the President wants to advance a health care spending agenda and Congress disagrees, Congress can vote to appropriate little money to the project, crippling the policy implementation process.

Legislation differs from policy directives in that legislation addresses a policy issue through the law permanently. Given that most policy issues are complex and cannot be fixed simply by legislation, Congress's legislative powers are not as strong as the President and the bureaucracy when implementing policy. If Congress passes legislation to address an issue and does not like how the bureaucrats are implementing it, little can they do. If the President does not like how the bureaucracy is implementing policy, the President can get directly involved by firing cabinet members and replacing heads of bureaucratic departments.

The Role of the Bureaucracy and the Courts in Policy Making

The judiciary is not involved in forming policy directly but can indirectly cause other government branches to act by issuing legal rulings and judgments. One of the judicial branch's central powers is to rule on whether an existing policy is legal or constitutional or not. If the Supreme Court determines that an existing policy contravenes the Constitution, the Supreme Court strikes it down, nullifying the policy. An example of this was the recent Supreme Court ruling overturning bans on same-sex marriage.

By striking down the policy and legislation created by governments, the Supreme Court is essentially establishing a new policy framework. As a result of the same-sex marriage decision, bureaucracies craft new policies related to handling local authorities who, for example, disobey the new law and refuse to issue marriage licenses to same-sex couples. The Supreme Court can rule that the policy created by Congress or the President is and should be upheld. While this does not "create" policy, it upholds it in a way that can embolden further action. If the Supreme Court rules in favor of an issue, the President may become less cautious in pursuing a policy agenda.

When the Supreme Court rules that policy is unconstitutional and overturns existing law, this is "legislating from the bench." Such rulings do not create new laws; they are invalidating old laws and are, in turn, creating a new policy direction. After the Supreme Court struck down state laws prohibiting abortion in *Roe v. Wade* (1971), then-current state statutes were not enforceable. However, an entirely new policy regime had to be created to ensure this right to provide access to and regulate abortions. With issues like this, where something previously banned became legal (more specifically, no longer illegal), the bureaucracy must spring into action to create a new policy framework to address issues that may arise from the new legal framework.

The policy enactment process is carried out through the bureaucracy, while the President and, to a lesser extent, Congress set the overall policy agenda. Since the bureaucracy is staffed with trained experts, they can better figure out how to implement a policy than politicians. Technically, the bureaucracy has no power to create policy and implements what the government decides.

Pro-Life March for Life in Washington D.C. in 2008, protesting Roe v. Wade

However, there is some leeway for the bureaucracy to interpret what government policy means when implementing it. Depending on which theory of public policy formation one believes is most accurate, the bureaucracy's policy power varies. Elitist and pluralist theorists see the bureaucracy as merely carrying out government orders, while institutional theorists believe that bureaucratic policy implementation is where the real power lies.

While the President and Congress drive policy, implementation is mainly up to the bureaucracy; controlling how policy is implemented is difficult. The sheer size of the bureaucracy means many people are working on implementing policy. The President cannot oversee everything that is happening in his administration. Bureaucrats may interpret policy and implement it according to their idea of what the policy means.

In most cases, the bureaucracy has experts who know more about the issues than do the politicians; bureaucrats have the latitude to use their policy expertise to implement policy in a way they see fit. Bureaucrats are mostly immune from being fired, making it difficult for the President to fix a poorly implemented policy. For these reasons, Presidents have expressed frustration with the bureaucracy for not implementing policy in a way that they originally envisioned. The President works with the bureaucracy to persuade them to implement policy according to the President's vision.

The procedures and rules created to govern how a policy is implemented and thus administrated by public-facing civil servants give the bureaucracy some legal authority. When the bureaucracy decides how a program will function, these rules become *de facto* laws and must be followed by everyone. Once the bureaucracy decides on implementing a policy, it must wait 60 days before enforcing those rules, regulations, or administrative guidelines. During this time, Congress can review the rules and make suggestions for changes. The policy rules, especially regulations, can be contested.

In *administrative adjudication*, the federal departments function like courts to determine what precisely a regulation entails. For regulations, an individual or a company may present a case which they believe is unusual and not adequately covered by existing regulations.

Administrative law judges adjudicate the case and make a ruling by issuing an affirmative, negative, injunctive (prohibition of acting), or declaratory (obligation for acting) order. These rulings establish a precedent for how the bureaucratic rules apply to other cases with similar facts. The Supreme Court has ultimate jurisdiction, but the federal court often defers intervention, and rulings are mostly decided by administrative adjudication (i.e., legal ruling). Often, the litigant has an affirmative duty to exhaust all administrative remedies before the courts hear the dispute.

While this administrative adjudication function of the bureaucracy usually involves enforcing regulations, the general trend in policymaking has been alternating between deregulation and increased regulations. Then the cycle often begins anew with the appointment of senior-level bureaucracy by the incoming administration. The bureaucracy determines how to remove or implement regulations consistent with the administration's stated policies.

Notes for active learning

Linkages Between Policy Processes, Institutions, and Groups

In addition to a public policy being influenced by government institutions, policymaking is shaped by numerous factors. The relation between the federal and state governments is essential for policy. Additionally, political parties can have a tremendous impact on what policies are pursued.

Interest groups and lobbying are hugely influential within the policymaking process. Public opinion can drive the President and others to act on specific issues and neglect others. Elections can determine which policy agenda is acted on and in what manner. Finally, policy networks are essential to advancing agendas.

Political Institutions and Federalism

The role of federalism in the policymaking process has always been important. In the Federalist Papers, James Madison argued that the biggest problem facing the new country was factions. Madison was worried that one faction, or interest group, might control the government and thus pursue a policy against the wishes of the majority or the well-being of the minority.

Madison's federalism fosters checks and balances at the national level and provides leeway to state governments to enact their policy agendas. Through these various branches and government levels, Madison's goal was to diminish interest groups' influence over the government severely. Given how prominent interest groups have become, Madison's fears of factions having too much influence in the policymaking process have become a reality. Conversely, factions and interest groups represent people's wishes better than elected Representatives and can get the government to pay attention to (e.g., lobby) important issues.

In a federal system, there is an overlap between states and the federal government. While the national policy agenda has paramount authority, state governments have their policy agendas on issues that are under their authority. *Multilevel consultation* is another step in the policy process that is often introduced at the policy formation level for issues that overlap with other states or other federal national government agencies.

President James Madison, co-author of The Federalist Papers, c. 1810

An example of a multilevel consultation would be if Arkansas or Mississippi wanted to dump waste into the Mississippi River, with Louisiana being greatly affected since it is downstream. The upstream states would have to consult with Louisiana, and since environmental protection is federally regulated, they would have to consult with the federal government. Because the waste would drain into the Gulf of Mexico, Mexico and Cuba may be affected. This would mean that the federal government, specifically the State Department, would be involved.

Multilevel negotiations tend to be exceedingly difficult and often dramatically slow down the policy process. However, they are necessary because if Arkansas were to unilaterally decide to dump waste into the river without consulting others, there might be a severe backlash.

While it is generally a good idea for states to engage in multilevel engagement on issues that overlap with other states, the federal government, or even other countries, they sometimes simply set their policy agendas and purposely defy the federal government. The most obvious example of this was the issue of slavery, which led to the Civil War.

Southern states believed that slavery was an issue that should be left to state discretion and was not a concern for the federal government. The federal government saw this as a human rights issue and kept the country united under the federal government. While this conflict between states' rights and federal rights led to a war, there are often policy clashes between states and the federal government without such dramatic escalation.

Before the recent Supreme Court ruling, which decreed same-sex marriage to be legal across the country, this issue was regulated by national government policy. The Defense of Marriage Act (DOMA) outlawed same-sex marriage nationally. Some state governments, such as Vermont, developed policies for civil unions for same-sex couples. Massachusetts enacted laws resulting from the Massachusetts Supreme Judicial Court decision in *Goodridge v. Department of Public Health* (MA, 2004), permitting same-sex marriage in Massachusetts signed into law by Republican Governor Mitt Romney in opposition to the prohibition policy by the federal government.

Eventually, the federal government changed its position, following the policy initiatives of individual states. Sometimes the federal government concedes and changes policy to accommodate the needs of states. However, sometimes the federal government enforces federal law and restricts the policy agenda of state governments.

A same-sex couple celebrating the overturning of DOMA in San Francisco in 2013

Political Parties

In a democracy, policy formation begins in two places: the public or government. The public might inform the political parties of their desires on a specific issue or advance a new issue which has never been debated in the legislature before. The government can create new agendas in the political party caucuses.

The goal of political parties is to get a public policy to match their beliefs. Political parties want to be galvanizing action on policies that they campaign on and which their supporters believe in. Political parties are enormously influential in the policy formation process. Given that political parties run campaigns on a specific set of issues and ask voters to choose them because of their proposed solutions, a policy is significant to how voters see political parties.

If a political party runs on a platform but cannot implement policies, voters are skeptical of future promises. As a result, political parties are incredibly motivated to move the policy process along on issues that they ran on during the election.

Political parties have a complex interaction with the first policy step of agenda formation. Since political parties run campaigns on a set of existing issues, it can seem like these are the only issues a party cares about. The President or Congress may not want to address new issues that have arisen until they have advocated for the campaign issues.

Thus, political parties can impede the policy agenda process by pushing politicians to disregard critical issues that were not part of their campaign. Since political parties are a group of like-minded people all in government, they can get rapid policy action on the issues they ran on. Political parties can both impede the policy agenda and help push it along, depending on whether the issue was part of their election campaign.

A party's strategies to get a new policy enacted depend on how strong the opposition is and how high a priority it is for the party. The new legislation is proposed, debated, and then voted on. Before it comes to a vote, the party which wants it to pass may revise it according to the suggestions of those who oppose it. If that is not acceptable, they might engage in the process of "log rolling." This means that parties make a trade. The party, which is opposed to a new policy, may agree to vote for it in exchange for a vote on their favored bill.

Note that a significant consideration in these negotiations is the other party's "preference intensity," in other words, how strongly each party opposes each of the policies involved. A modern tactic in Congress is a "rider clause." Suppose the policy does not pass a vote. In that case, the party may attach it to an unrelated bill favored by the opponents, so passing their legislation requires accepting the unfavored policy as part of the same bill.

An essential element of the way Congress changes government policy is "incrementalism." This was described as a theory introduced in the 1950s by political science and economics Yale professor Charles Lindblom. Incrementalism states that when there is too much opposition to a policy to get it enacted at once, the agenda can be advanced in small bites over a long period – incrementally. This has worked either because the public's attitude about an issue changes over time with politicians' loyalties or because smaller parts of a broader agenda are acceptable to the opponents while others are not. Incrementalism is particularly suited to the American system because it is already designed to ensure that government policy changes slowly.

Political parties do not only play a decisive role in policy. Parties that oppose a new policy can obstruct it at all stages. Political parties can obstruct new policies aggressively by challenging them in political campaigns or threatening to support the other party on other issues. However, they can do so more passively and constructively by proposing alternative legislation that addresses some of the other party's concerns while neutralizing the more controversial parts of the proposed policy. Political parties can obstruct the enactment of a new policy in many ways, the most obvious of which is voting against it. They can stall it in congressional committees.

Political parties become involved in the policy implementation stage only indirectly. Since this stage is directed mainly by the bureaucracy, which is not aligned to one party or the other, political parties can use Congress's control to adjust funding levels. If they do not like how the bureaucracy is implementing a program, the House's majority party may move to cut its funding. Political parties can make public critiques in the media of policy implementation media to sway public opinion. The same is valid for policy evaluation, which may be conducted internally by political parties to determine if their support of an individual policy has widespread support.

Political parties can obstruct implementation through the courts if their members file legal challenges. The Affordable Care Act (ACA or Obamacare) was challenged in several federal circuit courts. Federal circuit courts are appeals courts located in different regions in the country. Several circuit courts decided the issue differently. In 2011, the Supreme Court heard the argument that one clause in the ACA represented a new tax, which was not appropriately enacted. The Supreme Court permitted the unenforceable (violative) clause to be stricken from the law without, as is often the case, invalidating the Act. Invalidating the Act requires Congress to draft and enact new legislation. On March 2, 2020, the Supreme Court granted the *writ of certiorari* for upcoming judicial review.

A policy can be obstructed in the bureaucracy when the specific bureaucratic department responsible for implementing the new policy is staffed with people who oppose it: Two of the possible strategies are delaying and diversion. They can delay a policy by taking extreme amounts of time to process claims or do other critical tasks to implement the policy. They can divert the policy's objectives by reinterpreting the language to mean something other than intended.

An instance of obstruction by a bureaucrat recently was Kim Davis, a government clerk in Kentucky. She refused to issue marriage licenses to gay couples, in breach of the current law. She claimed religious reasons for doing so and was held in contempt of court for refusing a judge's order to begin issuing marriage licenses.

President Obama discusses health care reform in a speech to Congress, c. 2009

Political parties convene focus groups to ask people about their views about a specific policy program. Political parties use this information to evaluate what policies they should support in the future and what issues should be included in campaigns.

If political parties find that the public is not supportive of the policies they favor, they may begin a public relations campaign to move public opinion. Representatives from the party may go on political talk shows, get news shows to interview them, or try to get invited to lighter talk shows that typically interview celebrities. In this way, political parties can change the public's perception of a policy program's effectiveness.

Interest Groups

Domestic issues are the primary focus of interest groups. When the government engages with interest groups and brings them into the public policymaking process, they are stakeholders.

Lobbying attempts to influence policy in a certain way. It is usually a multi-step process. For many interest groups, their primary form of lobbying is through raising awareness. These groups feel the government is completely ignoring their issue – or approaching the issue incorrectly – and trying to garner interest in their cause.

Attempting to raise awareness relates to the policy cycle's first step and involves trying to get an issue onto policymakers' radar. This is the most crucial step for many interest groups. If the government is merely unaware of their issue, no policy is enacted.

The second aspect of lobbying in the policy process is attempting to have the government adopt a favorable policy once the issue has been raised on the policy agenda. Interest groups provide information to policymakers guiding policy specifics.

In the example of environmental protection, raising awareness, and getting the government to pay attention to the issue may be driven entirely by just one or two organizations dedicated to environmental protection. However, when the issue gets on the policy agenda, new interest groups emerge.

An interest group may have successfully lobbied legislators to pay attention to their issue; however, this does not mean that the government adheres to that input when making policy. For example, the government's awareness of environmental issues may have been raised by an interest group such as Greenpeace. However, they could make environmental policy (or refrain from doing so) because of lobbying by oil industry groups.

Once a policy is decided, interest groups lobby Congress to change funding for the policy. For environment protection, if the policy favors Greenpeace's agenda, the oil industry may lobby Congress to reduce funding for the environmental policy initiative. Thus, the goal is to undermine the policy from a financial standpoint.

Even if the presidential and congressional leadership are firmly in favor of acting on a policy agenda, those opposed to it can undermine it by reducing its appropriations in Congress. Since individual Congress members are more susceptible to being swayed by large financial donations or other offers of re-election help, the policy is often undermined at the funding stages. It is here that *Public Action Committees* (PACs) play a prominent role. PACs target sympathetic members of Congress with substantial financial support in exchange for taking their preferred policy position.

With the Supreme Court's *Citizens United* favorable ruling, Super PACs have become prominent. A *Super PAC* is an interest group, often with corporate or labor union donations, that can spend an unlimited amount of money helping their preferred candidates. While there are legal restrictions on traditional PACs regarding how much money they can spend, where they get their funding and rules related to revealing where this funding comes from, Super PACs are not subject to these same rules.

Unlike a regular PAC, Super PACs cannot directly contribute to a candidate's election campaign. They can spend unlimited amounts to help the candidate indirectly. This includes running attack ads against the opposing candidate or sponsoring "information" commercials designed to sway voters toward their preferred candidate.

Since Super PACs are legally considered separate from political parties, they must not coordinate with the candidate during the election. Despite this rule, donations to Super PACs can mainly be anonymous means that political parties could funnel money into Super PACs to skirt election financing laws. Although many states have now passed laws requiring Super PAC donors' disclosure, these disclosures may not occur until after an election, opening avenues for corruption.

Critics call this capacity of labor unions and corporations to spend unlimited amounts of money corruption of democracy. When elections are influenced by such dramatic spending, this provides a considerable media voice to those with money and can sway voters. Super PACs have been criticized for corrupting Congress members. Politicians may advocate for a policy position they disagree with, hoping to attract the attention of a Super PAC that might spend heavily in support of their election campaign.

Interest groups are also at the center of direct democracy campaigns. Many states have ballot initiatives or referenda. A ballot initiative is when the citizens write and propose legislation without the involvement of the legislature. If a minimum number of citizens endorse it, the initiative is put on the ballot at the next election for voters to pass or reject.

For a ballot initiative, a lengthy public opinion campaign ensues for and against the initiative. Each side tries to persuade the public to vote with them. Although the federal government has no direct democracy, the passage of a law in a state puts direct pressure on the federal government in many ways. It might put the federal law in direct opposition to state law, which forces one side or the other to change their legislation. It can embarrass Congress by making them look ineffective.

Interest groups can play a prominent role in policy evaluation. Continuing with the environmental policy example, both Greenpeace and the oil industry lobby might write the policy's evaluations. This can be for internal and external use. Internal evaluations look at how the policy affected their specific interest in the issue. Greenpeace would evaluate how effective the policy was at protecting the environment, and the oil lobby group would evaluate if the policy cost their member corporations any loss in profit.

These organizations may write external-facing evaluations, which tend to be less honest and more biased, to sway the government's policy analysts' opinion. So even if the policy did not cost the oil industry much money, they may release an external evaluation claiming that the environmental policy was very costly to their industry as a technique to try to dampen environmental regulations.

Interest groups have less of a role with implementation, but a strong one, nonetheless. As an interested party that has worked hard to see their agenda get passed and which benefits from the policy directly, they are a natural watchdog to ensure that implementation is not obstructed in any way. Activists work on challenging an unfavorable policy at every step and having their voices heard in the media. Interest groups provide legal funding for their side should a policy confrontation come to court. They may become the employees responsible for implementation, as was often the case for Southern blacks when voting rights legislation was enacted in the 1960s.

Public Opinion

In a democracy, public opinion preferences are supposed to be the only factor that determines public policy. The reality is that there are many different competing interests, factions, and actors at work in the policy process that can overshadow public opinion. The role of public opinion in the policy process depends on how one views democracy. The most general theory of representative democracy is that the people elect politicians to represent their national interests.

In an *indirect democracy,* a Representative is supposed to faithfully uphold the Constitution and represent public opinion once in office, not merely do what they feel is the best course of action. Conversely, the theory of representative democracy, known as *competitive elitism*, argues that public opinion only matters for electing Representatives.

When elected, Representatives are free to ignore public opinion and do what they feel is the best course of action.

Both understandings of representative democracy have advantages and disadvantages when interpreting their effect on the policymaking process. In the first theory, politicians act democratically by putting public opinion interests ahead of their personal views. The government, in theory, is always making public policy in response to what the public wants.

A quandary with representative democracy is that public opinion is not always distinct or easily discernible. Even with modern polling methods, which use statistical sampling to provide an accurate picture of public opinion, there are questions about how well the sample represents the populace.

If the public has not deliberated on specific complex issues and discussed this issue to educate themselves and understand it, their opinion can be ignorant or prejudiced. Should politicians listen to public opinion when it is uninformed? At the same time, what about opinions that are in the minority? If the elected representative's job is only to pursue policy supported by the majority, it leaves the minority unrepresented, contrary to the spirit of representative democracy.

In response to these problems, the *competitive elitism* theory of representative democracy arose. It argues that people get their say on Election Day, but representatives should not be beholden to public opinion once in government. While this corrects the problems mentioned above, it makes the government wholly undemocratic. The adherence to the competitive elitism theory is simply an elected dictatorship. Once in power, politicians are permitted to do as they wish regardless of what their constituents want. This permits possible abuses and corruption, promoting lying to get elected, and policy that may harm the public interest.

A variety of factors can motivate shifts in public opinion. However, one of the things politicians and political parties monitor to predict public opinion changes is demographics. *Demographics* is the study and collection of characteristics of the residents of a given area. By monitoring population transitions, regional public opinion shifts may be predicted.

If the population of cities increases while the rural population decreases, this may indicate future public opinion shifts. Demographics involve monitoring the political engagement of groups of people. Recently, political parties realize that Hispanic Americans are an influential group that is becoming more politically involved. By using demographics, political parties can identify how this might impact specific issues (e.g., immigration from Mexico and Central America). Another crucial demographic consideration for public opinion is age; older people tend to be more conservative. A shift in the age distribution can indicate a shift in support for specific policies.

Regarding the policy cycle, the policy agenda is where public opinion should have the most effect. The President and Congress want to be responding to issues people care about, even if their actions do not match their words. Public opinion can be conveyed to policymakers to help them set the agenda through a variety of outlets. In addition to public opinion polls, the media plays a significant role in forming and reporting public opinion. If the media plays up an issue, then people care more about it and demand policy action.

While the President may ignore public opinion on some issues, it becomes tough to ignore the media-driven opinions. In the media, there is a linkage between policymakers, public opinion, and interest groups. If interest groups do not have access to politicians to influence them directly, they rely on influencing public opinion. Interest groups often focus on major news networks to gain access to airtime and get reporters to cover their stories. By raising awareness in the media, interest groups hope to shape public opinion, forcing the government to address the issue by placing it on its policy agenda.

Public opinion can be consulted in the second step of the policy process, which involves determining options. When it comes to determining the public's opinion on an issue with multiple sides, it can be difficult for politicians to follow public opinion since there is not a majority.

Suppose an issue has four possible solutions, and public opinion is split between the four options, no matter what option the policymakers decide to choose. In that case, it goes against the wishes of much of the population. Thus, making decisions based on public opinion tends to be rare unless public opinion favors one option.

The policy implementation process is subject to public opinion as well. Even if the public brought an issue to policy awareness and supported the government's decision on what to do about it, if the policy program is poorly implemented, then public opinion can turn against it. An example was the invasion of Vietnam, which was at the time supported by a slim majority. The war continued without a significant advance in achieving the stated goals for the intervention in Southeast Asia. Public opinion began to change to oppose the war due to implementation, rather than the primary underlying reasons for intervention.

Even when the public may agree with a specific policy in principle, the public can turn against it and force the government to cancel it if it is implemented poorly. This step relates to policy evaluation. While public opinion is generally ill-equipped to determine a policy's effectiveness, interest groups can advertise and use the media to shape public opinion about a policy's outcome.

In many cases, interest groups had convinced Americans that the policy was ineffective, even when it was a success. A modern example of this is the opposition to the Affordable Care Act (known as "Obamacare"), which was widely characterized as a failure by interest groups. Public opinion is linked to all aspects of the political system and can be rallied in the name of democracy and public interest or manipulated to undermine democracy. This speaks to the notion that the only way to have a healthy democracy is to ensure that people are well-informed and not prone to the influences of biased political propaganda.

President Obama receives an update on the Affordable Care Act, c. 2010

Elections

Elections are essential to the policy cycle as they enable voters to choose which parties control the local and federal government. Voting is how citizens express a choice in the public policy direction of the country and the locality. By having political parties with different approaches to what should be on the policy agenda and how to address that issue, the election is when voters get a say in the public policy process.

Since parties campaign on a platform of policy issues, these issues become the most critical issues on the policy agenda. These issues are the most important because they matter to the political party and voters. By winning the election, the people mandate the government to pursue these issues.

While parties generally set the policy agenda and choose which agenda they prefer by voting in an election, the election campaign can sometimes drive the policy agenda. If a significant event happens during an election campaign, voters want to know how each party will deal with the issues that arise from it. Such unexpected events are often the most critical policy issues for deciding an election, as these are issues that require immediate responses. Parties have not had time to run focus groups and poll public opinion, and thus their response to such events is the best measure of what a candidate or a party believes. In this manner, the electorate drives the policy agenda and rewards parties that respond to changing circumstances by electing them.

While elections allow the people to choose between different policy options, elections have increasingly become more about personality in the modern era than issues. With the Democrats and Republicans converging into a consensus on most big-picture issues (hidden by bitter disagreements on minor issues), the parties have increasingly promoted their leaders' qualities overusing the election campaign to present a policy agenda for voters to decide.

Many political scientists lament the decline of issue-based elections as an erosion of democracy. If people are voting based on the leader's personality rather than their policy agenda, then elections no longer give citizens the ability to choose which policy agenda should be followed. This diminishes democracy, as people cannot choose what issues are essential and how policies should be enacted.

The two major theories of representative democracy can clash. The *representative democracy* theory argues that the current system undermines representation and democracy itself, as politicians are supposed to represent the people's wishes determined by the people voting in an election. However, if people do not vote based on issues, politicians can no longer represent the majority. The theory of *competitive elitism* asserts that candidates running on personality rather than issues is what representative democracy should be, as people should elect the most qualified people to make decisions for them.

Once a government is elected, it is considered to have a mandate from the people. Thus, in theory, its policy agenda represents the wishes of the majority. Some states have recall mechanisms that make it possible for the electorate to remove the governor from office if they do not focus on their election platform's issues.

Recall mechanisms give the citizens the ability to intervene in the policy decision and implementation stages by removing a politician who is poorly implementing policy. At the national level, however, there are no recall mechanisms. The President and Congress are free to pursue any policy, even if it is contrary to what they promised during an election. Once voters set the policy agenda through an election, they have limited influence until the next election; representative democracy is not very representative.

Seattle recall petitions in 1910

Political scientists have argued that politicians who do not implement the policy agenda were elected to undermine confidence in the political system and are among the significant reasons why voter turnout has dropped to just over half the population in the 1990s and 2000s. When citizens do not trust politicians to enact their policy promises, faith in the entire political system is undermined.

While the electorate is excluded from policy formulation, decision-making, and implementation stages, they come back into play in the evaluation stage. Citizens can study the implementation of policies they are interested in and develop their evaluations of how effective the previous government's solutions were. Then in the next election, citizens can render judgment on an incumbent government.

If a citizen feels that an important policy issue was handled well by an incumbent, the citizen can reward them with re-election. If the incumbent made a mess of implementing the policy, the citizen, mindful of their policy failure, votes for someone else. Citizens must know and understand politics' nuances to evaluate prior governmental performance and make an informed choice on Election Day.

Policy Networks

Policy implementation is described either in terms of an Iron Triangle or through issue networks. *The Iron Triangle theory* has Congress, the bureaucracy, and interest groups as the three points of a triangle that all interact to implement policy. Alliances are formed between prominent members of issue-related committees in Congress, members of interest groups wanting a specific implementation on a policy issue, and prominent appointees in positions at the top of the bureaucratic hierarchy.

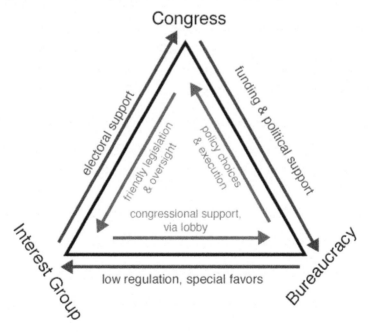

Chart of the Iron Triangle theory

The direction of policy implementation is then driven by these informal alliances in the three different sectors. They can control the policy implementation process and get the results they are after. Many people see iron triangles as a corruption of the bureaucracy. Instead of letting experts in the bureaucracy use their skills to make the best policy implementations, power networks control how policy is shaped.

In which iron triangles may form, *issue networks* can explain the bureaucratic policy implementation process. A group of people dedicated to implementing an issue will form and rally members of the government, media, bureaucracy, and regular citizens to support specific policy implementations. Issue networks are more open and broader than iron triangles. They are not necessarily dominated by political insiders but are open to action by those outside the government and bureaucracy. If the President's advisors, senior members of Congress, the media, the public, and prominent bureaucrats are all part of the same issue network, then policy implementation tends to move faster.

The main difference between an issue network and an Iron Triangle is that issue networks promote the public good. In contrast, iron triangles tend to be more focused on advancing private interest. For cases where public good and private interest conflict, issue networks and iron triangles can conflict.

For example, environmental issues are a public good and are promoted by issue networks. Oil industry lobbyists seek a private advantage for their industry and form into an Iron Triangle with like-minded supporters seeking personal gain within the bureaucracy and Congress. An environmental issue network might directly conflict with an oil industry iron triangle in such a situation.

While issue networks tend to be looser collections of groups and individuals and thus have less vested power like an iron triangle, the fact that an issue network can rally public opinion and appeal to the common good can make them indirectly powerful.

Notes for active learning

Notes for active learning

Appendix

Court Systems Within the United States: Federal and State Courts

There are two kinds of courts in the USA – federal courts and state courts.

Federal courts are established under the U.S. Constitution by Congress to decide disputes involving the Constitution and federal laws passed by Congress. A state establishes state and local courts. There are state courts with specific jurisdiction (e.g., probate, housing) courts established by counties, cities, and other municipalities.

The jurisdiction defines the differences between federal courts and state courts.[1] Jurisdiction refers to the kinds of cases that a specific court is authorized to hear and adjudicate (i.e., a pronouncement of a legally binding judgment upon the disputing parties).

Federal court jurisdiction is limited to the types of cases listed in the Constitution and expressly provided by Congress. For the most part, federal courts only hear:

- cases in which the United States is a party[2];

- cases involving violations of the U.S. Constitution or federal laws (under federal question jurisdiction[3]);

- cases between citizens of different states if the amount in controversy exceeds $75,000 (under diversity jurisdiction[4]); and

- bankruptcy, copyright, patent, and maritime law cases.

In contrast, state courts have broad jurisdiction, so the cases individual citizens are likely to be involved in (e.g., robberies, traffic violations, contracts, and family disputes) are usually heard and decided in state courts. The cases state courts cannot adjudicate are lawsuits against the United States, between states, and those involving specific federal laws: criminal, antitrust, bankruptcy, patent, copyright, and some maritime law cases.

In many cases, both federal and state courts have concurrent jurisdiction (i.e., either forum may adjudicate a case) whereby the plaintiff (i.e., the party initiating the suit) can choose whether to file their claim in state or federal court.

Criminal cases involving federal laws can be tried only in federal court, but most criminal cases involve violations of state law and are tried in state court. Robbery is a crime, but what law makes it is a crime? Except for certain exceptions, state laws, not federal laws, make robbery a crime. There are only a few federal laws for robbery, such as the law that makes it a federal crime to rob a bank whose deposits are insured by a federal agency. Examples of other federal crimes are the transport of illegal drugs into the country or across state lines and the U.S. mail system's use to defraud consumers.

Crimes committed on federal property (e.g., national parks or military reservations) are prosecuted in federal court. Federal courts may hear cases concerning state laws if the issue is whether the state law violates the federal Constitution. Suppose a state law forbids slaughtering animals outside of certain limited areas. A neighborhood association brings a case in state court against a defendant who sacrifices chickens in his backyard. When the court issues an order (an injunction[5]) forbidding the defendant from further sacrifices, the defendant challenges the state law in federal court as an unconstitutional infringement of his religious freedom.

Some kinds of conduct are illegal under both federal and state laws. For example, federal laws prohibit employment discrimination, and the states have added additional legal restrictions. A person can file their claim in either federal or state court under the federal law or both the federal and state laws. Cases about only a state law must be brought in state court.

Appeals for review of actions by federal administrative agencies are federal civil cases. For example, suppose that the Environmental Protection Agency issued a permit to a paper mill to discharge water used in its milling process into the Scenic River, over area residents' objection. The residents could ask a federal court of appeals to review the agency's decision.

---

[1] *jurisdiction* – (1) the legal authority of a court to hear and decide a specific type of case; (2) the geographic area over which the court has the authority to decide cases.

[2] *parties* – the plaintiff(s) and the defendant(s) in a lawsuit.

[3] *federal-question jurisdiction* – the federal district courts' authorization to hear and decide cases arising under the Constitution, laws, or treaties of the United States.

[4] *diversity jurisdiction* – the federal district courts' authority to hear and decide civil cases involving plaintiffs and defendants who are citizens of different states (or U.S. citizens and foreign nationals) and meet specific statutory requirements.

[5] *injunction* – a judge's order that a party takes or refrain from taking a specific action. An injunction may be preliminary until the outcome of a case is determined or permanent.

Organization of the Federal Courts

Congress has divided the country into 94 federal judicial districts, with each having a U.S. district court. The U.S. district courts are the federal trial courts -- where federal cases are tried, witnesses testify, and juries serve. Each district has a U.S. bankruptcy court, which is part of the district court that administers the U.S. bankruptcy laws.

Congress uses state boundaries to help define the districts. Some federal judicial districts cover an entire state, like Idaho, while other districts cover just part of a state, like the Northern District of California. Congress placed each of the ninety-four districts in one of twelve regional circuits whereby each circuit has a court of appeals. The losing party or litigant may petition the U.S. Circuit Court of Appeals for the Federal Circuit to review the case to determine if the district judge applied the law correctly.

There is the U.S. Court of Appeals for the Federal Circuit, whose jurisdiction is defined by subject matter rather than by geography. It hears appeals from certain courts and agencies, such as the U.S. Court of International Trade, U.S. Court of Federal Claims, U.S. Patent and Trademark Office, and some district court cases (mainly lawsuits alleging patent infringement).

In Washington, D.C., the Supreme Court of the United States is the highest in the nation. In a case in the federal court of appeals (or, sometimes, the state supreme court), the losing party can petition the Supreme Court to hear an appeal. However, unlike a court of appeals, the Supreme Court does not have to hear the case. The Supreme Court hears only a small percentage of the cases it is asked to review.

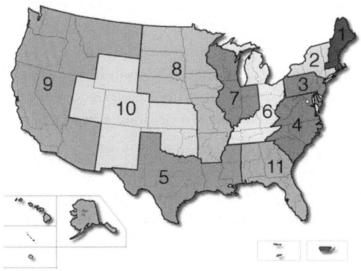

Twelve regional federal circuit courts

Judicial Independence

The United States founders recognized that the judicial branch must remain independent to fulfill its mission effectively and impartially. Article III of the Constitution protects certain types of judges by providing that they serve "during good behavior" and prohibits reducing their salary.

These constitutional protections allow judges to make unpopular decisions without fear of losing their jobs or having their pay cut. For example, the Supreme Court's decision in *Brown v. Board of Education* (1954), argued twice before the Supreme Court, declared racial segregation in public schools unconstitutional. This decision was unpopular with large segments of society. Some Congress members even wanted to replace the justices who rendered the decision, but this Constitutional protection would not allow them to do so.

An Article III Judge

"Article III judge" denotes federal judges under Article III of the Constitution are enabled to exercise "the judicial power of the United States" without fear of losing their jobs. They serve for "good Behaviour," which means they can be removed from office only by the rare process of impeachment and conviction. Article III provides that their compensation cannot be reduced. Almost all federal judges hold office for as long as they wish. "Article III judges" are those on the U.S. Supreme Court, the federal courts of appeals and district courts, and the U.S. Court of International Trade.

Federal judges appointed under Article III of the Constitution are guaranteed what amounts to life tenure and unreduced salary, not to be afraid to make an unpopular decision.

In *Gregg v. Georgia* (1976), the Supreme Court held it is constitutional for the federal and state governments to impose the death penalty if the statute is carefully drafted to provide adequate safeguards. Even though some people are opposed to the death penalty, Article III protections allowed the Judge to decide without fear of reciprocity.

The constitutional protection that gives federal judges the freedom and independence to make politically and socially unpopular decisions is one of the essential elements of our democracy. According to the Declaration of Independence, one reason the American colonies wanted to separate from England was that King George III "made judges dependent on his will alone, for the tenure of their offices, and the amount and payment of their salaries."

Federal Judges Other Than Article III Judges

Bankruptcy judges and magistrate judges conduct some of the proceedings held in federal courts. Bankruptcy judges handle almost all bankruptcy matters in bankruptcy courts that are technically included in the district courts but function as separate entities. Magistrate judges carry out various responsibilities in the district courts and help prepare the district judges' cases for trial. They may preside over criminal misdemeanor trials. They may preside over civil trials when both parties agree to have the case heard by a magistrate judge instead of a district judge.

Unlike district judges, bankruptcy and magistrate judges do not exercise "the judicial power of the United States" but perform duties delegated to them by district judges. Bankruptcy and magistrate judges serve for fourteen and eight-year terms, respectively, rather than "during good Behaviour." Bankruptcy judges and magistrate judges do not have the same protections as judges appointed under Article III of the Constitution. In contrast, bankruptcy judges may be removed from office by circuit judicial councils, and magistrate judges may be removed by the district judges of the magistrate judge's district.

Appointment of Federal Judges

Congress authorizes a set number of judge positions, or judgeships, for each court level. Since the 1869 "Circuit Judges Act," Congress has mandated that the Supreme Court would consist of 9 judges. As of 2019, Congress mandated 179 court of appeals judgeships and 667 district court judgeships. (In 1950, there were only 65 courts of appeals judgeships and 212 district judgeships). As of 2007, Congress mandated 352 bankruptcy judgeships and 551 full-time and part-time magistrate judgeships. All judgeships are rarely filled at any one time as judges die or retire, causing vacancies until judges are appointed to replace them. In addition to judges occupying these positions, retired judges often continue to perform some administrative work.

Supreme Court justices and the court of appeals and district judges are appointed to office by the President, with the U.S. Senate's approval. Presidents often appoint judges and justices who are members, or at least generally supportive, of their political party, but that does not mean that judges are partisan appointments.

The professional qualifications of prospective federal judges are carefully evaluated by the Department of Justice, which consults with others, such as lawyers who can evaluate the prospect's abilities. The Senate Judiciary Committee undertakes a separate examination of the nominees. Magistrate judges and bankruptcy judges are not appointed by the President or subject to Congress's approval. The court of appeals in each circuit appoints bankruptcy judges for fourteen-year terms. District courts appoint magistrate judges for eight-year terms.

Although there are almost no formal qualifications for federal judges, there are some strong informal ones. While federal magistrate judges and federal bankruptcy judges are required by statute to be lawyers, there is no statutory requirement that federal district judges, federal circuit judges, or Supreme Court justices be lawyers. However, there is no precedent for a President to nominate someone who is not a lawyer. Before their appointment, most judges were private attorneys, but many were judges in state courts or other federal courts. Some were government attorneys, and a few were law professors.

Most federal judges retire from full-time service at around sixty-five or seventy years of age and become senior judges. Senior judges are still federal judges, eligible to earn their full salary and continue hearing cases if they and their colleagues want them to do so, but they usually maintain a reduced caseload. Full-time judges are active judges.

Judicial Conduct

Judges follow the ethical standards set out in the *Code of Conduct for United States Judges.* The Code of Conduct contains guidelines to help avoid situations that might limit their ability to be fair or make it appear to others (i.e., the appearance of impropriety) that their fairness is in question. The Code of Conduct informs judges to be careful not to do anything that might cause people to think they would favor one side in a case over another. This includes giving speeches that urge voters to pick one candidate for public office or asking people to contribute money to civic organizations.

Congress has enacted laws requiring judges to withdraw or recuse themselves from any case in which a close relative is a party or in which they have any financial interest, even one share of stock. Congress requires judges to file an annual financial disclosure form. A judge's stock holdings, board memberships, and other financial interests are a matter of public record.

Congress has enacted a law allowing anyone to file a complaint alleging that a judge (other than a Supreme Court justice) has engaged in conduct "*prejudicial to the effective and expeditious administration of the business of the courts.*" Complaints can allege that a judge has a mental or physical disability that makes them unable to adequately discharge the office's duties. A complaint is filed with the clerk of the court of appeals of the respective judge's circuit. This complaint is considered by the chief judge of the court of appeals. If the chief judge determines that the complaint deserves attention, the chief judge appoints a select committee of the circuit judicial council to investigate.

If the committee concludes that the complaint is valid, it may recommend actions, such as temporarily removing the judge from hearing cases. However, it may not recommend that an Article III judge be removed from office. Only Congress may do that, through the impeachment process.

Chief Judges dismiss most complaints filed law because the complaints involve judges' decisions on cases. This process should not be used to complain about decisions. This prohibition applies to what may appear to be a wrong decision or unfair treatment of a party in a case. Parties in a lawsuit who believe the judge issued an incorrect ruling may appeal the case to a higher court, under the rules of procedure.

Each court, with more than one judge, must determine a procedure for assigning judges to cases. Most federal district and bankruptcy courts use random assignment. A random assignment helps to ensure a fair distribution of cases and prevents "judge shopping." Judge shopping (or court shopping) refers to parties' attempts to have their cases heard by the judge (or court) whom they believe will act most favorably. Other courts assign cases by rotation, subject matter, or geographic division within the court. In courts of appeals, cases are usually assigned randomly to temporary three-judge panels.

The Supreme Court of the United States

The Supreme Court of the United States is the highest in the nation. It is a different kind of appeals court; its principal function is not correcting errors made by trial judges but clarifying the law in cases of national importance or when lower courts disagree about interpreting the Constitution or federal laws.

The Supreme Court does not have to hear every case that it is asked to review. Each year, losing parties ask the Supreme Court to review about 8,000 cases. Almost all these cases come to the Court as petitions for *writ of certiorari*. The Supreme Court selects only about 80 – 120 of the most significant cases to review with oral arguments.

The Supreme Court decisions establish precedent for the interpretation of the Constitution and federal laws, precedents that all state and federal courts must follow.

The power of judicial review makes the Supreme Court's role in our government vital. Judicial review is the power of any court when deciding a case, to declare that a law passed by a legislature or an action of the executive branch is invalid because it is inconsistent with the Constitution.

Although federal district courts, federal courts of appeals, and state courts can exercise the power of judicial review, their decisions about the federal law are subject, on appeal, to review by the Supreme Court. When the Supreme Court declares a law unconstitutional, its decision can only be overruled by a Supreme Court's later decision or Amendment to the Constitution.

Seven of the twenty-seven Amendments to the Constitution have invalidated decisions of the Supreme Court. However, most Supreme Court cases do not concern the constitutionality of laws, but Congressional laws' interpretations.

Although Congress has steadily increased the number of district and appeals court judges, it has remained the same size since 1869. The Supreme Court consists of a required Chief Justice and eight associate justices. Like the federal court of appeals and federal district judges, the Supreme Court Chief Justices and Associate Justices are appointed by the President with the Senate's *advice and consent*. However, unlike the judges in the federal courts of appeals, the Supreme Court justices never sit on panels. Absent recusal, all nine justices hear every case, and a majority ruling decides cases.

The Supreme Court begins its annual session, or term, on the first Monday of October. The term lasts until the Court has announced its decisions in all the cases in which it has heard the argument that term—usually late June or early July.

During the term, the Supreme Court, sitting for two weeks at a time, hears oral arguments on Monday through Wednesday. The justices then hold private conferences to discuss the cases, debate the merits of the legal arguments, vote, reach decisions, and begin preparing the written opinions explaining its decision's legal reasoning. Most decisions, along with their opinions, are released in the late spring and early summer.

THE U.S. NATIONAL ARCHIVES & RECORDS ADMINISTRATION

www.archives.gov

The Declaration of Independence: A Transcription

IN CONGRESS, July 4, 1776.

The unanimous Declaration of the thirteen united States of America,

When in the Course of human events, it becomes necessary for one people to dissolve the political bands which have connected them with another, and to assume among the powers of the earth, the separate and equal station to which the Laws of Nature and of Nature's God entitle them, a decent respect to the opinions of mankind requires that they should declare the causes which impel them to the separation.

We hold these truths to be self-evident, that all men are created equal, that they are endowed by their Creator with certain unalienable Rights, that among these are Life, Liberty and the pursuit of Happiness.--That to secure these rights, Governments are instituted among Men, deriving their just powers from the consent of the governed, --That whenever any Form of Government becomes destructive of these ends, it is the Right of the People to alter or to abolish it, and to institute new Government, laying its foundation on such principles and organizing its powers in such form, as to them shall seem most likely to effect their Safety and Happiness. Prudence, indeed, will dictate that Governments long established should not be changed for light and transient causes; and accordingly all experience hath shewn, that mankind are more disposed to suffer, while evils are sufferable, than to right themselves by abolishing the forms to which they are accustomed. But when a long train of abuses and usurpations, pursuing invariably the same Object evinces a design to reduce them under absolute Despotism, it is their right, it is their duty, to throw off such Government, and to provide new Guards for their future security.--Such has been the patient sufferance of these Colonies; and such is now the necessity which constrains them to alter their former Systems of Government. The history of the present King of Great Britain is a history of repeated injuries and usurpations, all having in direct object the establishment of an absolute Tyranny over these States. To prove this, let Facts be submitted to a candid world.

He has refused his Assent to Laws, the most wholesome and necessary for the public good.

He has forbidden his Governors to pass Laws of immediate and pressing importance, unless suspended in their operation till his Assent should be obtained; and when so suspended, he has utterly neglected to attend to them.

He has refused to pass other Laws for the accommodation of large districts of people, unless those people would relinquish the right of Representation in the Legislature, a right inestimable to them and formidable to tyrants only.

He has called together legislative bodies at places unusual, uncomfortable, and distant from the depository of their public Records, for the sole purpose of fatiguing them into compliance with his measures.

He has dissolved Representative Houses repeatedly, for opposing with manly firmness his invasions on the rights of the people.

He has refused for a long time, after such dissolutions, to cause others to be elected; whereby the Legislative powers, incapable of Annihilation, have returned to the People at large for their exercise; the State remaining in the mean time exposed to all the dangers of invasion from without, and convulsions within.

He has endeavoured to prevent the population of these States; for that purpose obstructing the Laws for Naturalization of Foreigners; refusing to pass others to encourage their migrations hither, and raising the conditions of new Appropriations of Lands.

He has obstructed the Administration of Justice, by refusing his Assent to Laws for establishing Judiciary powers.

He has made Judges dependent on his Will alone, for the tenure of their offices, and the amount and payment of their salaries.

He has erected a multitude of New Offices and sent hither swarms of Officers to harass our people, and eat out their substance.

He has kept among us, in times of peace, Standing Armies without the Consent of our legislatures.

He has affected to render the Military independent of and superior to the Civil power. He has combined with others to subject us to a jurisdiction foreign to our constitution, and unacknowledged by our laws; giving his Assent to their Acts of pretended Legislation:

For Quartering large bodies of armed troops among us:

For protecting them, by a mock Trial, from punishment for any Murders which they should commit on the Inhabitants of these States:

For cutting off our Trade with all parts of the world:

For imposing Taxes on us without our Consent:

For depriving us in many cases, of the benefits of Trial by Jury:

For transporting us beyond Seas to be tried for pretended offences For abolishing the free System of English Laws in a neighbouring Province, establishing therein an Arbitrary government, and enlarging its Boundaries so as to render it at once an example and fit instrument for introducing the same absolute rule into these Colonies:

For taking away our Charters, abolishing our most valuable Laws, and altering fundamentally the Forms of our Governments:

For suspending our own Legislatures and declaring themselves invested with power to legislate for us in all cases whatsoever.

He has abdicated Government here, by declaring us out of his Protection and waging War against us.

He has plundered our seas, ravaged our Coasts, burnt our towns, and destroyed the lives of our people.

He is at this time transporting large Armies of foreign Mercenaries to compleat the works of death, desolation and tyranny, already begun with circumstances of Cruelty & perfidy scarcely paralleled in the most barbarous ages, and totally unworthy the Head of a civilized nation.

He has constrained our fellow Citizens taken Captive on the high Seas to bear Arms against their Country, to become the executioners of their friends and Brethren, or to fall themselves by their Hands.

He has excited domestic insurrections amongst us, and has endeavoured to bring on the inhabitants of our frontiers, the merciless Indian Savages, whose known rule of warfare, is an undistinguished destruction of all ages, sexes and conditions.

In every stage of these Oppressions We have Petitioned for Redress in the most humble terms: Our repeated Petitions have been answered only by repeated injury. A Prince whose character is thus marked by every act which may define a Tyrant, is unfit to be the ruler of a free people.

Nor have We been wanting in attentions to our British brethren. We have warned them from time to time of attempts by their legislature to extend an unwarrantable jurisdiction over us. We have reminded them of the circumstances of our emigration and settlement here. We have appealed to their native justice and magnanimity, and we have conjured them by the ties of our common kindred to disavow these usurpations, which, would inevitably interrupt our connections and correspondence. They too have been deaf to the voice of justice and of consanguinity. We must, therefore, acquiesce in the necessity, which denounces our Separation, and hold them, as we hold the rest of mankind, Enemies in War, in Peace Friends.

We, therefore, the Representatives of the united States of America, in General Congress, Assembled, appealing to the Supreme Judge of the world for the rectitude of our intentions, do, in the Name, and by Authority of the good People of these Colonies, solemnly publish and declare, That these United Colonies are, and of Right ought to be Free and Independent States; that they are Absolved from all Allegiance to the British Crown, and that all political connection between them and the State of Great Britain, is and ought to be totally dissolved; and that as Free and Independent States, they have full Power to levy War, conclude Peace, contract Alliances, establish Commerce, and to do all other Acts and Things which Independent States may of right do. And for the support of this Declaration, with a firm reliance on the protection of divine Providence, we mutually pledge to each other our Lives, our Fortunes and our sacred Honor.

The 56 signatures on the Declaration appear in the positions indicated:

Georgia: Button Gwinnett, Lyman Hall, George Walton

North Carolina: William Hooper, Joseph Hewes, John Penn

South Carolina: Edward Rutledge, Thomas Heyward, Jr., Thomas Lynch, Jr., Arthur Middleton

Massachusetts: John Hancock

Maryland: Samuel Chase, William Paca, Thomas Stone, Charles Carroll of Carrollton

Virginia: George Wythe, Richard Henry Lee, Thomas Jefferson, Benjamin Harrison, Thomas Nelson, Jr., Francis Lightfoot Lee, Carter Braxton

Pennsylvania: Robert Morris, Benjamin Rush, Benjamin Franklin, John Morton, George Clymer, James Smith, George Taylor, James Wilson, George Ross

Delaware: Caesar Rodney, George Read, Thomas McKean

New York: William Floyd, Philip Livingston, Francis Lewis, Lewis Morris

New Jersey: Richard Stockton, John Witherspoon, Francis Hopkinson, John Hart, Abraham Clark

New Hampshire: Josiah Bartlett, William Whipple

Massachusetts: Samuel Adams, John Adams, Robert Treat Paine, Elbridge Gerry

Rhode Island: Stephen Hopkins, William Ellery

Connecticut: Roger Sherman, Samuel Huntington, William Williams, Oliver Wolcott

New Hampshire: Matthew Thornton

THE U.S. NATIONAL ARCHIVES & RECORDS ADMINISTRATION

www.archives.gov

The Constitution of the United States: A Transcription

Note: The following text is a transcription of the Constitution as it was inscribed by Jacob Shallus on parchment (displayed in the Rotunda at the National Archives Museum.) Items that are hyperlinked have since been amended or superseded. The authenticated text of the Constitution can be found on the website of the Government Printing Office.

We the People of the United States, in Order to form a more perfect Union, establish Justice, insure domestic Tranquility, provide for the common defence, promote the general Welfare, and secure the Blessings of Liberty to ourselves and our Posterity, do ordain and establish this Constitution for the United States of America.

Article. I., Section. 1.

All legislative Powers herein granted shall be vested in a Congress of the United States, which shall consist of a Senate and House of Representatives.

Section. 2.

The House of Representatives shall be composed of Members chosen every second Year by the People of the several States, and the Electors in each State shall have the Qualifications requisite for Electors of the most numerous Branch of the State Legislature.

No Person shall be a Representative who shall not have attained to the Age of twenty five Years, and been seven Years a Citizen of the United States, and who shall not, when elected, be an Inhabitant of that State in which he shall be chosen.

Representatives and direct Taxes shall be apportioned among the several States which may be included within this Union, according to their respective Numbers, which shall be determined by adding to the whole Number of free Persons, including those bound to Service for a Term of Years, and excluding Indians not taxed, three fifths of all other Persons. The actual Enumeration shall be made within three Years after the first Meeting of the Congress of the United States, and within every subsequent Term of ten Years, in such Manner as they shall by Law direct. The Number of Representatives shall not exceed one for every thirty Thousand, but each State shall have at Least one Representative; and until such enumeration shall be made, the State of New Hampshire shall be entitled to chuse three, Massachusetts eight, Rhode-Island and Providence Plantations one, Connecticut five, New-York six, New Jersey four, Pennsylvania eight, Delaware one, Maryland six, Virginia ten, North Carolina five, South Carolina five, and Georgia three.

When vacancies happen in the Representation from any State, the Executive Authority thereof shall issue Writs of Election to fill such Vacancies.

The House of Representatives shall chuse their Speaker and other Officers; and shall have the sole Power of Impeachment.

Section. 3.

The Senate of the United States shall be composed of two Senators from each State, chosen by the Legislature thereof, for six Years; and each Senator shall have one Vote.

Immediately after they shall be assembled in Consequence of the first Election, they shall be divided as equally as may be into three Classes. The Seats of the Senators of the first Class shall be vacated at the Expiration of the second Year, of the second Class at the Expiration of the fourth Year, and of the third Class at the Expiration of the sixth Year, so that one third may be chosen every second Year; and if Vacancies happen by Resignation, or otherwise, during the Recess of the Legislature of any State, the Executive thereof may make temporary Appointments until the next Meeting of the Legislature, which shall then fill such Vacancies.

No Person shall be a Senator who shall not have attained to the Age of thirty Years, and been nine Years a Citizen of the United States, and who shall not, when elected, be an Inhabitant of that State for which he shall be chosen.

The Vice President of the United States shall be President of the Senate, but shall have no Vote, unless they be equally divided.

The Senate shall chuse their other Officers, and also a President pro tempore, in the Absence of the Vice President, or when he shall exercise the Office of President of the United States.

The Senate shall have the sole Power to try all Impeachments. When sitting for that Purpose, they shall be on Oath or Affirmation. When the President of the United States is tried, the Chief Justice shall preside: And no Person shall be convicted without the Concurrence of two thirds of the Members present.

Judgment in Cases of Impeachment shall not extend further than to removal from Office, and disqualification to hold and enjoy any Office of honor, Trust or Profit under the United States: but the Party convicted shall nevertheless be liable and subject to Indictment, Trial, Judgment and Punishment, according to Law.

Section. 4.

The Times, Places and Manner of holding Elections for Senators and Representatives, shall be prescribed in each State by the Legislature thereof; but the Congress may at any time by Law make or alter such Regulations, except as to the Places of chusing Senators.

The Congress shall assemble at least once in every Year, and such Meeting shall be on the first Monday in December, unless they shall by Law appoint a different Day.

Section. 5.

Each House shall be the Judge of the Elections, Returns and Qualifications of its own Members, and a Majority of each shall constitute a Quorum to do Business; but a smaller Number may adjourn from day to day, and may be authorized to compel the Attendance of absent Members, in such Manner, and under such Penalties as each House may provide.

Each House may determine the Rules of its Proceedings, punish its Members for disorderly Behaviour, and, with the Concurrence of two thirds, expel a Member.

Each House shall keep a Journal of its Proceedings, and from time to time publish the same, excepting such Parts as may in their Judgment require Secrecy; and the Yeas and Nays of the Members of either House on any question shall, at the Desire of one fifth of those Present, be entered on the Journal.

Neither House, during the Session of Congress, shall, without the Consent of the other, adjourn for more than three days, nor to any other Place than that in which the two Houses shall be sitting.

Section. 6.

The Senators and Representatives shall receive a Compensation for their Services, to be ascertained by Law, and paid out of the Treasury of the United States. They shall in all Cases, except Treason, Felony and Breach of the Peace, be privileged from Arrest during their Attendance at the Session of their respective Houses, and in going to and returning from the same; and for any Speech or Debate in either House, they shall not be questioned in any other Place.

No Senator or Representative shall, during the Time for which he was elected, be appointed to any civil Office under the Authority of the United States, which shall have been created, or the Emoluments whereof shall have been encreased during such time; and no Person holding any Office under the United States, shall be a Member of either House during his Continuance in Office.

Section. 7.

All Bills for raising Revenue shall originate in the House of Representatives; but the Senate may propose or concur with Amendments as on other Bills.

Every Bill which shall have passed the House of Representatives and the Senate, shall, before it become a Law, be presented to the President of the United States; If he approve he shall sign it, but if not he shall return it, with his Objections to that House in which it shall have originated, who shall enter the Objections at large on their Journal, and proceed to reconsider it. If after such Reconsideration two thirds of that House shall agree to pass the Bill, it shall be sent, together with the Objections, to the other House, by which it shall likewise be reconsidered, and if approved by two thirds of that House, it shall become a Law. But in all such Cases the Votes of both Houses shall be determined by yeas and Nays, and the Names of the Persons voting for and against the Bill shall be entered on the Journal of each House respectively. If any Bill shall not be returned by the President within ten Days (Sundays excepted) after it shall have been presented to him, the Same shall be a Law, in like Manner as if he had signed it, unless the Congress by their Adjournment prevent its Return, in which Case it shall not be a Law.

Every Order, Resolution, or Vote to which the Concurrence of the Senate and House of Representatives may be necessary (except on a question of Adjournment) shall be presented to the President of the United States; and before the Same shall take Effect, shall be approved by him, or being disapproved by him, shall be repassed by two thirds of the Senate and House of Representatives, according to the Rules and Limitations prescribed in the Case of a Bill.

Section. 8.

The Congress shall have Power To lay and collect Taxes, Duties, Imposts and Excises, to pay the Debts and provide for the common Defence and general Welfare of the United States; but all Duties, Imposts and Excises shall be uniform throughout the United States;

To borrow Money on the credit of the United States;

To regulate Commerce with foreign Nations, and among the several States, and with the Indian Tribes;

To establish a uniform Rule of Naturalization, and uniform Laws on the subject of Bankruptcies throughout the United States;

To coin Money, regulate the Value thereof, and of foreign Coin, and fix the Standard of Weights and Measures;

To provide for the Punishment of counterfeiting the Securities and current Coin of the United States;

To establish Post Offices and post Roads;

To promote the Progress of Science and useful Arts, by securing for limited Times to Authors and Inventors the exclusive Right to their respective Writings and Discoveries;

To constitute Tribunals inferior to the Supreme Court;

To define and punish Piracies and Felonies committed on the high Seas, and Offences against the Law of Nations;

To declare War, grant Letters of Marque and Reprisal, and make Rules concerning Captures on Land and Water;

To raise and support Armies, but no Appropriation of Money to that Use shall be for a longer Term than two Years;

To provide and maintain a Navy;

To make Rules for the Government and Regulation of the land and naval Forces;

To provide for calling forth the Militia to execute the Laws of the Union, suppress Insurrections and repel Invasions;

To provide for organizing, arming, and disciplining, the Militia, and for governing such Part of them as may be employed in the Service of the United States, reserving to the States respectively, the Appointment of the Officers, and the Authority of training the Militia according to the discipline prescribed by Congress;

To exercise exclusive Legislation in all Cases whatsoever, over such District (not exceeding ten Miles square) as may, by Cession of particular States, and the Acceptance of Congress, become the Seat of the Government of the United States, and to exercise like Authority over all Places purchased by the Consent of the Legislature of the State in which the Same shall be, for the Erection of Forts, Magazines, Arsenals, dock-Yards, and other needful Buildings;—And

To make all Laws which shall be necessary and proper for carrying into Execution the foregoing Powers, and all other Powers vested by this Constitution in the Government of the United States, or in any Department or Officer thereof.

Section. 9.

The Migration or Importation of such Persons as any of the States now existing shall think proper to admit, shall not be prohibited by the Congress prior to the Year one thousand eight hundred and eight, but a Tax or duty may be imposed on such Importation, not exceeding ten dollars for each Person.

The Privilege of the Writ of Habeas Corpus shall not be suspended, unless when in Cases of Rebellion or Invasion the public Safety may require it.

No Bill of Attainder or ex post facto Law shall be passed.

No Capitation, or other direct, Tax shall be laid, unless in Proportion to the Census or enumeration herein before directed to be taken.

No Tax or Duty shall be laid on Articles exported from any State.

No Preference shall be given by any Regulation of Commerce or Revenue to the Ports of one State over those of another: nor shall Vessels bound to, or from, one State, be obliged to enter, clear, or pay Duties in another.

No Money shall be drawn from the Treasury, but in Consequence of Appropriations made by Law; and a regular Statement and Account of the Receipts and Expenditures of all public Money shall be published from time to time.

No Title of Nobility shall be granted by the United States: And no Person holding any Office of Profit or Trust under them, shall, without the Consent of the Congress, accept of any present, Emolument, Office, or Title, of any kind whatever, from any King, Prince, or foreign State.

Section. 10.

No State shall enter into any Treaty, Alliance, or Confederation; grant Letters of Marque and Reprisal; coin Money; emit Bills of Credit; make any Thing but gold and silver Coin a Tender in Payment of Debts; pass any Bill of Attainder, ex post facto Law, or Law impairing the Obligation of Contracts, or grant any Title of Nobility.

No State shall, without the Consent of the Congress, lay any Imposts or Duties on Imports or Exports, except what may be absolutely necessary for executing it's inspection Laws: and the net Produce of all Duties and Imposts, laid by any State on Imports or Exports, shall be for the Use of the Treasury of the United States; and all such Laws shall be subject to the Revision and Controul of the Congress.

No State shall, without the Consent of Congress, lay any Duty of Tonnage, keep Troops, or Ships of War in time of Peace, enter into any Agreement or Compact with another State, or with a foreign Power, or engage in War, unless actually invaded, or in such imminent Danger as will not admit of delay.

Article. II., Section. 1.

The executive Power shall be vested in a President of the United States of America. He shall hold his Office during the Term of four Years, and, together with the Vice President, chosen for the same Term, be elected, as follows

Each State shall appoint, in such Manner as the Legislature thereof may direct, a Number of Electors, equal to the whole Number of Senators and Representatives to which the State may be entitled in the Congress: but no Senator or Representative, or Person holding an Office of Trust or Profit under the United States, shall be appointed an Elector.

The Electors shall meet in their respective States, and vote by Ballot for two Persons, of whom one at least shall not be an Inhabitant of the same State with themselves. And they shall make a List of all the Persons voted for, and of the Number of Votes for each; which List they shall sign and certify, and transmit sealed to the Seat of the Government of the United States, directed to the President of the Senate. The President of the Senate shall, in the Presence of the Senate and House of Representatives, open all the Certificates, and the Votes shall then be counted.

The Person having the greatest Number of Votes shall be the President, if such Number be a Majority of the whole Number of Electors appointed; and if there be more than one who have such Majority, and have an equal Number of Votes, then the House of Representatives shall immediately chuse by Ballot one of them for President; and if no Person have a Majority, then from the five highest on the List the said House shall in like Manner chuse the President. But in chusing the President, the Votes shall be taken by States, the Representation from each State having one Vote; A quorum for this Purpose shall consist of a Member or Members from two thirds of the States, and a Majority of all the States shall be necessary to a Choice. In every Case, after the Choice of the President, the Person having the greatest Number of Votes of the Electors shall be the Vice President. But if there should remain two or more who have equal Votes, the Senate shall chuse from them by Ballot the Vice President.

The Congress may determine the Time of chusing the Electors, and the Day on which they shall give their Votes, which Day shall be the same throughout the United States.

No Person except a natural born Citizen, or a Citizen of the United States, at the time of the Adoption of this Constitution, shall be eligible to the Office of President; neither shall any Person be eligible to that Office who shall not have attained to the Age of thirty five Years, and been fourteen Years a Resident within the United States.

In Case of the Removal of the President from Office, or of his Death, Resignation, or Inability to discharge the Powers and Duties of the said Office, the Same shall devolve on the Vice President, and the Congress may by Law provide for the Case of Removal, Death, Resignation or Inability, both of the President and Vice President, declaring what Officer shall then act as President, and such Officer shall act accordingly, until the Disability be removed, or a President shall be elected.

The President shall, at stated Times, receive for his Services, a Compensation, which shall neither be increased nor diminished during the Period for which he shall have been elected, and he shall not receive within that Period any other Emolument from the United States, or any of them.

Before he enter on the Execution of his Office, he shall take the following Oath or Affirmation:—"I do solemnly swear (or affirm) that I will faithfully execute the Office of President of the United States, and will to the best of my Ability, preserve, protect and defend the Constitution of the United States."

Section. 2.

The President shall be Commander in Chief of the Army and Navy of the United States, and of the Militia of the several States, when called into the actual Service of the United States; he may require the Opinion, in writing, of the principal Officer in each of the executive Departments, upon any Subject relating to the Duties of their respective Offices, and he shall have Power to grant Reprieves and Pardons for Offences against the United States, except in Cases of Impeachment.

He shall have Power, by and with the Advice and Consent of the Senate, to make Treaties, provided two thirds of the Senators present concur; and he shall nominate, and by and with the Advice and Consent of the Senate, shall appoint Ambassadors, other public Ministers and Consuls, Judges of the supreme Court, and all other Officers of the United States, whose Appointments are not herein otherwise provided for, and which shall be established by Law: but the Congress may by Law vest the Appointment of such inferior Officers, as they think proper, in the President alone, in the Courts of Law, or in the Heads of Departments.

The President shall have Power to fill up all Vacancies that may happen during the Recess of the Senate, by granting Commissions which shall expire at the End of their next Session.

Section. 3.

He shall from time to time give to the Congress Information of the State of the Union, and recommend to their Consideration such Measures as he shall judge necessary and expedient; he may, on extraordinary Occasions, convene both Houses, or either of them, and in Case of Disagreement between them, with Respect to the Time of Adjournment, he may adjourn them to such Time as he shall think proper; he shall receive Ambassadors and other public Ministers; he shall take Care that the Laws be faithfully executed, and shall Commission all the Officers of the United States.

Section. 4.

The President, Vice President and all civil Officers of the United States, shall be removed from Office on Impeachment for, and Conviction of, Treason, Bribery, or other high Crimes and Misdemeanors.

Article III., Section. 1.

The judicial Power of the United States shall be vested in one supreme Court, and in such inferior Courts as the Congress may from time to time ordain and establish. The Judges, both supreme and inferior Courts, shall hold their Offices during good Behaviour, and shall, at stated Times, receive for their Services, a Compensation, which shall not be diminished during their Continuance in Office.

Section. 2.

The judicial Power shall extend to all Cases, in Law and Equity, arising under this Constitution, the Laws of the United States, and Treaties made, or which shall be made, under their Authority;—to all Cases affecting Ambassadors, other public Ministers and Consuls;—to all Cases of admiralty and maritime Jurisdiction;—to Controversies to which the United States shall be a Party;—to Controversies between two or more

States;—between a State and Citizens of another State,—between Citizens of different States,—between Citizens of the same State claiming Lands under Grants of different States, and between a State, or the Citizens thereof, and foreign States, Citizens or Subjects.

In all Cases affecting Ambassadors, other public Ministers and Consuls, and those in which a State shall be Party, the supreme Court shall have original Jurisdiction. In all the other Cases before mentioned, the supreme Court shall have appellate Jurisdiction, both as to Law and Fact, with such Exceptions, and under such Regulations as the Congress shall make.

The Trial of all Crimes, except in Cases of Impeachment, shall be by Jury; and such Trial shall be held in the State where the said Crimes shall have been committed; but when not committed within any State, the Trial shall be at such Place or Places as the Congress may by Law have directed.

Section. 3.

Treason against the United States shall consist only in levying War against them, or in adhering to their Enemies, giving them Aid and Comfort. No Person shall be convicted of Treason unless on the Testimony of two Witnesses to the same overt Act, or on Confession in open Court.

The Congress shall have Power to declare the Punishment of Treason, but no Attainder of Treason shall work Corruption of Blood, or Forfeiture except during the Life of the Person attainted.

Article. IV., Section. 1.

Full Faith and Credit shall be given in each State to the public Acts, Records, and judicial Proceedings of every other State. And the Congress may by general Laws prescribe the Manner in which such Acts, Records and Proceedings shall be proved, and the Effect thereof.

Section. 2.

The Citizens of each State shall be entitled to all Privileges and Immunities of Citizens in the several States.

A Person charged in any State with Treason, Felony, or other Crime, who shall flee from Justice, and be found in another State, shall on Demand of the executive Authority of the State from which he fled, be delivered up, to be removed to the State having Jurisdiction of the Crime.

No Person held to Service or Labour in one State, under the Laws thereof, escaping into another, shall, in Consequence of any Law or Regulation therein, be discharged from such Service or Labour, but shall be delivered up on Claim of the Party to whom such Service or Labour may be due.

Section. 3.

New States may be admitted by the Congress into this Union; but no new State shall be formed or erected within the Jurisdiction of any other State; nor any State be formed by the Junction of two or more States, or Parts of States, without the Consent of the Legislatures of the States concerned as well as of the Congress.

The Congress shall have Power to dispose of and make all needful Rules and Regulations respecting the Territory or other Property belonging to the United States; and nothing in this Constitution shall be so construed as to Prejudice any Claims of the United States, or of any particular State.

Section. 4.

The United States shall guarantee to every State in this Union a Republican Form of Government, and shall protect each of them against Invasion; and on Application of the Legislature, or of the Executive (when the Legislature cannot be convened), against domestic Violence.

Article. V.

The Congress, whenever two thirds of both Houses shall deem it necessary, shall propose Amendments to this Constitution, or, on the Application of the Legislatures of two thirds of the several States, shall call a Convention for proposing Amendments, which, in either Case, shall be valid to all Intents and Purposes, as Part of this Constitution, when ratified by the Legislatures of three fourths of the several States, or by Conventions in three fourths thereof, as the one or the other Mode of Ratification may be proposed by the Congress; Provided that no Amendment which may be made prior to the Year One thousand eight hundred and eight shall in any Manner affect the first and fourth Clauses in the Ninth Section of the first Article; and that no State, without its Consent, shall be deprived of its equal Suffrage in the Senate.

Article. VI.

All Debts contracted and Engagements entered into, before the Adoption of this Constitution, shall be as valid against the United States under this Constitution, as under the Confederation.

This Constitution, and the Laws of the United States which shall be made in Pursuance thereof; and all Treaties made, or which shall be made, under the Authority of the United States, shall be the supreme Law of the Land; and the Judges in every State shall be bound thereby, any Thing in the Constitution or Laws of any State to the Contrary notwithstanding.

The Senators and Representatives before mentioned, and the Members of the several State Legislatures, and all executive and judicial Officers, both of the United States and of the several States, shall be bound by Oath or Affirmation, to support this Constitution; but no religious Test shall ever be required as a Qualification to any Office or public Trust under the United States.

Article. VII.

The Ratification of the Conventions of nine States, shall be sufficient for the Establishment of this Constitution between the States so ratifying the Same.

The Word, "the," being interlined between the seventh and eighth Lines of the first Page, The Word "Thirty" being partly written on an Erazure in the fifteenth Line of the first Page, The Words "is tried" being interlined between the thirty second and thirty third Lines of the first Page and the Word "the" being interlined between the forty third and forty fourth Lines of the second Page.

Attest William Jackson Secretary, done in Convention by the Unanimous Consent of the States present the Seventeenth Day of September in the Year of our Lord one thousand seven hundred and Eighty-seven and of the Independence of the United States of America

the Twelfth In witness whereof We have hereunto subscribed our Names, G°. Washington, *Presidt and deputy from Virginia*

Delaware
Geo: Read
Gunning Bedford jun
John Dickinson
Richard Bassett
Jaco: Broom

Maryland
James McHenry
Dan of St Thos.
Jenifer
Danl. Carroll

Virginia
John Blair
James Madison Jr.

North Carolina
Wm. Blount
Richd. Dobbs Spaight
Hu Williamson

South Carolina
J. Rutledge
Charles Cotesworth
Pinckney
Charles Pinckney
Pierce Butler

Georgia
William Few
Abr Baldwin

New Hampshire
John Langdon
Nicholas Gilman

Massachusetts
Nathaniel Gorham
Rufus King

Connecticut
Wm. Saml.
Johnson
Roger Sherman

New York
Alexander
Hamilton

New Jersey
Wil: Livingston
David Brearley
Wm. Paterson
Jona: Dayton

Pensylvania
B Franklin
Thomas Mifflin
Robt. Morris
Geo. Clymer
Thos. FitzSimons
Jared Ingersoll
James Wilson
Gouv Morris

Notes for active learning

Bill of Rights of the United States of America (1791)

The first ten Amendments to the Constitution are the Bill of Rights. Written by James Madison in response to calls from several states for greater constitutional protection for individual liberties, the Bill of Rights lists specific prohibitions on federal governmental power. The Virginia Declaration of Rights, written by George Mason, strongly influenced Madison.

A point of contention between Federalists and Anti-Federalists was the Constitution's lack of a bill of rights that would place specific limits on federal government power. Federalists argued that the Constitution did not need a bill of rights because the people and the states kept any powers not explicitly given to the federal government. Anti-Federalists held that a bill of rights was necessary to safeguard individual liberty.

Madison, then a member of the U.S. House of Representatives, went through the Constitution itself, making changes where he thought most appropriate. However, several Representatives, led by Roger Sherman, objected that Congress had no authority to change the Constitution's wording. Therefore, Madison's changes were presented as a list of amendments that would follow Article VII.

The House approved 17 Amendments. Of these 17, the Senate approved 12. Those 12 were sent to the states for approval in August of 1789. Of those 12, ten were quickly ratified. Virginia's legislature became the last to ratify the Amendments on December 15, 1791. These ten amendments are the Bill of Rights.

The Bill of Rights is a list of limits on federal government power. For example, what the Founders saw as individuals' natural right to speak and worship freely was protected by the First Amendment's prohibitions on Congress from making federal laws establishing a religion or abridging freedom of speech. The Fourth Amendment's warrant requirements safeguarded the natural right to be free from the government's unreasonable intrusion in one's home.

Other precursors to the Bill of Rights include English documents such as the Magna Carta[1] (1215), the Petition of Right (1628), the English Bill of Rights (1689), and the Massachusetts Body of Liberties (1641).

The Magna Carta illustrates Compact Theory[1] as well as initial strides toward limited government. Its provisions address individual rights and political rights. Latin for "Great Charter," the Magna Carta was written by Barons in Runnymede, England, and forced on the King John of England. Although the protections outlined in the Magna Carta were generally limited to the prerogatives of the Barons, the Magna Carta embodied the general principle that the King accepted limitations on his rule. These included the fundamental acknowledgment that the King was not above the law.

Included in the Magna Carta are protections for the English church, petitioning the King, freedom from a forced quarter of troops and unreasonable searches, due process and fair trial protections, and freedom from excessive fines. These protections are in the First, Third, Fourth, Fifth, Sixth, and Eighth Amendments to the Constitution.

The Magna Carta is the oldest compact in England. The Mayflower Compact (1620), the Fundamental Orders of Connecticut (1639), and the Albany Plan (1754) are examples from the American colonies. The Articles of Confederation was a compact among the states, and the Constitution creates a compact based on a federal system between the federal government, state governments, and the people. The Hayne-Webster Debate focused on the compact created by the Constitution.

[1] Philosophers, including Thomas Hobbes, John Locke, and Jean-Jacques Rousseau, theorized that peoples' condition in a "state of nature" (outside of society) is one of freedom. However, that freedom inevitably degrades into war, chaos, or debilitating competition without the benefit of a system of laws and government. Therefore, they reasoned that for their happiness, individuals willingly trade some of their natural freedom in exchange for the government's protections.

The Bill of Rights

Amendment I

Congress shall make no law respecting an establishment of religion, or prohibiting the free exercise thereof; or abridging the freedom of speech, or of the press; or the right of the people peaceably to assemble, and to petition the government for a redress of grievances.

Amendment II

A well regulated Militia, being necessary to the security of a free State, the right of the people to keep and bear arms, shall not be infringed.

Amendment III

No soldier shall, in time of peace be quartered in any house, without the consent of the owner, nor in time of war, but in a manner to be prescribed by law.

Amendment IV

The right of the people to be secure in their persons, houses, papers, and effects, against unreasonable searches and seizures, shall not be violated, and no warrants shall issue, but upon probable cause, supported by oath or affirmation, and particularly describing the place to be searched, and the persons or things to be seized.

Amendment V

No person shall be held to answer for a capital, or otherwise infamous crime, unless on a presentment or indictment of a grand jury, except in cases arising in the land or naval forces, or in the militia, when in actual service in time of war or public danger; nor shall any person be subject for the same offense to be twice put in jeopardy of life or limb; nor shall be compelled in any criminal case to be a witness against himself, nor be deprived of life, liberty, or property, without due process of law; nor shall private property be taken for public use, without just compensation.

Amendment VI

In all criminal prosecutions, the accused shall enjoy the right to a speedy and public trial, by an impartial jury of the state and district wherein the crime shall have been committed, which district shall have been previously ascertained by law, and to be informed of the nature and cause of the accusation; to be confronted with the witnesses against him; to have compulsory process for obtaining witnesses in his favor, and to have the assistance of counsel for his defense.

Amendment VII

In suits at common law, where the value in controversy shall exceed twenty dollars, the right of trial by jury shall be preserved, and no fact tried by a jury, shall be otherwise reexamined in any court of the United States, than according to the rules of the common law.

Amendment VIII

Excessive bail shall not be required, nor excessive fines imposed, nor cruel and unusual punishments inflicted.

Amendment IX

The enumeration in the Constitution, of certain rights, shall not be construed to deny or disparage others retained by the people.

Amendment X

The powers not delegated to the United States by the Constitution, nor prohibited by it to the states, are reserved to the states respectively, or to the people.

Constitutional Amendments 11-27

Amendment XI

Passed by Congress March 4, 1794. Ratified February 7, 1795.

Note: Article III, section 2, of the Constitution was modified by amendment 11.

The Judicial power of the United States shall not be construed to extend to any suit in law or equity, commenced or prosecuted against one of the United States by Citizens of another State, or by Citizens or Subjects of any Foreign State.

Amendment XII

Passed by Congress December 9, 1803. Ratified June 15, 1804.

Note: The 12th amendment superseded a portion of Article II, section 1 of the Constitution.

The Electors shall meet in their respective states and vote by ballot for President and Vice-President, one of whom, at least, shall not be an inhabitant of the same state with themselves; they shall name in their ballots the person voted for as President, and in distinct ballots the person voted for as Vice-President, and they shall make distinct lists of all persons voted for as President, and of all persons voted for as Vice-President, and of the number of votes for each, which lists they shall sign and certify, and transmit sealed to the seat of the government of the United States, directed to the President of the Senate; -- the President of the Senate shall, in the presence of the Senate and House of Representatives, open all the certificates and the votes shall then be counted; -- The person having the greatest number of votes for President, shall be the President, if such number be a majority of the whole number of Electors appointed; and if no person have such majority, then from the persons having the highest numbers not exceeding three on the list of those voted for as President, the House of Representatives shall choose immediately, by ballot, the President. But in choosing the President, the votes shall be taken by states, the representation from each state having one vote; a quorum for this purpose shall consist of a member or members from two-thirds of the states, and a majority of all the states shall be necessary to a choice. [And if the House of Representatives shall not choose a President whenever the right of choice shall devolve upon them, before the fourth day of March next following, then the Vice-President shall act as President, as in case of the death or other constitutional disability of the President. --]* The person having the greatest number of votes as Vice-President, shall be the Vice-President, if such number be a majority of the whole number of Electors appointed, and if no person have a majority, then from the two highest numbers on the list, the Senate shall choose the Vice-President; a quorum for the purpose shall consist of two-thirds of the whole number of Senators, and a majority of the whole number shall be necessary to a choice. But no person constitutionally ineligible to the office of President shall be eligible to that of Vice-President of the United States.

*Superseded by section 3 of the 20th amendment.

Amendment XIII

Passed by Congress on January 31, 1865. Ratified December 6, 1865.

Note: The 13th amendment superseded a portion of Article IV, section 2, of the Constitution.

Section   **1.**
Neither slavery nor involuntary servitude, except as a punishment for crime whereof the party shall have been duly convicted, shall exist within the United States or any place subject to their jurisdiction.

Section 2.
Congress shall have the power to enforce this article by appropriate legislation.

Amendment XIV

Passed by Congress June 13, 1866. Ratified July 9, 1868.

Note: Section 2 of the 14th amendment modified Article I, section 2, of the Constitution.

Section 1.

All persons born or naturalized in the United States, and subject to the jurisdiction thereof, are citizens of the United States and the State wherein they reside. No State shall make or enforce any law which shall abridge the privileges or immunities of citizens of the United States; nor shall any State deprive any person of life, liberty, or property, without due process of law; nor deny to any person within its jurisdiction the equal protection of the laws.

Section 2.

Representatives shall be apportioned among the several States according to their respective numbers, counting the whole number of persons in each State, excluding Indians not taxed. But when the right to vote at any election for the choice of electors for President and Vice-President of the United States, Representatives in Congress, the Executive and Judicial officers of a State, or the members of the Legislature thereof, is denied to any of the male inhabitants of such State, being twenty-one years of age,* and citizens of the United States, or in any way abridged, except for participation in rebellion, or other crime, the basis of representation therein shall be reduced in the proportion which the number of such male citizens shall bear to the whole number of male citizens twenty-one years of age in such State.

Section 3.

No person shall be a Senator or Representative in Congress, or elector of President and Vice-President, or hold any office, civil or military, under the United States, or under any State, who, having previously taken an oath, as a member of Congress, or as an officer of the United States, or as a member of any State legislature, or as an executive or judicial officer of any State, to support the Constitution of the United States, shall have engaged in insurrection or rebellion against the same, or given aid or comfort to the enemies thereof. But Congress may by a vote of two-thirds of each House, remove such disability.

Section 4.

The validity of the public debt of the United States, authorized by law, including debts incurred for payment of pensions and bounties for services in suppressing insurrection or rebellion, shall not be questioned. But neither the United States nor any State shall assume or pay any debt or obligation incurred in aid of insurrection or rebellion against the United States, or any claim for the loss or emancipation of any slave; but all such debts, obligations and claims shall be held illegal and void.

Section 5.
The Congress shall have the power to enforce, by appropriate legislation, the provisions of this article.

Changed by section 1 of the 26th amendment.

Amendment XV

Passed by Congress February 26, 1869. Ratified February 3, 1870.

Section 1.

The right of citizens of the United States to vote shall not be denied or abridged by the United States or by any State on account of race, color, or previous condition of servitude.

Section 2.
Congress shall have the power to enforce this article by appropriate legislation.

Amendment XVI

Passed by Congress July 2, 1909. Ratified February 3, 1913.

Note: Article I, section 9, of the Constitution was modified by amendment 16.

The Congress shall have the power to lay and collect taxes on incomes, from whatever source derived, without apportionment among the several States, and without regard to any census or enumeration.

Amendment XVII

Passed by Congress May 13, 1912. Ratified April 8, 1913.

Note: The 17th amendment modified Article I, section 3, of the Constitution.

The Senate of the United States shall be composed of two Senators from each State, elected by the people thereof, for six years; and each Senator shall have one vote. The electors in each State shall have the qualifications requisite for electors of the most numerous branch of the State legislatures.

When vacancies happen in the representation of any State in the Senate, the executive authority of such State shall issue writs of election to fill such vacancies: *Provided*, That the legislature of any State may empower the executive thereof to make temporary appointments until the people fill the vacancies by election as the legislature may direct.

This amendment shall not be so construed as to affect the election or term of any Senator chosen before it becomes valid as part of the Constitution.

Amendment XVIII

Passed by Congress December 18, 1917. Ratified January 16, 1919. Repealed by amendment 21.

Section 1.

After one year from the ratification of this article the manufacture, sale, or transportation of intoxicating liquors within, the importation thereof into, or the exportation thereof from the United States and all territory subject to the jurisdiction thereof for beverage purposes is hereby prohibited.

Section 2.
The Congress and the several States shall have concurrent power to enforce this article by appropriate legislation.

Section 3.

This article shall be inoperative unless it shall have been ratified as an amendment to the Constitution by the legislatures of the several States, as provided in the Constitution, within seven years from the date of the submission hereof to the States by the Congress.

Amendment XIX

Passed by Congress June 4, 1919. Ratified August 18, 1920.

The right of citizens of the United States to vote shall not be denied or abridged by the United States or by any State on account of sex.

Congress shall have the power to enforce this article by appropriate legislation.

Amendment XX

Passed by Congress March 2, 1932. Ratified January 23, 1933.

Note: Section 2 of this amendment modified Article I, section 4, of the Constitution. Also, a portion of the 12th amendment was superseded by section 3.

Section 1.
The terms of the President and the Vice President shall end at noon on the 20th day of January, and the terms of Senators and Representatives at noon on the 3d day of January, of the years in which such terms would have ended if this article had not been ratified; and the terms of their successors shall then begin.

Section 2.
The Congress shall assemble at least once in every year, and such meeting shall begin at noon on the 3d day of January, unless they shall by law appoint a different day.

Section 3.
If, at the time fixed for the beginning of the term of the President, the President elect shall have died, the Vice President elect shall become President. If a President shall not have been chosen before the time fixed for the beginning of his term, or if the President elect shall have failed to qualify, then the Vice President elect shall act as President until a President shall have qualified; and the Congress may by law provide for the case wherein neither a President elect nor a Vice President elect shall have qualified, declaring who shall then act as President, or the manner in which one who is to act shall be selected, and such person shall act accordingly until a President or Vice President shall have qualified.

Section 4.
The Congress may by law provide for the case of the death of any of the persons from whom the House of Representatives may choose a President whenever the right of choice shall have devolved upon them, and for the case of the death of any of the persons from whom the Senate may choose a Vice President whenever the right of choice shall have devolved upon them.

Section 5.
Sections 1 and 2 shall take effect on the 15th day of October following the ratification of this article.

Section 6.
This article shall be inoperative unless it shall have been ratified as an amendment to the Constitution by the legislatures of three-fourths of the several States within seven years from the date of its submission.

Amendment XXI

Passed by Congress February 20, 1933. Ratified December 5, 1933.

Section 1.

The eighteenth article of amendment to the Constitution of the United States is hereby repealed.

Section 2.

The transportation or importation into any State, Territory, or possession of the United States for delivery or use therein of intoxicating liquors, in violation of the laws thereof, is hereby prohibited.

Section 3.

This article shall be inoperative unless it shall have been ratified as an amendment to the Constitution by conventions in the several States, as provided in the Constitution, within seven years from the date of the submission hereof to the States by the Congress.

Amendment XXII

Passed by Congress March 21, 1947. Ratified February 27, 1951.

Section 1.

No person shall be elected to the office of the President more than twice, and no person who has held the office of President, or acted as President, for more than two years of a term to which some other person was elected President shall be elected to the office of the President more than once. But this Article shall not apply to any person holding the office of President when this Article was proposed by the Congress, and shall not prevent any person who may be holding the office of President, or acting as President, during the term within which this Article becomes operative from holding the office of President or acting as President during the remainder of such term.

Section 2.

This article shall be inoperative unless it shall have been ratified as an amendment to the Constitution by the legislatures of three-fourths of the several States within seven years from the date of its submission to the States by the Congress.

Amendment XXIII

Passed by Congress June 16, 1960. Ratified March 29, 1961.

Section 1.

The District constituting the seat of Government of the United States shall appoint in such manner as the Congress may direct:

A number of electors of President and Vice President equal to the whole number of Senators and Representatives in Congress to which the District would be entitled if it were a State, but in no event more than the least populous State; they shall be in addition to those appointed by the States, but they shall be considered, for the purposes of the election of President and Vice President, to be electors appointed by a State; and they shall meet in the District and perform such duties as provided by the twelfth article of amendment.

Section 2.

The Congress shall have power to enforce this article by appropriate legislation.

Amendment XXIV

Passed by Congress on August 27, 1962. Ratified January 23, 1964.

Section 1.

The right of citizens of the United States to vote in any primary or other election for President or Vice President, for electors for President or Vice President, or for Senator or Representative in Congress, shall not be denied or abridged by the United States or any State by reason of failure to pay any poll tax or other tax.

Section 2.

The Congress shall have power to enforce this article by appropriate legislation.

Amendment XXV

Passed by Congress on July 6, 1965. Ratified February 10, 1967.

Note: Article II, section 1, of the Constitution, was affected by the 25th amendment.

Section 1.

In case of the removal of the President from office or of his death or resignation, the Vice President shall become President.

Section 2.

Whenever there is a vacancy in the office of the Vice President, the President shall nominate a Vice President who shall take office upon confirmation by a majority vote of both Houses of Congress.

Section 3.

Whenever the President transmits to the President pro tempore of the Senate and the Speaker of the House of Representatives his written declaration that he is unable to discharge the powers and duties of his office, and until he transmits to them a written declaration to the contrary, such powers and duties shall be discharged by the Vice President as Acting President.

Section 4.

Whenever the Vice President and a majority of either the principal officers of the executive departments or of such other body as Congress may by law provide, transmit to the President pro tempore of the Senate and the Speaker of the House of Representatives their written declaration that the President is unable to discharge the powers and duties of his office, the Vice President shall immediately assume the powers and duties of the office as Acting President.

Thereafter, when the President transmits to the President pro tempore of the Senate and the Speaker of the House of Representatives his written declaration that no inability exists, he shall resume the powers and duties of his office unless the Vice President and a majority of either the principal officers of the executive department or of such other body as Congress may by law provide, transmit within four days to the President pro tempore of the Senate and the Speaker of the House of Representatives their written declaration that the President is unable to discharge the powers and duties of his office. Thereupon Congress shall decide the issue, assembling within forty-eight hours for that purpose if not in session. If the Congress, within twenty-one days after receipt of the latter written declaration, or, if Congress is not in session, within twenty-one days after Congress is required to assemble, determines by two-thirds vote of both Houses that the President is unable to discharge the powers and duties of his office, the Vice President shall continue to discharge the same as Acting President; otherwise, the President shall resume the powers and duties of his office.

Amendment XXVI

Passed by Congress March 23, 1971. Ratified July 1, 1971.

Note: section 1 of the 26th amendment modified amendment 14, section 2, of the Constitution.

Section 1.

The right of citizens of the United States, who are eighteen years of age or older, to vote shall not be denied or abridged by the United States or by any State on account of age.

Section 2.

The Congress shall have power to enforce this article by appropriate legislation.

Amendment XXII

Originally proposed Sept. 25, 1789. Ratified May 7, 1992.

No law, varying the compensation for the services of the Senators and Representatives, shall take effect, until an election of Representatives shall have intervened.

Notes for active learning

Notes for active learning

Glossary

A

Absentee ballot — a ballot, usually sent in the mail, allows those who cannot go to their precinct on election day to vote.

Absolute majority — a term used to compare the least votes a winning candidate may need in a preferential, single-member voting system (known as "50% + 1 vote"). This compares to the first-past-the-post systems of other countries. A "majority" may be less than 50%; this concept is used in some parliamentary votes where a simple majority of members present is not sufficient.

Absolutism — the belief that the government should have all the power and do whatever it wants.

Accord — a diplomatic agreement that does not have the same binding force as a treaty.

Act — a bill that has been signed into law by the executive officer (e.g., governor or President).

Acquisitive model — a view of bureaucracies that argues agency heads always seek to expand their agency's size, budget, and power.

Acts and Resolves — a compilation of the bills and resolutions enacted and passed by the legislature and signed by the governor. Bound in a volume every year.

Actual malice — knowingly publishing falsehoods (whether in print, on radio, TV, or the internet) to harm a person's reputation.

ad hominem **[Latin, to the man]** — attacking the presenter of an argument rather than the argument itself (known as "playing the man, not the ball").

Adjournment — temporary interruption during a parliamentary session; with the intent to resume.

Administrative adjudication — the bureaucratic function of settling disputes by relying on rules and precedents.

Administrative law — the segment of public law used to challenge government officials' decisions, excluding policy decisions made by the people's elected representatives deemed popular electoral support authorizes office holders to be unrestrained within the law. Public servants can be challenged in court (if the plaintiff has standing) on the "reasonableness" of their administrative actions or failure to act. Over time, the administrative law authority has been extended to quasi-public bodies (e.g., NGOs, Quangos, and other organizations that otherwise have discretionary power over their members' rights).

Adverse report — a committee recommendation that a matter ought not to pass.

Affirm — an action by a higher court (e.g., Supreme Court) to uphold a ruling by a lower court; that ruling now becomes legally binding as a precedent.

Affirmative action — legislative programs that aim to create minority equality in employment, university placements, housing, and other government-influenced beneficial situations.

Agency capture — the gaining of control (direct or indirect) over a government regulatory agency by the industry it regulates.

Agency representation — a type of representation in which representatives act on behalf of the district's voters and held accountable if they do not do as the constituents wish.

Agenda-setting — the power of the media to determine which issues are discussed and debated.

Agitprop — less-than-subtle political propaganda disseminated through the media and performing arts; the term derived from the Department of Agitation and Propaganda of the Soviet Union.

Agrarian socialist — initially applying to non-urban, pre-Industrial Revolution people with traditional, conservative attitudes; belief in the collective ownership and control of primary industries and, to a lesser extent, secondary industries for the benefit of all; otherwise are not that committed to other socialist beliefs such as progressive/liberal approaches to domestic or international social concerns.

Alinsky, Saul — (1909-1972), through his book *Rules for Radicals* (1971), propagated ideas for needy communities to politically organize; widely used in the 1970s by college students and other counter-culture movements.

Altruism — the devotion to others' interests above that of the self; the opposite of egotism.

Amendment — a change to the Constitution.

American conservatism — believes freedom trumps all other political considerations; the government should play as small a role as possible in people's lives.

American exceptionalism — the view that the United States is markedly different from and better than other countries.

American liberalism — the belief that government should actively promote political and economic equality.

Americans with Disabilities Act — the first law (1990) banning discrimination against the disabled; it requires employers to make all reasonable accommodations to disabled workers.

amicus curiae **brief [Latin, friend of the court]** — a brief submitted to the court by a group not involved in the case; presents additional arguments of the issue for one side.

Anarchism — the belief that governments are repressive and should be dismantled.

Anarchy — a condition of lawlessness and disorder brought about in the absence of any controlling authority.

Anti-clericalism — opposition to the influence of religion in government and legislative affairs.

Anti-Federalists — group opposed to the Constitution's ratification because it gave too much power to the federal government at the states' expense; later became one of the first two major political parties in America; see *Federalists*.

Antitrust policy — a collection of federal and state laws (including the Sherman Antitrust Act of 1890) to prevent a business from gaining monopoly control over an economic sector.

Appellate jurisdiction — authority to hear appeals of cases arising from a geographic area or legal issue. The Supreme Court has appellate jurisdiction over all cases arising under the United States Constitution; see *Original jurisdiction*.

Appointment power — the President's power to appoint people to crucial federal offices.

Appropriation — the act of Congress formally specifying the money an agency is authorized to spend.

Approval voting — first-past-the-post voting with the added concept that one can vote for as many candidates' names as one wishes. A more straightforward form of preferential voting eliminating the chances of minority candidates winning when too many mainstream candidates are running against each other.

Articles of Confederation — a document that established a "firm league of friendship" or weak federal Congress between the original thirteen states during the Revolutionary War.

Attack journalism — journalism that aims to undermine political leaders.

Authoritarian regime — a government that can do whatever it wants, without limits.

Authority — the ability of the government to exercise power without resorting to violence.

Authorization — a formal declaration by a congressional committee that a certain amount of money is available to an agency.

Autocracy — a form of government where an individual or regime holds unlimited power.

B

Bad tendency doctrine — interpretation of the First Amendment that would allow Congress or state legislatures to prohibit or limit speech or expression that incites illegal activity.

Bad-tendency rule — a rule to judge if speech can be limited (i.e., if the speech could lead to some "evil," it can be prohibited).

Bakke **case** — the Supreme Court (1978) held that quota systems are unconstitutional, but affirmative action (i.e., preferential treatment) is legal if race is not the only factor considered.

Balance of power — the leverage a small party in the legislature possesses by voting support to a significant (albeit still minority) party to allow it to have a majority on a vote.

Balanced budget — when a government spends precisely as the revenue (i.e., taxes) raised.

Ballot — a method of secret voting, generally in a written form; a form provided to each voter on election day to be marked, showing the candidates' names (and sometimes the parties) standing for election.

Ballot initiative — a public policy question to be decided by a general vote; the placement of the question on the ballot is initiated by the people (usually by petition); used only at the state level.

Bell the cat — an impractical suggestion that highlights the theorist's short-sightedness advocating a problem's solution that will not work in practice or politically lethal for the party proposing it. It is derived from a fable about a group of mice who decide the best way to be warned when the cat is near is for someone to place a bell around its neck, only to find there are no volunteers to perform that task.

Bellwether — a small entity whose characteristics reflect that of the whole nation (a bellwether is a ram with a bell attached to indicate to the farmer where the flock is when not in sight). For example, Nevada is a bellwether state for American presidential elections in that it has voted the same as the whole country for a century with only one exception.

The Beltway — describes the politically and socially insular community of Washington, D.C.; derived from Interstate Highway 495, which circumnavigates Washington, forming a "belt;" the term is sometimes used in other countries. In Britain, the equivalent is "the Westminster Bubble."

Bicameral (legislature) — describes a legislative branch divided into two Houses (e.g., the United States Congress, which consists of the House of Representatives and the Senate).

Bigot — a person who refuses to discuss, consider or listen to beliefs or theories contrary to their own; derived from the French term of abuse in the Middle Ages for religious Normans who would frequently use the term "By God."

Bilateral — a state is acting in cooperation with another state.

Bill — the name for proposed legislation entered to Congress to be debated and then voted upon for approval; if approved at all stages, it becomes an Act and enacts a law. The document accompanying a petition usually asking for legislative action of a permanent nature.

Bill of attainder —a no-longer practiced ancient *writ* (i.e., act) of Parliament to declare someone guilty of a crime or subject to punishment without the benefit of a trial. Attainder means tainted-ness, meant someone guilty of a capital crime lost all civil rights including property and, if not life, then right to reputation. A bill passed by a legislature imposing a penalty on a particular individual or group is forbidden by Article I, Section 9 of the U.S. Constitution.

Bill of Rights —a list of entrenched fundamental human rights as perceived by the declarer (known as Charter of Rights or Declaration of Rights); whereas a nation's enacted laws protect people from their fellow citizens' malevolent deeds. Bill of Rights protects the citizenry from the excesses of their rulers; a term derived from the 1689 Bill of Rights enacted by the British Parliament after the Glorious Revolution; the first ten Amendments to the U.S. Constitution safeguard specific rights of the American people and the states.

Bipartisan(ship) — cooperation and collaboration between members of the two major political parties (e.g., Republicans and Democrats) to agree on an initiative.

Bipartisan Campaign Finance Reform Act — a 2002 law that banned soft money, put limits on issue advertising, and increased the amount people can donate to candidates. See *McCain-Feingold bill.*

Bipolar system — an international system characterized by two superpowers that balance.

Blanket primary — a primary in which voters can choose candidates from more than one party; declared unconstitutional by the Supreme Court.

Block grant — a grant-in-aid with few restrictions or rules about how it can be spent.

Block voting — in multi-member electorates; each voter has the same number of votes as the number of vacant seats; this minimizes the chances of minority candidates winning seats.

Boondoggle — a wasteful government-financed infrastructure developed at a cost much higher than its value, undertaken for territorial or political gain.

Bourgeois — Marxist term for middle-class professionals living a relatively luxurious lifestyle.

Brief — a document submitted to a court that presents one side's argument in a case.

Brinksmanship — hostile diplomatic relations where at least one party is prepared to risk all and go to the brink of war, economic ruin, or whatever calamitous situation to get what they want (e.g., the present government of North Korea).

Broadcast media — media that is distributed over the airwaves.

Brown v. Board of Education — a 1954 Supreme Court decision ending segregation and holding "separate but equal" schools and facilities unconstitutional.

Bundling — the practice of lumping campaign donations from several donors together, sometimes to disguise contributors' identities.

Bureaucracy — an administrative way of organizing large numbers of people to work together; usually relies on specialization, hierarchy, and standard operating procedure.

Buying power — one's ability to purchase things; it is undermined by inflation.

By-law —a government rule or regulation; see *Delegated legislation*.

C

Cabinet — a group, composed of the heads of federal departments and critical agencies that advises the President; the President as the head and each Secretary responsible for the relevant government departments (e.g., Defense, Environment, Commerce).

Caesaropapism — the belief that the powers of church and state should be united in one person.

Candidate — an individual who stands for election to political office.

Candidate-centered politics — campaigns that focus on the candidates, not party labels.

Capitalism — an economic system based on the recognition of private property rights, where prices are dictated by supply and demand and the means of production and distribution of goods and services derived from privately owned resources, or capital, operating within a minimally regulated or unregulated market.

Caretaker government — governance where those in power refrain from significant actions (e.g., undertaking major legislative programs) and only maintain necessary administrative duties. This is because power would be in transition due to an election or other situation where the legitimate democratic government has to be restored.

Carpetbagger — a pejorative term to describe outsiders taking advantage of a situation where others would generally be expected to benefit. A carpet bag was a popular form of luggage used by northern "Yankees," political appointees, or opportunistic businessmen. They moved down to southern states during the American post-Civil War Reconstruction era. These migrants took advantage of the instability, power vacuum, and fire-sale prices of the property market.

Case law — the collection of court decisions (i.e., precedence) that shape legal decisions.

Casework — work was done by a member of Congress or their staff on behalf of constituents.

casus belli — the alleged justification for acts of war.

Categorical grants — money allocated for a specific purpose that comes with restrictions concerning how the money should be spent; there are two types of categorical grants: *project grants* and *formula grants*.

Caucus (legislative) — a group of legislators unified by common goals or characteristics; the largest congressional caucuses are the Republican and Democratic party caucuses. Other caucuses include the Black Caucus, the Hispanic Caucus, and other issue-oriented caucuses.

Caucus (local party) — a closed meeting of members of a political party to make decisions, such as which candidate to nominate for an office; to set policy, and to plot strategy. Also, the term for a group of people within an establishment with a shared political leaning.

Cause célèbre — French for "famous case," a controversy (often a court case) arousing high public interest because of "sensitive" policy issues (e.g., Scopes Monkey Trial, *Roe v. Wade* Supreme Court cases).

Census — counting the population to determine representation in the House of Representatives; the Constitution mandates one every ten years.

Central bank — the institution with the power to implement monetary policy.

Centralization — the process by which law and policymaking become centrally located.

Centrally planned economy — an economy where the government makes all decisions.

Charter — a document issued by state government granting certain powers and responsibilities to a local government.

Checks and balances — the ability of government branches to stop each other from acting, designed to prevent one branch from gaining too much power (e.g., the President's ability to veto legislation and the judicial authority to declare acts unconstitutional).

Chief diplomat — the President's role as the primary representative between the United States and other nations.

Chief of state — the ceremonial head of government; the President serves as the chief of state.

Citizen — a legal member of a political unit.

Citizens initiated referendum — a democratic vehicle for legislative or constitutional enactment in some states. Suppose a specific proposition petition garners a certain number of signatures. The legislature is compelled to put it to the people at a referendum vote and enact it in law if passed.

Civic education — education geared toward training the young to be good citizens.

Civil liberties — individual freedoms that the government cannot take away, including free speech, freedom of religion, and the accused's rights.

Civil Rights Act of 1964 — the primary civil rights legislation in the modern era; banned discrimination and segregation in public accommodations.

Civil Rights Cases — an 1883 Supreme Court decision that the Fourteenth Amendment only made discrimination by the government illegal; private citizens were not restrained.

Civil service — government employees hired and promoted by merit, not political connections.

Civil Service Commission — the first federal personnel agency; an impartial, independent board that hears and decides appeals filed by individual state and municipal workers.

Civil Service Reform Act of 1883 — a law that established the federal civil service; see *Pendleton Act.*

Civil Service Reform Act of 1978 — a law that updated and reformed the civil service.

Civil society — the network of community relationships that builds social capital.

Civil war — a war fought within a country between or among different groups of citizens who want to control the government and do not recognize another group's right to rule.

***civis romanus sum* [Latin, I am a Roman citizen]** — ancient Romans claimed full rights and protection in foreign lands because the Roman military responds to any violations.

Classical conservatism — a view that arose in opposition to classical liberalism; it claims tradition is precious, human reason limited, and stability essential.

Classical liberalism — a political philosophy that arose in the early modern era in Europe that individual human beings are autonomous with inviolable rights and that government powers arise from the people. It argues for the value of the individual, the necessity for freedom, the importance of rationalism, and free markets.

Clear and present danger — a concept in American constitutional law to describe a situation where fundamental constitutional principles can be ignored in exigent circumstances.

Client state — a country that is economically or militarily dependent upon another but not controlled politically by the patron state, a "puppet state."

Closed rule — a rule in the House of Representatives which forbids amendments to a bill being considered on the floor

Closed primary — a primary election in which only voters who belong to a political party are permitted to vote (e.g., only registered Democrats can vote in a closed Democratic primary).

Closed shop — a place of work where the union has arranged that the employer only employ those people who are union members.

Cloture — a motion to end debate in the Senate; requires Senate vote.

Coattail effect — a boost in electoral support realized by candidates lower down the ballot when a successful candidate of their party runs strong at the top of the ballot (e.g., a popular presidential candidate who wins a large percentage of the vote might carry other Party candidates into office on their "coattails").

Codetermination — a policy in some countries with strong social democratic parties that forces large corporations to have substantial representation from their workers on the board of directors.

Cold war — between the United States and the former Soviet Union which involved no direct conflict between the two nations. Instead was characterized by a multibillion-dollar nuclear arms race and numerous aggressive acts against secondary (or "satellite") nations backed (sometimes publicly, sometimes secretly) by each nation.

Commander-in-Chief — constitutional role of the President as leader of the armed forces.

Command economy — compared to the free market, an economy that is mostly under the government's command.

Commerce clause — a clause in Article I, Section 8 of the U.S. Constitution grants Congress the power to regulate interstate commerce.

Committee on Bills in the Third Reading — a committee of three which is empowered to examine and correct bills and resolutions before their final reading in the Senate or House; resolutions for adoption, and amendments to bills, resolves, and resolutions adopted and before the body for concurrence.

Common-carrier role — the media's role as an intermediary between people and the government.

Common law — the law comes from neither statute nor the constitution, but from court law reports. Initially, that body of law, which was common to all parts of England (not customary or local law) and developed over centuries by the English courts. It was subsequently adopted by and developed in countries using that system. In contrast to democratically maintained law, common law is judge-maintained and modified law and is valid unless it conflicts with statute (legislative) law or constitutional underpinnings.

Communism — a form of socialism advocating violent revolution to create a socialist state.

Communitarianism — the concept of collective, rather than individual, ownership of the nation's assets and the duty by those able to create and manage those assets.

Comparative advantage — a state's ability to produce a good or service at a lower marginal or opportunity cost than another. For example, suppose country A can produce cars and electronics cheaper than country B, with cars significantly cheaper. In that case, it is more efficient for it to build and export only cars while importing electronics, even though the imported electronics are more expensive than if they were domestic.

Comparative politics — an academic discipline comparing states to evaluate how they work.

Concurrence — agreement by one branch with an action originating in the other branch.

Concurrent powers — powers shared and exercised jointly under the Constitution by federal and state governments (e.g., taxation, law enforcement).

Concurrent resolution — a statement of the Congress's opinion, passed by both the House and the Senate; not legally binding.

Concurring opinion — an opinion issued by a judge who votes with the prevailing side but in some way disagrees with the majority or plurality opinion.

Confederacy — a loose relationship among some smaller political units.

Confederalism — a form of federalism where the individual regions that make up the sovereign state exercise a more substantial degree of autonomy. Often claiming the right to secede and sole right to raise taxes. The pre-Civil War slave states of America united to form the Confederate States of America to maintain their states' rights.

Confederate system — a system of government with a weak central and strong state government.

Conference committee — a committee comprised of House and Senate members charged with reconciling the House and Senate versions of a bill. Consisting of three members from each body (one senator and one representative acting as chairpersons) appointed by the legislative leaders to resolve differences between the two bodies concerning a specific matter. Failure of the committee to agree or failure of one body to accept the committee's recommendation results in a new conference committee's appointment.

Conformism — a tendency for people to behave similarly (e.g., read the same news sources).

Conservatism —political philosophy favoring limited government with minimal regulation and governmental interference in the economy. In general, conservatives favor giving power to state and local governments rather than to the federal government. This term is synonymous with "right-wing," protecting against "immoral" behavior; a belief in the established order.

Constituent — a citizen residing in a legislator's area or district.

Constituency — the people in a district represented by a legislator.

Constitution — the structures and fundamental principles of how power will be distributed and used legitimately by an organization, state or nation. It is usually written (Great Britain is notable for its "unwritten" constitution). The United States Constitution is the *supreme law of the land*, meaning other laws (including state laws), executive actions, and judicial decisions must be consistent. By granting power to the government from the people, the Constitution can only be changed by Congress and state legislatures' ratification.

Constitutional amendment — a formally proposed and ratified change to the Constitution that becomes a fully binding provision of the Constitution.

Constitutional democracy — a system of governance based on popular sovereignty in which the structures, powers, and limits of government are set forth in a constitution.

Constitutional government — a regime in which the use of power is limited by law.

Constitutional law — a law that finds its basis in the Constitution; more broadly, "constitutional law" is the interpretations of constitutional questions rendered by the Supreme Court and lower courts in published court opinions.

Constitutional powers — the powers of the President granted explicitly by the Constitution.

Constitutional convention —a gathering to write a new constitution or amend an existing constitution.

Consumer price index — a measurement of inflation arrived at by comparing, at regular intervals, the price (taking weighting into account) of a set of essential consumer goods and services purchased by households.

Consumption tax — a tax levied on goods and services such as sales tax, GST, VAT, or an excise tax. A tax on the spending of income rather than its earnings includes people who might evade paying income tax (e.g., underground economy).

Continuing resolution — a temporary spending bill that funds government programs until funds are appropriated for them.

Continuing resolution — a measure passed by Congress that temporarily funds an agency while Congress completes its budget.

Conventional participation — political participation in activities deemed appropriate by most people (e.g., voting, donating to a campaign, writing letters to officeholders).

Convention delegate — a party member or official who goes to the national convention to vote for the party's presidential nominee and ratify the party's platform.

Cooperative federalism — a term used to describe federalism for most of the twentieth century (and into the twenty-first), where the federal government and the states are partners, not competitors, in the exercise of governmental authority; see *Marble-cake federalism*.

Corrupt practices acts — a series of laws in the early twentieth century that were the first attempts to regulate campaign finance.

coup d'état — the sudden and often violent overthrow of a government.

Credentials committee — party officials who decide which delegates may participate in the national convention.

Critical election — an election that marks the advent of a realignment.

Crossing the aisle — a legislator crossing the floor of Congress to vote with the opposition party.

Crossover voting — members of one party voting for candidates of another; encouraged by open primaries; see *Split-ticket voting*.

Cumulative voting — a type of block voting; where the voter can choose from a list of candidates running for fewer seats, their ranked preference for each candidate. In such decisions, the selected candidates would get one-quarter of a vote each, half a vote, or where only one candidate received the vote, the whole vote.

D

Daily list — inventory of committee hearings with the committee name, its matters, and the time and room number of each hearing.

Damage control — the concerted defensive response a politician adopts to offset negative publicity about an embarrassing situation (e.g., controversial comment, scandal).

Darkhorse candidate — an unexpected candidate with little public exposure who can win an election against established candidates; the term originated by British Prime Minister and author Benjamin Disraeli.

Dealignment — the loosening of party ties as more voters are independent.

Debt — the accumulated amount of unpaid budget deficits.

Decision — a document issued by the court stating who prevails in litigation.

Declaration of Independence — the document written by Thomas Jefferson in 1776 formally broke the colonies away from British rule.

Deficit — the shortfall in a nation's income compared to its expenditure and the total unpaid accumulated debt of the government over time; see *National debt*.

Deficit spending — the government intentionally spending more money than raised in taxes in a fiscal year.

de facto **segregation** — segregation due to economic and behavioral patterns, not because of law.

Defamation of character — unfairly hurting a person's reputation.

de jure **segregation** — segregation imposed by law.

Delegate — a representative who bases their votes on the majority of the people they represent.

Delegated legislation — rules, regulations, by-laws, and ordinances made by a government official under the authority of a specific act of parliament; sets out the overall purpose of what is desired but delegates to that official's office the authority to create the minutiae (the delegated legislation) necessary. In contrast, all parliamentary legislation is final and cannot be challenged in court (apart from constitutional inconsistencies). Delegated legislation can be challenged in court if it violates the Act's purpose; see *Enabling legislation*.

Delegated powers — powers granted by Congress to help the President fulfill their duties.

Demagogue — a leader who gains popularity by appealing to prejudice and basic instincts, often considered manipulative and dangerous.

Demand-side economics — an approach to economic policy that stresses the stimulation of demand by putting more money at the disposal of consumers.

Democracy — a form of government in which policy alternatives are voted on by the people with the majority determining the outcome (i.e., rule by the people); from the Greek "demos" for the ordinary, everyday people and "*Kratos*" for power or strength.

Democratic socialism — a form of socialism that works within democratic governments to attain socialism gradually.

Demosclerosis — the U.S. government's inability to legislate because interest groups impede major change.

Denial of power — declaring that an individual or group does not have a specific power.

Deontology — the concept of moral obligation and binding duty; the goodness and righteousness are evaluated by the act alone (the means justify the means). Compare to *consequentialism*, where an act is judged by its consequences (the ends justify the means).

Depression — a severe economic downturn that lasts a long time, more severe than a recession.

Deregulation — the repeal or reduction of regulations to boost efficiency, increase competitiveness, and benefit consumers.

Descriptive / normative ethics —the study of what people think is moral. Normative, or prescriptive, ethics is the study of what is moral. Meta-ethics is the study of what "moral," or any other term, means.

Deterrence — threatening to use military force to prevent another state from a course of action.

Devolution — the federal government giving increased responsibilities and powers to the state, local, or regional governments.

Dictatorship — an absolute government in which one person holds all the power and uses it for their self-interest.

Diplomacy — the act of negotiating with other nations; trying to achieve goals without force.

Direct democracy — a system or process that depends on the voice of the people (and not representatives), usually through referendums or initiatives, to make public policy decisions; government by the people rather than merely in principle, with the citizenry themselves voting on all issues affecting them (practiced in ancient Greece, some cantons of Switzerland and some small towns in New England); considered to be a highly abstract form of government.

Direct primary — an election in which rank-and-file members (and not the leaders) of a political party select nominees to represent their party in the general election.

Discharge petition — a measure in the House forcing a bill out of a committee for consideration by the House.

Discretionary spending — spending raised, lowered, kept even, or eliminated by Congress.

Disinformation — false or misleading information disseminated for strategic gain.

Dissenting opinion — a court opinion written by the minority (i.e., losing) side explains why it disagrees with the majority (i.e., prevailing) decision.

Dissolved — termination of a session of the legislature (e.g., the first Wednesday in January).

Diversity — a mix of different cultural, ethnic, and religious traditions and values.

Divided government — a situation in which one party controls the presidency while the other controls at least one House of Congress (known as "divided-party government").

Divine right theory of kingship — the view that God chooses the monarch to rule with absolute power over a country.

Division of labor — the practice of dividing a job into smaller parts and assigning each part.

Donkey vote — the excess votes a candidate at the top of the ballot paper receives because some voters do not bother to consider their decision but tick the first box on the ballot (known as the "unthinking vote").

Doublespeak — using language that intentionally distorts or obscures the meaning of unpalatable information or policy; sometimes the real meaning is the exact opposite; allegedly the amalgam of two terms invented by George Orwell in his novel *1984*, "doublethink" and "newspeak."

Dual federalism — belief that the federal government and state governments have distinct realms of authority that do not overlap and the other should not intrude. Describes federalism throughout most of the nineteenth century, when the federal and state governments rarely overlapped. See *layer-cake federalism*.

Due process clause — the Fourteenth Amendment declares that no person can be deprived of life, liberty, or property without due process of law.

Duopoly — describes the overwhelming power of the two major parties in American politics.

duumvirate / triumvirate / quadrumvirate — Latin terms to describe a group of two, three, or four people (respectively) joined in authority or office.

Dynasty — a sequence of hereditary rulers.

Dystopia — a nightmare vision of society beyond failed, a dysfunctional state where the system is planned by those in power, creating (most often) a totalitarian society (fictional examples are Jack London's *The Iron Heel* and George Orwell's *1984*); alternative to "utopia."

E

Earned Income Tax Credit — a federal welfare program that refunds all or part of a low-income family's social security tax.

Economic aid — assistance to other countries designed to help the recipient's economy.

Economic group — an interest group that seeks material benefits for its members.

Economic growth — the expansion of the economy, leading to more jobs and more wealth.

Effective tax rate — the percentage of one's income paid in taxes after deductions and tax credits.

Elastic clause — a clause in Article I, Section 8 of the Constitution that says Congress has the power to do anything necessary and proper to carry out its expressed powers. See *necessary and proper clause.*

Elector — a member of the Electoral College. The voters in elections or to those appointed to a certain level to vote their choice to a higher office (e.g., members of the Electoral College that choose the President). Technically, a voter who is successful in helping to get their preferred candidate elected.

Electorate — all the people in a country, state, or district who are entitled to vote in an election.

Electoral College — the body that elects the President of the United States; composed of electors from each state equal to that state's Representation in Congress; a candidate must get the most electoral votes to win.

Elitism/elite theory — the view that a small, capable group should rule over the rest.

Emergency powers — inherent powers exercised by the President to solve emergencies.

Emergency preamble — an expressionary statement to a bill setting forth the facts constituting an emergency. The statement that the law is necessary for the immediate preservation of the public peace, health, safety or convenience. Matters with emergency preambles become law immediately upon approval by the governor. Either the governor or the legislature may attach a preamble.

Emigrate — one who leaves their home country to settle in another permanently.

Empire — a state that governs more than one national group, usually from conquest.

Enabling legislation — a law passed by Congress describing the general purposes and powers of an agency but grants the agency power to determine the policy's details.

Enactment — final passage of a bill in identical form by the House and Senate, signed into law by the President (or governor) or passed over their veto.

Engrossed bill — the final version of a bill for enactment or resolve before the House or Senate after typing and certification by the clerk.

Enlightenment — the 18th-century epoch of intellectual advances where humanity entered the light of reason from the darkness of tradition (i.e., "the Age of Reason"). The term originated in the U.K. but developed most fully in continental countries such as France, with thinkers such as Baruch Spinoza (1632-1677), Voltaire (1694-1778), and Rousseau (1712-1778).

Entitlement programs — benefits extended to individuals who meet legislatively-established eligibility requirements; any individual who meets the requirements is considered "entitled" to the benefit, regardless of the overall amount spent on providing the benefit to all eligible individuals.

Enumerated powers — explicit powers of Congress in Article I, Section 8 of the Constitution.

Environmental impact statement — a statement prepared by the federal government before acting describes how the environment will be affected.

Environmentalism — believes humans must protect the world from the excesses of human habitation, including pollution and the destruction of wilderness.

Equality — the state of being equal, especially in status, rights, and opportunities; impartiality.

Equality of opportunity — when all have equal chances to compete and achieve so that those with talent and diligence succeed, whereas others will not.

Equality of finish — equal outcomes, generally measured regarding socioeconomic status; the "finish" in question generally refers to accomplishments after entering adulthood.

Equality of outcome — when people achieve the same result, regardless of talent or effort.

Equality of start — equal opportunity, generally measured regarding equal access to quality education and training.

Equal protection clause — a provision in the 14th Amendment to the Constitution that guarantees all people "equal protection under the law."

Equal Rights Amendment — a proposed amendment that would have ended gender discrimination; it failed to be ratified by the state since 1972.

Equal time rule — a broadcast media regulation that requires media outlets to give equal amounts of time to opposing candidates in an election.

Equity — when all parties to a transaction are treated fairly.

Equity law — an auxiliary part of the common law where the courts have the authority to modify existing common law to adapt to modern times. The courts have the power to create original law, overriding existing common law in circumstances where it is deemed that without it, "unconscionable" conduct would occur.

Establishment clause — the First Amendment forbids the governmental establishment of religion.

Excess demand — an economic situation in which the demand for something exceeds the supply.

Exchange rate — the relationship between the values of two countries' currencies. Any one-off reading is informative when considering what each country's currency unit will buy in its domestic market. When the rate changes over time, it indicates one country's economy is not doing and the other.

Exclusionary rule — a rule that excludes from a trial any evidence obtained in an illegal search.

The Executive — that part of the government which put into effect (i.e., execute) the law, as compared to the legislature which creates laws (i.e., statutes); comprises public service officials from the Presidential branch responsible for the daily administration of the state.

Executive agreement — an agreement made between the President of the United States and the leader of another country or countries; it has the same effect as a treaty but does not need to be ratified by the Senate.

Executive branch — a branch of government charged with "executing" or implementing and enforcing the laws.

Executive leadership — the view that the President should have a strong influence over the bureaucracy.

Executive Office of the President — a set of agencies working closely with the President to help them perform their job.

Executive order — an order issued by the President that has the effect of law.

Executive privilege — claim that the President, as the Executive Branch leader, has the prerogative to divulge or refuse to divulge information in a manner that they believe most consistent with the national interest. The executive branch's right to refuse to disclose some information to the other branches or the public.

ex officio **[Latin, by virtue of one's office]** — the power to do something or hold an office because one holds an earlier office (e.g., the Vice President is, ex officio, the President of the Senate).

ex post facto **law** — a law that declares something illegal after it has been done.

Expressed powers — the specific powers given to Congress or the President by the Constitution. See *enumerated powers*.

F

Fabian Society — a movement founded in 1884 by intellectuals Sidney Webb (1859-1947) and Beatrice Webb (1858-1943), and George Bernard Shaw (1856-1950). They believed the only way to introduce socialism is incremental, using education and gradual legislative changes. It was named after the Roman general Fabius Cunctator ("the delayer") who possessed the patience to defeat the Carthaginian Hannibal (247-184 B.C.) using a slow war of attrition and harassment.

Faction — a group united in pursuing shared political values; a political party is a large faction.

Fairness doctrine — a broadcast media regulation that requires broadcast media airing a controversial program to provide airtime to those with an opposing view.

Faithless elector — an Electoral College elector who votes for someone other than the candidate who won the most votes in the state.

Fascism — an authoritarian and nationalist political ideology that embraces strong leadership, singular collective identity, and the will to commit violence or wage war to further the state's interests. Averse to concepts such as individualism, pluralism, multiculturalism, or egalitarianism.

Favorable report — a committee recommendation that a matter ought to pass; a matter takes its first reading at this time.

Federal budget — detailing how the federal government will spend money during a fiscal year.

Federal Communications Commission (FCC) — the federal agency that regulates the broadcast media.

Federal Election Campaign Act — a law passed in 1971 that limited media advertising expenditures and required disclosure of donations above $100; made more stringent following the Watergate scandal.

Federal Election Commission (FEC) — the independent regulatory agency created in 1974 to enforce campaign finance laws.

Federal Register — a federal publication that lists all executive orders.

Federal Reserve Bank — the name of the central bank of the United States, called the Fed.

Federal system — a government system with shared power between the central, state, and local governments; see *Federalism.*

Federalism — a system under which governmental powers are divided (e.g., national, state, local) between the central government and the states or provinces, all within the same geographical territory; opposite to the unitary system of the U.K., New Zealand, and Japan. See also: *cooperative federalism, horizontal federalism, layer-cake federalism, marble-cake federalism, new federalism.*

Federalist Papers — a series of essays written to support ratifying the Constitution, written by Alexander Hamilton, John Jay, and James Madison.

Federalists —supporters of the Constitution during the battle for its ratification; one of the first two major political parties in the United States (opposed by the Anti-Federalists).

Fellow traveler — mid-20th-century term to describe someone who allegedly sympathized with Communism but would not go so far as to declare themselves a Communist or join the party.

Feminism — the belief that women are equal to men and should be treated equally by the law.

Fence mending — a politician returning to his electorate, hoping to restore his reputation with the voters.

Fifth column — in a military or political environment, a person who surreptitiously undermines a group or entity from within. A term derived from a Nationalist General during the Spanish Civil War (1936-1939) who boasted he had four columns of troops attacking Madrid and the fifth column of sympathizers inside the city. Sometimes described as "entryism," the Alec Guinness (1914-2000) character in the film *Dr. Zhivago* (1965) was a wartime fifth columnist.

Filibuster — a form of legislative obstruction by a Congress member through prolonging a speech for merely preventing a vote. The agenda calendar allocates the business of reading, debating, and voting on a bill on its allotted day; it may a long time before it again comes before the House. A Senator in the minority opposing a bill holds the floor, speaking incessantly (in effect shutting down the Senate) until the majority backs down and kills the bill.

First Continental Congress — a gathering of representatives from all thirteen colonies in 1774; called for a total boycott of British goods to protest taxes.

First-past-the-post — an electoral system where the winning candidate needs only the most votes, even if well below a majority (known as "pluralist voting").

Fiscal federalism — states spending federal money to administer national programs.

Fiscal policy — policies and programs establishing budgetary policy, including types and rates of taxation and types and amounts of spending.

Fiscal year — a twelve-month period that does not coincide with the calendar year (beginning October 1 and ending September 30). A term used for accounting and budget purposes by the federal government.

527 groups — a political organization not affiliated with a party that can raise and spends soft money. It is named after a section of the Internal Revenue Code (IRS).

Fixed-term — describes the set term of office (e.g., U.S. House of Representatives is two years). Compare with other democracies like the U.K., where the House of Commons term of office is for a maximum of five years but can be shorter at the Prime Minister's discretion.

Flat tax — tax collected at the same rate or percentage regardless of income level (e.g., 15%).

Food stamps — coupons issued by the government used to purchase food.

Foreign policy — a state's international goals and its strategies to achieve those goals.

Formal session — meeting to consider and act upon reports of committees, messages from the governor, petitions, orders, enactment papers from the other branch, matters in the Orders of the Day, and other matters which may be controversial and during which roll-call votes may be taken.

Formalized rules — the standard operating procedure.

Formula grants — grants in which a formula determines how much money each state receives.

Fourth estate — the unofficial political institution and authority comprising the press and media; the term comes from the first three estates of the French States-General: the church, the nobility, and the townsmen.

Framers — the 55 appointed delegates to the 1787 Constitutional Convention and took part in drafting the United States' proposed Constitution.

Franchise — the right to vote; see *Suffrage*.

Franking — Congressional members mail informational literature to constituents free of charge.

Free exercise clause — the part of the First Amendment forbidding the government from interfering in the free exercise of religion.

Free rider — someone who can receive government policy benefits without incurring any of the costs; an individual who chooses not to contribute to an interest group but benefits from the group's activities.

Friday news dump — the practice of governments releasing embarrassing or unpopular news before the weekend when few people pay attention to the news. The act of lumping together stories to minimize the effect of each one); known as "take out the trash day."

From each according to his ability... — "*From each according to his ability to each according to his needs,*" slogan made famous by Karl Marx (1818-1883) in an 1875 publication highlighting a fundamental tenet of communism. Allegedly a retort to capitalism.

Front-loading — moving primaries up in the campaign calendar to be early in the cycle.

Front-runner — the candidate perceived to be in the lead in an election campaign.

Full faith and credit clause — a clause in Article IV of the Constitution that declares that state governments must give *full faith and credit* to other state governments' decisions.

Fundamentalism — the belief that a religious document is infallible and trustworthy.

G

Gag order — an order by a court to block people from talking or writing about a trial.

Gender discrimination — treating people differently and unequally because of gender.

Gender gap — the difference between women and men in political ideology or political party preferences; in recent years, women have been more likely than men to support the Democrats.

General election — either an election that is not local but is for the state or federal government or an election that is the final arbiter after the primaries.

General jurisdiction — a court's power to hear cases, which is mostly unrestricted.

General law — legislative act generally applying to the State and its citizens.

General laws — all of the laws of a state of a general and permanent nature as embodied in the Official Edition of General Laws (e.g., updated monthly), together with all amending and related general statutes subsequently enacted down through the current session of the legislature.

Georgism —a philosophy created by the 19th-century American economist Henry George (1839-1897) advocating things found in nature (e.g., land) remains the state's property. Government revenue would be raised by fees (e.g., rents on land, mineral and mining rights, fishing licenses).

Gerrymandering — the redrawing of a political district to favor a candidate or kind of candidate (e.g., an incumbent, a member of a political party or a racial minority). Intended to have a partisan and unfair effect on the total vote. The concept is named after Elbridge Gerry (1744-1814), governor of Massachusetts from 1810-1812.

Gibbons v. Ogden — an 1824 Supreme Court ruling on federal government's extensive powers through the *commerce clause* of Article I, Section 8, Clause 3.

Gideon v. Wainwright — a 1963 Supreme Court decision ordering governments to provide an attorney to indigent criminal defendants.

Glad-hander — an excessively "friendly" person, typically a politician, who greets another effusively but insincerely to gain popularity.

Glasnost — Russian for "publicness," a policy that commits the government to greater accountability and visibility, such as freedom of information laws.

Globalization — the trend toward the breakdown of state borders and the rise of international and global organizations and government bodies.

Godwin's Law — theory by American journalist Mike Godwin that as an online discussion or argument grows longer, one party's compares the other to Nazis approaches.

Going negative — a campaigning style where an election candidate emphasizes the opponent's negative attributes rather than their positive plans for future governance. Sometimes a legitimate action if the opponent has character or competency issues, but otherwise used to compensate for the fact the candidate has little to offer in experience, vision, or plans.

Government — the organization of power within a country.

Government Accountability Office — Congress's principal investigative agency; investigates government agencies' operations as part of congressional oversight.

Government bond — a promissory note issued by the government paying the original price plus interest.

Government corporation — a federal agency that operates like a corporation (following business practices and charging for services) but receives some federal funding.

Grandfather clause —a voting law that stated that a person could vote if their grandfather were eligible to vote before 1867. It was designed to keep African Americans from voting; an exemption to a new law which accommodates already existing entities (metaphoric "grandfathers") not having to comply (e.g., the law increasing the drinking age from 18 to 21 but exempting those under 21 who were legally entitled to consume alcohol).

Grant-in-aid — a general term that describes federal aid given to the states for a matter.

Grant of power — declaring that a person or group has a specific power.

Grassroots activism — efforts to influence government by mobilizing people.

Grassroots — the everyday people; the term generally refers to movements or political parties created by them rather than by professionals, elitists, or established leaders.

Great Compromise — the compromise plan on representation in the constitutional convention; created a bicameral legislature with representation determined by population in one House and compelling equality in the other (with each state getting two Senators); see *Connecticut Compromise.*

Gross domestic product (GDP) — the monetary value of all economic activity (goods and services produced) in a nation during one calendar year. The total amount produced onshore, whether by local or foreign entities. The total value of all economic transactions within a state.

Gross national product (GNP) — the monetary value of the goods and services produced in a nation during one calendar year; the total output of goods and services annually produced by a country, whether on or offshore.

Group benefits — incentives such as mementos (e.g., calendars, mugs) or financial benefits (e.g., insurance discounts) given to people who join a group; these benefits are often unrelated to the primary purposes and goals of the group.

Groupthink — an attitude that exists in academia or the media with unanimity in approaches to specific issues, either due to laziness in research or fear of the consequences of going against the prevailing wisdom.

Gubernatorial — of or relating to a state governor or the office of the state governor.

Guerrilla war — a war in which combatants use small, lightly armed militia units rather than professional, organized armies. Guerrilla fighters usually seek to topple their government, often having peoples' (sometimes covert) support.

Gun control — policies that aim at regulating and reducing the use of firearms.

H

habeas corpus **[Latin, deliver the body]** — a writ, issued by a court upon request, for a government authority to present a person it is detaining to the court and give justification as to why they should continue to be detained.

Hack — a derogatory term for a journalist of very ordinary, unexceptional talents employed to do routine work. It is derived from the term for an old saddle horse still performing basic duties.

Hatch Act — a 1939 law restricting federal civil servants' participation in political campaigns.

Hegemony — dominance or leadership of one state or social group over another.

Hierarchy — an arrangement of power with a small number of people at the top issuing orders through a chain of command to lower-level workers; each is responsible to someone above them.

Hoi polloi — the ordinary people, as compared to the wealthy, higher educated or elite.

Hollow men — conviction-free, consensus-driven politicians who live by the polls and desiring to achieve and maintain political power; found in major parties on both sides. A term derived from the 1925 T.S. Eliot (1888-1965) poem describing *"men of straw."*

Home rule — the granting of significant autonomy to local governments by state governments.

Homestyle — the way a member of Congress behaves in their district.

Honeymoon — period shortly after an election, particularly a presidential election, during which the winning candidate enjoys a surge in public and political support. The first few months of an administration in which the public, Congress members, and the media tend to give the President their goodwill.

Horizontal federalism — how state governments relate to each another.

House and Senate Rules — rules of order and procedure adopted by that branch at the beginning of each biennial session.

House of Representatives (U.S.) — the lower House of Congress, consisting of at most 435 members, each state has members proportional to its population.

House Rules Committee — the committee in the House of Representatives that creates a "rule" for each bill to be debated on the floor; establishes the time, extent of debate, and what amendments can be offered.

Humanism — cultural movement during the Renaissance (i.e., 14th to 17th centuries) emphasizing secularism and classical learning from ancient Greece and Rome; the doctrine emphasizes the human capacity for self-fulfillment without religion.

Hyperpluralism — the idea that there are too many interest groups competing for benefits.

I

Idealism — the view that states should act in the global arena to promote moral causes and use ethical means to achieve them.

Identity politics — political advocacy which, rather than proposing better ways (e.g., fight crime, improve the economy, save the environment), orient towards the victimhood (or alleged victimhood) of certain people because of demographics (e.g., age, religion, gender, race).

Ideologue — an individual with strong philosophical or ideological leanings; generally unwilling to compromise or work with others with differing views.

Ideology — a set of beliefs a person holds that shapes the way they behave and see the world.

Illegal participation — a political activity that includes illegal actions, such as vandalism, revolution, or assassination.

Impeachment — the legislative equivalent of a criminal prosecution, where a high government official is subject, by Congress, to an investigation, indictment, and subsequent trial. It is the power of the House of Representatives to charge an officeholder with crimes. The Senate then holds a trial to determine if the officeholder should be removed from office.

Implementation — the act of putting laws into practice.

Implied powers — powers not explicitly stated in the Constitution but suggested or implied by the "general welfare," the "necessary and proper," and the commerce clauses in the Constitution.

Income distribution — the way income is distributed among the population.

Income transfer — a government action that takes money from one part of the citizenry and gives it to another part; usually, the transfer goes from the well-off to the poor.

Incorporation — federal courts forcing state governments to abide by the Bill of Rights.

Incrementalism — the tendency of policy to change gradually, rather than dramatically.

Incumbent — the current holder of a seat in the legislature or an office of authority.

Independent — a person who does not profess affiliation for any party.

Independent executive agency — a federal agency that is not part of any department; its leader reports directly to the President.

Independent regulatory agency — a federal agency charged with regulating some part of the economy; in theory, such agencies are independent of Congress and the President.

Individualism — the idea that people are different and should be able to make their own choices.

Inflation — the increase in prices that accompanies a decline in a currency's purchasing power.

Informal sessions — meeting designated by the Speaker of the House and Senate President to consider reports of committees, enactments, amendments, matters in the Orders of the Day, and other non-controversial matters. Any session may be declared an informal session with prior notice given, or in cases of an emergency.

Informational benefits — the educational benefits people derive from belonging to an interest group and learning more about the issues they care about.

Inherent powers — powers not explicitly delegated to the President or Congress but are reasonable and logical derivatives needed to carry out national objectives; see *Implied powers*.

Initiative — a public policy question initiated by the people, usually by petition, and decided by voters at the ballot box.

Initiative petition — request by a specified number of voters to submit a constitutional amendment or law to the people for approval or rejection. The petition is introduced into the legislature if signed by many citizens (e.g., equal to three percent of the total vote for governor in the preceding gubernatorial election). If a proposed initiative law fails to pass the legislature, additional signatures must be placed on the ballot. A proposed initiative constitutional amendment approved by at least one-quarter of the legislature, sitting in joint sessions by two consecutively elected legislatures, shall be placed on the voters' ballot for approval.

In-kind subsidies — government aid to the poor not given as cash but in other forms (e.g., food stamps, fuel assistance, rent vouchers).

Inside game — interest groups' efforts to influence government policy by direct contact with government officials (known as "lobbying").

Interest group — an organization that shares a common interest and works to protect and promote that interest by influencing the government.

International agreement — an understanding between states to restrict their behavior and set up rules governing international affairs.

Internationalism — the view that the United States should play an active role in world affairs.

International law — a set of agreements, traditions, and norms built up over time, restricts what states can do, not always binding.

International organization — an institution by agreements between nations, such as the United Nations (UN) and the World Trade Organization (WTO).

International system — the underlying structures that affect how states relate to others, including rules and traditions.

Internet media — media distributed online.

Interpretive reporting — reporting that states the facts and provides analysis and interpretation.

Interregnum — an interval of seemingly "directionless" government, such as between administrations.

Intervention — when a state sends military forces to help a country that is already at war.

Invisible hand — the free market theory of the 18th-century economist Adam Smith that there is an "invisible hand," which guarantees that, without government intervention, there will be a supply to meet demand.

Iron triangle — an alliance of groups with an interest in a policy area (e.g., bureaucrats, legislators from the appropriate committee, and interest groups affected by the issue).

Isolationism — a policy of isolating one's country from military alliances or other commitments with all other countries as the best resort to avoiding foreign entanglements.

Historically, a strong sentiment in the USA; President Woodrow Wilson won a second term in 1916 by promising to keep America out of WWI. It subsequently entered the war; the U.S. was conspicuous for not joining the newly formed League of Nations after the War.

Issue advertising — advertising paid for by outside groups that can criticize or praise a candidate but cannot explicitly advocate for or against them.

Issue network — a collection of actors who agree on policy and work together to shape it.

J

Jim Crow laws — laws passed by southern states imposing inequality and segregation on African Americans.

Jingoism — a nineteenth and twentieth-century term describing chauvinistic, bellicose expressions of nationalism, especially in warlike pursuits. The term is associated with President Teddy Roosevelt; it derives from the bellicose. The British slang expression is "By Jingo."

Jobs for the boys — a type of political nepotism where prestigious government jobs are given to party members rather than because of merit. The term had a legitimate meaning in the early 20th century to express public gratitude for demobilized soldiers returning home from war.

Joint Chiefs of Staff — a group of the most senior uniformed leaders that helps the President make strategy decisions and evaluates the military's needs and capabilities.

Joint committees — consist of Senators and Representatives, responsible for holding public hearings and reporting on all legislative matters referred to them.

Joint rules — rules for the governing of the two bodies adopted by both branches.

Judicial activism — a judicial philosophy advocating that courts can take an active role not supported by existing law to remedy alleged wrongs in society.

Judicial branch — the branch of government that hears and settles legal disputes.

Judicial implementation — the process of enforcing a court's ruling.

Judicial philosophy — a set of ideas that shape how a judge or lawyer interprets the law and the Constitution.

Judicial restraint — a judicial philosophy that believes the court's responsibility is to interpret the law, not set policy.

Judicial review — the power of the courts to declare laws and presidential actions unconstitutional.

junta [Latin, join] — a clique, faction, or cabal, often military, taking power after an overthrow of the government.

Jurisdiction — a court's power to hear and adjudicate cases of a type (e.g., housing court).

jus ad bellum — the alleged justification a country will use to go to war.

Justiciable question — a matter that the courts can review and fashion a remedy.

Just-war theory — a theory of ethics defining when war is morally permissible and what means of warfare are justified.

K

Keynesian economics, Keynesianism — a demand-side economic policy, first presented by British economist John Maynard Keynes (1883-1946) after World War I, encourages governments' deficit spending during economic recessions to provide jobs and boost personal income.

Kitchen Cabinet — an informal name for the chief executive's closest advisers.

Kleptocracy — a cynical term that describes highly corrupt governments where politicians, bureaucrats, and their protected friends engage in sales of government licenses, perquisites, and other frauds.

Kyoto Protocol — an international treaty effective from 2005 aimed at reducing greenhouse gas emissions.

L

Laissez-faire — French for "allow to do," an economic system with abstinence of state interference.

Lame-duck — a political office holder who, because of term limits, retirement or defeat, are ending their present term of office; Presidents serving in their second terms are not eligible for a third term and are, therefore, "lame-duck" Presidents.

Lawmaking — the power to make rules that are binding on everyone in society.

Lay on the table — to temporarily postpone considering a specific bill, resolve, report, amendment, or motion. Consideration is postponed until a subsequent motion taking the item off the table succeeds.

Layer-cake federalism — a term used to describe federalism through most of the nineteenth century. The federal and state governments each had their issue areas that rarely overlapped. See *dual federalism*.

Leader of the House — a lower House member of the majority (ruling) party, elected to organize and arrange that House's proceedings.

Left-wing — the liberal or socialist side of a political system. "On the left" is a so-called "womb to tomb" (or "cradle to grave") approach to social welfare and an internationalist worldview. "On the right" describes a political philosophy favoring conservative, pro-market attitudes with a preference for individual rights instead of an "interventionist" government, a strict approach to law and order, a strong defense force, and a sense of nationalism. The terms originated in the French Estates-General in 1789 when the nobility who favored the peasant's conditions' complacency sat on the King's right. Those wanting to ameliorate the peasant's conditions sat on the left.

Legislative agenda — a series of laws a person wishes to pass.

Legislative branch — branch of government with authority to change the laws of the land.

Legislative Bulletin on Committee Work — a complete listing of all matters and the committees they are assigned. A short description of each matter, its number, hearing date, and committee report are included.

Legislative record — numerical listing of all numbered matters filed for consideration by the legislature (e.g., General Court); includes a brief description of the matter and its full legislative history.

Legitimacy — acceptance by citizens of the government.

Lemon test — a three-part test to determine if the First Amendment's establishment clause has been violated; named for the 1971 Supreme Court decision in *Lemon v. Kurtzman.*

Libel — printing false statements that defame a person's character.

Liberal democracy — reflects restraints that only allow the seemingly good (e.g., a Constitution or entrenched common law protecting freedom of speech, the press, a moderately free market, an independent judiciary, the rule of law, separation of powers, minority rights, and the notion of the individual).

Liberalism — a theory of international relations that deemphasizes the importance of military power in favor of economic power, trade, and international institutions.

Liberalism (classic) — a philosophy advocating the rights of the individual against the state or church as espoused by such eighteenth-century English writers like John Locke (1632-1704) and John Stuart Mill (1806-1873). They advocated for *laissez-faire* economics, freedom of speech, the rule of law, an extension of the franchise, amelioration in disciplinary practices, and changing views on relations between the sexes and children's upbringing. In modern times Classic Liberals have become either libertarians or "small 'l'" liberals.

liberalism (small 'l') — a modern philosophy that favors change for change's sake; encompasses a compromising and compassionate attitude to personal lifestyle, law and order, foreign affairs, and immigration; policy decisions tilt toward those in more straitened circumstances.

Libertarianism —political philosophy of self-reliance, reason, and maximum non-interference by the state in economic and personal affairs (i.e., limited government). Straddling both the left and right, a libertarian might believe in the right to bear arms, access to recreational drugs for adults, a free-market capitalist economy, and the abolition of censorship.

Liberty — the freedom to do what one chooses if it does not harm or limit others' freedom.

Limited government — a right-wing concept that espouses the practice that any public service that could reasonably be solely supplied by the market, or any potentially harmful action that could be self-regulated or otherwise controlled by public censure, should be.

Limited jurisdiction — a court's power to hear only certain kinds of cases.

Limited war — a war, often not formally declared, fought to obtain a specific political or territorial objective, rather than to obtain the enemy's unconditional surrender.

Limousine liberal — a derogatory term for a supposed socialist who maintains a luxurious lifestyle (British equivalent: *Champagne socialist, Bollinger Bolshevik*; Italian: *radical chic*; Australian: *Chardonnay socialist*).

Line-item veto — rejects specific legislation passed by the Congress; Congress attempted to give the President a line-item veto authority in 1995. However, the Supreme Court ruled it unconstitutional because it transferred legislative authority from the Legislative to the Executive Branches. Congress proposed the President use the line-item veto to remove or lower excessive spending from Congressional legislation.

Line organization — in the government bureaucracy, an agency whose head reports directly to the President.

Literacy test — historically, a written test must be passed before a person can vote; designed to disenfranchise voters.

Lobbying — the practice of talking with Congress members to persuade them to support a position or piece of legislation; initially conducted in hotel "lobbies" near the White House.

Lobbyist — serves as a go-between for people or businesses with a definite pro or con position about legislation. It is in politicians' interest to keep abreast of the problematic effects (i.e., unintended consequences) of legislation communicated efficiently by a knowledgeable advocate. The propensity for corruption in the lobbying process does not invalidate its legitimate function.

Logrolling — two or more members of Congress agree to support each other's bills.

Long, Huey P. — the quintessential populist, a corrupt demagogue of modern times who served as Louisiana governor from 1928 to 1932 and as Senator until 1935; a master of political patronage who became the model for the Robert Penn Warren (1905-1989) novel (1946) and the film adaptation (1949) *All the Kings Men*; assassinated by a victim's relative.

Loophole — a part of the Internal Revenue Service (IRS) tax code that allows individuals or businesses to reduce their tax burden.

Loose constructionism — a judicial philosophy that believes the Constitution should be interpreted openly and not be limited to things explicitly stated.

Lower House — the House of Representatives or (statewide) the Legislative Assembly.

Lumpenproletariat — those in society Marx identified as miscreants, lacking class consciousness, and useless to the revolutionary struggle. These include beggars, prostitutes, gangsters, racketeers, petty criminals, and the chronically unemployed or unemployable).

M

Mace — large and intimidating medieval hand-held weapon; appears in lower Houses as a symbol of authority.

Machine — a powerful party organization that turns favors and patronage into votes.

Machiavellian — adjective to describe manipulative and cynical political activity in which morals and principles figure but little; attributed to Italian Renaissance political theorist Niccolo Machiavelli (1469-1527) who wrote *The Prince* (1532) when government and statesmanship had dire life or death consequences.

Madisonian Model — a government structure proposed by James Madison (1751-1836) that avoided tyranny by separating power among different branches and building checks and balances into the Constitution. See *separation of powers*.

Maiden speech — the first-ever speech given by a Congress member, traditionally granted a no interjections courtesy.

Majority leader — in the House, the second-ranking member of the majority party; in the Senate, the majority party's highest-ranking member.

Majority opinion — a court opinion that reflects the reasoning of the majority of justices.

Majority party — in a legislative body, the party with more than half of the seats.

Majority preferential — preferential voting in single-member electorates.

Majority rule — the idea that the government should act by the will of most of the people.

Malapportionment — an apportionment of seats in Congress that is unfair due to population shifts; violating the concept of "one person one vote," the existence of electorates of the unequal population still has the same number of Representatives.

Malthus, Thomas — a clergyman and political economist of the eighteenth century, theorized that the world's population grows faster than its food supply. Rather than alleviating perpetual hunger by misguided compassion, allow the inevitable famine, disease, and war to act as natural retardants to population growth. Malthus (1766-1834) argued against the ideological, theoretical ideas of the philosopher William Godwin (1756-1836) and other supporters of the French Revolution (May 5, 1789, to November 9, 1799).

Mandate —the alleged command and authority a winning political party must institute its promised pre-election policies because of the convincing win. When the federal government requires states to perform or refrain from specific actions.

Mandatory retirement — an employment policy that states that when an employee reaches a certain age, they must retire.

Mandatory spending — spending that is mostly out of the control of Congress. Primarily "entitlements," paid to people on a formula basis regardless of how much money is available.

Marble-cake federalism — describes federalism for most of the twentieth century (and into the twenty-first), where the federal government and the states work closely and are intertwined; see *Cooperative federalism*.

Marginal seat — a single-member vote electorate where the winning candidate or party barely won the last election and may lose the next election.

Markup — when a congressional committee revises a bill in session.

Massachusetts ballot — a ballot that groups candidates by the office (all candidates for an office are listed together); also called "Office-block ballot."

Material incentive — the lure of a concrete benefit, usually money, attracts people to join.

McCain-Feingold bill — the informal name for the Bipartisan Campaign Finance Reform Act of 2002; named after its sponsors, Arizona Republican Senator John McCain (1936-2018; 1987-2018) and Wisconsin Democratic Senator Russell Feingold (b. 1953; 1993-2011).

McCulloch v. Maryland — an 1819 Supreme Court decision granting the federal government extensive power to carry out its enumerated powers.

Means testing — limiting government benefits, such as a baby bonus or health care, to those below a certain income or accumulated wealth. Basing benefits from a policy on a person's financial status, so that poor people get more benefits than rich people.

Media — information and the organizations that distribute that information to the public.

Media bias — occurs when the media (individually or collectively) reports something that is inaccurate or one-sided because of ideology, political favoritism (not treating both sides equally); bias can show up in coverage (or lack thereof) or the content and analysis of stories.

Media consolidation — the trend toward a few corporations owning most media outlets.

Mediating institution — an institution that stands between and connects people with the government (e.g., the media, political parties, and interest groups).

Mercantilism — an economic doctrine practiced from the 16th to the 18th centuries, proposed state power the supreme goal for international affairs. Policies included export subsidies, positive balance of payments, developing colonies, forbidding trade with foreign ships, restricting colonies' trade to the mother country, maintaining large precious metal reserves, and limiting domestic consumption, such as with sumptuary laws.

Merit system — the practice of hiring and promoting people based on skill.

Merit System Protection Board — investigates charges of wrongdoing in the federal civil service.

Midterm election — a congressional election that does not coincide with a presidential election.

Military aid — assistance to other countries designed to strengthen the recipient's military.

Military-industrial complex — the alliance of defense contractors, military elites, and some Congress members that promotes ever-larger defense budgets to profit themselves.

Minority leader — an individual elected to lead a party in the House or Senate that does not hold most seats in the body.

Minority party — in a legislative body, the party with fewer than half of the seats.

Miranda v. Arizona — a 1966 case in which the Supreme Court ruled that police must inform suspects of their rights, under the Fifth Amendment, when arrested.

Mixed economy — an economic system embracing aspects of free enterprise and socialism.

Monarchy — a regime in which a person holds all power (e.g., king or queen).

Monetarism — the theory of economic control by increasing or reducing the money supply.

Monetary policy — policies aimed at controlling inflation and unemployment through the money supply and interest rates; primarily established by the Federal Reserve Board.

Money bill — a law that transfers money or property from the people to the government (e.g., a bill that imposes a tax). These bills must be taken up in the House of Representatives first.

Monocracy — rule by one person; not necessarily anti-democratic.

Monopoly — a situation where there is only one seller of a good or service due to either protection by legislation or impractical for others to compete.

Monopolistic model — a view of the bureaucracy that says bureaucracies have no incentive to reform or improve performance because they face no competition.

Monopsony — a single buyer market for goods or services; the opposite of a monopoly.

Monroe doctrine — an American policy promulgated by President James Monroe in 1823, claims America's right to intervene in Western Hemisphere nations' affairs and a reluctance to intervene in the Eastern Hemisphere (e.g., Europe).

Moral relativism — a philosophical concept whereby an act identified as immoral in the home country is excusable when observed in another country because of culture or history.

Motherhood statement — a "feel good" platitude supporting an uncontroversial case that few dare disagree.

Muckraker — a journalist or author whose primary goal is to uncover adverse character history. Teddy Roosevelt coined the term about a *Pilgrim's Progress* character with a muckrake who could only look down.

Multiculturalism — the perspective that all cultures within a society are of equal merit and should be respected.

Multilateralism — the idea that nations should act together to solve problems.

Multinational corporation — a business that operates in more than one country.

Multiple-member district — a district sending more than one representative to the legislature.

Multipolar system — an international system with more than two major powers.

N

Nation — a large group of people linked by similar culture, language, and history.

National convention — a convention held by a political party every four years to nominate candidates for President and Vice President and to ratify the party platform.

National debt — money owed by a government.

National interest — things that benefit and protect a nation-state.

Nationalism — a belief in the goodness of one's nation and a desire to help make the nation more robust and better.

National Security Council — a part of the White House Staff that advises the President on security policy.

Nation-building — the task of creating a national identity through the promotion of a common culture, language, and history.

Nation-state — a state that rules over a nation.

Naturalist law —legal philosophy which judges use to aid decision making. The naturalist law theory is the ageless, unchanging law of nature, as deduced by the interpreter's reasoning process or the teachings of God, and should be followed even if it conflicts with duly constituted legislation. Contrast with the positivist law theory that follows the democratically instituted law no matter how rational and just it may be.

Nazism — political ideology originating in the 1930s that stressed the German race's superiority, authoritarian rule by one party, military expansion, and taking inspiration from a mythical past.

Necessary and proper clause — a clause at the end of Article I, Section 8 of the U.S. Constitution granting Congress the power to do what is *necessary and proper* to carry out its duties. It strongly suggests that the federal government has powers other than those explicitly stated in the Constitution; see *Elastic Clause.*

Necessary evil — is believed to be needed but not right in and of itself; many Americans see the federal government as a necessary evil.

Negative rights / positive rights — the right to do, or refrain from, action or otherwise be free from interference, compared to the right to gain a specific benefit that would have a monetary value. The right to speak freely and the right to having legal representation supplied when in court; an affirmative obligation to supply the cost of a lawyer while there is no (negative) cost to allow someone the right of free association; term derives from the obligation on society for supplying those rights.

Negotiated rule-making — a federal rule-making process including those affected by the rules.

Neoconservatism — a recent development in American conservatism that believes the state's power should promote conservative goals.

New Deal coalition — the supporters of Franklin Roosevelt's New Deal; the coalition included labor unions, Catholics, southern whites, and African Americans. This policy helped the Democrats dominate politics from the 1930s until the 1960s.

New federalism — an American movement, starting in the 1970s, to return power to state and local governments, thereby decreasing the federal government's power.

New Jersey Plan — a plan at the constitutional convention that gave each state equal representation in the legislature.

Nihilism — the belief that life and all the things that make it up are meaningless; the rejection of all moral and religious notions.

Nimby — stands for "not in my backyard," a pejorative term used to describe opposition to a public policy decision, which in itself is considered beneficial but causes discomfort. For example, airports, prisons, nearby nuclear power plants, austerity measures affecting those who thought they would be excluded).

Nineteenth Amendment — passed in 1920, it gave women the right to vote.

No Child Left Behind Act — a law passed in 2001 that expanded federal funding to schools while linking them to increased testing and accountability.

Nomination — a prerequisite to standing as a political candidate; made only after the primary election concludes.

Noneconomic group — an interest group that works on noneconomic issues; also called a "citizens' group."

Nongovernmental actor — a participant in the international arena that is not part of a government (e.g., nongovernmental organizations, multinational corporations).

Nongovernmental organization (NGO) — a political actor not affiliated with a government; many NGOs are nonprofit institutions run by private citizens (e.g., Red Cross, Doctors Without Borders, Catholic Church).

Nonprobability sampling — a non-random selection of respondents for a survey; problematic because the group chosen to respond to the survey is unlikely to represent the broader population.

Normative / descriptive ethics —the study of what people think is moral. Normative, or prescriptive, ethics is the study of what is moral. Meta-ethics is the study of what "moral," or any other term, means.

Nuclear Non-Proliferation Treaty — an international treaty, signed in 1968, intended to prevent nuclear weapons spread.

O

Objective reporting — reporting only the facts with no opinion or bias.

Office-block ballot — a ballot that groups candidates by the office (all candidates for an office are listed together); also called "the Massachusetts ballot."

Office of Management and Budget (OMB) — the federal agency that compiles and reviews budget figures on the President's behalf.

Office of Personnel Management — the central federal personnel office, created in 1978.

Oligarchy — a form of government where the rule is by the few and in their interest.

Ombudsperson — a concept, originally Swedish, where Parliament appoints a person to act as an official watchdog over bureaucracy on behalf of the public. By its initiative or public complaints, the Ombudsman investigates government officials and reports its findings to the government, after which action may be taken. The Ombudsman office has limited power to penalize, although, in some jurisdictions, the Ombudsman can launch criminal prosecutions.

Open primary — election held to choose the nominee for a political party in which voters of any party are eligible to vote.

Open rule — a rule in the House of Representatives that allows an unlimited number of amendments to a bill.

Opinion — a document issued by a court explaining the reasons for its decision.

Opinion leader — a person whose opinion can shape the opinions of others.

Optional preferential voting is preferential voting, marking only the number of preferences.

Order — formal motion in writing, not requiring the governor's signature, which is temporary and establishes investigative committees, change rules, and other parliamentary actions.

Orders of the Day (Calendar) — listing of matters to be considered by the Senate and House at each sitting.

Ordinary vote — a vote cast at a polling place in the elector's home division on polling day compared with a mail-in or absentee ballot.

Organization for Economic Co-operation and Development (OECD) — founded in 1961 to stimulate world trade and economic progress. A group of 34 first world countries committed to democracy and the market economy who organize mutual plans to maintain taxation conventions and fiscal stability, combat corruption and bribery, and endeavors such as issuing annual publications on the world economic outlook.

Original intent — a judicial philosophy that states that judges should interpret the law and the Constitution according to the founders' intent.

Original jurisdiction — authority to hear a case for the first time in a geographic area or sphere of the law; courts of original jurisdiction are generally trial courts where juries make decisions; see *Appellate jurisdiction*.

Outside game — a term used to describe grassroots activism and other means to influence elections and policymaking.

Overregulation — an excess of regulation that hurts efficiency.

Override — to overturn the governor's veto by a 2/3 vote of members present in both the House and Senate.

Oversight — Congress's power to make sure laws are being correctly enforced.

Overton window — modern concept advanced by political theorist Joseph Overton (1960-2003), whereby there is a small window of acceptable political approaches on a given subject at a specific time. Any policies advanced not within the window are likely to be considered "extreme" and politically unsafe. Most politicians only support policies within the window.

P

Pack journalism — journalists and news outlets' tendency to cover the same stories, driven by the fear of being "scooped" by other reporters. The idea that journalists frequently copy and imitate each other rather than doing independent reporting.

Pairing of votes — procedure (in some state legislatures) allowed in the Senate only, whereby a member, before the vote is taken, announces that they have paired their vote with an opposing vote of an absent member. The two votes do not affect the outcome of the final tally.

Palm tree justice — expedient justice applied in good faith but absent of the rule of law; paying little attention to the existing law, precedent, or fundamental principles; comes from primitive societies where justice was dispensed by a wise older man sitting under a palm tree.

Parachute in (a candidate) — a political party's central office appoints the candidate for an electorate, rather than the local branch's usual practice.

Paradox of participation — when people vote because they wish to make a difference, but the chances of making a difference are infinitesimally small.

Pardon — a release from punishment for a criminal conviction; the President has pardon power.

Parliamentary democracy — a regime in which the legislature chooses the executive branch.

Parliamentary government — a government system where ultimate authority is vested in the legislative body; the cabinet, including the chief executive, is from, appointed by, and responsible to the legislature (the Parliament). This is an alternative to a presidential system, where the voters independently elect both the legislature and the executive.

Participation rate — the share of the eligible workforce (15-65, not institutionalized) working or seeking work.

Partisan journalism — journalism that advances the viewpoint of a political party.

Party activist — a person who is deeply involved with a party; usually more ideologically committed than an average party voter.

Party-centered politics — campaigns and politics that focus on party labels and platforms.

Party-column ballot — a ballot that groups candidates by the party; called "the Indiana ballot."

Party identification — feeling connected to a political party.

Party in government — the role and function of parties in government, particularly in Congress.

Party in the electorate — party identification among voters.

Party line voting — even though politicians "represent" the citizens of their specific electorates, at voting, they mostly vote (unless an independent) according to their party's call (i.e., as directed by their leader rather than according to constituents' wishes).

Party-list voting — "above the line" only proportional representation voting; voters do not cast preferences, but the candidates or parties themselves choose (before the election) the list of preferred other candidates to which their unused votes will go.

Party organization — the formal structure and leadership of a political party.

Party platform — a proclamation of the beliefs, values, and policy positions of a political party; specific statements or positions in a platform are sometimes called "planks" (e.g., the "abortion plank" of a party's platform).

Party platform — the collection of issue positions endorsed by a political party.

Party reform — measures aimed at opening party leadership adopted by the major parties following the 1968 election.

Pass a resolve — the final passage of a resolve by the House or Senate.

Patronage — the practice of rewarding jobs in government to political allies after an electoral victory; government jobs and contracts are given to political allies in exchange for support.

Payroll tax — paid in equal amounts (12.4% for 2020) by employers and employees to fund Social Security and Medicare; known as FICA.

Pendleton Act — another name for the Civil Service Reform Act of 1883.

Perestroika — denotes political, bureaucratic, or economic restructuring; first coined by Mikhail Gorbachev (b. 1931) about the former Soviet Union (i.e., 1922-1991).

Pericles — esteemed Athenian leader (c. 495-429 B.C.) of ancient Greece who, while advancing the material and cultural aspects of his city-state, also did much to enhance democracy.

Permissive federalism — view that because the federal government is supreme, the states only have those powers which the federal government permits them to exercise.

per curiam — an unsigned decision issued by an appellate court; not considered binding as a precedent.

Petition — a request describing the nature of the proposed legislation and the objects sought by it, signed by the petitioner, and accompanied by a draft of the bill or resolve embodying the legislation proposed.

Pettifogging — a member of the legislature holding up a debate by quibbling over trivial, irrelevant matters.

Photo op — a situation where a politician arranges or accepts an invitation to an event (or pseudo-event) where the setting and circumstances are. They attract the media and give the politician exposure.

Pigeonholing — the ability of a committee to kill a bill by setting it aside and not acting.

Platform — the political agenda of a candidate or party.

Plausible deniability — the position a member of the executive or some person in charge of an organization attempts to maintain; created by keeping a distance from certain operations or practices. An operation "goes south" and attracts unfavorable publicity has no evidence linking them to the chain of command.

Plebeian / patrician — the two citizen classes of ancient Rome; the allegedly coarse and crude ordinary plebeians and the wealthy, educated, and aristocratic "born to rule" patricians; both terms used today in a derogatory manner. For example, U.S. President G.H.W. Bush was a patrician due to his being born into a wealthy political family and treating political life as a duty rather than an opportunity for reformist zeal concerning ordinary Americans.

Plebiscite — a public vote to gauge public opinion on an issue (such as conscription), which does not affect the Constitution nor is otherwise legally binding.

Plessy v. Ferguson — a 1896 Supreme Court decision upholding a Louisiana law segregating passengers on trains creating the "*separate but equal*" doctrine.

Pluralism — the view that society contains numerous centers of power, and many people decide for society.

Plurality — more votes than any other candidate but not a majority.

Plurality opinion — an opinion written by the majority of the justices on the prevailing side.

Plutocracy — government, controlled by, or greatly influenced by, the wealthy.

Pocket veto — if Congress adjourns before ten days have passed since the passage of a bill, the President can allow the legislation to die by neither signing nor vetoing the bill. Results from the President's or governor's failure to sign a bill following prorogation or dissolution of the legislature's second annual session. Because the session has ended, the bill will not automatically become law after ten days, and the legislature has no opportunity to override the veto. See *veto*.

Point of order — a challenge to a possible breach of order or rule.

Poison the well — when made aware of a new topic or program an opponent is about to discuss, to get in early and publicly criticize or deride the issue to "poison" the public against having an open mind to your opponent's suggestion.

Political action committee (PAC) — an interest group legally permitted to give money to political candidates competing for federal elected office.

Political appointees — federal bureaucrats appointed by the President, as a reward for loyalty.

Political culture — the set of beliefs, values, shared myths, and notions of a good polity that a group of people holds.

Political economy — the study of how politics and economics interact.

Political efficacy — the belief that the government listens to ordinary people and that their participation can make a difference in government.

Political equality — treating everyone the same way in the realm of politics.

Political participation — engaging in actions to achieve political goals.

Political party — a team of office-seekers and their supporters; generally unified by a prevailing ideology, philosophy, set of values, and political beliefs; usually outlined in a party platform.

Political party status — candidates register at an election as a party and receive certain privileges such as "above the line" placement and public funding if they attain a certain percentage of the vote (as long as they can present to officials the signatures and addresses of a sufficient number of supporters). Certain privileges apply to the winning party candidates if their votes reach a certain threshold.

Political science — the systematic, rigorous study of politics.

Political socialization — the process by which political culture passes to the young.

Politico — one interested or engaged in politics.

Politics — the process by which government decisions are made.

Polity — form or process of civil government; organized society; the state.

Poll — a research survey; another word for an election.

Polling — assessing public opinion by asking people what they think and feel.

Polling place/booth — centers in each division to take the votes of the local people.

Pollster — a person who conducts polls.

Poll tax — a voting fee; designed to keep poor people and African Americans from voting.

Popular sovereignty — the notion that political power is derived from the people. The people retain the right to rescind any grant of power to the government, a regime in which the government must respond to the peoples' wishes.

Populace — the people living in a specific area.

Populism — political campaigning oriented toward real democracy by soliciting votes by promising specific benefits. Contrast with representative democracy where voters select a team of (allegedly) responsible politicians who, after due deliberation, institute a program with a general theme for specific legislation. Populists promise to bring about their agenda despite institutional obstructions. Non-populists take a more conservative approach respecting the judiciary, the Constitution, the bureaucracy, and the international approaches to the same issues.

Populist democracy — ultimate democracy not restricted by a constitution or other reviewing authority as legislation or executive orders; an alternative to liberal democracy.

Populist politician — a politician who offers the people what they want irrespective of how moral, feasible or practical it is for such promises to be carried out; cynically, it is how a losing candidate is likely to describe the candidate he lost to.

Populists — a political movement in the late nineteenth century that fought on behalf of the poor workers and farmers; fused with the Democratic Party in 1896.

Pork-barrel spending — politicians arranging for big-spending government contracts in their district to enhance their reputation with their constituents; not in the nation's interest as a whole.

Positivist law — two opposing branches of legal philosophy which judges use to aid decision making. The naturalist law theory is the ageless, unchanging law of nature, as deduced by the interpreter's reasoning process or the teachings of God, and should be followed even if it conflicts with duly constituted legislation. The positivist law theory follows the democratically instituted law no matter how rational and just it may be.

Poverty line — the minimum income needed to cover the necessities (e.g., fuel, food, clothing, shelter, basic household, personal items); as in "relative poverty," whereby the reference value is a percentage of the country's median income, immaterial of the nation's GDP.

Power — the ability held by individuals or institutions to create and enforce policies and manage resources for society.

Power of the purse — the ability of Congress to raise taxes and authorize spending. Congress must authorize all federal expenditures.

Pragmatism — a non-ideological approach to political issues where "the merits of the particular case" may take a higher than normal precedence.

Pravda — Russian for "truth," state-owned and controlled newspaper of the Soviet Union and an official organ of the Central Committee of the Communist Party between 1921 and 1991; a derogatory term for media organizations which are owned or controlled by the government.

Precedent — a court ruling bearing on subsequent court cases.

Preemption — the invalidation of state law if it conflicts with federal law.

Preferential voting — when voters vote for several candidates by preference, so at least one choice is elected.

Pre-poll votes — voting before election day by mail or appearing at an Election Commission or Clerk's office; permitted when the voter will be elsewhere on election day.

Presidential Commission — a body that advises the President on some problem and makes recommendations; some are temporary; others are permanent.

Presidential democracy — a regime in which the President and the legislators must be entirely separate.

President *pro tempore* — acting President of the Senate in the absence of the Vice President, the Constitutionally authorized President of the body.

Presidential system — as opposed to parliamentary government, a constitutional framework where the executive is directly chosen by and responsible to the people (e.g., France, South Korea, the Philippines, and the U.S.).

Primary election — mostly occurring in America, an election where the successful candidate wins no office but becomes eligible to run in the upcoming official election as a party's candidate. An election within a party to choose the party's nominee for the office.

Primary vote — the number of first-choice votes a candidate receives in preferential voting systems; see two-party-preferred votes.

Print media — media distributed via printed materials.

Prior restraint — stopping free expression on a sensitive (usually "national security") issue before it can happen.

Private bill — a bill that offers benefit or relief to a person named in the bill.

Private good — a good that benefits only some people, such as members of a group.

Privatization — the practice of private companies providing government services.

Privileges and immunities clause — part of the Fourteenth Amendment, which forbids state governments from taking away any of the privileges and immunities of American citizenship.

pro tem [**Latin, for the time being**] — describes a person who temporarily takes the role of an absent superior.

Probability sample — a sampling technique in which each member of the population has a known chance of being chosen for the sample.

Professional legislature — a state legislature that meets in session for long periods, pays its members well, and hires large support staff for legislators.

Progressive tax — progressive income tax, as espoused in "plank" two of Karl Marx's (1818-1883) *The Communist Manifesto* (1848), is a graduated tax where the rate increases as the income of the taxpayer get higher.

Prohibited powers — the powers explicitly denied to the federal government by the Constitution.

Project grants — categorical grant programs in which states submit proposals for projects to the federal government, and the federal government choose which to fund on a competitive basis.

Proletariat — a term used in Marxist ideology to describe the working class who do not own property and whose only value is their labor.

Property right — the right to use, control, benefit, and exclude others.

Proportional representation — an electoral system in which each party gets some seats in the legislature proportionate to its percentage of the vote. A voting system where the whole state is just one electorate and parties win seats in proportion to the total votes they receive in an election. Hybrid systems exist where the state is divided into several multi-member electorates whereby seats won are approximately proportional to the votes cast).

Proposal — document accompanying a petition introducing legislative amendments to the Constitution of the Commonwealth.

Prorogation — termination of a legislative year by agreement of the Governor, with the advice of both legislative bodies.

Prorogue —temporarily bring a legislative session to an end (e.g., summer recess) compared with a dissolution before an election.

Prospective voting — voters choosing by looking to the future; voters choose the candidate(s) they believe will help the country the most in the next few years.

Provisional vote — votes cast at an election in circumstances where a voter's name cannot be found on the roll or has already been marked off the roll; they are not counted until a check of enrollment records.

Proxy war — a war instigated by enemy states in which third parties fight rather than the enemy states themselves.

Psephology — Greek for "*voting with pebbles*," the statistical and predictive study of elections.

Public administration — the task of running the government and providing services through policy implementation.

Public assistance — government benefits provided to those who meet specific criteria (e.g., low income).

Public choice theory — the study of politics from an economic perspective; rather than assuming that politicians, civil servants, and voters are all motivated by "*what should be done*," analyzing how all three take self-interest into account when making decisions.

Public education — informing the public about critical issues and what Congress is doing about those issues.

Public good — a good that benefits everyone, not just some; called a "collective good."

Public interest group (PIG) — a group that exists for the express purpose of promoting public interests that would not otherwise be pursued (e.g., Public Citizen, a broad consumer advocacy group).

Public opinion — the underlying attitudes and opinions of the public.

Public policy — any rule, plan, or action about issues of domestic national importance.

Public representative role — the media's role acting as a representative of the public, holding government officials accountable to the people.

Pundit — Hindi for "learned one," a commentator with a supposedly keen knowledge of issues.

Purposive incentive — a lure designed to promote a cause that might otherwise not have much appeal.

Q

Quadratic voting — an untested theory by academic economist Glen Weyl (b. 1985). For referenda or plebiscites (i.e., ballot question), a voter not only pays to vote but may pay a higher amount for multiple votes, accommodating more input for those with a more significant stake in the issue. To prevent simple vote-buying, each extra vote's cost is not linear but quadratic. For example, if one vote costs a dollar, then two votes cost the square of two or four dollars; three votes, nine dollars; four votes 16 dollars, etc.). Not a counter to "*the tyranny of the majority*" but a counter to the tyranny of the indifferent majority.

Quango (Quasi-Autonomous Non-Government Organization) — a body financed by a government but not under its direct control.

Quorum — set by the Constitution or bylaws for the minimum number in attendance for a duly called session.

Quota preferential — preferential voting used in conjunction with proportional representation.

R

Rally 'round the flag effect — a significant boost in presidential popularity when a foreign crisis or threat of war arises.

Random sampling — selecting individuals to participate in a public opinion poll (or another kind of study) in an unbiased way.

Random selection — a sampling technique to ensure that each person in the population has an equal chance of being selected for the sample.

Ranking member — the senior committee member from the minority party.

Rapprochement — the renewal or establishment of friendly relations between states which were previously hostile towards each other.

Ratings game — the practice of organizations rating Congress members based on how they voted on issues of concern to the organizations and their members, usually expressed as a percentage (e.g., a Senator given a 100% rating always voted the way the organization rating them wanted).

Rational choice theory — an approach that assumes people act rationally in their self-interest, seeking to maximize value.

Rationalism — the belief that human reason can find solutions to problems.

Reaganomics — economic strategy promoted by Ronald Reagan during his time in office based on supposing that cutting taxes would make individual taxpayers more productive and wealthy. The taxes paid by the wealthy, although collected at a lower percentage, would, in theory, be equal to or greater than before the tax cuts.

Realignment — a dramatic shift in the balance between the two parties that changes where they stand on the key issues dividing them.

Realism — a theory of international relations that stresses the importance of power, particularly military power, claims that states act in their national interest.

Realpolitik — the politics of realism; rather than from principle, a self-interested approach to politics either from the standpoint of what benefits one's party or one's country.

Reapportionment — the process of reallocating representation in the House of Representatives after a census; some states (the more newly populous) gain seats, while others (with dwindling populations) lose them.

Recall — electoral procedure practiced in Canada and in many American states whereby an elected official, including the chief executive, can be recalled from office by the voters if there are sufficient signatures on a petition; there is no provision for a national recall.

Recess — temporary delay in proceedings.

Recession — a country's economic status achieved after two consecutive quarters of a decrease in the gross national product (GNP); milder than a depression.

Reconsideration — motion to reconsider a vote on action previously taken. Any member may propose reconsideration, and if the motion prevails, the matter is voted on again. Must be moved before entering upon the Orders of the Day on the next legislative session.

Redistribution — the periodical redrawing of electoral boundaries (i.e., ten-year census) ensures each electorate conforms to the electoral laws' prerequisites, making the number of Representatives consistent with the district's current population.

Redistributive policy — a government action that takes money from one part of the citizenry and gives it to another part; usually, the transfer goes from the well-off to the poor; see *Income transfer*.

Redistricting — redrawing district boundaries so that a state loses or gains seats in the House of Representatives. Usually occurs after the 10-year census.

Referendum — a public policy decision referred to the people's vote by a legislative body; used only at the state level.

Referendum Petition — a petition signed by a specified number of voters to repeal a law enacted by the legislators and requesting that the legislation be suspended until the people take a vote at the next state election.

Refile — a petition like the one which was presented to the legislature in the previous session.

Regime — a word used to describe a government.

Regressive tax — tax collected at increasingly lower rates as income level increases high earners pay more tax than low earners.

Regulated federalism — the practice of the federal government imposing standards and regulations on state governments.

Regulatory policy — government policies limiting what businesses can do (e.g., minimum wages, workplace safety measures).

Remand — sending a case back to a lower court for a new trial or proceeding.

Rent-seeker —someone who attempts to make an income by manipulating the social, political, or economic environment, rather than creating goods or services. The "rent" coming to them is usually from government-enforced monopoly privileges or government grants paying for "services" which the free market might not otherwise see as of any value. A term created by American economist Anne Krueger (b. 1934).

Rent voucher — a voucher issued by the government that can be used to pay all or part of a person's rent.

Repatriation — the sending back of someone to their country of origin, such as an illegal immigrant or prisoner of war.

Report of a committee — recommendation on a legislative matter by the committee to which it was referred.

Representative democracy — a government system where citizens do not directly vote on issues and laws but surrender that right to their duly elected representatives; in modern times, it is commonly known as a democracy.

Representative sample — a sample that resembles the population.

Reprieve — a formal postponement of a criminal sentence; the President has the power to grant reprieves.

Republic — a regime that runs by representative democracy; a form of government in which representatives chosen by the people make decisions. Defined as a democracy but loosely described as a form of government where the rule is constrained by institutional frameworks and not by the selected few. It is not an oligarchy but not necessarily a democracy; the Roman

Republic was the original precedent for republicanism; apartheid South Africa, by this definition, was a republic.

Reregulation — significantly changing government regulations on industry.

Reserved powers — the powers reserved to the states and the people by the Tenth Amendment.

Resolutions — documents that may or may not accompany a petition expressing the sentiment of one or both legislature branches. They are used for congratulations, memorializing the Congress of the United States regarding general questions, etc. Resolutions do not require the governor's signature.

Resolve — document accompanying a petition, usually asking for legislative action of a temporary or immediate nature (e.g., establishing temporary investigative commissions).

Retention election — a state election using the merit plan for selecting judges, in which voters decide whether a judge should keep his or her job.

Retrospective legislation — laws defining behavior for criminal or civil liablity (e.g., taxation), even when that behavior happened before the law was enacted. This is more prevalent in autocracies as it violates the traditional concept of the *rule of law*, but happens in democracies; see *Ex post facto laws*.

Retrospective voting — making a vote choice by looking to the past; voters support incumbents if they feel that the country has done well over the past few years.

Revenue agency — a government agency that raises money by collecting taxes or fees.

Revenue sharing — the federal government's practice giving money to the states with no strings attached; started by the Nixon Administration and ended by the Reagan Administration.

Reverse — when a court overturns a lower court's ruling, declaring it void.

Reverse discrimination — discrimination against majority-status people due to affirmative action policies.

Revolution — a significant event causing a fundamental change in a state.

Rider — an attachment to a piece of legislation that is generally unrelated to the rest of the bill.

Right of rebuttal — a media regulation that requires broadcasters to allow people to reply to criticisms aired on the outlet.

Rights of the minority — rights held by the minority that must be respected by the majority.

Right-wing — "on the right" describes a political philosophy favoring conservative, pro-market attitudes with a preference for individual rights instead of an "interventionist" government, a strict approach to law and order, a strong defense force, and a sense of nationalism. "On the left" is the opposite with a so-called "womb to tomb" (or "cradle to grave") approach to social welfare and an internationalist worldview. The terms originated in the French Estates-General in 1789 when the nobility who favored the peasant's conditions' complacency sat on the King's right. Those wanting to ameliorate the peasant's conditions sat on the left.

Roe v. Wade — a 1973 Supreme Court decision legalizing abortion during the first trimester.

Rogue state — a state that does not follow international law or rules of the global arena.

Roll — the list of voters eligible to vote at an election.

Roll-call vote — occurs when each member's vote is recorded.

Rugged individualism — a form of individualism that emphasizes self-reliance and ignoring what others want and think.

Rule-making — the bureaucratic function of creating rules needed to implement policy.

Rule of law — the traditional legal concept, dating back to Aristotle, that societies live under a set of predetermined rules rather than the arbitrary "wise guidance" of any contemporary judge, king, or chief executive. It does not necessarily imply democratically or just rules, but merely a stable government where the law is proclaimed, applied equally to all; a term derived by the 19th-century British jurist Albert Venn Dicey (1835-1922). The tenets are 1) all people are subject equally to the privileges and penalties of the law, 2) people are ruled by laws and not by individuals (i.e., the judiciary and executive must act only according to the law rather than their beliefs of what is justice), 3) the law shall be prospective, visible, clear, and relatively stable., and 4) due process must be afforded to all before the law (following the law's letter and procedures).

Rule of four — an informal Supreme Court rule whereby four of the nine justices must agree to hear a case for the Court to issue a *writ of certiorari.*

S

Safe seat — a congressional seat that is highly likely to be held by the incumbent (the current occupant of the seat) after the next election; known as a "blue ribbon seat."

Sample — a group representing the whole population in a research study (e.g., opinion polls).

Sampling error — an error that arises as a matter of chance in selecting individuals for participation in a research study (e.g., public opinion poll).

School vouchers — government money given to parents to use for tuition at private schools.

Scrutiny — the checking and counting of ballot papers to ascertain the result of an election; political parties are allowed representatives on such occasions.

Second Continental Congress — the governing body over the colonies during the American Revolution that drafted the Articles of Confederation to create the first national government.

Selective incentives — the lure of benefits that only group members will receive.

Selective incorporation — forcing states to abide by only certain parts of the Bill of Rights.

Self-selected candidate — a person who chooses to run for office on their initiative.

Semantic infiltration — a concept first highlighted by Senator Daniel Patrick Moynihan (1927-2003) where someone succeeds in persuading opponents to accept their terms in the discussion of specific subjects and, by extension, the policies, and beliefs that accompany them. For example, compare freedom fighters/terrorists, benefits/entitlements, or illegal immigrants/asylum seekers.

Senate (U.S.) — the upper legislative chamber in the bicameral legislature of the United States, and together with the House of Representatives, makes up the U.S. Congress; consists of 100 elected U.S. Senators, two from each state.

Senate and House Journals — record of proceedings in each chamber for each legislative day, including matters considered, amendments offered, and votes taken.

Senatorial courtesy — a tradition in which a Senator can have input into whom the President nominates for federal judgeships in their state if they are of the President's party.

Separation of powers — derived by Charles Montesquieu, a traditional concept of liberalism where, for limiting abuse of power, the three branches of government (executive, legislature, and judiciary) remain independent. In modern times, the best examples are some American states where all branches have real power, and because of separate elections, no branch is appointed by nor can be removed by another. The executive appoints the judiciary; see the *Madisonian Model*.

Sexual harassment — unwanted and inappropriate physical or verbal conduct of a sexual nature creates a hostile work environment.

Shared powers — powers that are held and exercised by more than one level of government.

Shays' Rebellion — a 1786 uprising of Massachusetts farmers against high taxes and debt.

Signing message — a message attached to a bill that the President signs, explaining their understanding of the bill, sometimes with specific instructions on how it should be implemented.

Single-member district — a legislative district that sends only one person to the legislature.

Single-member voting (SMV) — as opposed to proportional representation, the system where only one candidate represents all the citizens of an electorate or geographical area (known as Majoritarian voting when preferences are allowed on the ballot).

Single transferable vote (STV) — a proportional representation voting system where there is no "above the line" option to vote for a party but only for individual candidates in the preferred order. A party's winning candidates may not be in the same order as on the party's "ticket," and the voters' preferences may not necessarily be what the party would have liked. Due to the relative complexity of voting and vote counting, there are likely to be more invalid ballots, and the election results would take longer to ascertain.

Skewed sample — a sample that is not representative and leads to inaccurate polling results; a deceptive practice used to manipulate public opinion.

Slander — explicitly stating knowingly untrue statements that hurt a person's reputation.

Social capital — mutual trust and cooperation acquired by people through involvement in community organizations and volunteer groups.

Social contract — an 18th-century philosophical concept used to explain how people originally left their solitary, wilderness existence and came together under government auspices. Theorist Thomas Hobbes (1588-1679) first posited that the "contract" entailed each surrendering all their rights, saving that of life, in exchange for the Crown's protection. A half-century later, philosopher John Locke (1632-1704) proposed that people retained life and certain other fundamental rights and were legitimate in overthrowing any state that violated those rights.

Socialism — a method of government in which the means of planning and producing goods and services are controlled by a central government that seeks to collect the wealth of the nation and distribute it evenly amongst its citizens. A philosophy based on the notion that the governmental authority ought to promote fair and equal socioeconomic outcomes in education, income distribution, and other vital ways. Socialistic governments generally own or exercise substantial control over the economic sectors and engage in wealth and income redistribution programs.

Social engineering — the practice that it is not enough for governments to create an environment for the citizenry where there is an adequate standard of living together with good health care, low crime, and fundamental freedoms. The governments must engineer or program the beliefs, attitudes, and practices of the citizenry to conform to what is decreed, at the time, to be socially, physiologically, and intellectually acceptable.

Social security — a social insurance program to keep the retired and disabled out of poverty.

Sociological representation — a type of representation in which the representative resembles most of their constituents in ethnicity, religion, race, or social or educational background.

Soft money — political contributions not regulated by federal campaign finance laws; money is given directly to political parties for "party building;" not to be used for or given directly to candidates in support of election efforts; banned by the 2002 Bipartisan Campaign Reform Act, known as the *McCain-Feingold bill.*

Solicitor general — a high-ranking Justice Department official who submits requests for *writs of certiorari* to the Supreme Court on behalf of the federal government; they usually argue cases for the government before the Court.

Solidarity incentive — the lure of social benefits (e.g., friendship) by an organization's members.

Sortition — an electoral system whereby candidates do not win office by popular choice but by lottery; popular in ancient Greece but rarely used today, occasionally advocated by reformists.

Sovereignty — the right to exercise political power in a territory.

Speaker of the House — leader of the House of Representatives, elected by the majority to preside over the House's proceedings in formal sessions; the Speaker of the House is almost always a member of the majority party.

Special district — a type of local government designed to meet a need.

Special election — an election to replace a member of Congress who leaves office between regular elections.

Special law — a legislative act applying to a particular county, city, town or district, individual or group of individuals and not general.

Specialization — the practice of a group or person becoming extraordinarily knowledgeable and skilled at one specific task.

Speech and debate clause — a clause in Article I of the U.S. Constitution granting Congress members a privilege from arrest and legislative immunity for any speech or debate made in either of the houses.

Spin — to frame a news story in such a way as to shift the emphasis in the most politically favorable direction.

Splinter party — a third party, created when a faction from a major party forms its party.

Split-ticket voting — the practice of casting votes for candidates of different political parties on the same ballot (e.g., casting a vote for the Democratic presidential candidate while voting for the Republican congressional candidate).

Spoiler — a losing candidate who costs another candidate the election.

Spoils system — the practice of elected officials rewarding supporters with government jobs.

Staffer — a person who works for a Senator or Congressman in a supporting capacity.

Standard operating procedure — a set of rules established in a bureaucracy that dictates how workers respond to different situations to respond in the same way.

Standing — the legal right to bring a claim (i.e., lawsuit) in court. To have standing, an individual must show harm, not merely that they might be harmed in the future.

Standing committees — permanent legislative committees in the House and Senate with established issues and policy jurisdictions. For example, permanent Senate committees (Administration, Rules, Ways and Means, Bills in Third Reading, Ethics, Post Audit and Oversight, Science and Technology, Steering and Policy) and in the House (Rules, Ways and Means, Bills in Third Reading, Ethics, Counties, Post Audit and Oversight, Personnel and Administration, Science and Technology) which serve their respective legislative bodies.

stare decisis **[Latin,** *let the decision stand***]** — a legal principle recognizing previous court decisions when deciding current cases.

State — a political unit that has sovereign power over a piece of land.

State of nature — the natural condition of humankind living in a primitive environment before governments developed. Existence was a perpetual struggle for sustenance, shelter, and protection from potential harm. According to the English philosopher Thomas Hobbes, life was "*solitary, poor, nasty, brutish and short.*"

Statecraft — the exercise of power, guided by wisdom, in pursuit of the public good.

State of the Union address — a Constitutionally mandated message, given by the President to Congress, in which the President lays out plans for the coming year.

Statute — a law passed by Congress, a state legislature, or other government body.

Stewardship theory — a view of presidential power advanced by Theodore Roosevelt, arguing that the President is uniquely suited to act for the nation's well-being because it elected them.

Straight-ticket voting — voting for only candidates from one party.

Straw man (argument) — addressing and refuting an opponent's argument not stated, even though it might appear they could make it. A human-like figure made of straw, such as a military target dummy, easily destroyed or knocked down.

Strict constructionism — a judicial philosophy that argues that constitutional interpretation should be limited to the specific wording of the document.

Stump— involved political campaigning, especially making speeches. The expression "on the stump" derived from the 19th-century practice of speaking while standing on a tree stump.

Subcommittee — smaller, more specialized committees organized and operate under the authority of standing committees.

Subnationalism — identification with small ethnic and regional groups within a nation.

Subsidy — an economic benefit given by the government to an individual, business, or group that engages in behavior deemed beneficial by policymakers; subsidy payments can take the form of direct cash payments, tax credits, or tax deductions.

Substitution for an adverse report — a procedure by which a committee's adverse report is overturned. The original or a new but similar bill, resolve, or resolution is substituted for the adverse report.

Suffrage — the right to vote. See *franchise.*

Sunset clause — a provision or clause inserted in legislation to declare its expiry date; most legislation does not contain such clauses. The intention is that laws are permanent, at least until subsequent modification or repeal.

Sunset provisions — expiration dates written into some federal programs; Congress can renew the program if it is satisfied that it achieves its objectives.

Sunshine laws — laws that require government agencies to hold public proceedings.

Superdelegate — a party leader or elected official who is automatically granted delegate status for the national convention. Superdelegates do not have to be chosen in primaries.

Super Tuesday — describes primary elections held in many states on the same day.

Supplemental Security Income — a federal program that provides a minimum income to seniors and the disabled who do not qualify for social security.

Supply-side economics — the economic theory that when the supply side of the economy (the producers, capitalists) is taxed less and subject to less regulation, it creates more profit (and taxes on that increased profit); even at a lower rate, it should be equivalent to or even surpasses the original tax; the apotheosis of SSE is the flat-rate income tax); see *Trickle-down economics*.

Supremacy clause — the part of Article VI of the Constitution that specifies that the federal Constitution, and laws passed by the federal government, are the supreme law of the land.

Surplus — the amount by which the available funds exceed spending during a fiscal year.

Swing — how electoral results change between elections (e.g., "There was a 15% swing toward the Republicans in this district since the 2001 election").

Swing voters — voters who are not loyal but who swing between parties according to circumstances.

Symbolic speech — actions intended to convey a belief.

Syndicalism — early 20th-century revolutionary political doctrine whereby the means of production are taken over in a general strike by workers' unions, who then effectively take over the government.

System of government — how power is distributed among different parts and levels of the state.

T

Talk radio — a radio format featuring a host who interviews guests; often very partisan.

Tammany Hall — the New York headquarters of the Democratic Party in the 19th century became notorious for political corruption.

Tax credit — a reduction in one's tax burden designed to help certain people.

Tea Party — a grassroots American political movement (not a political party) advocating adherence to the Constitution as well as reining in alleged excessive taxing and spending by the government; the term derived by advocates sending tea bags (symbolizing the Boston Tea Party) to Congresspersons with a reputation for supporting large spending bills.

Temporary Assistance to Needy Families — a federal welfare program that provides money to low-income families.

Term limit — a legal prohibition against running for a political office after holding it for a prescribed number of years or terms.

Terrorism —violent tactics creating fear and destabilizing government; often targets civilians.

Theocracy — a government controlled by the church/priesthood or a proclaimed living god (e.g., ancient Egypt and modern-day Iran).

Think tank — a non-government, non-profit research institute comprised of scholars and physical scientists generally dedicated to advocating (and finding rationales for) some widespread political, economic, or social belief.

Third party — in American politics, any political party other than Democrats or Republicans.

Three-fifths compromise — a compromise between the Northern and Southern states at the Constitutional Convention stipulating that slaves count as 3/5 of a person for purposes of representation and taxation.

Totalitarian — a government that wishes to subordinate the individual to the state by controlling not only all political and economic matters but the attitudes, values, and beliefs of its population.

Total war — a highly destructive total war in which combatants use every resource available to destroy the enemy's social fabric.

Tragedy of the commons — the concept espousing the impracticality of communally owned resources (e.g., grazing land, fishing ponds). Individuals act independently to maximize benefits at others' expense, thus depleting common resources. Alternatively, where resources are privately owned, there is an incentive to moderate their exploitation to preserve the owner's further use.

Transfer value — in preferential-voting proportional-representation elections, a winning candidate's surplus votes are transferred to the next available candidate; this is achieved by transferring all the ballot papers at a fraction of their value.

Transnational — something that lies beyond the boundaries of a nation-state or consists of several nation-states.

Treason — crime committed against one's country (e.g., spying for an enemy nation).

Treaty — legally binding agreement between two nations; United States treaties are generally negotiated by the President or Secretary of State and must be ratified by the Senate.

Trial balloon — a novel idea put forward (or "floated") but not embraced by a politician to gauge its popularity.

Trickle-down economics — an attempt to improve the economy by providing tax cuts to businesses and wealthy individuals (the supply side). These cuts encourage investment and entrepreneurship, which then creates jobs so; allegedly, the effect will be felt throughout the economy; see *Supply-side economics*.

Trojan horse — an organization with an innocuous or "motherhood statement" type title intended to gain public acceptance to introduce programs, funding, or legislation of a more partisan nature than one is led to believe.

Trustee — a representative who bases their decision not on public opinion but on what they believe is right or best.

Trustee representation — a type of representation in which the people choose a representative whose judgment and experience they trust; the representative votes for what they think is right, regardless of the constituents' opinions.

Two presidencies — the distinction between the President's domestic and foreign policymaking; Presidents generally have more discretion in the foreign policy arena.

Turkey farm — a government agency or department of less than priority status, staffed primarily with political appointees and other patronage hires.

Turnout — the percentage of enrolled citizens who vote.

Two-party-preferred — the final tally for the two most popular candidates or parties of all the votes (regardless of whether they were first, second, or third choices) in single-member preferential voting systems.

Tyranny of the majority — when the majority violates the rights of the minority. A concept first coined in the nineteenth century by French writer Alexis de Tocqueville (1805-1859) and embraced by John Stuart Mill (1806-1873), who claimed that even democracies had limitations because minority rights could be forfeited for favored causes. Possible solutions to such tyranny are a Constitutionally entrenched bill of rights, proportional representation, or a democracy divided into a federation where people of different beliefs and values could gravitate to separate geographical areas that maintained their specific practices and associated laws.

U

Unconventional participation — a political activity that, although legal, is considered inappropriate by many people; includes demonstrations, boycotts, and protests.

Underemployment — when people who seek work can only find part-time jobs.

Unemployment — when not everyone who wants a job can find one.

Unfunded mandate — a mandate for which the federal government gives the states no money.

Unicameral — government with a single-house legislature (e.g., France, Sweden, South Korea).

Unilateral — a state acting alone in the global arena.

Unipolar — an international system with a single superpower dominating other states.

Unitary system — a system of government where power is concentrated in the central government.

Unity — the idea that people overwhelmingly support the government and share certain common beliefs, even if they disagree about policies.

Universe — the group of people about which a research survey is trying to generalize when conducting a public opinion poll.

Useful idiot — description for people of influence who support a cause they fail to understand the leaders of that cause exploit the full ramifications, attributed initially to Vladimir Lenin (1870-1924). He described H.G. Wells (1866-1946), George Bernard Shaw (1856-1950), Paul Robeson (1898-1976), and journalist Walter Duranty (1884-1957), who visited during a famine. They were restricted where they visited and returned home, reporting the new "workers' paradise."

Utilitarianism — consequentialist philosophy initially espoused by the 18th-century writer Jeremy Bentham (1748-1832), whereby the best policy provides the greatest happiness to the highest number.

User fee — a government fee to do certain things (e.g., tunnel toll, fishing license).

V

Veto [Latin, *I forbid*] — the President's power to stop a bill passed by both Houses of Congress if they disapprove of it. See *line item veto* and *pocket veto*. A governor's objection in writing to legislation enacted by the legislature. The legislation is returned to its branch of origin.

Veto message — a message written by the President and attached to a bill they have vetoed; explains the veto's reasons.

Veto override — if the President vetoes a bill, Congress may override the veto by a two-thirds majority vote in both Houses; the bill becomes law, the President's objections notwithstanding.

Virginia Plan — a plan at the Constitutional Convention to base representation in the legislature on population.

Voter turnout — the percentage of citizens who vote in an election.

Voting behavior — a term used to describe the motives and factors that shape voters' choices.

Vote of no confidence — in parliamentary systems, where the executive can only continue to serve at the behest of the majority of the legislature, a vote of no confidence (generally by the lower House) would be a death knell for the current administration; unless another coalition of parties could form a majority, it would precipitate an election.

Voting Rights Act — a law passed in 1965 that banned discrimination in voter registration.

W

War Powers Resolution — passed by Congress in 1973, demands that the President consult with Congress when deploying troops; it gives Congress the power to force troops' withdrawal.

Washington community — the "inside the beltway" group that closely follows politics and continually evaluates the relative power of politicians.

Watchdog journalism — journalism that attempts to hold government officials and institutions accountable for their actions.

Watergate — a hotel and office complex in Washington, D.C., was home to the Democratic Party's campaign headquarters, which were broken into by operatives of the Richard Nixon campaign of 1972; the resulting scandal, known as "Watergate," led to Nixon's resignation.

Watermelon — a derogatory term for a Green politician or supporter who is more concerned with socialist policies than with the environment ("green on the outside but red in the center").

Weberian model — the model of bureaucracy developed by sociologist Max Weber (1864-1920) that characterizes bureaucracy as a rational and efficient means of organizing people.

Welfare — the term for policies designed to help those in economic need.

Welfare state — describes a government that provides aid to the poor and helps the unemployed.

Whip — a political party official in a legislative body, charged with the duty of encouraging party members to vote with their parties on critical pieces of legislation; ensures that their party members do the right thing, such as being in attendance for crucial votes; the notice sent by political parties to legislative members.

Whistleblower — a person who reports wrongdoing in a government agency.

White House staff — the people with whom the President works every day.

White primary — the practice of political parties only allowing whites to participate in their primaries.

Winner-take-all — an electoral system in which the person with the most votes wins everything (and everyone else loses); most states have winner-take-all systems for determining electoral votes.

Wonk — someone engrossed in the technicalities of some aspect of public policy.

writ — a formal written order issued by a body with administrative or judicial jurisdiction. In electoral terms, a document commanding an electoral officer to hold an election and contains dates for the close of rolls, the close of nominations, the polling day, and the writ's return; the issue of a writ triggers the electoral process.

writ of certiorari — the legal document issued a higher court (i.e., appellate court, Supreme Court) ordering a lower court to send a case for review.

writ of habeas corpus — (literally to "produce the body") is a court order to an individual (e.g., prison warden) or agency (institution) holding someone in custody to deliver the imprisoned to the court to determine whether the custodian has lawful authority to detain the prisoner.

writ of mandamus — a judicial order directing a government official to perform a duty of their office.

Y

Yellow journalism — journalism that focuses on shocking, sordid, sometimes near-libelous stories to sell newspapers.

Z

Zeitgeist — German for "the spirit of the time," the prevalent beliefs and attitudes of a place or country at any period.

Notes for active learning

Image Credits

Chapter 1

Thomas Hobbes, English philosopher and political theorist. Wright, John Michael. Thomas Hobbes. C. 1669-1670. Oil on canvas. National Portrait Gallery, London. Wikimedia Commons.

Locke (left) and Montesquieu (right), Enlightenment philosophers. Sir Godfrey Kneller. *Portrait of John Locke.* 1697. Oil on canvas. Hermitage Museum, St. Petersburg. Wikimedia Commons.

French School. *Portrait of Montesquieu.* 1728. Oil on canvas. Palace of Versailles, Versailles. Wikimedia Commons.

Rousseau (left) & Paine (right), French Enlightenment philosophers. Quentin De La Tour, Maurice. *Portrait of Jean-Jacques Rousseau.* Late 18th Century. Pastel on paper. Musée Antoine-Lécuyer, Saint-Quentin. Wikimedia Commons. Milliere, August, George Romney, and William Sharp. *Thomas Paine.* c. 1876. Oil on canvas. National Portrait Gallery, London. Wikimedia Commons.

Drafting the Declaration of Independence. Pratt, Mara L. *American's Story for America's Children: The Early Colonies.* Boston: D.C. Heath & Company, 1901.

Portraits of Daniel Shays and Job Shattuck, leaders of the Massachusetts "Regulators."

"Shays' Rebellion." The Portraits of Daniel Shays and Job Shattuck, Leaders of the Massachusetts "Regulators" 1787. Smithsonian Institution: National Portrait Gallery, Washington, D.C. *Bickerstaff's Boston Almanack.* Bickerstaff, 1787. Wikimedia Commons.

James Madison (left) and Edmund Randolph (right). Bryant, William Cullen, and Sydney Howard Gay. *A Popular History of the United States.* New York: Charles Scribner's Sons, 1881.

Brumidi, Constantino. *Portrait of Edmund Randolph.* 19th century. Wikimedia Commons.

William Paterson, Supreme Court justice and pioneer of the New Jersey Plan. Sharples, James, Gregory Stapko, Thomas Addis Emmet, and Max Rosenthal. *Portrait of William Paterson (1745-1806) When He Was a Supreme Court Justice (1793-1806).* 1794. Oyez: IIT Chicago-Kent College of Law, Illinois Institute of Technology. *The History of the Supreme Court of the United States.* 1902. Wikimedia Commons.

Title page of the Federalist Papers by Alexander Hamilton, James Madison, and John Jay. Hamilton, Alexander, James Madison, and John Jay. *The Federalist: A Collection of Essays, Written in Favour of the New Constitution, as Agreed upon by the Federal Convention, September 17, 1787.* Vol. 1. New York: J. and A. McLean, 1787. *America's Story from America's Library.* The Library of Congress. Wikimedia Commons.

Alexander Hamilton, political theorist and author of the Federalist Papers. Bryant, William Cullen, and Sydney Howard Gay. *A Popular History of the United States.* New York: Charles Scribner's Sons, 1881.

Seals of the House of Representatives (left) and Senate (right). The United States. Congressional Relations. U.S. Government Publishing Office. *U.S. Government Publishing Office.* By U.S. Federal Government. Federal Digital System. Wikimedia Commons. The United States. Senate. *United States Senate.* By Congress. Internet Archive. Wikimedia Commons.

Chief Justice John Marshall of McCulloch v. Maryland. Inman, Henry. 1832. Oil on canvas. Library of Virginia, Richmond, Virginia. Wikimedia Commons.

Thomas Jefferson, U.S. President, and political theorist. Scott, David B. *A School History of the United States.* New York: Harper & Brothers, 1883.

Supreme Court building, Washington, D.C. The United States Department of Agriculture. *Supreme Court Building in Washington, DC.* By Ken Hammond. Wikimedia Commons.

Plato, philosopher of ancient Greece. Raphael. *The School of Athens (detail).* 1509. Fresco. Stanza Della Segnatura, Palazzi Pontifici, Vatican, Rome. Wikimedia Commons.

Constitutional Convention of 1787. Juengling, Frederick, and Alfred Kappes. *The Convention at Philadelphia, 1787.* 19th Century. New York Public Library: Mid-Manhattan Picture Collection, New York. *Our First Century.* N.p.: R.M. Devin, 1881. Wikimedia Commons.

Chapter 2

Roosevelt signs the declaration of war against Japan in 1941, starting America's involvement in WWII. Rowe, Abbie. *United States President Franklin D. Roosevelt signing the Declaration of War against Japan in the Wake of the Attack on Pearl Harbor.* 1941. National Archives and Records Administration, Washington, D.C. Wikimedia Commons.

President Ronald Reagan and Vice President George H. W. Bush. President Ronald Wilson Reagan and Vice President George Herbert Walker Bush Work in the Oval Office of the White House, July 20, 1984. 1984. Executive Office of the President of the United States, Washington, D.C. Wikimedia Commons.

President Franklin Delano Roosevelt at his fourth inaugural address. 1945. National Archives and Records Administration: Harry S. Truman Library, Independence, Montana. Wikimedia Commons.

U.S. President Gerald Ford. United States. *Gerald Ford, Official Presidential Photograph.* Executive Office of the President of the United States. *Gerald R. Ford Presidential Library and Museum.* By David Hume Kennerly. National Archives and Records Administration. Wikimedia Commons.

U.S. Senate in session during the impeachment trial of President Bill Clinton. Floor Proceedings of the U.S. Senate, in Session during the Impeachment Trial of Bill Clinton. 1999. *C-SPAN Archives.* Wikimedia Commons.

Founding members of the Congressional Black Caucus. U.S. Congress. Founding Members of the Congressional Black Caucus. Black Americans in Congress. Office of the Clerk, U.S. House of Representatives. Wikimedia Commons.

Logo for the U.S. Senate Select Committee on Intelligence. Digital image. U.S. Government, 2013. Wikimedia Commons.

Supreme Court building. Architect of the Capitol. *U.S. Capitol – Sunny Afternoon at the Supreme Court.* 2012. U.S. Capitol, Flickr. Wikimedia Commons.

Seal of the United States Court of Appeals for the First Circuit. U.S. Government. Digital image. District of Columbia Court of Appeals Seal. 2015. Wikimedia Commons.

Members of the Warren Court, who made the unanimous decision for Brown v. Board of Education. United Press International Telephoto. *The Members of the Warren Court.* 1953. Library of Congress, Washington, D.C. Wikimedia Commons

Max Weber, German sociologist. 1894. *Live Journal.* Live Journal, Inc. Wikimedia Commons.

President Lyndon B. Johnson at the University of Michigan commencement in 1964, where he made his first public reference to his Great Society policies. LBJ Great Society Speech. University of Texas Photography Lab, Austin. Wikimedia Commons.

Assassination of President James Garfield. Berghaus, A., and C. Upham. *An Engraving of James A. Garfield's Assassination. 1881. Frank Leslie's Illustrated Newspaper. Images of American Political History.* Wikimedia Commons.

Seal of the C.I.A. United States Federal Government. Digital image. Wikimedia Commons.

President Ronald Reagan. American Forces Radio and Television Service. *Official Portrait of President Ronald Reagan.* 1981. University of Texas: Ronald Reagan Presidential Library and Museum. Wikimedia Commons.

Montesquieu, French political theorist. Bayard, Émile-Antoine. 1889. *Album of the Centenary: Great Men and Great Events of the French Revolution.* By Augustin Challamel and Desire Lacroix. Paris: Jouvet & Cie, 1889. Wikimedia Commons.

President Richard Nixon. 1935-1982. National Archives and Records Administration: Still Picture Records Section, Special Media Archives Services Division. Department of Defense. Department of the Army. Office of the Deputy Chief of Staff for Operations. U.S. Army Audiovisual Center. Wikimedia Commons.

Abraham Lincoln with his cabinet. Carpenter, Francis Bicknell. *First Reading of the Emancipation Proclamation of President Lincoln.* 1864. Oil on canvas. United States Capitol: West Staircase, Senate Wing, Washington, D.C. Wikimedia Commons.

U.S. President Barack Obama with Canadian Prime Minister Stephen Harper.

The United States. White House. Executive Office of the President of the United States. *Barack Obama, President of the United States of America, with Stephen Harper, Prime Minister of Canada.* By Pete Souza. The White House: President Barack Obama. Wikimedia Commons.

Logo for the Gallup Corporation, one of the leading polling firms of the U.S. Gallup, Inc. Standard logo for Gallup, Inc. Digital image. Wikimedia Commons.

President John F. Kennedy Meets with Representatives from the National Association for the Advancement of Colored People (NAACP). Dr. E. Franklin Jackson, President of Washington, D.C. NAACP Branch; Bishop Stephen G. Spottswood, Chairman of NAACP Board of Directors; President Kennedy; Arthur B. Spingarn, Former NAACP Vice-President. Oval Office, White House, Washington, D.C. 1961. Knudsen, Robert. White House Photographs Collection. John F. Kennedy Presidential Library and Museum, Boston. Wikimedia Commons.

Internal Revenue Service Building on Constitution Avenue in Washington, D.C. U.S. Department of the Treasury. Wikimedia Commons.

Logo of the Federal Communications Commission. The United States. Federal Communications Commission. Office of Engineering and Technology. *Understanding the FCC Regulations for Computers and Other Digital Devices.* By U.S. Government. 1996. Print. Ser. 62. Wikimedia Commons.

Painting of Thomas Jefferson (leader of the anti-federalists) and Alexander Hamilton (author of The Federalist Papers) with George Washington in the Capitol building. Architect of the Capitol, and Constantino Brumidi. *US Capitol – George Washington with Thomas Jefferson and Alexander Hamilton.* 1872. Oil on plaster. Capitol Building Room S-213, Washington, D.C. Wikimedia Commons.

Seal of the U.S. Bureau of Indian Affairs. Department of the Interior. *Seal of the U.S. Department of the Interior, Bureau of Indian Affairs (1824).* Digital image. 2012. Wikimedia Commons.

Chapter 3

Slave auction in America. Ellis, Edward S. *The Youth's History of the United States.* New York: The Cassell Publishing Company, 1887.

William Lloyd Garrison, leader of the abolitionist movement. American Abolitionist William Lloyd Garrison, Three-quarter-length, Seated. National Archives and Records Administration. Wikimedia Commons.

U.S. Colonel Robert E. Lee. Vannerson, Julian. *Portrait of Gen. Robert E. Lee, Officer of the Confederate Army.* 1864. Library of Congress: Prints and Photographs Online Catalog, Washington, D.C. Wikimedia Commons.

Medals that commemorate the leaders of the desegregation of public schools that led directly to Brown v. the Board of Education. The United States. United States Mint. Authorized by Public Law 108-180, *This Medal Commemorates Reverend Joseph A. DeLaine, Harry and Eliza Briggs and Levi Pearson for Their Contributions to the Nation as Pioneers in the Effort to Desegregate Public Schools That Led Directly to the Landmark Desegregation Case of Brown Et Al. v. the Board of Education of Topeka Et Al.* By Charles L. Vickers and Donna Weaver. 2003. Print. Wikimedia Commons.

Suffragettes Elizabeth Cady Stanton (left) and Susan B. Anthony (right). Elizabeth Cady Stanton (seated) with Susan B. Anthony (standing). c. 1900. Library of Congress: Prints and Photographs Division, Washington, D.C. Wikimedia Commons.

Feminist and suffragette Victoria Claflin Woodhull Martin (1838-1927). 1880. Everything Paweks Online Magazine. Wikimedia Commons.

Eleanor Roosevelt (left) and Esther Peterson (right) of the Presidential Commission on the Status of Women. 1962. National Archives and Records Administration: Franklin D. Roosevelt Library, Hyde Park, New York. Wikimedia Commons.

A COINTELPRO document outlining the FBI's plans to 'neutralize' activist Jean Seberg for her support of the Black Panther Party. Held, Richard W. *A COINTELPRO Document Outlining the FBI's Plans to 'neutralize' Jean Seberg for Her Support for the Black Panther Party.* 1970. *Pink Noise Studio.* Wikimedia Commons.

President George H. W. Bush signs the Americans with Disabilities Act of 1990. 1990. The White House Historical Association, Washington, D.C. Wikimedia Commons.

U.S. Supreme Court Justice William Rehnquist. Oakes, Robert S. 1972. Library of Congress, Washington, D.C. Wikimedia Commons.

Politician and activist Harvey Milk. Nicoletta, Daniel. *Harvey Milk Filling in for Mayor Moscone for a Day in 1978.* 1978. Wikimedia Commons.

Elbridge Gerry, American politician, and Anti-Federalist. Bogle, James, and John Vanderlyn. *Elbridge Gerry (1744-1814), American Statesman.* 1861. Monmouth College. Wikimedia Commons.

Eugene Debs, political activist. University of Iowa Libraries: Redpath Chautauqua Collection: Special Collections Department, Iowa City, IA. Wikimedia Commons.

James Madison, fourth President of the United States. Stuart, Gilbert. c. 1821. Oil on panel. National Gallery of Art: Gallery 60 A, Washington, D.C. Wikimedia Commons.

The burning of Washington during the War of 1812. Capture and Burning of Washington by the British. 1876. Wood engraving. Library of Congress: American Memory, Washington, D.C. Wikimedia Commons.

Throwing tea overboard during the Boston Tea Party. Stephens, Alex H. *A Comprehensive and Popular History of the United States.* Chattanooga: Hickman and Fowler, 1882.

House Committee on Un-American Activities. Harris, and Ewing. *While Newsmen Take Notes, Chairman Dies of House Committee Investigating Un-American Activities, Proofs and Reads His Statement Replying to President Roosevelt's Attack on the Committee.* 1938. Library of Congress: Prints and Photographs Division, Washington, D.C. Wikimedia Commons.

Sandra Day O'Connor, American jurist and Supreme Court Justice. American Jurist Sandra Day O'Connor (b. 1930), Justice of the Supreme Court of the United States. c. 1981-1983. Library of Congress: Prints and Photographs Division, Washington, D.C. Wikimedia Commons.

Guard tower at Abu Ghraib Prison. United States. U.S. Army. *Local Host Images.* By Michael J. Carden. 2005. Wikimedia Commons.

U.S. Justice Arthur Goldberg. Arthur Goldberg, U.S. Supreme Court Justice, and UN Ambassador. Lyndon B. Johnson Library Collection. Wikimedia Commons.

U.S. President Lyndon B. Johnson. Okamoto, Yoichi. *Portrait of President Lyndon B. Johnson.* 1969. University of Texas: LBJ Presidential Library. Wikimedia Commons.

Print celebrating the passage of the Fifteenth Amendment to the United States Constitution. Kelly, Thomas. *The Fifteenth Amendment.* 1870. Hand-colored lithographs. Library of Congress: Prints and Photographs Division, Washington, D.C. Wikimedia Commons.

Representative John A. Bingham of Ohio, Principal Framer of the Fourteenth Amendment. Congressman John Bingham of Ohio Was the Principal Framer of the Equal Protection Clause. Rep. John A. Bingham. Library of Congress: Prints and Photographs Division, Washington, D.C. Wikimedia Commons.

Chapter 4

The First Federal Congress, 1789, where the Bill of Rights was created. Executive Office of the President of the United States. *U.S. Capitol – The First Federal Congress, 1789.* 1973-1974. Oil on canvas. Great Experiment Hall Cox Corridors. Wikimedia Commons.

Aristotle, ancient Greek philosopher. Anzenbacher, Arno. *Engraving of the Philosopher Aristotle.* Picture Archive of the Austrian National Library, Vienna. *Introduction to Philosophy.* Freiburg and Herder. Wikimedia Commons.

U.S. President Dwight D. Eisenhower. The United States General Services Administration. National Archives and Records Administration. National Archives. *Photograph of Dwight D. Eisenhower.* Wikimedia Commons.

General Washington in the American Revolution. Lossing, Benson J. Our Country. New York: Johnson and Bailey, 1895. Wikimedia Commons.

Presidential portrait of George W. Bush. Sanden, John Howard. *The Official Portrait of George W. Bush, 43rd President of the United States (2001–2009).* 2012. The White House Historical Association, Washington, D.C. *John Howard Sanden: American Portrait Painter.* Wikimedia Commons.

U.S. President Franklin Delano Roosevelt. Franklin D. Roosevelt. 1940. *National Archives and Records Administration*, Hyde Park, New York. Wikimedia Commons.

Portrait of Hitler at an SS meeting during the German occupation of WWII. Belgian Flemish Nationalist Politician (VNV), Writer and Poet Ward Hermans (1897-1992) as a Speaker at a Meeting of General SS Flanders in Ghent, during the German Occupation in World War II, Above Him Large Portrait of Hitler. 1941. National Archives, The Netherlands. *Nationaal Archief.* Wikimedia Commons.

Occupy Wall Street poster. Cochran, Seth. *A "We Are The 99%" Poster Created by an Occupy Wall Street Group.* 2011. Wikimedia Commons.

Stephen Colbert at the 71st Peabody Awards. Krusberg, Anders. *71st Annual Peabody Awards Luncheon Waldorf Astoria Hotel.* 2012. Peabody Awards. Wikimedia Commons.

Electoral College map of the 2012 United States presidential election. Skidmore, Gage. "Electoral College Map for the 2012 United States Presidential Election." 2012. Wikimedia Commons.

Friends of the NRA logo. Greene, Jeremy. *New Friends of NRA Logo as of December 2011.* Digital image. *Friends of NRA.* Wikimedia Commons.

Nineteenth Amendment passed in 1920. The United States. National Archives and Records Administration. *The Charters of Freedom.* The U.S. National Archives and Records Administration. Wikimedia Commons.

U.S. voting booths. Buckawicki, Mark. *The Polling Station of Ward 1.* 2013. Nashua, New Hampshire. Wikimedia Commons.

Watergate Complex. The United States. U.S. Department of Justice. National Archives and Records Administration. *Record Group 21: Records of District Courts of the United States, 1685-1991. Gerald R. Ford Library & Museum "The Watergate Files" Exhibit.* Wikimedia Commons.

Canadian Prime Minister Justin Trudeau. Radio Television Malacañang (RTVM). *Justin Trudeau and Benigno Aquino III at the APEC Philippines 2015 (cropped for Use in Election Infoboxes).* 2015. *Asia-Pacific Economic Corporation.* Wikimedia Commons.

Seal of the Supreme Court of the United States. The United States. United States Federal Court. *Seal of the Supreme Court of the United States.* 2008. Wikimedia Commons.

Civil Rights movement protest. Wolfson, Stanley. *Photograph Shows Marchers Carrying Banner "We March with Selma!" on Street in Harlem, New York City, New York.* 1965. Library of Congress, Washington, D.C. *New York World Telegram & Su*n. Wikimedia Commons.

Seattle Ministerial Conference in 1999. Seattle Ministerial Conference, November 30–December 3, 1999. 1999. Switzerland. *World Trade Organization.* Wikimedia Commons.

Civil Rights leader Martin Luther King Jr. Reyneau, Betsy G. National Archives and Records Administration: Donated Collections: Records Group 200. *Teachers' Resources.* National Archives. Wikimedia Commons.

Campaign poster for William J. Bryan, American politician. Williams, Neville. *Campaign Poster for William J. Bryan.* c. 1900. Campaign poster. Library of Congress, Washington, D.C. Wikimedia Commons.

Chapter 5

Logo of the Republican Party of the United States of America. Abbreviation GOP stands for "Grand Old Party." By Republican Party (http://gop.com/) [Public domain], via Wikimedia Commons.

The official logo of the United States Democratic Party. By United States Democratic Party [Public domain], via Wikimedia Commons.

The official logos of the Libertarian party of the United States and the Green Party of the United States. By Libertarian Party of the United States [Public domain], via Wikimedia Commons.

The official logo of the Green Party of the United States. By Green Party of the United States (http://www.gp.org/rebranding-campaign) [Public domain].

Thomas Jefferson, founder of the Democratic Republicans. Beach, Chandler B., A.M., and Frank Morton McMurry, Ph.D., eds. *The New Student's Reference Work for Teachers, Students, and Families.* Chicago: F.E. Compton, 1914. Wikimedia Commons.

Andrew Jackson, presidential candidate of 1824. Beach, Chandler B., A.M., and Frank Morton McMurry, Ph.D., eds. *The New Student's Reference Work for Teachers, Students, and Families.* Chicago: F.E. Compton, 1914. Wikimedia Commons.

Theodore Roosevelt (left) and William Howard Taft (right),26th and 27th Presidents of the United States. Theodore Roosevelt. [Public domain], via Wikimedia Commons. *William Howard Taft.* Library of Congress Prints and Photographs online collection. [Public domain], via Wikimedia Commons.

Ross Perot, an American businessman. The United States. Department of Veterans Affairs. *Ross Perot at the United States Department of Veterans Affairs.* 2008. Wikimedia Commons.

1916 Democratic Party National Convention held at the St. Louis Coliseum in St. Louis, Missouri. 1916. Library of Congress, Washington, D.C. Wikimedia Commons.

Presidential candidate Rick Santorum campaigning for Iowa Caucus, January 2012. By *IowaPolitics.com* (http://creativecommons.org/licenses/by-sa/2.0), via Wikimedia Commons.

The United States Electoral College map. Copyright by Sterling Education.

Al Gore, American politician and environmentalist. Al Gore, Former Vice President of the United States. c. 1994. *American Forces Radio and Television Services.* Wikimedia Commons.

Political cartoon shows the newly drawn Massachusetts State Senate district of South Essex created by the legislature to favor the Democratic-Republican Party candidates of Governor Elbridge Gerry over the Federalists (1812). By Elkanah Tisdale (1771-1835) (often falsely attributed to Gilbert Stuart). Originally published in the *Boston Centinel*, 1812. [Public domain], via Wikimedia Commons.

American Medical Association headquarters building in Chicago, Illinois. Crocker, J. *IBM Building, Chicago, IL, USA.* 2004. Wikimedia Commons.

Justice Anthony Kennedy, author of the Supreme Court's decision in Citizens United v. Federal Election Commission. Collection of the Supreme Court of the United States. *Anthony Kennedy, Associate Justice of the Supreme Court of the United States.* Oyez: IIT Chicago-Kent College of Law. Wikimedia Commons.

Logo for the 24-hour news channel, CNN. Turner Broadcasting, Inc. *Digital image.* 2015. Wikimedia Commons.

U.S. Federal Communications Commission Inspector General badge. Federal Communications Commission. Digital image. *Office of the Inspector General. Federal Communications Commission.* Wikimedia Commons.

Chapter 6

Official logo of the Executive Office of the President of the United States. Public domain.

Guantanamo Bay map. Public domain via Wikimedia Commons.

President Bush signs the Homeland Security Appropriations Act of 2004. United States. Department of Homeland Security. White House. By Tina Hager. Washington, D.C., in 2003. Wikimedia Commons.

U.S. President Bill Clinton signs the Defense of Marriage Act in 1996. Public domain (government works).

President Bush signs the Patriot Act. Draper, Eric. *President George W. Bush Signs the Uniting (and) Strengthening America (by) Providing Appropriate Tools Required (to) Intercept (and) Obstruct Terrorism (USA PATRIOT) Act, Anti-Terrorism Legislation, in the East Room Oct. 26.* 2001. Washington, D.C. *The White House.* Wikimedia Commons.

Leaders of the Civil Rights March on Washington (1963). August 28, 1963. By Unknown or not provided author (U.S. National Archives and Records Administration) [Public domain], via Wikimedia Commons.

Counter Terrorist Unit seal for the Department of Homeland Security. The United States. Department of Homeland Security. Counter Terrorist Unit. *CTU.* By U.S. Department of Homeland Security. Wikimedia Commons.

President Roosevelt signs the Tennessee Authority Act, part of the New Deal. The United States Tennessee Valley Authority. *United States President Franklin D. Roosevelt Signs the T.V.A. Act, Which Established the Tennessee Valley Authority.* 1933. *Tennessee Valley Authority.* Wikimedia Commons.

The Federal Reserve headquarters in Washington, D.C. By Dan Smith (http://creativecommons.org/licenses/by-sa/2.5)], via Wikimedia Commons.

President Barack Obama and Vice President Joe Biden meet with members of the National Security Council in 2014. Souza, Pete. Washington, D.C. *The White House Flickr.* Wikimedia Commons.

The USS Arizona burning after the Japanese attack on Pearl Harbor on December 7, 1941. U.S. Navy. 1941. National Archives and Records Administration, Washington, D.C. Wikimedia Commons.

Saddam Hussein, Iraqi dictator and terrorist shortly after his capture (2003). Armed Forces Radio and Television Service, 2003. Washington, D.C. Wikimedia Commons.

The Joint Chiefs of Staff photographed in the Joint Chiefs of Staff Gold Room, more commonly known as The Tank, in the Pentagon on December 14, 2001. From left to right are: U.S. Air Force Chief of Staff Gen. John P. Jumper, U.S. Marine Corps Commandant Gen. James L. Jones Jr., Vice Chairman of the Joint Chiefs of Staff Gen. Peter Pace, U.S. Marine Corps, Chairman of the Joint Chiefs of Staff Gen. Richard B. Myers, U.S. Air Force, U.S. Army Chief of Staff Gen. Eric K. Shinseki, U.S. Navy Chief of Naval Operations Adm. Vern E. Clark. By Mamie Burke [Public domain], via Wikimedia Commons.

President Lyndon B. Johnson signs the Economic Opportunity Act. U.S. Government. 1964. LBJ Presidential Library, Austin, TX. Wikimedia Commons.

The official logo of the Environmental Protection Agency. Public domain.

President George W. Bush signs the No Child Left Behind Act. Morse, Paul. *Visiting Hamilton High School in Hamilton, Ohio, Jan. 8, 2002, President George W. Bush Signs into Law the No Child Left Behind Act.* 2002. Executive Office of the President of the United States. *The White House.* Wikimedia Commons.

Barack Obama signing the Patient Protection and Affordable Care Act at the White House. Souza, Pete. 2010. Executive Office of the President of the United States. *Nancy Pelosi Flickr.* Wikimedia Commons.

Pro-Life March for Life in Washington D.C. in 2008, protesting Roe v. Wade. Martin, Eric. *Pro-Life, March for Life 2008 U.S. Capitol, U.S. Supreme Court, Washington, D.C., Constitution Avenue.* 2008. Wikimedia Commons.

President James Madison, co-author of The Federalist Papers. *James Madison, Half-length Portrait, Seated, Facing Right, with Documents in Hand.* 1828. Pendleton's Lithography. Library of Congress, Washington, D.C. Wikimedia Commons.

A same-sex couple is celebrating the overturning of DOMA in San Francisco in 2013. Dombrowski, Quinn. *Mommy, Mama, and Baby Georgie.* 2013. Wikimedia Commons.

President Obama discusses health care reform in a speech to Congress. The United States. White House. Executive Office of the President of the United States. *The White House: President Barack Obama.* By Pete Souza. United States Federal Government. Wikimedia Commons.

President Obama receives an update on the Affordable Care Act. The United States. The White House. Executive Office of the President of the United States. By Pete Souza. 2014. Wikimedia Commons.

Seattle recall petitions in 1910. Presenting Recall Petitions against Seattle, Washington Mayor Hiram Gill. The Recall Election Took Place February 1911. 2010. Seattle Public Library: Seattle Room. McClure's. 1911. Wikimedia Commons.

Chart of the Iron Triangle theory. Diagram of an Iron Triangle in Government. Digital image. 2004. Wikimedia Commons.

Everything you always wanted to know about...

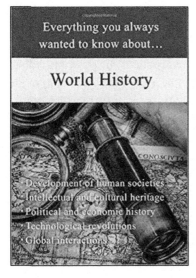

World History

ISBN-13: 9781947556881

Learn the world history starting from the early Neolithic period to the present-day events. This guide is a must-have book for anyone who wants to be knowledgeable about the history of human civilizations. As it goes through the sequence of the major events of the past, it provides readers with the analysis necessary to make them more educated and appreciative participants in the global future. Develop a better understanding of important civilizations, their economic and cultural growth and declines, the political and social challenges they went through, as well as the relationships between different historical events. Learn about historical figures and important events that set the foundations of influential civilizations, the meaning and significance of the historical shifts, as well as how each important historical event shaped its country's cultural heritage and political development.

American History

ISBN-13: 978-1947556553

From the founding of the United States of America government to the present-day challenges, this guide is perfect for anyone who wants to be knowledgeable about the history of America and its democracy. As it goes through the sequence of the events of the past, it provides readers with the analysis necessary to make them more engaged and appreciative participants in the American future. This book was designed for those who want to develop a better understanding of America's founding, economic and cultural growth, the political and social challenges it went through, as well as the relationships between different historical events. Learn about historical figures and important events that established the foundations of American government, the meaning and significance of the various social movements, as well as how each important historical event shaped the country's cultural heritage and political development.

European History

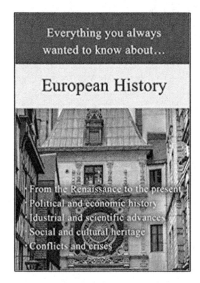

ISBN-13: 978-1947556980

Perfect guide for anyone who wants to learn about European history. From the rise of humanism and Renaissance to the 21st century developments, it goes through the sequence of the events of the past, providing readers with the information necessary to make them more engaged and knowledgeable learners of European history. This book was designed to help readers develop a better understanding of what shaped European governments, their economic and cultural underpinnings, political and social challenges they went through, as well as the causal relationships between different historical events. Learn about historical figures and important events that established the foundations of the European governments, the meaning and significance of the social movements, and how each important historical event shaped regional cultural heritage and political development.

Comparative Government and Politics

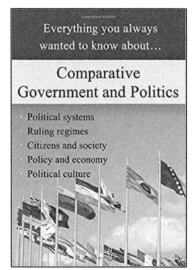

ISBN-13: 978-1947556584

Why different countries have different forms of government and political institutions? Why some countries exist as democracies and others are authoritarian regimes? Why are some revolutions successful and others fail? This book was designed for those who want to develop a better understanding of political systems and regimes that affect the lives of people around the world, as well as political cultures, structures, governmental functions, and the relationships between the governments and the governed. Readers will learn about major events that shaped how governments function, the different institutions of government and political cultures that exist around the world, how branches of governments interact with each other and the governed, and how these institutions may be affected by the input from the populace. This clearly explained text is a perfect guide for anyone who wants to be knowledgeable about comparative government and politics.

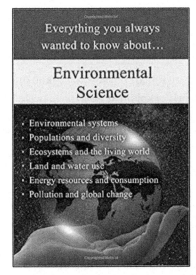

Environmental Science

ISBN-13: 978-1947556645

From the foundations of Earth systems to the present-day climate challenges, this book is aimed at providing readers with the information necessary to make them more engaged and appreciative participants in the global environment. This guide is designed to help develop a better understanding of ecosystems, population dynamics, use of natural resources, as well as the political and social landscape of environmental challenges. The content is focused on an essential review of all the important facts and events shaping the natural world we live in. You will learn about Earth's biochemical cycles, land, and water use, energy resources and their consumption, the significance of the various environmental movements and global initiatives, as well as how different human actions affect the overall balance within ecosystems.

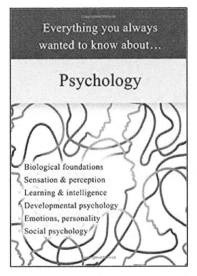

Psychology

ISBN-13: 978-1947556560

This book was designed for those who want to develop a better understanding of the human mind, emotions, feelings and behaviors, as well as the relationships between different historical events. Readers will learn about historically significant psychology researchers, the biological basis of human behavior, basic principles of consciousness and cognition, what drives human emotions and motivations, how early childhood psychological development affects human behavior, as well as develop the ability to compare and interpret theories and scientific methods, and to apply different theoretical frameworks to analyze a given situation. The book also describes all major groups of psychological disorders and covers the foundations of social psychology. From the foundations of human mind theories to the modern neuropsychology challenges, this clearly explained text is a perfect guide for anyone who wants to be knowledgeable about human psychology.

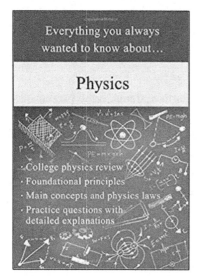

Physics

ISBN-13: 978-1947556621

From the foundations of Newtonian physics to atomic and nuclear theories, this clearly explained text is a perfect guide into standard college physics topics. As it navigates through the material, it provides readers with the information necessary to define and understand physics concepts, develop the ability to comprehend basic physical laws that govern our universe and skills to apply the theoretical knowledge to solving conceptual and quantitative problems. This book was designed for those who want to develop a better understanding of our physical universe, as well as the relationships between different laws of physics. The book describes all major topics covered in a standard college physics course and walks you through solving different types of problems. You will learn about kinematics and dynamics, statics and equilibrium, foundations of gravity, energy, work, sound and light, electricity and magnetism, basic principles of atomic physics, as well as heat and thermodynamics.

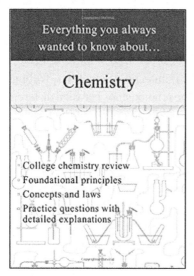

Chemistry

ISBN-13: 978-1947556874

From the foundations of the chemical reactions to the complex mechanisms of atomic particles, this general chemistry guide provides readers with the information necessary to be better equipped to understand these multifaceted chemistry topics. This book is a detailed review of all the fundamental processes and mechanisms affecting general chemistry and physical processes at the atomic level. The content was designed for those who want to develop a better understanding of the electronic structure of elements, principles of chemical bonding, phases of matter, types and mechanisms of chemical reactions, as well as essential principles of solution chemistry and acid-base equilibria. Learn about rate processes in chemical reactions, empirical and molecular formulas, bond dissociation energy for the heats of formation, Gibbs free energy, enthalpy, entropy, oxidation number, the laws of thermodynamics, and electrochemistry.

Cell and Molecular Biology

ISBN-13: 978-1947556683

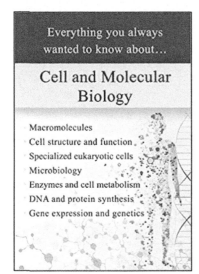

Created by highly qualified science teachers, researchers, and education specialists, this book educates and empowers both the average and the well- informed readers, helping them develop and increase their understanding of biology. From the foundations of a living cell to the complex mechanisms of gene expression, this self-teaching guide provides readers with the information necessary to make them better equipped for navigating these multifaceted biology topics. This book was designed for those who want to develop a better understanding of cell structure and function, cell metabolism, DNA and genetics, as well as the technological and ethical challenges of modern science. The content is focused on an essential review of all the important processes and mechanisms affecting organisms on the cellular and molecular levels. You will learn about macromolecules, enzymes, cell cycle, photosynthesis, the significance of the various DNA mutations and heredity, as well as how different cell processes affect the overall well-being of an organism.

Organismal Biology

ISBN-13: 978-1947556690

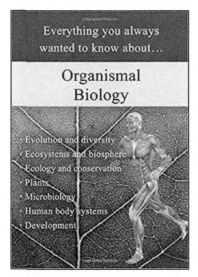

Organismal biology is the study of structure, function, ecology and evolution at the organismal level. From the origin of life to the complex anatomical systems of humans, this clearly explained text was designed for those who want to develop a better understanding of ecosystems, diversity and classification, as well as anatomy and physiology. The content is focused on an essential review of all the important events and mechanisms affecting populations and communities. You will learn about evolution, comparative anatomy, plants, microorganisms, as well as human anatomical systems, along with physiological processes affecting the overall organism. Created by highly qualified science teachers, researchers, and education specialists, this book educates and empowers both the average and the well- informed readers, helping them develop and increase their understanding of biology.

Made in the USA
Monee, IL
05 August 2021